"That's right—you simply pick them up like this and
move them about on the little squares."

The Fireside Book of
CHESS

By IRVING CHERNEV
and FRED REINFELD

Simon and Schuster - New York

ACKNOWLEDGMENTS

THE EDITORS are grateful to the following publishers, authors and artists for permission to reproduce copyrighted material:

Billy Rose for *Don't Quote Me, But . . .* Reprinted from WINE, WOMEN AND WORDS by Billy Rose. Copyright 1946, 1947, 1948 Glenmore Productions, Inc., Simon and Schuster, Inc.

Alfred Kreymborg for *Chess Reclaims a Devotee.* Copyright 1949 Alfred Kreymborg.

Story Magazine, Inc. for *Exchange of Men* by Joseph Cross. Copyright 1946 by Story Magazine, Inc.

Gerald Kersh for *The Devil That Troubled the Chessboard.* Reprinted from October 1945 ESQUIRE, copyright 1945 Esquire, Inc.

Jay Wilson and Sydney A. Sanders for *Check . . . and Mate* by Jay Wilson. Copyright 1946 The Crowell-Collier Publishing Company, permission of the author.

C. J. S. Purdy for *History of the Game* which appeared in *Among These Mates.*

Solomon Hecht for *Telling Off the World Champion* which appeared in THE GAMBIT in 1930 under the title *How Emanuel Lasker Refutes his own Chess Principles by Wholesale Violations.*

Frontispiece cartoon by Leslie Starke, reprinted by special permission of *The Saturday Evening Post.* Copyright 1949 by The Curtis Publishing Co.

For Melvin, Don and Judy

Table of Contents

Table of Contents

Part One

STORIES AND ARTICLES

"I don't see how he does it. My feet would be killing me."

Cartoon by Barney Tobey, by permission of the artist. Copyright 1948 The
New Yorker Magazine, Inc.

Don't Quote Me, But . . .

BY BILLY ROSE

♛ I TALK a pretty good game of chess. A lot of years ago I could even play one. At least that's my story.

Except for foot-racing and wife-beating, chess is the oldest known sport. The knights of old were so daffy about it they'd sometimes bet a finger or toe on a game. At the East Side coffeehouse where I learned how to play, the stake was usually a cup of tea in a glass. I could have memorized the Five-Foot Shelf in the hours I spent learning how to think five moves ahead. I never won many games—in this particular coffeehouse the chair-warmers thought ten moves ahead.

Yesterday afternoon the telephone in my office kept ringing like crazy. The twentieth time it rang I hollered into the mouthpiece, "No spik Engleesh." I got my hat and skedaddled via the back elevator.

On Sixth Avenue a friendly breeze was blowing kisses at the pretty gals. I ducked into a side street, fished half a dozen pennies out of my pocket and started pitching them at a crack. Only fair. I remembered back a hundred years ago when I could come within an inch of the line, ten times out of ten. By this time the telephone had stopped ringing in my head.

I ambled over toward Broadway. Near 50th Street, I saw a sign on a second-floor store window over a garage—"Budnick's Chess Club." I walked up. Like my coffeehouse on the East Side, it featured a low ceiling and a set of high foreheads. The air was foggy with the tobacco smoke which generally goes with masculine brainwork.

At a couple of long tables, half a dozen housemen were taking on all comers. If you lost a game, it cost you a quarter. If you won, you paid nothing.

Budnick came over and introduced himself. "It's about time," he said, in a Lower Slobbovian accent. "Hays tells me you play."

"What Hays?" I asked.

"Arthur Garfield Hays, your lawyer. He comes quite often. So does David Stern, the newspaper publisher, and when he's in town, Harry Warner, the movie fellow."

I decided to stay. If these Joseph McGeniuses could step away from their empires and sit around Budnick's for a couple of hours, I figured it wouldn't do my popcorn machines any harm if I did likewise. Besides, if I could remember some of the gambits out of the old Morphy book, I might beat the house out of twenty-five cents.

Over in a corner one of the pros was available. I dropped down in the chair opposite him.

"Want to move first?" he said, lighting a brown-paper cigarette.

"Anything you say," I answered.

"Take the whites and move," he shrugged. "It's your quarter."

I tried a fancy opening—tournament stuff out of the book. Around the fourth move I got the feeling the pro didn't recognize the gambit. He moved his men quickly, almost carelessly—and chess is a game where players have been known to wear out a two-pants suit between moves.

The first five minutes I thought I was doing fine. I knocked off two of his pawns and a bishop. Suddenly, as if from left field, his queen came into play. Protected by a knight, the lady dusted off the pawn to the left of my king. "Check and mate," said the little pro. "Want to try another?"

I tried six others. It was like Mortimer Snerd arguing relativity with Einstein. By game No. 7, I was so shattered that I fell into the old trap—the Fool's Mate in four moves.

I got up from the table feeling pretty low. "Not my day, Capablanca," I sighed.

"That's five games you owe for," said the pro.

"Seven," I told him.

He took out a pencil stub and a little pad. He put down 25 and under it a 7. He multiplied and got $1.25.

"You're cheating yourself," I pointed out.

He tried again and got $2.25. He did a lot of crossing out. Then he put down 25 seven times and added. This time it came out right—$1.75.

I took out a five-dollar bill. He frowned and went back to the paper. He wrote down $5.00 and put $1.75 under it with a big minus sign. The answer came out $4.85.

He looked up wistfully and said, "I don't think that's right. Haven't you got the even change?"

I laid the five on the chessboard where I had been humiliated. "Keep it," I told him. "I feel a lot better now."

Cartoon by H. T. Webster, by permission of the artist. Copyright 1937 New York Herald Tribune, Inc.

Chess Reclaims a Devotee

BY ALFRED KREYMBORG

♛ RECENTLY, after an absence of nearly twenty years from the chess world, I returned to the game of my first love, and may now be seen at the Manhattan Chess Club, along with many another ex-expert, college champion or duffer, puffing away at a pipe, stogie or cigarette, and shoving or banging white or black figures through a dreamy atmosphere, the while onlookers or kibitzers indulge in gratuitous comments at the expense of the losing players.

No game of chess in the old days had the least zest unless it was encircled by spectators infinitely wiser than the unhappy combatants; and for some time after my retirement from action I sat with the kibitzers and vied with the ancient fraternity in showing a defeated player, much against his will, how he could have won a lost game. The fraternity is open to any tyro with the requisite impudence for loosing his tongue in the face of the masters themselves; and the post-mortem is usually opened with some expletive such as *Potzer! Pfuscher! Nebich!* Ultimately, I drifted away from the game altogether. It had savagely reduced my energies, lost its nocturnal fascination and never earned for me more than a few dollars a week—my sole livelihood for a number of years. All in all, the mad, intricate, logical, ferociously difficult combat had subjected me to too many heartbreaks.

I played my game as most other men played theirs: with passionate intensity. To the ignorant outside world, two men over a chessboard look like a pair of dummies. And yet, inside the pale automata, dynamos pound incessantly. Here is nothing less than a silent duel between two human engines using and abusing all the faculties of the mind—the will, the imagination, logic, memory, caution, cunning, daring, foresight, hindsight, perspective, detail, unity and courage—in an effort to outwit, corner and demolish the not-less-than-hateful opponent. It is warfare in the most mysterious jungles of the human character. Chess has also its lighter, jocular, outrageously funny aspects; but first I wish to revert to its tragedies; and anyone who has ever participated in tournaments will know at once what I mean.

Those in which I took part from boyhood on—I made my debut at eleven—were absolute nightmares. In my last tournament—a national contest won by Frank Marshall, with José Capablanca half a game behind—I lost nine pounds over a simple oversight I committed in a game against Chajes—then the Western champion and an East Side idol. I broke down near the close of a combination some seventeen or eighteen moves deep with all the pieces on the board, excepting a pawn or two on each side. To my king's pawn opening—a pawn which has given way to the queen's in present-day chess—Chajes retorted with the Sicilian defense: a delightfully risky game involving both players in counter-attacks from the outset. Counter-attack, the basis of chess of the classical or romantic era, gave way, about twenty years ago, to the growing inroads of safety first, conservatism and science—a movement ushered in by queen's pawn openings, a movement we'll come to later. At the moment, I must once more relieve myself of that everlasting bugaboo: the game with Chajes. Before I plunged into the mazes of the combination, I spent about fifty minutes working out in advance all the possible ramifications involving both sides of the board.

I have to explain to the layman that tournament games must be conducted with time-clocks in order to force the combatants to move at reasonable intervals. Time-clocks had to be invented against old-time players who won their games through a preponderance of *Sitzfleisch*—or as my old friend, Dr. Siff, used to say: "What you need for chess isn't brains, but buttocks." During the classical era, a man with a lost position could wear down his opponent by sitting like Buddha and refusing to move—except once every hour or two. Staunton, the old British champion, won many a lost game in that fashion.

Time-clocks were the only means of keeping such devils within gentlemanly bounds, and, in the course of events, all tournaments, international, national or local, were conducted with the little double clocks ticking in accordance with which player's turn it was to move. World championships and international contests are run at the rate of fifteen moves an hour; contests of lesser importance at the rate of twenty: a fairly fast rate for players congenitally slow. I was one of these, and the tournament in question was run at the twenty-move rate. I now look upon that oversight of mine as the luckiest break in my whole existence. But at the time it was an overpowering tragedy.

Having spent fifty minutes on the first move of the combination, I would have only ten minutes to make my next nineteen moves. This, however, was a safe matter: I knew the combination by heart and, one by one, Chajes was making the anticipated moves. But I was deeply excited. Each time he made his next move and I made mine, I got up from the table and flitted about the room. My state was intensified by the interest in our game shown by the other contestants. Whenever they were free to leave their tables, they came over and followed the course of the combination—Capa and Marshall no less than the others. No one spoke to anybody else, but I could see experts nudge each other and eye me amazedly.

The whole thing went to my head. For years and years, I'd had a consuming chess ambition to rise by degrees to the New York State championship, the American, and finally, nothing less than the world crown—then held by Emanuel Lasker. A year or two before, I had tied with Capa for the State championship and only lost the play-off after a long, heartrending end game in which a mere tempo defeated me. Had it been his move, we would have drawn, but since it was mine I lost: the result, I swore, of defending the damned queen's pawn opening. Here was young Capa again; "fools" were already predicting he was destined to defeat Dr. Lasker. And here was Marshall, the American champion—and here was I, after having drawn an uphill battle, with two pawns down, against Hodges, a former American champion—and having won a game against the tantalizing Rice Club champion, Tenenwurzel. En route to victory over Chajes—the dark horse of the tournament—I would close the third round in the lead—providing I made my moves by heart. Veteran that I was at twenty-five, how could I possibly go wrong?

But I did. The general excitement was too much for my nerves. My hand began shaking with each successive move. The silence, above all, was unendurable. If I could have spoken to someone or someone could have spoken to me—but no. Chess contestants are pledged to non-communication as if they were prisoners under sentence for committing egregious crimes.

I shoved my pieces mechanically. The time-clock dangers were reduced. My opponent, beginning to detect the outcome of the combination, moved with increasing deliberation. But no matter how he pondered, he still had to make the moves I had figured on, once he'd entered the trap. They were the best at his disposal. By the time we neared the close of the combination, all the unengaged players were seated about the table, surrounded by practically all the spectators in the long, gray room. Capa and Marshall had been forgotten. I was the center of the chess world and I paced up and down outside the dark ring, a prey to frenzied emotions. After Chajes made his sixteenth move, I would only have to make my seventeenth and he his seventeenth. Then my eighteenth, the *coup de grâce*, would force him to resign.

I kept looking at the ring for a sign that the East Side veteran had made his sixteenth move. The sign came. A number of men looked my way and respectfully opened a path. Capa was one of the men who stepped aside. I could see him smile a little. I don't quite recall what followed. I was in a tingling haze and through the haze I saw that Chajes had made the necessary move. He shook his stoical head as he made it. I haven't the slightest idea why I didn't sit down and deliberate before making my penultimate move. I remember looking at my clock: I had ample time. But I didn't take it. Nor did I sit down. Exultantly, I made the move leaning over the table and then sat down. And then—to my frozen horror—I saw I had made, not my seventeenth, but my eighteenth move! I had transposed the moves and blundered outright!

9

A few moves later I resigned. Instead of an immortal game, a game for chess history—as Marshall assured me later—I had blundered like a tyro. An infinitesimal aberration cost me the game, my chances in the tournament and my whole chess career. Throughout the remaining rounds, people reverted to that strange oversight. They buttonholed me in off hours and again and again I had to explain how it had happened, from the first move to the last. And abed at night, each time I lost another game—I lost game after game—I rehearsed the cause of my collapse. Instead of finishing at the head or near the head of the contestants, I finished next to last.

But I had already reached a solemn determination. While sitting petrified in a chair which should have been a throne, and accepting Chajes' cordial condolence, I resolved to have done with chess tournaments, chess clubs and chess forever after. I lost nine pounds over that oversight. And thanks to a constant devotion to poetry, side by side with chess, there wasn't another pound I could afford to lose. I was about thirty pounds underweight and poorer than a sparrow. So I gave up chess for poetry. But that is another story.

II

Ultimately, I caught the serene view of the Chajes tragedy. Had I won the game, I would have been lured on to further victories and defeats, only to end in a chess master's grave—a dismal profession withal. The invincible Steinitz had fallen before the invincible Lasker, and Lasker before the invincible Capablanca, and Capa before the invincible Alekhine. Chess mastery—possibly like any other mastery— is a thing to keep away from. The people who usually enjoy chess are the dubs and duffers, experts who have resigned their ambitions and now play for the pastime, and the fraternity of kibitzers.

One uncertain day, rather bored with the self-centered world of poetry and the self-centered world at large, I found myself in the neighborhood of the Manhattan Chess Club and, being able to "resist anything but temptation," I dropped in. I was greeted with a delight I could not have received anywhere else on earth. And here, scarcely a day older than when I had last beheld them, were some of the friendly enemies of my youth: Rosen, Rosenthal, Meyer, Warburg,

Beihoff, Tenner. In chess, the Rosens bloom on and on. In the old days, over on Second Avenue, the crack players numbered Rosen, Rosenbaum, Rosenfeld, Rosenthal, Rosenzweig—the last truly a twig compared with the others.

Well, I was at home again, more at home than ever before. No time-clock was in evidence; no tourney in progress. Safe from the past, was I safe from the present? What was going on here? What had happened to chess? "Pots—" Rosen ventured.

"What are pots?"

I was swiftly initiated. Pots is a game invented by a fellow named Calladay— "Cal, he's called"—by way of destroying serious chess. And who is this Cal? A third-class goy who's just as poor at this game as he was at the old game. But pots are now the rage all over the chess world.

I watched the marvelous invention. Three players take turns playing one another the while the odd or disengaged player acts as the referee calling time. He calls time, not at the rate of fifteen or twenty moves an hour, but at ten seconds a move! I never saw so many blunders in my life—it was delightful. And the best of players blundered—still more delightful. No wonder Cal had invented Pots. If a fellow didn't move on time, "Forfeit!" the referee called and took the place of the offender, who took the place of the referee. The stakes are always a quarter a game. They are called "union rates." And shades of Caissa, what a noise—noise of all things at a chess club! It was all most alluring.

We had played rapid-transit chess in the past, but never with such wholesale gusto. In the earlier days on the East Side, where chess could be seen at its best and grimiest, a man named Louis Hein invented a game called the Marathon, in which twenty, thirty or forty dynamos engaged in a round-robin the while Hein bellowed "Move!" That was also ten-second chess, but Marathons used to drag on for hours, and long sessions of any sort were precisely the torture most old-timers had begun to revolt against.

Before I knew where I was at, I was seated at one of these crazy tables—"Try it and see, you old duffer," I was challenged. Never a fast player, and long out of practice, I could barely see two moves ahead.

Still worse, my lack of ambition undermined the will to win. I lost often and didn't mind losing. What had happened to me? I dropped in at the club again, merely to look on—and then to play, always to the friendly greeting, "you old duffer!" The name didn't nettle me. There were always old experts who recalled my former exploits to the youngsters who derided me. One day, I won a quick game from the Intercollegiate champion and the old-timers chortled. A large, grave gentleman, watching proceedings, remarked: *"Das war wie Eisen gespielt!"* The speaker was Alexander Alekhine. I thanked him and fled the table.

No one could rouse my ambition again, least of all the new world's champion. I'd sought the old haunt in pursuit of that momentary Nirvana which chess clubs afford to any profession: the law, medicine, music, commerce, religion or what not. I recalled a chess proverb: You can lose your wife one day and come here and forget her the next. Each of these men came here for relaxation, had always done so and always would. Best of all, these pots had buried the cut and dried queen's pawn opening. Chess was irregular again, adventurous, delirious, novel, absurd, human. The mummies who formerly shoved pieces about were flesh and blood again. And the laughter I heard had not been heard in my world for years. The rude explosion was neither ironical nor cynical. It had nothing to do with modernity, psychology, reasoning. It was forthright. And no one laughed louder than the dubs.

Men who rarely won a game before won many a game now, and won it from many a master. The master resigned with grace and then proceeded to trounce the potzer as the potzer had never been trounced before. Nothing pleased me more than the momentary rise of the duffers. Among my chess memories—or memories in general—none cling more tenaciously, or with more enduring affection, than those which shadow underdogs I have known. Here I have to revert again to the Second Avenue of my youth and young manhood.

III

I was then the queer little shaver who earned his livelihood by playing anyone and everyone at so much a game at all hours of the day and night. One thing that attracted me to the East Side was the fact that most men earned their living in just the same way. Another thing—most of the men were older than I, much older, some of them patriarchs. Still another—they were cultivated. When we weren't playing or talking chess, we talked about music and books: I went to school over there. And I learned philosophy without calling it such. We had no abstract words for what we felt and thought. When we wearied of talk, "Let's have another game—" there was always that. And no one was so hard up that there wasn't someone worse off. I remember the proprietor of a chess café who let the addicts sleep on or under tables overnight. I remember a potzer too proud for such beds. If he lost instead of won, he'd sleep on park benches. None of us found that out till he died on one. Then we chipped in to save him from Potter's Field. A witty fellow he was; none wittier over there where wit is an essential weapon to losers.

I remember a game I played with a rabbi old enough to be my father's grandfather. He had a beard longer than the beard of Moses. He combed it with care and let it hang at ease over one corner of the board. It was too long to hang anywhere else. We were in the midst of an exciting game in the midst of an excited band of kibitzers. I noticed nothing at the time but the game itself. The old rascal had "swindled" me out of the first game: a legitimate swindle, a coffeehouse trap. I vowed vengeance and dug myself into the table. The smoke was terrific—I didn't smoke in those days. The pieces we handled were heterogeneous: queens looked like bishops, bishops like pawns, and some of the knights had no heads. I was nearsighted, but I didn't mind. I'd got the hang of the pieces. And I'd got the hang of the position. But I didn't get the hang of the beard. I paid no attention to that.

The game was going my way. The rabbi was attacking on all sides, but I revelled in such tactics. I was always at my best building up walls against attacks, and then forcing a hole with a pawn, another pawn and then the counter-attack. The counter-attack was at work; it was working beautifully. The old fellow shook his head; so did the other old fellows. They began poking fun at him, unmerciful fun. "Warte nur," he said, but kept on retreating. "Warte nur yourself," I retorted, and went on advancing.

Suddenly, I detected a mate in three and cried, "Check!" He moved his king. Then I shouted, "Check again!" and he moved his king. Then I grabbed my queen, banged her down and crowed, "Checkmate, my friend!" The rabbi shook his head calmly. "Not yet, my friend," he replied, lifting his magnificent beard off the corner of the board. Out came a rook that removed my queen!

Then there was an old fellow named Ziegenschwarz who hated to win games that didn't end in checkmates. He took a sadistic delight in encouraging his victims to struggle on to the very end. He simply wouldn't let them resign. He'd even make bad moves to keep them going awhile longer, and chattered away in an effort to keep them cheerful. His favorite opponent was a melancholy soul named Levkowitz.

Levkowitz was an ideal loser: he not only lost as a rule, but he lost with a series of groans that deepened and lengthened with each hopeless move. One evening I watched the pair: Levkowitz looked not alone forlorn, but ill, very ill. He kept complaining about his *Magen*: he'd eaten some indigestible herring.

"There's nothing the matter with herring," Ziegenschwarz argued; "it's your game disagrees with you."

"I've got a lost game!"

"No, you haven't, move, you *Pfuscher!*"

Levkowitz made a lame move—"I've got a lost game, I resign."

"No, you don't—" and Ziegenschwarz made a weak move.

Levkowitz brightened a little, but suddenly scowled and moaned: "I feel sick."

"No, you don't—move, *Dummkopf!*"

Levkowitz made a heroic effort, moved—and was sick in earnest. He tried to get up, but Ziegenschwarz wiped off the board with his sleeve, made a move and grabbed his victim's sleeve.

"I'm nearly mate."

"No you're not. Move, move!"

Levkowitz moved and was violently sick again. His tormentor wiped and moved with mad acceleration.

"I'm lost, lost," Levkowitz moaned.

"Move once more, just once more."

Levkowitz moved and staggered from the table.

"*Schachmatt!*" howled Ziegenschwarz without wiping the table and hustled after his friend: "Come, I'd better take you home."

IV

The crown prince of East Side chess was and still is Charles Jaffe. It is impossible to convey the weird type of game he used to play and the respect it won him among the cohorts along the avenue. If ever a man held court around a table, it was this very dark, slender, cigarette-smoking gypsy. The moment he arrived and sat down with some dub, most other tables were deserted. I venture to say that if Capa and Lasker had fought out their battles on the avenue and Jaffe and his dubs sat down near by, the world warriors would have been deserted by the kibitzers.

Jaffe kept up a running fire of caustic badinage and could give amazing odds to the potzers. I never saw any high-class player give such odds and get away with them. The reverence in which he was held was mainly due to this faculty. He was a genius against weaker players. And they measured the rest of the chess world accordingly. If a better player than Jaffe (there were, of course, none better!) failed to win games at the odds the prince gave, he was treated with comparative contempt.

The ability to play coffeehouse chess was one in which Jaffe surpassed any master. Coffeehouse chess depends on an alert ingenuity in waylaying the opponent through subtle little traps or swindles. Usually the trap is baited with a sacrificial pawn no potzer can resist smelling and seizing. Were the pawn a consequential piece, the fellow would hesitate and look around. But the little pawns overwhelm his appetite. It is almost an axiom that most games have been lost and won through hastily grabbing those innocent pawns.

Jaffe was a veritable devil in leaving them about and in keeping up an undercurrent of teasing cajolery, mock-heroics, encouragement, quips and puns. No wonder Second Avenue held him in awe! And no wonder the avenue held the outside masters in comparative contempt! Even Lasker, king of the whole chess world, was held in doubt where Jaffe was concerned. As for Capa, he was a duffer by comparison. "Jaffe could beat Capa blindfolded!"

Unhappily, once the crown prince left the avenue he was not so invulnerable. Invite him to a tournament among his peers, take away his magic banter and force him to face sound, scientific chess, and his traps proved of little avail. Traps were often his own undoing. What we call playing for position—a damnable modern invention—was something his valiant combinations couldn't penetrate. The extreme caution of modern chess wore down his temperamental inspirations. He belonged to the school of Paul Morphy, giant meteor of the romantic era.

Jaffe, in truth, should have been born among the Labourdonnais and MacDonnells who never defended themselves, but went on attacking till the other fellow's attacks demolished them. Even inferior players, by playing book openings and developing "according to Hoyle," could defeat him by letting him defeat himself. Jaffe seldom disgraced himself in tournaments. He had the habit of defeating superiors and losing to inferiors which seems to be the outcome of taking chances. No matter how he fared, he was always defended by the cohorts.

I recall the international tournament in Europe he embarked on some years ago. He didn't have the fare abroad and had to raise it through subscription—so I was told at the time. Doubtless, most of it was raised east of Third Avenue and south of Fourteenth Street. Over on Second Avenue, newspapers were scanned as they had never been scanned before, and there was only one daily event the readers turned to. I'm not in the mood for rehearsing those long days of silent gloom. Jaffe went abroad to show the *Schachmeister* what duffers they were and finished, not on top, nor anywhere near the top. When he returned, did the avenue upbraid him or drape itself in mourning? I went across town with that question in mind, ready to say what I could if necessary. I didn't have to say it. Jaffe was surrounded by a ring of laughing, gossiping kibitzers. Opposite him sat a time-honored potzer.

The potzer was eying and trying not to eye a terribly tempting pawn. I prayed to all the gods that the fellow would nab it. He didn't nab it. He hesitated, circled the board with his eyes and looked at everything but the little pawn. The suspense was growing quite awful. It silenced the kibitzers. It silenced Jaffe himself. He looked rather drawn after the foreign debacle. I wanted to shake hands with him, wring his arm off, slap his back, hug him—but I'd have to wait.

He was smoking away as usual. His side of the board was strewn with cigarette stubs, ashes and burnt matches. The famous lurking smile was absent. Confound that *Pfuscher!* Why didn't he relieve our suspense? All he'd lose would be a dime, and that pawn was worth a fortune to us. His glance no longer circled, but concentrated on one spot. The spot, confound him, was far removed from the pawn. Then he smiled slyly and lifted his left hand. Why did he lift that hand— he always moved with the other?

Then, praise Elohim, the hand closed round his queen and quietly clipped off the pawn. Jaffe smiled, lifted a knight and put it down ever so gently—forking the duffer's king, queen and two rooks. Hysteria rent the air. Jaffe raised his hand—"Wait, let him look!"

"I have to lose the exchange," sighed the duffer.

"Look again."

"I have to lose one of my rooks or the queen—"

"Look again."

"I'm in check—wait—I'll move my king—but wait—I don't want to lose my queen—why didn't you say check?"

"I didn't have to say check, potzer! Where are your ears? Didn't you hear me say mate?"

The hysteria revived. Pandemonium smote the table. *"Rinnsvieh, Nebbich, Dummkopf, Schlemiel!"* the cohorts clamored. . . .

V

Well, here I am, here I am again, a ghost unashamed of his past. The game I now play is less than the shadow of the game I used to play. Fellows I formerly gave odds to, now play me even, or have the impudence to offer me odds. Worst of all, I'm no longer a hard loser; and if I leave a rook *en prise* in one game, I leave my queen in the next. *Sic transit etcetera!*

Luckily, I'm in first-class company. Other old-timers who sit down with me are not much better than I. Sometimes I pay them a quarter; sometimes they pay me—and we always play Pots. We open our sessions with a few plausible alibis. One man has a headache from trying to sell life insurance policies; another looks weary from having done nothing all day, and the third—I mention actual cases—had read a rotten review of his latest poems.

Somehow, on the evening in question, the weary gentleman had won three pots in a row: an unheard of record for him. The life-insurance salesman—who is none other than George Beihoff—let it go at that and shrugged his shoulders. Throughout chess history, vanquished players are entitled to the immortal post-mortem: "I had a won game." The third time I sang the slogan, Anonymous—I have to call him that —shot back: "You had a won game, but I won it." We started to sputter and argue. Beihoff finally cut us short and turned on Anonymous: "Why shouldn't you beat us at chess? You've retired from business, you live on your income and your sex-life is over."

Without further ado, I rejoined the Manhattan Club in earnest. I entered my name for a life-membership. But there's a special clause in my application. It provides that if I'm ever caught starting anything remotely resembling a serious game, I'm to be expelled without trial by the board of governors.

Exchange of Men

BY JOSEPH CROSS

♛ WHEN the train pulled slowly out of Grand Central, Francis Baron took the miniature chessboard from his pocket and began to contemplate it. He did not set out the pieces, but simply studied the sixty-four black and white squares on which, you might say, he played not only chess but his whole life as well. Already as he watched the vacant board, invisible pieces moved and combined in his mind's eye, developing of themselves the studied complexities of his games. It was as he had once said, "When one passes a certain stage, one no longer moves the pieces, but simply watches them move." Francis Baron had passed that stage by the time he was twenty years old. What he was doing now, and expected to be doing until the train reached Boston, might be compared to the five-finger exercises which a great virtuoso performs faithfully every day. A discipline, a regimen, and more: he knew that from these simple diversions might come the inspiration that would save a game, the subtle but definite variation that had never appeared in books. It had happened so before, and the books had modified themselves agreeably: "The following brilliant line of play was employed for the first time in any tournament by the American master, Francis Baron. . . ."

Now, at the age of forty, on his way to the International Tournament, his appearance certainly suggested nothing so artistic and out of the way as a chess master. He was a small man, neatly and not distinctively dressed, and his only peculiarity was a rather oversize round head from which large eyes peered through silver-rimmed glasses. This anonymity of appearance, coupled with his magnificent play, had caused someone to nickname him "the mighty pawn," a title which, with that other more grandiose one of "master" he had retained since his early tournaments.

Conductors and people passing through the car glanced curiously at the little man who nursed in his lap the unoccupied chessboard as though it were a treasure or a secret sorrow; and a personable young man, who sat with a pretty girl across the aisle, leaned over and asked, "Would you care to have a game?"

Baron looked up in some annoyance. "Thank you, no," he said primly, and while he spoke he exchanged queens with his invisible opponent, and came out with the advantage of a pawn. That was one thing about being a master: you could not play with anybody you happened to meet. Even a master dropped games surprisingly often, and such a loss to an unknown opponent in a railroad car would be embarrassing, not to mention the detriment to one's reputation. Also, though Baron was a young man compared to most of the masters he would meet in tournament play, he already had a strong respect, which soon would become fear, for the rising generation. He himself must have looked like a naive innocent when, at twenty-three, he defeated Orimund in the first of many games. Now he could not blame Orimund for behaving so ungraciously afterward.

Fearing he might have been rude, he said now, "I'm terribly busy, you see," and realized that it must have sounded ridiculous.

"Are you going to watch the tournament in Boston?" the young man asked.

Baron hesitated. "Yes," he said finally. "Yes, I expect to be there." Firmly his mind told him, rook takes rook, pawn takes rook, check . . . the ending would be simplicity itself.

"I guess it's really between Orimund, Savard, and Baron," said the young man. "No one else has much chance against those three."

The mate, Baron thought, would be accomplished with a very small force, because the white king was blocked in three directions by his own pawns.

"I admire Orimund very much," the young man continued. "He's the last of the old grand masters. He has the most intense attack I've ever seen. I rather hope he becomes champion again. It would be a victory not only for himself but for his style of play as well."

"You don't care for the modern way?" asked Baron.

"Too much subtlety, too much caution," said the young man. "Modern chess isn't playing, it's waiting."

"It wins."

"Look," the young man offered. "How about a game? I'll spot you whatever you like—a rook, even."

Baron smiled slowly. "I don't think that will be necessary."

"Well, I feel I should tell you; I'm Richard James, that is—I don't suppose you've heard of me. I won the intercollegiate championship last year."

So this was Richard James. Baron remembered a piece in the papers, not about the intercollegiate tournament, but about another, a small affair in Chicago, in which a young man named Richard James had lost rather badly to Max Tarnes but carried off the brilliancy prize all the same for a rather exciting combination against Jacob Goldman. He could see the familiar old pattern as it began to repeat itself. In a year, or two years, or three, he would be facing the brilliant young master, Richard James, across the tournament board, and everything would be at stake. But nothing need be given away at this moment. He began to set up the pieces.

"I'd still prefer to play even," he said.

"Now are you satisfied?" asked the pretty girl. "You've trapped the innocent bystander into a game. That's what's such fun about being married to Dick," she explained to Baron, "you meet such a lot of interesting people. But by a strange coincidence, they all play chess."

The young man laughed. "I want you to meet my wife, Sally, Mr.—?"

Baron looked at the board. "Springer, John Springer," he said, using the German name for knight. His use of a pseudonym, he told himself, was not in the least disreputable. After all, he had a standing which must be jealously guarded at every moment. Suppose there should be a slip, an accident, the distraction of being aboard a rattling train, the disturbingly informal conditions generally—he did not intend that such an accident should affect the reputation or the tournament play of Francis Baron during the next week.

But in trying, temporarily, at least, to conceal his identity, he must not, he knew, employ his own style of play, which to an expert would at once reveal both his name and his quality. He must accept, then, the disadvantage of meeting Richard James on the latter's own ground, which would probably be the ground of a violent attack, initiated as rapidly as possible. Ordinarily Baron would withdraw before such an attack and use his whole development for defense, for subtle probing and slow exploiting of weaknesses, occupying more and more space in the long wait for his opponent's critical mistake, which must come in time. Then, rapidly, the complexion of the match would change. From the reticence of his beginnings and his control of strategic area, Baron would open out the penetrating, incisive, and fatal counterattack. That was the way, the modern style, which had made Baron a master. But now he must fight by older and riskier methods.

Young James drew the white and opened with the Max Lange attack, quick and straight down the center of the board. It was evident that he was trying for immediate victory, and accepting a disadvantageous position if the attempt failed.

Baron countered along conventional lines, vigorously fighting for the center, for the points from which well-masked and defended powers could extend their grasp on positions within the enemy's lines. Both men were slightly nervous. There was a quality of chess, thought Baron, which made it absurd to say, "It's only a game." On the contrary, as you could judge from the way people played it, it was a warlike and representative struggle for mastery. It was a conspectus of life itself, with the illusion of power over life, which is why, though unthinking people laugh to hear of it, the chess master often dies worn out, overstrained from an incredible depth and complexity of concentration prolonged over a period of years.

As they entered the end game with an exchange of queens, James was a pawn behind, but occupied better immediate attacking position.

"You play extremely well, sir," he said deferentially to Baron, who nodded and smiled. The position, he saw, was critical. If Richard James possessed perfect book knowledge, he had what amounted to a winning game. On the other hand, he was nervous, just about trembling with eagerness for success. If that nervousness could be exploited properly, or improperly, for that matter, but exploited somehow—Francis Baron regretted exceedingly having been drawn into the match. This young man would be present at the tournament, he would recognize his opponent of the railroad car, there would surely be some publicity. He could imagine Savard's wry, crooked grin; and not alone Savard. Baron was not so well liked among the masters; they resented his youth and perhaps his manner as well. There would be a good deal of laughter over this.

Abruptly he said, "I'm afraid I didn't tell you my real name." He smiled in apology, held out his hand. "I'm Francis Baron."

On the surface it was all right. It was even a compliment to the younger man. The master, by revealing his identity, seemed to be acknowledging a worthy opponent. And Richard James tried desperately to take the acknowledgment in that spirit. But there was now too much at stake. He was no longer playing a chess game. He was playing, with a chance to win, against Francis Baron himself. He blushed and stammered, "I hope you didn't think me rude—about Orimund, I mean. I had no idea—"

"Of course not." Francis Baron smiled. "Orimund plays his way, I play mine. It's your move, Mr. James."

Two moves later Richard James moved the pawn that cost him the game. His famous antagonist was gracious in triumph, quiet and assured as he complimented the younger man on playing a very strong game.

"We shall be seeing you in tournament play very soon, I fear," he said cordially when they parted in Back Bay Station.

"You're very kind to say so; we look forward to watching your games."

Both men knew what had happened. For Baron the victory was rather empty, achieved by a trick in a class with blowing smoke in your opponent's face throughout a game (this being the favorite stratagem of one Russian master), or whistling, or tapping your fingers on the table. And worst of all, he did not know if he could have won that particular game without such a device.

As for Richard James, he said to his wife, "I don't know why he had to pick that moment to tell me who he was. I was doing all right until then, but Lord! to be up against Francis Baron! I just collapsed right there."

"And that," said Sally, "is just about what he wanted. Your Francis Baron may be a great master, but it strikes me he's just a little bit of a heel at the same time."

"Now, darling, he could have beaten me anyhow."

"Don't 'now darling' me. I don't know much about chess, and he may have been able to beat you hollow; but from what I saw of his face at the time, he didn't think so."

The players in the tournament, thought Baron, had all the solemnity and high seriousness of a conclave of cardinals met to elect a new Pope, and all the jealousy, to be sure, of a boy's ball team electing a captain. It was the first international tournament since before the war, and the meeting was marked by the absence of a few faces formerly well known: Estignan, who was dead; Zinuccio, who had turned Fascist and was in prison; Einrich, who was not allowed to leave his country. But the others he knew well enough: the English master, Cranley, looking in his rich tweeds like an aged schoolboy; Savard, the Frenchman, a dumpy little man who resembled a chef and played the most eccentric games of any master; Jasoff, from Russia, looking more than usually peaked and unhappy; and several other masters from all over the world. Second-rate, thought Baron. And yet, not really second-rate: so little distance, in chess, separated the master from the expert, the merely brilliant player. It was more than probable, he reflected with distaste, that he would lose games to more than one of them. But fortunately, in a chess tournament one was not eliminated for losing a game. Elimination occurred at definite stages, on the basis of point score: one for a win, one-half for a draw. After a complete round, the contestants with the lowest scores went out and the remainder began again.

And there was Orimund, at last. The aged master whose white hair stood out like a wiry halo over his head, who always wore a high white collar and shiny black suit. Orimund, nearing seventy, with his trembling hands, his gentle voice and perfect manners, and that mind whose keenness had probably suffered somewhat during the last years. They said he had spent time in a concentration camp, and looking at him now, Baron found it easy to believe this. He had not remembered the old man as so gentle, so meek. They met in the lobby of the hotel, and Orimund seemed to have forgotten his resentment of Baron. They called each other, conventionally, Master, and were for a moment almost friendly.

"Ech, life passes, Master Baron," the old man said. "You, too, are no longer exactly of the youngsters."

Was that the way of it? Did one creep gently out of life, shedding the old antagonisms, ridding oneself gradually of the vicious desire for success?

"I am glad to have the honor once again, Master," he replied.

"Perhaps for the last time," Orimund said. "You know, years ago, when I was asked 'How can you waste your life playing chess?' I was able to reply 'How can you waste your life writing books, or making money, or painting pictures, or whatever?' And it was a good, an acceptable answer. Now, I confess, I begin to wonder, what have I done? I was given my life, and what have I made of it?"

"You leave an immortal name," replied Baron gravely.

"An immortal name—better to have died ten years ago, much better. Perhaps you will understand that someday, Master." This last, Baron recognized, was said with the familiar cold, deadly anger that he remembered as an element in the former Orimund. But Baron understood what the old man meant: better to have died champion of the world, rather than face the failing of one's powers, the uprising of the young just when one is no longer able to oppose them with success. Better than the last cold years in which, if a master makes a mistake, he believes himself to be losing his mind.

That was the last time they spoke together except over the board. Almost angrily, Baron put down the pity he felt for the old genius. If that's the way it is, that's all, he told himself. When my time comes, I don't expect to weep on the conqueror's shoulder. That's what life is, and if we were the same age I would still be confident of winning. For that matter, if the position were reversed would he show any mercy to me? I doubt it.

The tournament was not easy. Few can go through the nervous strain of game after game against excellent players without feeling a sense of desperation, and Francis Baron was no exception. The competition grew progressively more severe, and in the last matches of the opening round one came up against players who, knowing already that they would be eliminated, played with violence and extravagance in the hope of taking home by way of consolation at least one victory over a possible world's champion. Baron was beaten in this way by Jasoff and Cranley, while Orimund dropped games to Savard and to Baron himself.

Baron, however, was superbly confident. In the first round he had beaten Savard, and his victory over Orimund was achieved, if not easily, at least with certainty and power from the opening move of a solid, invulnerable game. The old man played with a brilliance matching his former great tournament play, but finding his attack met at all points he overextended his defenses slightly and was unable to withstand the vicious counterattack when it finally came.

Richard and Sally were present at all his matches, and though Baron did not in any way acknowledge their interest, he felt intensely and uncomfortably that they had in some sense seen through what had occurred on the train, that it would give them pleasure if he lost, that they were in fact simply waiting for him to make a mistake. He smiled ironically to himself. There would be no mistakes, there must be none —perfection. And forthwith he proceeded roundly to trounce Dr. Anderson, his last opponent in the first round.

Orimund, Savard, Francis Baron, and an Irishman named Brian alone escaped elimination. In the second round Brian realized suddenly that he was very close to being world's champion, and simply collapsed, losing to everyone. Savard lost to Baron and Orimund, and these last drew their games and entered the final with a score of two and a half each for the round.

On the night before the last match, Baron was sitting in the hotel lobby, reading, when he was approached by the secretary of the local chess club.

"We have about ten people collected," this functionary said, "and we wondered if you'd care to give some sort of exhibition. We should be honored, greatly honored, Master, and I can say definitely that there will be no publicity. Of course, I realize that you may not feel inclined to make the effort on the eve of the final, but I was instructed to ask you all the same." He hesitated, looked apologetic, and seemed, as though realizing the enormity of his request, to be ready to retire without an answer; but Baron stopped him.

"Under the conditions you specify," he said, "I shouldn't object to the exercise. In fact, I'm grateful for the compliment of your interest. But understand, I'll hold you to strict silence on the subject. In the first place, it would be a reflection on my opponent if it got out that I was so careless of him as to play for fun on the night before our game. I can play tonight only if it is understood that the results don't matter, that it is simply a relaxation from the tournament."

"I quite understand," the secretary said. "This is the arrangement. The members will be told that a master, whose name will not be given, will play blindfolded against all ten of them simultaneously. The master will be in a room apart, and will not meet the other players either before or after the match. In that way the secret of your identity can be kept between the president and myself until after tomorrow night. And besides, the other players will be asked to keep silent about the whole event."

These terms proving to Baron's satisfaction, he was driven to the quarters of the Copley Chess Club, where he was placed in a small antechamber and left alone. Presently the secretary came in.

"It has been arranged," he said, "that you are to have white in the even-numbered games and black in the odd. Fair enough?"

"Fair enough," replied Francis Baron.

"Then the first move in all the odd-numbered games is pawn to king four," said the secretary.

"My reply is the same, and my opening move in the even-numbered games is pawn to queen four."

That was the way of it, he thought. In this blindfolded game one allowed the opponents to open up a little, and then when the weak sisters among them disclosed themselves, they must be whipped rapidly, allowing one to concentrate on the difficult games.

The amateurs did show themselves very soon. Games one, two, four, eight, and nine took less than fifteen moves for the establishment of overwhelming superiority on Baron's side. Few of the boards presented any great difficulty. There was the usual zealot who felt that the queen-side pawns could do everything necessary, one who thought that to *fianchetto* both bishops was to solve all his troubles, another who brought out his queen and proceeded to do damage to the extent of a rook and a pawn before falling into a cleverly prepared trap. Few of the games were in any way rewarding, except as an exercise in concentration for the master.

At last game number seven sorted itself out from the rest; there was something there. A Max Lange attack, with a curious variation in the placement of the queen's knight. Going over the position in his mind, Baron began to recognize the style. His opponent, he was almost certain, could be no one but Richard James. A few minutes later an astonishingly rapid attack confirmed his belief. Baron felt himself being pressed with some severity and marshaled his forces to defend. It would be a close game.

The other games expired in something over the fortieth move. He had won them all, but then, the competition had been very nearly nothing. The seventh game, however, was close and even threatening. James was playing for a brilliant win and as things stood it was well within the possible for him to achieve it. And this time there was no way of breaking the boy's nerve; instead, Baron knew, his own nerve might go. It was so easy to make a mistake; he was holding precariously in his mind the crossing, tangling threads of thirty-two pieces moving altogether more than eighty times over sixty-four squares. The possibilities were infinite. If one forgot a move, or misplaced a move in memory, it was over: defeat. One defeat, of course, in ten blindfold games, is nothing; but to lose to young James! And he was certain that James knew his opponent; he felt an intellectual rapport that enabled him to picture the handsome young face as it bent over the board, and realized that James knew perfectly that he was playing—and winning —against Francis Baron.

And then it came. The secretary entered, said, "Game number seven. Pawn to bishop six."

"Is he certain of that?" Baron asked, incredulous.

"That is his move, sir."

"My reply—queen takes rook."

Francis Baron breathed easily. Richard James had made a mistake, a subtle mistake, to be sure, and not immediately apparent, but the master could now foresee the imminent collapse of his opponent's game. After the sacrifice of the queen, knight and two rooks would accomplish the rest. He called after the secretary, "I announce checkmate in six moves."

It went as he planned, now. On the fifth move he forced the white rook to occupy the square adjacent to the white king, thus blocking all escape squares and enabling the knight to mate at bishop seven. He returned to his hotel.

But he was troubled in his mind. A mistake like that, it was unnatural, considering how masterful James's play had been up until then. It was tantamount to deliberate surrender, it was . . . it was deliberate surrender! He saw it now. James had recognized his adversary, had realized that Baron, strained by the tournament, could be upset beyond measure by a defeat of any sort at this moment, and he had deliberately opened up his board so as to be defeated. It was a gesture of the most subtle and keen sportsmanship; it was, in a way, a moral revelation. After all, he reflected, when you consider that he probably dislikes me intensely, and realized that he had it in his power to hurt my game and refrained—that shows the greatest delicacy.

Francis Baron found it difficult to get to sleep. His own face kept appearing to him, saying, "I am Francis Baron, I am Francis Baron," over and over with the utmost pomposity imaginable. "What was it for?" he asked himself. For a game of chess. Chess is not, after all, life itself. Chess, if you regard it properly, is a game. A great game, true; but is it worth the demands it makes? Fancy a man like Orimund, now, decrepit, feeling bitterly the decline of his powers, yet playing with the most religious courtesy and chivalry.

He could imagine Orimund after the final match, returning alone to Europe. There would still be many admirers, would still be the satisfaction of a good game, not a great game, mind; but deeply, essentially, he would be an old man, nearing death, alone.

Orimund won the final game. Francis Baron would never forget how the reporters gathered around after the game, nor how the old man wept far more over his success than he would have wept over his defeat. And how Orimund called him "Master" and said good-by in the most touching and friendly way, his hand on the younger man's shoulder. "After me," he had said, "in a year, less perhaps, who knows?"

Between dejection and satisfaction, Francis Baron, runner-up for the world's chess championship, packed his bag and prepared to return to New York. The analysis of that final game, he knew, would give many people reason enough to laugh at him.

"Come in," he said in response to a knock.

Richard and Sally James stood at the door. He invited them in, and Richard said, "We just wanted you to know we saw what you did in that game." Sally nodded in agreement. "And we'd like to tell you we thought it was wonderful."

"Did? I didn't do anything—except lose, of course."

"You gave him the game. You did it purposely, and you did it so that no one who didn't know both your styles perfectly would ever realize."

Francis Baron smiled at them. "There's no need to shout it all over the place," he said. "Anyhow, I've got you to thank for my quixotic behavior. You taught me a great deal about games and other things last night."

"Last night?" James looked blank.

"Yes. At the Copley Club, you know, game number seven."

"I don't get it," Richard James said, "I've never been to the Copley Club in my life."

Check . . . and Mate

BY JAY WILSON

It was generally conceded in the circles in which he traveled that the discovery of the atomic bomb had been something of a setback to Freddy Ferguson's chances of proving himself an acceptable son-in-law to General Lane. If it had been Freddy, for instance, who had made the discovery, the General might have been impressed. As it was, it was felt that just one more field had been closed to Freddy, and his chances of being regarded as other than a blithe sort of idiot by the father of the indisputably lovely Jo reduced by just that much. As a matter of fact, it was not entirely certain that Jo herself did not go along at least part way with the General's views on Freddy.

"And don't ever," Jo said one evening, "let Father see you swallow a lighted cigarette again. He was retired for ulcers."

They were dancing at El Morocco and Freddy completed an intricate little side step and glide of his own invention before answering. "I don't really swallow it," he said.

Jo tilted her sleek blond head back to look up into Freddy's serene countenance. Freddy's features, as standard assembly jobs went, were not unpleasant to look at. Well-fed, amiable and clean. A face one could get along with if one didn't expect too much.

"Don't be an ass," Jo said. A pleased expression came into her eyes as she followed another complicated little dance pattern Freddy had evolved. Then her mind went back to the problem at hand. "You've

31

got to do something about Father, you know. Assert yourself. Show him you've got something."

"Card tricks?"

Jo sniffed daintily. "Save those for the children."

"I've just learned the 'Donkey Serenade' on the harmonica."

"Freddy," Jo said impatiently, "are you really as big a chump as you sound sometimes? There is probably nothing Father would like to hear more than a harmonica selection than the sound of a harmonica player sizzling in hot oil."

"Stuffy old coot," Freddy sighed. "What's he want to be so grim for? Of all the millions of parents you could have had, why you had to select that old moose for is more than I can understand."

By the slight stiffening of the slim body in his arms he knew that somehow he had not said quite the right thing. "What I mean," he added quickly, "is that I don't know just what he expects in a man."

"Perhaps," Jo said coolly, "he just expects a man."

Freddy grunted. If there was one criticism he might have made of the girl he loved it was that deep within her there was a streak of the General. She could laugh at his jokes and listen to his harmonica. She danced like a spring breeze in his arms and he thought she was almost ready to love him as he loved her. But every so often the General came out in her and she would want him to prove something for the mere sake of proving it. Like taking a job. He hadn't needed a job. A pair of scissors and a trip to the bank once in a while to clip coupons gave him more than he required. But he had taken a job . . . and gotten three raises, much to his surprise. Lately Jo had become stiffish about the General. She wanted the General to approve of Freddy. He, Freddy, didn't care whether the General approved of him or not. Jo could be exasperating.

"And I suppose," Freddy growled, "that I'm not a man?"

"Would you care to have me quote Father?" Jo asked, still cold.

"You know, Jo," Freddy said, "your trouble is you're not satisfied with things as they are. You'd want a town car to pull like a truck and you'd want a truck to do seventy miles an hour . . . and you'd wreck them both trying to make them do what they weren't built to do. Why don't you relax? You can't make me over."

It was, he felt, a neat and pointed little speech. Something for Jo to think about. If she had a reasonable bone in her lovely body she'd see what he meant. The music stopped and they went back to their table. Jo was silent and Freddy congratulated himself upon having gained a point.

At the table Jo said, "You're rationalizing. You know perfectly well you'd like Father's respect. In fact, I insist on it."

Freddy sighed again. "Did it ever occur to you," he asked, "that perhaps your father does not measure up to all the things *I* think *he* should be?"

Jo stared at Freddy. "Don't be ridiculous!" she said.

"Sometimes he gets in my hair," Freddy muttered, ignoring all danger signals. "Sometimes I feel like telling him he's rude, uncivilized and . . ."

"He's home right now," Jo interrupted. "Why don't you tell him?"

As Freddy explained later, a form of madness came over him from which he awakened to find himself in the Lane library face to face with Jo's father. He describes that awakening as one of the more horrible moments of his life.

The General was playing chess. That is, the General was absorbed in working out a chess problem by himself, playing both the white and the black pieces. As always, and in spite of anything he had said to Jo, Freddy experienced the usual rubbery feeling about the knees. The General was not a large man but he gave the impression of vastness. His close-cropped mustache was white frost on a steeltrap mouth. Freddy had never before seen the General so absorbed and unaware of his presence. He was sitting forward in a deep leather armchair, leaning over an Oriental table on which was a large inlaid chessboard. The pieces were also large, intricately carved and beautiful. It was a set, Freddy knew, which only a devotee of the game would be likely to possess.

It was the first time that Freddy had known the General was that way about the game. At that moment, leaning so absorbed over the board, he looked like Freddy's grandfather. Freddy shuddered slightly. Grandfather Ferguson had been a master of the game—one who felt that all the mental training required to cope with anything that would come up in life could be taught on the chessboard. Among Freddy's more vivid memories of his younger years had been those chess lessons his grandfather had insisted on. During the war, at moments when things had been especially tense, Freddy had recalled those lessons and had been able to relax in the comparative peace of his shell-jarred foxhole.

Jo said, "Hello."

The General started. He looked up at her. "Oh, it's you. Home early, aren't you? Did that young jackanapes . . ." The General saw Freddy standing there shifting unhappily from one foot to the other and the northern lights flickered in his glacial eyes.

"Har!" he said so explosively that Freddy felt his vertebrae jolt violently up and down his spine like the cars of a suddenly braked freight train.

"Har!" Freddy heard himself echo weakly and involuntarily.

The General stared at him. "What did you say?"

"Uh . . . 'har' . . . I think."

"And precisely what in the goddam hell does that mean?"

Freddy felt a mild perspiration begin to ooze from his brow. At the same time a little irritation stirred within him, too. Short of using a lethal weapon he was at a disadvantage against anyone who didn't care a hoot about anyone else's sensitivities. Still, there were limits. Freddy noted that Jo was smiling a little. She was being a splintery little chip off the old block at the moment. Freddy pulled himself together.

"It means, I suppose, the same thing that it does when you say it."

An immediate and complete silence settled in the Lane library. Jo stopped smiling and her eyes widened. The General's eyes narrowed. He inhaled a long, slow breath. Freddy held his . . . and waited.

"Young man," the General demanded finally, "are you trying to intimate that I would make an asinine sound like that?"

Freddy swallowed. "You . . ."

"You cleared your throat, darling," Jo interrupted. "To say hello."

"I did not," the General snapped. He looked at Freddy. "What do you want anyway?"

There are two schools of thought regarding the appropriateness of

Freddy's reply to that question. There were those who felt that it was entirely out of order inasmuch as there had been nothing in the General's prior words to warrant any assumption of favorable reaction . . . and there were those who pointed out that while it was true that a more sympathetic mood could have been desired, it was also true that it was the first time the General had given Freddy enough consideration to utter intelligible sounds in his direction. The latter school felt that Freddy took advantage of the best opportunity which had or would be likely to present itself to go on record about what it was he really wanted.

"I want to marry your daughter, sir," he said in a remarkably firm but respectful manner.

The General made a sort of choking noise. Jo stared at Freddy.

"Good Lord!" the General finally said. "The man is crazy! Jo, why didn't you warn me?"

"Darling," Jo said to her father, "that was the last thing I ever expected him to say to you . . . tonight." She looked at Freddy. "Pinhead!"

Freddy's irritation increased. He looked at Jo. "Would you mind explaining that?"

"There isn't a damn' thing to explain, young man," the General cut in. "My daughter said you were a pinhead. It's perfectly clear. P-I-N-H-E-A-D, pinhead."

"Father!" Jo said. "I didn't really mean that." Jo was sorry now that she had let Freddy in for this. "Freddy is really very sweet in lots of ways."

"Har!" snorted the General.

"Oh, har yourself!" Freddy said.

Even a sweet nature could be pushed too far. Now his eye fell upon the chessboard again. "Don't tell me you've been having trouble with that little problem?"

The General came to his feet. "What?" he roared.

Freddy moved over to the chessboard without answering. He studied the problem that was so like the many Grandfather Ferguson had made him sweat out. While the General was obviously trying to decide whether to have the butler throw Freddy out or to indulge in the pleasure himself and Jo stood with her lovely lips forming a little O of amazement Freddy began moving pieces on the chessboard.

"There's your solution," he said. "Child's play."

The General looked at the board and then at Freddy. The General had been baffled for an hour before Freddy and Jo had come in.

"Any pinhead could see through that problem," Freddy went on, rubbing it in.

The emotions that were actually surging through the General at that moment were only feebly indicated by the flush raging on his cheeks. He stood frozen until at last he succeeded in pointing to the chair across the table.

"Sit down!" he whispered.

"Freddy!" Jo said.

The General drew the white pieces. In six moves Freddy knew that the General was really a keen player, probably one of the best, but that he was throwing caution to the wind to smash Freddy quickly. The General was a wounded bull pawing the dirt. Freddy developed carefully, waited for the premature attack he knew the General was bound to make in that mood and then smashed the attack. The General stared at the chessmen as if they were so many small cobras flicking their tongues at him.

He looked up at Freddy. "All right," he said hoarsely. "I resign."

"Why?" Freddy asked. "I could win with your pieces from that position."

"Freddy!" he heard Jo say. "Don't."

Freddy ignored her. He turned the board around. He was savoring triumph at its sweetest. Pinhead, was he? Freddy acknowledged that in a calm frame of mind the General would have been a far different opponent but tonight the General was getting it right in the teeth. It was a rare thing, indeed, when one could take the pieces a player had resigned with, turn the board around and beat him. In a sort of trance the General played the pieces that had been Freddy's, to lose the second time in ten more moves.

Freddy stood up. "Thank you," he said.

In that moment the General showed the stuff he was made of. He looked Freddy in the eye and said, "My boy, that has never been done to me before. I would appreciate an opportunity to play with you again. I hope that you will consider as unsaid anything which I may have carelessly let drop about your intelligence and . . . uh . . . . regarding that request about Jo . . . Well, I should say that was a matter entirely up to her. Good night." With a straight back and a head held high the General walked out of the room.

It was a moment before the full import of what had happened was clear to Freddy. But when it did dawn upon him that he had so easily done what must certainly be the last thing Jo could ask him to do by way of proving things for her, an exuberance exploded within him that made him cut several extremely sharp tap steps that culminated with a double heel click in midair.

"Like Hitler when France fell," Jo said.

It is too bad that it cannot be said that Freddy became instantly frozen in midair to remain suspended there with heels about to click once more. Because that was figuratively about the way Jo's words affected him. The cold blast of her voice froze his happiness on the spot. He looked at her in amazement. She was looking at him with frigid disapproval.

"Huh?" said Freddy.

"I said," Jo repeated, "like Hitler when France fell. Disgusting."

"But . . ."

"I suppose you think you're extremely smart. I suppose you think it was something to humiliate a beaten old man by turning his own pieces against him. I suppose you think I should come flying to your arms crying, 'My hero!'"

"Look . . ."

"I am looking, I'm glad I've had an opportunity to look before it was too late. You're a . . . a gloater. Good night."

During the course of a sleepless night Freddy persuaded himself that he'd been wrong, a cad and a heel. He called Jo at ten o'clock in the morning, beginning the conversation with a cheery hello as though all were well. It had worked before. There was no way for Freddy to know that Jo had not slept that night either; that after a long and stubborn struggle her conscience had convinced her that she had been unreasonable. Had he known he would have presumed that he was doing precisely the right thing in calling Jo. Like most men he would not have understood that the sound of his cheery "Good morning!"—as though the previous night's quarrel had not weighed upon his mind at all—was not the way to announce his existence to a girl who had struggled all night with herself over what she had considered to be a major emotional crisis, and who had prepared herself for a reconciliation of great tenderness. She could not have reacted with greater bitterness had she lost a leg, and Freddy's first words had been, "It's a nice day for a walk."

"Stop chirruping!" she said irritably.

"Huh? Who's chirruping?"

"Is there any point in going into it?"

"Look, Jo, stop being unreasonable."

He heard Jo draw in her breath. "*I* am being unreasonable?"

"Well, last night you jumped to conclusions."

"Indeed? As I remember it you were doing all the jumping. All over the place."

"That was because I was happy."

"That was obvious. Why don't you go kick some blind man's cup of pennies and go into a real ecstasy?"

Freddy counted ten slowly. "Look, darling, I was happy because . . ."

"There's no need to explain. I have eyes. I have ears. You succeeded in doing just what you set out to do when we left El Morocco. I hope it made you very happy to humiliate Father. To . . . to deliver a mortal wound to his pride. I can only say that I am more hurt than angry. Goodby."

Freddy stared at the dead instrument in his hand. He slammed it back on the hook. "Women!" he breathed with feeling. "Women!" . . .

The General evidenced no signs of mortal wounds when Freddy called that evening firmly resolved to accept whatever punishment Jo might have in mind and start out anew. The General placed an arm around Freddy's shoulder.

"Scotch?" he inquired. "Cigar? We're in luck. Jo has gone out. Have the evening to ourselves."

"Gone out?" Freddy echoed blankly.

"With some odd little monster. Squirmed all the time he was here. Jo said you'd understand if you happened to drop in."

"Oh!" said Freddy.

The General sat down and began setting up the chessmen.

"What was his name?" Freddy asked.

"Haven't the vaguest idea," the General replied absently. "Someone she gushed all over. Nauseating." He tossed a coin. "Call it for the whites."

Freddy called and lost to get the black pieces.

"Look, General, do you remember last night I said I wanted to marry Jo?"

"Eh? Oh, yes. So you did. All right with me."

"But she's out with someone!" Freddy protested. "You shouldn't have let her!"

The General regarded Freddy thoughtfully. "My boy, one does not 'let' Jo do anything. One just tries to keep out of the line of fire as much as possible. Sit down and let's begin the play."

"You don't even know who she's out with," Freddy went on, accusingly.

A slightly harassed look came over the General's face. "Isn't it enough if Jo knows? I'll open with the king's pawn. Your move."

"But . . ."

"My dear young man, we are playing chess."

"Do you know why she's out with him tonight?" Freddy demanded indignantly.

"Maybe he has tickets to *Oklahoma!*"

"No. To spite me. She thinks I humiliated you last night."

"And so you did," the General said cheerfully. "So you did. Thoroughly. Wouldn't be surprised if I'd mentioned it to her too."

Freddy groaned. "No wonder she's through with me!"

The General clucked regretfully. "Sometimes she takes things more seriously than she should. Oh well, there must be about seventy million more women in this nation to choose from if you must have one. Meanwhile, let's get on with the play."

"There isn't anyone in the world like Jo," Freddy said vehemently.

"Oh, come!" the General said. "And if there isn't it may be just as well. She has a nasty disposition before breakfast . . . not at all like the girls waking up in the toothpaste ads. She has deucedly expensive taste in clothes and I have to pay a devilish lot of traffic fines for her. Serve this little oaf she's out with right if she decides in favor of him. Even consider you fortunate."

"Fortunate!" Freddy said bitterly as he moved his king's pawn out to meet the General's opening move. The General had succeeded only in revealing to Freddy some further intimate and delightfully fascinating facets of Jo's character. He loved her the more for them. Freddy glared across the board at the General. He, Freddy, would sit there until Jo came home, and meanwhile treat the General to a real trimming.

The General played a gambit with his king's bishop's pawn to the bishop's four, Freddy accepted the gambit, the General came out with his king's knight to the bishop's three and a game began brilliantly with a daring opening.

It cannot be said that Freddy had ever enjoyed chess under the instruction of his grandfather but he had learned it. He knew the intricate patterns and combinations and how to achieve them in the face of keen opposition. Tonight he found himself slowly coming to enjoy his mastery of the game. The desire to defeat the General gave purpose to it all. It gave Freddy a tingling pleasure to build a careful defense against the General's equally well-developed attack; to counter and frustrate his opponent. The chessboard had become a medium for the expression of an urge to bat someone's ears off. The library became quiet . . . the atmosphere tense. In the middle game Freddy was still a pawn ahead with a knight and a bishop on both sides exchanged. But the General was beginning to crowd his attack, and Freddy sensed the danger of a loss of mobility. Neither was aware of the passing of time. Neither noticed Jo come in accompanied by a short, somewhat plump young man in evening clothes.

A grim little smile of satisfaction touched the corners of Jo's lips when she saw Freddy. She'd hoped he might be there so she could throw Hogarth Evans in Freddy's face and watch him squirm. She could have wished to appear with someone else, but Hogarth had been the only man available on short notice. "Hello," she said brightly. "We've had a perfectly marvelous time."

The General grunted and Freddy, looking up and, noting whom Jo had been out with, felt a great relief. "Hello, Jo," he said. "Hello, Hoggie."

"Your move," the General said. He glared at Jo and Hoggie. "You two be quiet."

"Playing chess?" Hoggie said conversationally.

The General looked at his daughter. "Keep him quiet!"

Jo bit her lip. This wasn't working out right. Freddy had already turned his attention back to the board. Hoggie might just as well have been her aunt for all the jealousy Freddy had indicated. She turned irritably to Hoggie.

"Bring over a chair, darling," she said with an effort of lightness. "We'll watch them."

"I don't know anything about chess," Hoggie said. "How about turning on the radio and . . ."

"Do as I say!" Jo snapped.

Jo sat in the chair, prepared to show immediate and great interest in Hoggie sitting uneasily on the arm, the instant Freddy should raise his head. But Freddy did not raise his head. The General was threatening to uncover a check and simultaneously attack his queen. Right at that point he could lose the game if he were not extremely careful. . . . He was aware of the warm bond which had developed between himself and the General during the game. It was something which had nothing to do with Jo. He would patch things up with Jo presently; apologize or anything else her little heart desired. But right at the moment he was aware of the eager glint in the General's eyes. The General thought he had the game cinched. He hadn't seen what Freddy suddenly noted with a feeling of exultation. Let the General uncover check and attack the queen. There was a knight move that would . . . Freddy was almost afraid to let his eyes follow the moves of the knight as he studied the possibilities for fear the General might look up and see him looking at the knight. But if that knight should . . .

"Aren't they beautiful pieces, Hogarth?" Jo said. There was nothing in the sweetness of her voice to indicate the fury she felt toward Freddy.

Freddy looked up. He looked up just in time to see Hoggie Evans lean forward to pick up one of the captured knights beside the board and lose his balance in doing so. He reached out to save Hoggie but he was too late. Hoggie saved himself . . . by placing his hand in the middle of the board and completely wrecking the game.

Neither the General nor Freddy moved. They sat silent and motionless . . . staring at the scattered men.

Hoggie retrieved himself and laughed a little nervously. At the sound both the General and Freddy turned their heads slowly to regard Hoggie.

The General said, "I believe it was your move, Freddy. Try not to get blood over everything."

Freddy nodded. "Thank you, sir. I'll be careful." And he stood up.

Hoggie backed away. Jo jumped to her feet. What she had seen in Freddy's eyes was the same thing she had seen in her father's.

"Freddy!" she squealed. "Don't!"

It was an unnecessary plea. Hoggie had gone. Freddy went out of the library and came back a moment later with Hoggie's hat and coat. "Guess he forgot them," he said. He went to the window and looked down at the traffic, fifteen stories below. Thoughtfully he opened the window and dropped the hat and coat down into the night. "At the rate he was going," he said, "he might catch them as he comes out on the street."

The General nodded his quiet approval. "That was a generous thought, my boy. Undoubtedly clothes that would fit a human malformation like that are expensive and hard to replace." He stood up and sighed. He looked at Freddy and Jo. Without knowing it, Jo was staring at Freddy with the back of her hand still pressed against her open mouth. A grim smile touched the General's lips. "Well, the game is over, so I think I'll retire. But it's still your move, Freddy . . . and please remember about the blood. Good night."

When the General had gone Freddy turned to Jo. She backed nervously away from him.

"Freddy . . . what are you going to do?"

"Oh," said Freddy, moving toward her, "I think maybe I'll wring your neck, or maybe break some arms and legs. I don't know . . . I haven't decided."

"I . . . I haven't done anything bad, Freddy—not really bad."

"Not really bad?" he shouted. "Not really bad? First you go out with that Hogboom. Hoghead, Hoggie—whatever his name is— Hogarth. Then you drag him back here and have him fall all over the chessboard, just when my knight—"

"Oh, Freddy, I'm really awfully sorry. Believe me, Freddy, I never thought—"

"Never thought, indeed. Bah! Double-bah! That fat little pig of a man!"

"I know it, Freddy. But don't rub it in. Please don't rub it in."

Freddy allowed himself to remain speechless. Jo backed away from him until she came up against the couch and could back no farther. Freddy put his finger on the tip of her small nose and pushed. Jo sat down.

"Rub it in?" he whispered heavily. "I suppose I'm gloating? Is that it? Am I gloating? Did I gloat at Hoggie? Did I?"

"No, you didn't. You were very restrained, and that was very nice of you."

"I know it was."

She laughed a nervous little laugh. "He did look funny," she said.

"He was born to look funny."

"So fat," Jo said. "So round and so plump."

"Comic," Freddy said.

"Fantastic," Jo said.

Freddy sat down beside her. He fixed a stern eye upon her. "Now who's gloating?" he demanded.

"Why . . . why . . . this is different, Freddy."

He laughed.

"Gloating at Father is no fair. Gloating at Hoggie—"

Freddy took her in his arms and kissed her on the mouth. She put her hands on his face and pulled him closer. It was an exceptional sort of kiss.

He let her go, and she sat up and clapped her hands and laughed.

"What's funny?" he said. "What are you doing?"

She moved closer to him on the couch and leaned her head on his shoulder. She looked up at him and she smiled a very sweet smile. "Gloating," she said.

"Har!" said Freddy.

"Careful!"

Cartoon by Fred Balk from *This Funny World* (1947), by permission of The McNaught Syndicate, Inc.

The Devil That Troubled the Chessboard

BY GERALD KERSH

♛ A SHOCKING book might be written about Pío Busto's apartment
house. It stands on a corner not far from Oxford Street. It stands. No
doubt Busto, who knows all the laws pertaining to real estate, has
managed to find some loophole in the Law of Gravity; I can think of
no other reason to account for the fact that his house has not yet fallen
down. Pío Busto knows how to make a living by letting furnished
rooms. He puts a sheet of wallboard across a small bedroom and calls
it two apartments. His house is furnished with odds and ends raked
from the junk heaps in the Cattle Market. No space is wasted. He
sleeps in a subterranean washhouse, and would convert even this into
a bed-sitting-room if the coal cellar were not crammed with spare
furniture and bed linen. He is something of a character, this Busto;
he looks like Lorenzo the Magnificent, and sleeps with a savage old
dog named Ouif; in case of burglars he keeps a service revolver under
his pillow, and a cavalry saber hung on a bootlace over his head. He
keeps evil spirits at bay with a rusty horseshoe, the lower half of a
broken crucifix, and a lithograph of the Mona Lisa, whom he believes
to be the Virgin Mary.

His rooms are dangerous. You sigh; they shake. You sneeze, and
down comes a little piece of ceiling. What is more, the walls are full
of little holes, bored by tenants of an inquisitive turn of mind. The
curiosity of these people is often highly irritating—your view is sometimes obscured by the eye of your neighbor, who is trying to peep

back at you. But Busto's tenants rarely stay long. They are mostly rolling stones, and by the time they come down to Busto's house, which is very far from the bottom of things, they have acquired momentum. They come, and they go.

As for me, I lived for more than three months in one of the cheapest of those spy-hole-riddled bedrooms. I completed my education there. Through three or four tiny holes, which must have been bored by some neglected genius of espionage, I watched people when they thought they were alone. I saw things which walls and the darkness were made to conceal; I heard things which no man was ever supposed to hear. It was degrading, but impossible to resist. I stooped. I stooped to the keyhole of hell, and I learned the secrets of the damned.

Among the damned was Shakmatko. Picture for yourself this terrifying man.

I saw him for the first time in the saloon bar of the "Duchess of Euoro"—long-drawn-out, somber, pallid and mysterious; dressed all in black. He had the unearthly, only partly human appearance of a figure in a Japanese print. I glanced at him, and said to myself, with a sensation of shock: "Good God, this man is all forehead!" Imagine one of those old-fashioned square felt hats without the brim: his skull was shaped exactly like that. It towered straight upwards, white and glabrous. His forehead conveyed an impression of enormous weight—it seemed to have pressed his face out of shape. You can reproduce something of his aspect if you model a human face in white plasticine, and then foreshorten it by squashing it down on the table. In plasticine that is all very well; but alive, in a public house, it does not look so good.

And if all this were not enough, his eyes were hidden behind dark-blue spectacles.

As I looked, he rose from his chair, stretching himself out in three jerks, like a telescope, and came towards me and said, in a hushed voice, with a peculiar foreign intonation:

"Can you please give me a match?"

"With pleasure."

He recoiled from the light of the match flame, shading his concealed eyes with a gloved hand. I thought of the Devil in Bon-Bon.

46

The tightly clamped mouth parted a little, to let out a puff of smoke and a few more words:

"I find the light hurts my eyes. Will you drink?"

"Oh, thank you."

He indicated a chair. When we were seated, he asked:

"Pardon me. You live in this vicinity?"

"Almost next door."

"Ah. In apartments?"

"That would be a polite name for them."

"You will excuse my asking?"

"Of course. Are you looking for a room?"

"Yes, I am. But it must be cheap."

"I live on the corner. They have one or two rooms vacant there. They're cheap enough, but—"

"Are there tables?"

"Oh! Yes, I think so."

"Then I will go there. One thing: I can pay in advance, but I have no references."

"I don't suppose Busto will mind that."

"You see, I never stay long at one place."

"You like variety, I suppose?"

"I detest variety, but I have to move."

"Ah, landladies are often very difficult to get on with."

"It is not that. A large number of people live in this house of yours?"

"A good few. Why?"

"I do not like to be alone." At this, he looked over his shoulder. "Perhaps you would be kind enough to tell me the address?"

"I'm going that way. Come along with me, if you like."

"You are far too kind." He reached down and picked up a great black suitcase which had been standing between his feet. It seemed to drag him down, as if it were full of lead. I said:

"Can I give you a hand?"

"No, no, no, thank you so very much." We walked to the house and asked Busto about the vacant rooms. "First afloor fronta vacant, thirteen bobs. Very nice aroom. Top floor back aten bob, electric light include. Spotless. No bug," lied Busto.

"Ten shillings. Is there a table in that room?"

"Corluvaduck! Bess table ina da world. You come up, I soon show you, mister."

"As long as there is a table."

We went upstairs. Straining at his suitcase, the stranger climbed slowly. It took us a long time to reach the top of the house, where there was a vacant bedroom next to mine. "Ecco!" said Busto, proudly indicating the misbegotten divan, the rickety old round table, and the cracked skylight, half blind with soot. He looked at the stranger and asked, "Hokay?"

"It will do. Ten shilling a week; here is a fortnight's rent in advance. If I leave within a week, the residue is in lieu of notice. I have no references."

"Hokay. What name, in case of letters?"

"There will be no letters. My name is Shakmatko."

"Good."

Shakmatko leaned against the door. He had the air of a man dying of fatigue. His trembling hand fumbled for a cigarette. Again he recoiled from the light of the match, and glanced over his shoulder.

Pity took possession of me. I put an arm about his shoulders, and led him to the divan. He sat down, gasping. Then I went back to pick up his suitcase. I stooped, clutched the handle; tensed myself in anticipation of a fifty-six-pound lift; heaved, and nearly fell backwards down the stairs.

The suitcase weighed next to nothing. It was empty except for something that gave out a dry rattling noise. I did not like that.

Shakmatko sat perfectly still. I watched him through the holes in the wallboard partition. Time passed. The autumn afternoon began to fade. Absorbed by the opacity of the skylight, the light of day gradually disappeared. The room filled with shadow. All that was left of the light seemed to be focused upon the naked top of Shakmatko's skull, as he sat with his head hanging down. His face was invisible. He looked like the featureless larva of some elephantine insect. At last, when night had fallen, he began to move. His right hand became gradually visible; it emerged from his sleeve like something squeezed out of a tube. He did not switch the light on, but, standing a little

48

night light in a saucer, he lit it cautiously. In this vague and sickly circle of orange-colored light he took off his spectacles, and began to look about him. He turned his back to me. Snick-snick! He opened the suitcase. My heart beat faster. He returned to the table, carrying an oblong box and a large square board. I held my breath.

He drew a chair up to the table, upon which he carefully placed the board. For a moment he hugged the box to his breast, while he looked over his shoulder; then he slid the lid off the box and, with a sudden clatter, shot out onto the board a set of small ivory chessmen. He arranged these, with indescribable haste, sat for a while with his chin on his clenched hands, then began to move the pieces.

I wish I could convey to you the unearthly atmosphere of that room, where, half buried in the shadows, with the back of his head illuminated by a ray of blue moonlight, and his enormous forehead shining yellow in the feeble radiance of the night light, Shakmatko sat and played chess with himself.

After a while he began to slide forward in his chair, shake his head and shrug his shoulders. Sometimes in the middle of a move his hand would waver and his head would nod; then he would force himself to sit upright, rub his eyes violently, look wildly round the room, or listen intently with a hand at his ear.

It occurred to me that he was tired—desperately tired—and afraid of going to sleep.

Before getting into bed I locked my door.

It seemed to me that I had not been asleep for more than a minute or so when I was awakened by a loud noise. There was a heavy crash —this, actually, awoke me—followed by the noise of a shower of small, hard objects scattered over a floor. Then I heard the shrill tones of Shakmatko's voice, raised in a cry of anguish and terror:

"You again! Have you found me so soon? Go away! Go away!"

His door opened. I opened my door, looked out, and saw him, standing at the top of the stairs, brandishing a small silver crucifix at the black shadows which filled the staircase.

"What is it?" I asked.

He swung round instantly, holding out the crucifix. When he saw me, he caught his breath in relief.

"Ah, you. Did I disturb you? Forgive me. I—I—May I come into your room?"

"Do," I said.

"Please close the door quickly," he whispered as he came in.

"Sit down and pull yourself together. Tell me, what's troubling you?"

"I must leave here in the morning," said Shakmatko, trembling in every limb. "It has found me again. So soon! It must have followed on my very heels. Then what is the use? I can no longer escape it, even for a day. What can I do? Where can I go? My God, my God, I am surrounded!"

"What has found you? What are you trying to run away from?" I asked in a calm voice.

He replied: "An evil spirit."

I shivered. There are occasions when the entire fabric of dialectical materialism seems to go sphut before the forces of nightmarish possibilities.

"What sort of evil spirit?" I asked.

"I think they call them poltergeists."

"Things that throw—that are supposed to throw furniture about?"

"Not all my furniture. Only certain things."

"Such as—"

"Chess pieces, and things connected with the game of chess. Nothing else. I am a chess player. It hates chess. It follows me. It follows me from place to place. It waits until I am asleep, and then it tries to destroy my chess pieces. It has already torn up all my books and papers. There is nothing left but the board and the pieces; they are too strong for it, and so it grows increasingly violent."

"Good heavens!"

"Perhaps you think that I am mad?"

"No, no. If you had told me that you had merely been seeing things I might have thought so. But if one's chessboard flies off the table, that is another matter."

"Thank you. I know I am not mad. My name may be unfamiliar to you. Are you interested in chess?"

"Not very. I hardly know the moves." I replied truthfully.

"Ah. If you were you would have heard of me. I beat Paolino, in the tournament at Pressburg. My game on that occasion has gone down in history. I should certainly have been world champion but for that Thing."

"Has it been troubling you for long?"

"My dear sir, it has given me no peace for twenty years. Conceive; twenty years! It visited me, first of all, when I was in Paris, training with Ljubljana. I had been working very hard. I think I had been working nearly all night. I took a hasty lunch, and then lay down and went to sleep. When I woke up I had a feeling that something was wrong: a malaise. I went quickly into my study. What did I see? Chaos!

"All my books on chess had been taken out of the bookcase and dashed to the floor, so violently that the bindings were broken. A photograph of myself in a group of chess players had been hurled across the room, torn out of the frame, and crumpled into a ball. My chess pieces were scattered over the carpet. The board had disappeared: I found it later, stuffed up the chimney.

"I rushed downstairs and complained to the concierge. He swore that nobody had come up. I thought no more of it; but two days later it happened again." He trembled as he lived the scene over again.

"And didn't you ever see it?"

"Never. It is a coward. It waits until nobody is looking."

"So what did you do?"

"I ran away, and took another flat, in another quarter of Paris. I thought that the house, perhaps, was haunted. I did not believe in such things; but how is it possible to be sure? From the Rue Blanche, I moved to the Boulevard du Temple. There, I found that I had shaken it off. I sighed with relief, and settled down once again to my game. Then, when I was once again absorbed, happy, it came again.

"My poor books! Torn to pieces! My beautiful notes—savagely torn to shreds! My beloved ivory pieces—scattered. Ah, but they were too strong for it. It could destroy books and papers; it could destroy the calm detachment and peace of mind necessary to my chess—but my ivory pieces and my inlaid ebony board; those, it has never been able to destroy!"

"But what happened then?"

"I ran away again. I found that by moving quickly, I could avoid it. I took to living in streets which were difficult to find; complicated turnings; remote back-alleys. So I often managed to lose it for a while. But just when I thought I had shaken it off forever I would awake, in horror, and find my papers fluttering in tiny fragments; my pieces in chaos.

"For years and years I have been driven from place to place, all over the world like a leaf on the wind. It has learned my scent, and now it does not have to look long for my track. Two days, three days, then it is with me. My God, what am I to do?"

"Couldn't you, perhaps, consult the Psychical Research people?"

"I have done so. They are interested. They watch. Needless to say, when they watch, it will not come. I, myself, have sat up for nights and nights, waiting for it. It hides itself. And then—the moment comes when I must sleep—and in that moment—

"Coward! Devil! Why won't it show its face? How can I ask anybody for help? Nobody would believe. They would lock me up in an asylum. No, no, there is no help for me.

"Look, I ran away from it last night. I came here today. Yet it found me, this evening. There is no escape. It has caught up with me. It is on my heels. Even at this moment, it is sitting behind me. I am tired of running away. Yet I dare not go to sleep. If I do, it will creep in.

"Oh my God, what can I do? It is with me now, tonight. If you don't believe me, come and see."

Shakmatko led me to his door, and clinging to my arm, he pointed.

The chessboard lay in the fireplace. The pieces were scattered about the room, with pieces of paper torn as fine as confetti.

"What can I do?" he asked.

I picked up the chessmen, and, replacing the board on the table, arranged them correctly. Then, turning to Shakmatko, I said:

"Listen, you need some sleep. Come sleep in my bed. I'll watch."

"You are a man of high courage," said Shakmatko. "God will bless you."

I took him back, and covered him with my blanket. Poor old man, he must have been nearly dead for want of rest! He gave a deep sigh, and was asleep as soon as his head touched the pillow.

I tiptoed to his room and sat down. I did not really believe in ghosts; but, for all that, I kept my eye on the chessboard, and turned up the collar of my coat so as to protect my ears in the event of flying bishops.

An hour must have passed. Then I heard a footstep. I clenched my fists and fixed my eyes on the door, my heart pounding. A floorboard creaked. The handle of the door turned, and the door opened.

I had already steeled myself to the expectation of some awful invisibility. What I actually saw proved to be far more horrible.

It was Shakmatko. His eyes were wide open, but rolled up so that only the bloodshot white was visible. His face was set in a calm expression, his hands were extended; he was walking in his sleep.

I meant to cry out: "Shakmatko!" but my tongue refused to function. I saw him walk steadily over to the table, sweep the pieces off the board with a terrific gesture, and fling the board itself against the opposite wall.

The crash awoke him with a shudder. His eyes snapped back to their normal positions, and blinked, in utter terror, while he cried:

"Damn you! Have you hunted me down again? Accursed—"

"Shakmatko," I cried, "you've been walking in your sleep."

His large, whitish eyes dilated. He brandished a skinny fist.

"You!" he said to me, "you! Are you going to say that too?"

"But," I said, "I saw you."

"They all say that," said Shakmatko, in a tone of abject hopelessness. "Oh, God, what am I to do? What am I to do?"

I returned to my room. The rest of the night was completely quiet, but it was nearly dawn before I managed to fall asleep.

I awoke at seven. I was drawn, as by a magnet, to Shakmatko's room. I went to his door and tapped very gently. There was no answer. Had he run away? I opened the door and looked in. Shakmatko was lying in bed. His head and one arm hung down. He looked too peaceful to be alive.

I observed, among the chessmen on the floor, a little square bottle labeled *Luminal!*

In that last sleep Shakmatko did not walk.

Capsule History of the Game

BY CHIELAMANGUS

♛ THE ORIGIN of chess is wrapped in the mists of obscurity.

Its invention has been variously ascribed to the Greeks, the Icelanders, the Australian blacks, the Chinese, the Parsees, the Pygmies, the Red Indians, the Irish Free State, the Bataks, and the Meetaks.

Chess pieces are said to have been found in ancient tombs, Ur and there. The conclusion to be drawn is that the game originated either in India, or not in India, between 10,000 B.C. and 2000 A.D. Practically all the opponents of this view have by now been discredited.

Rapidly spreading over the face of the globe, the game was enthusiastically taken up by Ruy Lopez, a Spanish bishop. He never, however, played the Ruy Lopez, which was therefore named after him, and is still popular among all classes of players at the present day. Incidentally, some authorities suspect that he was not a Bishop at all; but he mitre been.

The next great name in chess was Greco, an Italian, who published a book of faked games, which convincingly show what brilliant combinations were not played in his day.

In the eighteenth century, there arose the great Philidor, immortalized by the famous opening known as Philidor's Defense, so called because, as far as is known, he never played it. Philidor's theories were too much in advance of his time to be understood, and since then have become too far behind the times to receive any attention. He is therefore considered the first great chess thinker.

He was succeeded by Deschapelles, who, when he was no longer certain of beating everybody, refused to play at all unless his opponent would accept pawn and move. If Deschapelles lost he could say it was because of the odds. This was known as the Deschapelles coup.

The next great event was the hundred years' match between Labourdonnais and McDonnell. During the play, Labourdonnais swore, gesticulated, and burst into snatches of song. He won.

After the match both players died, and were succeeded by Staunton's "Handbook," which is noted for its author's shameful treatment of Paul Morphy.

This was the name given to a young genius from New Orleans, who flashed across the chess world like a meteor, defeating all he met with ridiculous ease, especially the Duke of Brunswick and Count Isouard in a Paris opera-box. After convincingly demonstrating that he was the pride and sorrow of chess, Morphy retired in disgust.

The next great figure was Wilhelm Steinitz; a very deep player—also wide, though short. He held the world's championship for twenty-six years, and was therefore considered by his rivals to be very obstinate and pig-headed.

Dr. Lasker then held the championship for another twenty-six years. Critics explained that this was because he made weak moves. This was psychology. Lasker thus became known as the apostle of common sense.

The next champion was José Raoul Capablanca, the Cuban genius. His perfect technique made him invincible, and he was defeated by A. A. A. A. Alekhine.

Alekhine was recognized as the greatest player of all time, but he drank some alcohol, and was defeated by AEIOU at Amsterdam, Rotterdam, Blaastendam, and the ague.

Alekhine then drank some sour milk, and defeated AEIOU by a decisive margin.

Then it was practically now, and history stopped.

Telling Off the World Champion

BY SOLOMON HECHT

♛ SHORTLY after he wrested the World's Championship from Steinitz, Emanuel Lasker delivered in London in 1895 a series of lectures, later published in book form under the title of *Common Sense in Chess*. In this work he undertakes to lay down principles of chess play of general application, that is, applicable supposedly to any and all kinds of games, and even with the game in all of its stages, including the opening, the middle game and the end game.

It is nothing short of astounding that a world's champion a century after the death of Philidor should thus presume to crowd this game of infinite resources into the space of a peanut shell. Without even reading his rules one would be justified in dismissing them in advance as an impossible pretension. But more astounding is that in this age which flatters itself that it is so chess-wise they should have been generally and slavishly adopted. Apparently, not even to his rival masters has it occurred, up to the present, that there must be something radically wrong with them. For have they not adopted the principles in their own books?

In his preface to *Common Sense in Chess* Lasker says: "It may be regarded as an attempt to deal with all parts of a game of chess by the aid of general principles." And, fortunately for my purposes, he accommodatingly admits that the work was not dashed off in a hurry, adding: "The games and positions given in this book are comparatively few, but have been selected with CARE" (capitals mine).

LASKER'S FOUR INFALLIBLE PRINCIPLES

"1. Do not move any Pawn in the opening of a game except the K and Q Pawns.

"2. Do not move any piece twice in the opening, but put it at once upon the right square. (In my practice I have usually found it strongest to post the Kts at B3, where they have a magnificent sway, and the KB somewhere on his original diagonal, if not exposed to exchange, at QB4.)

"3. Bring your Kts out before developing the Bishops, especially the QB.

"4. Do not pin the adverse KKt (by B—KKt5) before your opponent has castled.

"In regard to Rule 1 you will sometimes, especially in Q side openings, find it better to advance the QBP two squares before obstructing it with your QKt. This, however, is the only exception where the violation of the principles just laid down is unquestionably justified. You will see that according to this plan the mobilization takes six moves, consumed in the development of two Pawns, the two Knights, and the two Bishops. You may be obliged to spend some of your time in the beginning of a game for the exchange of a pawn or a piece, or it may be necessary to make one or two defensive moves. But the real business of development ought to be accomplished in no more than six separate moves devoted to that purpose."

A DOGMA WITHOUT PRECEDENT IN CHESS HISTORY

First, let me call to attention that in these four rules there is practically nothing new except making an iron-clad dogma of Rule 1, for which fortunately there is no precedent in chess history—praised be the gods! No Chinaman, no Hindu, no Persian, no Arab, no European, no American, has ever before ventured to lay down as a universal principle to utilize only two out of eight pawns. At least four pawns should be available for immediate service during the opening—the KBP to support the KP, and the QBP to support the QP. But all of the Pawns should be subject to call. Why should anybody voluntarily tie one arm and two legs and restrict himself to the use of one arm! Preposterous!

But even Rule 1 is not original, Steinitz in his "Modern Chess Instructor," suggesting to hold back the other pawns but wisely refraining from attempting to dogmatize it.

There is nothing novel in the 2nd Rule except that neither Lasker nor anybody else follows it. This is one of the unwritten rules of Philidor, who never moved a piece twice during the opening unless necessary.

The 3rd Rule is hardly new. It is only converting into a religious dogma another idea of Steinitz who did not feature it too strongly, perhaps because he was not sure that he was right. But let Lasker have the credit for this rule; it is not one that will win applause from future generations.

The 4th Rule is merely one of fifty maxims which do not at all belong in the class of universal principles. It originated with Philidor.

LASKER'S MODEL RUY LOPEZ DEFENSE

He prefaces his Model Ruy Lopez Defense with: "We have given in our former lecture the theory of the first part of a game of Chess . . . . It now remains to put it to a practical test."

Gladly! Let us see what these principles are worth when subjected to analysis in a game which he takes the pains to state was selected with CARE and is offered for practical test. Let us see how the author himself sticks to them. And if HE doesn't consider them worth practicing, why should anybody else?

1 P—K4, P—K4; 2 Kt—KB3, . . .

I shall not pause long over this move, being the keymove of modern chess practice, but will say that after it has been made I believe it will be exceedingly difficult to play any game of chess correctly. Lasker contends that obstructing the BP's is insignificant compared with the great advantage of having the Kt at B3. But in this very game we shall see that it is not insignificant, for this Knight accomplishes nothing at B3 and presently has to lose a move in order to free the KBP, thereby delaying the development of a piece. Further we shall see this Kt is appropriately punished, for at the end of the opening he will be found in a useless position at QKt3.

2 . . . Kt—QB3; 3 B—QKt5, . . .

In a previous article I pointed out that B—QKt5 is violative of a very correct principle laid down by Marshall & Macbeth not to move any piece into enemy territory during the opening. This strong KB is shortly going to exchange himself for the poor, weak QKt. He could have gone to QB4 and had a serious threat against Black's KBP, the most vital spot on the board.

3 . . . Kt—KB3; 4 Castles, . . .

SOMETHING GOES WRONG EARLY

Hold! What right has this Rook to move? Did Lasker not lay down the law that only the KP and QP, the two Knights and the two Bishops were to move in the opening? He said that the whole business of mobilization should require not more than six moves. Here at the 4th White is castling to bring the KR into play.

But let us also see whether this act of such extremely early castling may not in itself be violative of principles of correct play? In the preceding article I quoted Marshall & Macbeth as pointing out that in order to give mate it is necessary to know where to find the enemy King. Here White advertises in the newspapers that for the rest of the game his King will be receiving callers at the KKtsq. Philidor never was in an undue hurry to castle. He saw an advantage in waiting to see where the enemy was concentrating his forces, and then he might castle on the opposite side. It is no more in the nature of a Rook so early to get action than it is of an elephant to play tag. When we scramble to win in chess we are bound to overlook principles.

4 . . . Kt×P.

UNSPEAKABLE HUMILIATION FOR THE KING'S GUARDS

I am not interested in the ingenious thoughts behind the strategy that allows the Kt to capture this Pawn. What I do know is that Chess is supposed to be a war game and that any General who would leave the King's own Guards subject to unopposed capture should instantly be relieved from his command in disgrace. This Division of Infantry is composed of all of the young princes and nobles, the flower of the

Kingdom. I can hear the derisive shouts from Black's camp reaching to the high heavens. I can feel with poor White's King his inexpressible humiliation and anguish.

5 P—Q4, . . .

Lasker lays down the rule that only the KP and QP must be moved in the opening. The KP he gives away, so now one solitary Pawn must serve as the first line of offense and defense.

And how does White's bereaved King feel over no steps being taken to avenge the grievous insult? By this time Black's troops are nearly delirious with their shouts of derision.

5 . . . B—K2; 6 Q—K2, . . .

MORALE AT LOW EBB

Hold again! Where in the rules is there any provision for the Queen developing at the 6th Move? The two Pawns, the two Knights and the two Bishops were to develop, which requires a minimum of six moves. Instead of the QKt and QB developing, the Rook and the Queen have been brought into play. It seems that at least six pieces are needed in the opening.

By this time the morale of White's troops must be appreciably lowered. The King's Guard has been captured in disgrace, and the QKt and QB are muttering discontent over being kept in camp when they were promised early opportunities to win fame. The Queen is jealous of the Rook, and gets ahead of him.

6 . . . Kt—Q3.

This is the 3rd Move for this Knight.

7 B×Kt, . . .

THE BISHOP BREAKS A RULE

"As a general rule," says Lasker in the following chapter, "it is not good policy to exchange in the early stages of a game the long-reaching Bishop for the Knight, whose power does not extend beyond a certain circle."

Since he is playing for both parties in devising this opening, why did he play 3 B—QKt5 when he knew that at the 7th Move the Bishop would violate the rule against exchanging himself for the Queen's Knight—the weakest piece on the board?

This is a second move for this Bishop, made before the QKt and QB have had a chance to develop.

7 . . . KtP×B; 8 P×P, . . .

A Powerful Pawn Center?

A lone Pawn at K5 with no other Pawn in a position to support him does not exactly constitute a strong center. Right now it would be very desirable to have the KKt away from KB3 to free the KBP for support of his precariously advanced companion. It may be true that the Knight has a "magnificent sway," but he is in the way.

This is a 2nd Move for the QP.

8 . . . Kt—QKt2.

The Black Bandit Knight, a Reckless Law-Breaker

This is the 4th Move of this Knight, made while Black has only one other developed piece on the board. And note Black's position. There being practically not a Pawn advanced, the Knight had nowhere else to go. White is castled on the King's side, so this Knight in order to give mate retires as far as possible into the QR corner! There he is blocking the QB, making it impossible for Lasker to comply with his promise of quick development. Besides that, he is robbing the QR of the opportunity of commanding the open QKt file. Could a piece be worse placed? What compensation has Black now for the Knight's capture of the KP, a move discussed and approved by Lasker?

9 Kt—Q4, . . .

Not So Well Posted After All!

Oh, ho! It seems the Knight was not so well placed at KB3 after all! He has to lose a move to free the KBP. But for this lost move the QKt or QB could have developed. We are already at the 9th Move, and only two of the four specified pieces have developed, and one of them, the valuable KB, is off the board. The whole business of mobilization was to be done in six moves, but at this stage all that is visible in the field is a Knight and a too-far advanced Pawn.

9 . . . Castles.

Black at least is entitled to the credit of having castled with more kingly dignity. He did not rush to the newspapers at the first opportunity.

10 R—Qsq, . . .

A second move by this illegally developed Rook, made before the QKt and QB have developed. He is bound to move again because he doesn't belong there. He ought to be at Ksq and the QR at Qsq. But who knows when the QR will get into action under this rapid mobilization scheme?

10 . . . Q—Ksq.

The scheme of frozen Pawns in the opening does not look good. The Queen at this stage ought to be in the 2nd Row, not blocking the King Row, but where else is there breathing space? Are the two forces really fighting? How much would you pay to see a corresponding exhibition in a boxing ring? Remember, we are at the 10th Move!

11 R—Ksq, . . .

THE ROOK BECOMES A BANDIT, TOO!

What, this Rook moving again? It is the 3rd time, and the QKt and QB are still swapping their grievances. Eleven moves, and no mobilization yet!

11 . . . B—B4!

Lasker makes an exclamation mark, whether to call attention to a surprise move or to the fact that this is a 2nd Move for this Bishop, I do not know.

12 Kt—Kt3, . . .

The 3rd Move for this Knight, while the QKt and QB are still undeveloped, and to what a position! But no sympathy should be wasted on him. This is the same Knight who blocked the KBP at the 2nd Move, and he is only getting what he deserves.

Note the peculiar strategy. Both Kings are castled on the King's side, but instead of the Knights trying to worry the Kings, both parties are retiring them as far away as possible.

12 . . . B—Kt3.

This Bishop now has moved three times, while the QB is unable to develop because completely blocked.

13 Kt—QB3, . . .

Instead of developing during the first six moves, this Knight emerges from his tent at the 13th. Perhaps even now he would not have been allowed to develop except for the fact that his brother Knight is lonesome in that far-off corner.

These Knights have not yet learned their lesson, for now they are blocking the QBP and QKtP. It would seem that it would be convenient to have at least the QBP free for advance. If this Pawn is no good during the first 13 moves, when will he become useful? Philidor and Franklin K. Young considered P—QB3 the best 3rd Move. Young calls it the key move of an opening.

13 . . . P—Q4.

WHY THE BISHOP HASN'T DEVELOPED YET

This is as far as he carries the opening. But was there not a contract to show development of the QB? The Bishop is still undeveloped. Behold a mystery!

If White undertakes to free this Bishop at the next move, then 14 B—KKt5, P—Q5; 15 Kt—R4, P—QB4; 16 Kt×B, RP×Kt, and Black has a superior game.

So not yet will this Bishop develop. Instead, it is a safer guess that White will play (under a suspension of the rules) 14 Kt—R4, then 14 . . . P—QB4; 15 Kt×B, RP×Kt; 16 P—QB3—with the Bishop still undeveloped! Two principles would be violated at one stroke under this suspension of the rules, the Bishop having failed to develop during the opening, while a forbidden Pawn was forced to move.

Couldn't Get Along With Only Two Pawns

The Knights are a positive hoodoo, again blocking Pawns. The QKt is blocking the QBP, while the KKt is blocking the QKtP. We have seen that the KKt had to make two moves to a miserable position because the KBP was needed before the rapid mobilization could be effected, and that the QKt should immediately vacate QB3 to free the QBP, and at the cost of exchanging with the Bishop and strengthening Black's Pawn center. So we have proof that Lasker needs at least four Pawns in the opening as badly as anybody else, and that chess is governed by laws not to be violated with impunity by the mere dictum of world's champions.

Rule Violated Eleven Times

So the famous Rule 1, the only original one in the collection, is completely exploded. The hoodoo Knights themselves have exploded Rule 3, while Rule 4 is to be brushed aside as having no place among general principles of chess play. Now let us see what has become of Rule 2, and then we shall have disposed of all of the Principles, Laws, Rules, Dogmas, Articles of Faith.

"2. Do not move any piece twice in the opening."

White's KB moved 2 times, the KKt 3, the KR 3, and the QP 2. This is a total of 10 moves made by 4 pieces and Pawns which should have moved only once each; hence 6 violations. Black's KKt moved 4 times, and his KB 3 times. This is 7 moves by two pieces; 5 violations. There have been 11 violations in 26 moves, which means that nearly half of the moves were against the rule. Could it be violated any worse? But the fault is not with the rule, which is based on Philidor's play. It lies in the simple fact that there is no way of applying consistent principles to inconsistent openings.

But let it not be thought that this opening of Lasker is a very exceptional offender. Analyze almost any Knight opening, and you will also find wholesale violations, only perhaps never so thoroughly outrageous.

The Military Principles

But we are not through with Lasker's four Principles that are supposed to be a panacea for all chess ills. I propose to add a 5th, one of my own. It is:

"5. Chess should be played in strict accordance with the best military principles."

But how about the military principles here involved? Who ever heard of a war conducted like this? When

> "The King of France with 20,000 men
> Went up the hill, and then came down again,"

he did only once what was done twice in this game. White's KKt made three moves to get as far away as possible from Black's King because he heard that he had the smallpox, while Black's KKt, hearing a similar rumor about White's King, made four moves to a haven of safety. The rumor spread through the ranks, and all of the Pawns, except one on each side that had advanced before hearing the report, remained at their posts, frozen stiff with fear.

Move back White's KP, move back Black's QP, out of danger—quick! And then we shall be able to see more clearly that the parties have only been firing smoke-screen empty cartridges at each other—there never was an intention to mobilize. Why, mobilization in real warfare is supposed to mean something! In 13 moves all of White's pieces ought to be commanding powerful positions, each with a threat, and all together constituting a terrorizing menace. The atmosphere ought to be vibrating with tension. Who ever before heard of such a thing as the whole army standing still while one Knight on each side consumes weeks of time on a reconnoitering expedition—and in his own territory?

White has not the semblance of an attack.

> *Storm'd at with shot and shell,*
> *Boldly they rode and well,*
> *Into the jaws of Death,*
> *Into the mouth of Hell.*

> *When can their glory fade?*
> *O the wild charge they made!*
> *All the world wonder'd.*

Shade of General Sherman, who said "War is Hell"; shade of Tennyson, who wrote "The Charge of the Light Brigade"; shade of Philidor, shade of Labourdonnais, shade of Macdonnell, shade of Anderssen, shade of Morphy, rise, Oh rise, from your tombs—speak!

Cartoon by H. T. Webster, by permission of the artist. Copyright 1932 New York Herald Tribune, Inc.

Part Two

THE MAGIC OF CHESS

Cartoon by Martha Blanchard, by permission of the artist, from *The Saturday Review of Literature.* Copyright 1948 Saturday Review Associates, Inc.

Odd, But True

1

A game of chess can be won in two moves! Here's how:

WHITE	BLACK
1 P—KB4	P—K3
2 P—KKt4	Q—R5 mate

2

The shortest master game of all time is this snappy four-mover:

QUEEN'S PAWN OPENING
Paris, 1924

WHITE	BLACK
Gibaud	Lazard
1 P—Q4	Kt—KB3
2 Kt—Q2	P—K4
3 P×P	Kt—Kt5
4 P—KR3	Kt—K6!

And White resigned. He is threatened with loss of his Queen; if he takes the Knight, 5 . . . Q—R5ch forces mate.

3

The record for the longest number of moves in a master game is held by Makogonov and Chekover, who fought for four days (21½ hours of playing time) at Baku in 1945. The result of this titanic struggle was a draw on the 171st move. Such a battle is the equivalent of five tournament games rolled into one!

4

Runner-up for the longest-game record is the encounter between Wolf and Duras at Karlsbad 1907, which lasted 168 moves! Duras lost a Pawn in the opening, at his *seventh move*, but hung on grimly throughout six sittings (22½ hours of playing time) until he was checkmated by Wolf, who had *two Queens*. Duras, who had only his King on the board, must have been hoping for an earthquake (the atomic bomb had not yet been invented).

5

Other lengthy contests were: Duras—Janowski, San Sebastian 1911, 161 moves (another tortuous loss for Duras); Lipshutz—Bird, New York 1889, 159 moves; Mason—Tchigorin, Monte Carlo 1902, 144 moves; Pinkus—Denker, New York 1940, 141 moves. This last game was printed in the New York *Post* in three weekly installments!

To this list of long-drawn labors must be added the report of a game said to have been played in 1888 for the Australian Championship between W. Crane and H. Charlick which lasted 219 moves! Luckily for the editors, typesetters and readers of this book, the score of this game is unobtainable!

6

Many a miniature game owes its existence to an early mistake made by one of the players. But when four allies discuss their ideas with each other, and then get mated on the sixth move, that is unique.

CARO-KANN DEFENSE

Palma, 1935

WHITE	BLACK
Alekhine	Four Allies
1 P—K4	P—QB3
2 P—Q4	P—Q4

3 Kt—QB3   P×P
4 Kt×P   Kt—Q2
5 Q—K2   KKt—B3??
6 Kt—Q6 mate

7

A correspondence player can take a day or two for each move. One would expect him to make blunders rarely, and the games so played to be long drawn-out affairs. The world's record for brevity in chess by mail must therefore be this quickie:

BUDAPEST DEFENSE
Correspondence, 1930

WHITE	BLACK
Warren	Selman
Dublin	*Amsterdam*
1 P—Q4	Kt—KB3
2 P—QB4	P—K4
3 P×P	Kt—K5
4 P—QR3	P—Q3
5 P×P	B×P
6 P—KKt3	Kt×BP
Resigns	

On 7 K×Kt, B×Pch wins the Queen; on other moves, Black wins the exchange.

8

Many a good player would like to try his skill against the masters in a tournament, but dreads the possible outcome—a long string of zeros. Not so Colonel Moreau, who played in the Monte Carlo Tournament of 1903. He played two games with each of 13 opponents, and lost 26 times in succession. Not even so much as one measly draw could he get!

9

What is the best move to begin a game? At one time the masters began automatically with 1 P—K4; then they switched to 1 P—Q4. Paul Morphy, considered by many critics the greatest chess genius that ever lived, never played 1 P—Q4. In contrast, Ernest Gruenfeld, one of the greatest living authorities on opening play, ventured on 1 P—K4 only once in his entire tournament career (against Capablanca at Karlsbad 1929). When asked why he avoided 1 P—K4, he answered, "I never make a mistake in the opening!"

10

Chess is thought of so highly in the Soviet Union that it is taught in the public schools. Yet, blindfold play is forbidden by law! (Do they realize, we wonder, that a master player analyzing a combination ten moves deep is really playing blindfold chess?)

11

Franz Gutmayer wrote a book on how to become a chess master, but could never become one himself! Gutmayer never won a *Hauptturnier* first prize, a requisite in Germany for the title of master.

12

Dr. Lasker was certainly a hard man to beat. Marshall won from him in May 1900, and then once again on another May day. But that second victory came after forty years of tournament and match play, in the course of which they had met many times.

13

Humorists who poke fun at some of the strange names of chess players may add this item to their collection:

The St. Petersburg tournament of 1903 had *three* players who rejoiced in the surname Znosko-Borovsky. Evidently their names occasioned them no complexes, as they all won prizes.

14

A book was once published in German with the title, *Advice to Spectators at Chess Tournaments.* All the pages, with one exception, were completely blank. On this page there were only two words, *Halt's Maul!"* which means "Keep your mouth shut!"

15

The first eight moves between Capablanca and Reshevsky in a game they played at AVRO in 1938 took exactly one hour. Nothing startling in that, but this was the breakdown:

Reshevsky, 58 minutes
Capablanca, 2 minutes

16

Beethoven astonished the world of music by composing masterpieces when he was deaf. Arthur Ford Mackenzie matched this miracle by composing chess problems when he was blind.

17

Chess critics are almost unanimous in the opinion that the three greatest chess masters that ever lived were Alekhine, Capablanca and Lasker. Rarely did any of them lose a game, and yet, Akiba Rubinstein defeated each in turn the first time he played them!

18

Capablanca played 103 games simultaneously at Cleveland in 1922. His percentage of wins in this exhibition has never even been approached before or since, by any other master. He won 102 games, drew 1, lost none!

19

Mr. A. P. Barnes once gave an amateur Rook and Knight odds and won easily. Nothing startling in that, but in this case his opponent finished up with more pieces than he started with originally!

| REMOVE WHITE'S QUEEN | 11 R—K1 | P×P |
| ROOK AND QUEEN KNIGHT | 12 R—Q1 | P×B(Q) |

WHITE	BLACK
Barnes	Amateur
1 P—K4	P—K4
2 P—Q4	P×P
3 P—QB3	P×P
4 B—QB4	Kt—QB3
5 P—QR3	QKt—K2
6 Kt—B3	P—QR3
7 O—O	P—QKt4
8 B—R2	P—QB3
9 Kt—Kt5	Kt—R3
10 Q—Kt3	Q—R4

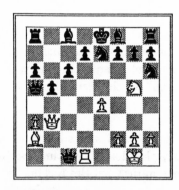

White announced mate in three moves, as follows: 13 Q×Pch!, Kt×Q; 14 B×Ktch, K—Q1; 15 Kt—K6 mate!

20

In 1851 the Chess Champion of the world was A. Anderssen; the Checker Champion of the world was A. Anderson!

21

The year 1894 was a disastrous one for board champions. William Steinitz, who had held the chess title for twenty-eight years, lost it in his World Championship match with Emanuel Lasker. In the same year, James Wyllie, who was World's Checker Champion for the almost incredible period of forty years, lost his title to James Ferrie.

22

Norwood Potter once gave an amateur the tremendous odds of a Queen. After only six moves were played, he announced a forced checkmate in nine moves! The game follows:

REMOVE WHITE'S QUEEN

WHITE Potter	BLACK Amateur
1 P—K4	P—K4
2 Kt—KB3	Kt—QB3
3 B—B4	Kt—B3
4 Kt—B3	Kt—QR4
5 Kt×P	Kt×P
6 P—Q3	Kt—B4

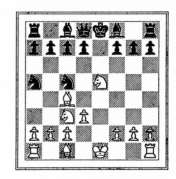

White announced mate as follows: 7 B×Pch, K—K2; 8 B—Kt5ch, K—Q3; 9 Kt—Kt5ch, K×Kt; 10 P—B4ch, K—B4; 11 Kt—Q4ch, K—Kt5; 12 P—R3ch, K—Kt6; 13 Kt—K2ch, K×P; 14 B—Q5ch, Kt—K5; 15 B×Kt mate.

Mates of all sorts have been announced before and since this game, but never one which, as here, is longer than the rest of the game itself!

23

The capped Knight . . . Much more difficult even than giving Queen odds is it to undertake to give mate with a specific Pawn or piece. Clearly, the opponent can afford to give up any amount of material just to rid himself of the only piece that has the power to checkmate him. Here is a rare example of this stipulation being carried out successfully.

Max Lange contracts to checkmate with his Queen Knight.

MUZIO GAMBIT			
WHITE Lange	BLACK Von Schierstedt	8 B×Pch	K×B
		9 Q—R5ch	K—Kt2
		10 R×P	Kt—R3
1 P—K4	P—K4	11 B—K3	P—Q3
2 Kt—QB3	Kt—QB3	12 Kt—K2	Q—K2
3 P—KB4	P×P	13 K×P	B—K3
4 Kt—B3	P—KKt4	14 QR—KB1	B—B2
5 B—B4	P—Kt5	15 Q×Ktch	K×Q
6 O—O	P×Kt	16 R—Kt4ch	K—R4
7 P—Q4	P×P	17 Kt—Kt3ch	K×R

18	R—B5	P—KR3
19	P—R3ch	K—R5
20	R—R5ch	B×R
21	Kt—B5 mate!	

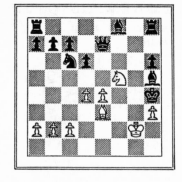

In the course of completing his task, Lange sacrificed his Queen, two Rooks, a Knight and a Bishop!

24

Cambridge University once played a game by correspondence with an insane asylum, and lost!

SICILIAN DEFENSE

Correspondence, 1883–1885

WHITE	BLACK
Cambridge	Bedlam
1 P—K4	P—QB4
2 Kt—QB3	P—K3
3 Kt—B3	Kt—QB3
4 P—Q4	P×P
5 Kt×P	B—Kt5
6 Kt—Kt5	Kt—B3
7 P—QR3	B×Ktch
8 Kt×B	P—Q4
9 P×P	P×P
10 B—KKt5	B—K3
11 B—K2	O—O
12 O—O	Kt—K2
13 B×Kt	P×B
14 B—Q3	K—R1
15 Q—R5	P—B4
16 Kt—K2	Q—Q3
17 Kt—Q4	Q—K4

18 Kt—B3	Q—Kt2
19 Kt—R4	R—KKt1
20 P—KKt3	Q—B3
21 P—KB4	R—Kt5
22 QR—K1	QR—KKt1
23 Kt—Kt2	R(Kt1)—Kt3
24 R×B	P×R
25 B—K2	R—R3
Resigns	

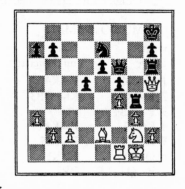

25

The first exhibition of simultaneous blindfold play in chess history occurred in January of 1266. The Saracen master Buzecca opposed three Florentine experts, playing two games blindfold, and the third over the board. The result of this séance has been handed down to posterity in somewhat vague form—two wins for the Saracen, and one draw. In spite of the loose reporting, one important fact was determined—a world's record for playing chess without sight of board or pieces had been established. Not until centuries later (517 years, to be exact) was this record broken!

26

When Philidor played three blindfold games simultaneously in 1783, affidavits were drawn up attesting to the fact that this performance had really taken place. Chess players of that day doubted that future generations would believe that such an astounding feat was possible. Not until three quarters of a century had passed was Philidor's mark eclipsed. Louis Paulsen ventured on four simultaneous *sans voir* games in 1857, then five, seven, ten, and finally fifteen games. Paulsen was a hard-working performer, and his exhibitions generally took the better part of two days. At about the same time, the peerless Paul Morphy was astounding the natives with the speed, accuracy and brilliancy of his blindfold play. Morphy never tried more than eight boards at a time, but there is no doubt that he could have handled many more with ease.

Blackburne, a few years after learning the moves, managed ten boards effortlessly. Later, he raised his mark to sixteen, which record was subsequently equaled by Zukertort.

This branch of the game reached such a stage of perfection that Pillsbury played 12 and 16 games as a matter of routine. Old-timers who have seen him in action still get misty-eyed as they recall the smooth, easy technique with which Pillsbury created his elegant combinations. Pillsbury increased the number of his simultaneous blindfold games to 17, 20, 21 and finally 22 at Moscow in 1902.

His record stood for seventeen years until Reti surpassed it with 24 games, played at Haarlem in 1919. Reti's triumph was short-lived, as

Breyer outdistanced him with 25 games two years later. In 1924, after the great New York tournament, Alekhine played 26 games in this style, scoring 16 wins, 5 draws and 5 losses. Prominent among the opposition were such strong players as Kashdan, Steiner, Tholfsen and Pinkus! The following year at Paris, Alekhine shattered his own record with an exhibition on 28 boards. A few months later at São Paulo, Reti raised the number to 29, only to be topped by Koltanowski with 30. Along came Alekhine again, to raise the standard to 32 games. Nothing daunted, Koltanowski lifted the mark still higher by playing 34 games at Edinburgh in 1937. He seemed quite safe, and was—until the year 1943. In 1943, Naidorf played 40 boards at Rosario, in a display which lasted 17½ hours. Despite the fact that he opposed two players at each board, he achieved the impressive result of winning 36 games, drawing one and losing three. Just to make sure that his name would go ringing down the corridors of chess history, Naidorf played . . . but this deserves another paragraph . . .

In 1947 at São Paulo, Naidorf established a world's record for simultaneous blindfold play. Without sight of the board or pieces, he pitted himself against 45 opponents—as remarkable a feat as any in the realm of mnemonics! This phenomenal exhibition lasted 23½ hours, at the end of which Naidorf had compiled a score of 39 wins, 4 draws and only 2 losses!

27

William Steinitz defended the World's Chess Championship against all comers for twenty-eight years—an astonishing achievement! His conqueror, Dr. Emanuel Lasker, proved a worthy successor; he held the title for twenty-seven years!

28

In 1940 Reuben Fine toured North America, giving exhibitions of his skill at blindfold play, "ordinary" simultaneous chess, and serious games against single opponents. He played 418 games altogether, of which 21 were conducted blindfold. Of these last, Fine won 17, drew four and lost none. Of the remaining 397, Fine won 376, drew 18 and lost only three games!

29

Devotees of the Philidor Defense who are interested in seeing how the great Frenchman himself managed its intricacies will look through the scores of his games in vain.

In all his life, Philidor never played the Philidor Defense!

30

Can you win a game of chess without moving a piece? It sounds impossible, but here is how Hans Bruening once did it!

QUEEN'S GAMBIT DECLINED

WHITE	BLACK
Amateur	Bruening
1 P—Q4	P—Q4
2 P—QB4	P—K3
3 Kt—QB3	P—QB4
4 B—B4	BP×P
5 B×Kt	P×Kt
6 B—K5	BP×P

White resigned! Black threatens 7 . . . P×R(Q), as well as 7 . . . B—Kt5ch winning the Queen.

31

All sorts of sacrifices have been made in order to force checkmate; Queens, Rooks, Knights, Bishops and Pawns have been offered up. But to Dr. Ballard belongs the unique distinction of giving away all eight of his Pawns in the course of an odds game!

REMOVE WHITE'S QUEEN KNIGHT			
WHITE	BLACK	5 P—Kt3	P×P
Ballard	Fagan	6 O—O	Kt—KR3
		7 P—Q4	O—O
1 P—K4	P—K4	8 P×P	B×P
2 P—KB4	P×P	9 K—Kt2	B—Q3
3 Kt—B3	B—K2	10 R—R1	Q—B3
4 B—B4	B—R5ch	11 P—K5	Q—Kt3ch
		12 K—B1	Kt—B4
		13 KR—Kt1	Kt—Kt6ch

14 K—B2	Kt—K5ch	*29* Q—R8ch	K—B2
15 K—K1	B—Kt5ch	*30* Kt—Kt5 mate	
16 P—B3	Kt×P		
17 P×Kt	B×Pch		
18 K—B2	Q—QB3		
19 B—Q3	B×R		
20 P—Q5	Q—Kt3ch		
21 B—K3	Q—Kt7ch		
22 K—B1	P—KB4		
23 B—Q4	Q×P		
24 B×B	Q×P		
25 P—K6	P—KKt3		
26 P—K7	R—K1		
27 Q—K2	Q—B4		
28 Q—QKt2	R×P		

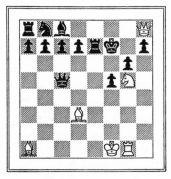

The final position

32

Immediately after the conclusion of the U. S. A.–U. S. S. R. radio match in 1945, Reuben Fine gave a startling demonstration of mental gymnastics. He undertook to play four blindfold games simultaneously at a speed time-limit of ten seconds a move! He made short work of his "seeing" opponents, chalking up a score of 4–0.

33

Solving Otto Blathy's problems is no picnic. In a booklet of his compositions, the *shortest* problem requires that White is to mate in 30 moves! The longest specifies that mate is to be forced in 292 moves!

34

"Only one or two Pawn moves in the opening," says Lasker. Tarrasch said, "Nothing so easily ruins a position as Pawn moves" and, jokingly to his pupils, "Never move a Pawn and you will never lose a game." Steinitz says, "The King Pawn and the Queen Pawn are the only ones to be moved in the early part of the game."

But genius knows no restrictions; here is how Marshall played ten consecutive Pawn moves, won a piece, and later the game!

SICILIAN DEFENSE
New York, 1940

WHITE	BLACK
Marshall	*Rogosin*
1 P—K4	P—QB4
2 P—QKt4	P×P
3 P—QR3	Kt—QB3
4 P×P	Kt—B3
5 P—Kt5	Kt—Q5
6 P—QB3	Kt—K3
7 P—K5	Kt—Q4
8 P—QB4	Kt(Q4)—B5
9 P—Kt3	Kt—Kt3
10 P—B4	

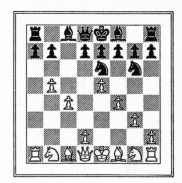

Not a single piece of Marshall's has been brought into play, and yet he has a won game! Rogosin played 10 . . . Kt(Kt3)×P and quickly lost. The alternative 10 . . . Kt—B2 would also lose a piece after 11 P—B5, Kt×P; 12 P—Q4, and the Knight has no retreat!

35

Show this diagram to any chess master! Just say, "White to play," and before you finish telling him the stipulations, he will polish off the Black King by a smothered mate in five moves.

The reason? It is one of the oldest and prettiest tricks in the expert's repertoire. The position in the diagram was first published by Lucena in 1496! The winning idea is useful, as it comes up quite often. The solution is 1 Q—K6ch, K—R1; 2 Kt—B7ch, K—Kt1; 3 Kt—R6ch, K—R1; 4 Q—Kt8ch!, R×Q; 5 Kt—B7 mate!

36

In an end-game competition sponsored by *Sydvenska Dagbladet Snaellposten* in 1924, Henri Rinck won 1st prize, 2nd prize, 3rd prize, first honorable mention, 2nd honorable mention and 3rd honorable mention! A remarkable achievement, but—

In 1936, in an end-game competition, Grigoriev shared first and second prizes, won 3rd, 4th and 5th prizes; shared 1st and 2nd honorable mentions, and was awarded 3rd, 4th, 5th and 6th honorable mentions!

37

In the first 13 moves of a game against Forgacs, Maroczy sacrificed his Queen, won his opponent's Queen Rook, and promoted a Pawn to a new Queen. Within the next eight moves Forgacs duplicated the feat! He sacrificed his Queen, promoted a Pawn to a new Queen, and won Maroczy's Queen Rook. The score of this extraordinary game:

IRREGULAR DEFENSE
Budapest, 1902

WHITE	BLACK
Forgacs	Maroczy
1 P—K4	P—QR3
2 P—Q4	P—K3
3 P—KB4	P—Q4
4 P—K5	P—QB4
5 P—B3	P—QKt4
6 B—Q3	Kt—QB3
7 Kt—B3	B—Q2
8 B—K3	Kt—R3
9 P×P	P—Kt5
10 Kt—Q4	Q—R4
11 P—QR3	P×BP
12 Kt×Kt	P×Pch
13 Kt×Q	P×R(Q)
14 P—B6	B—B1

15 Q—R4	Kt—B4
16 B—R7	B×P
17 P—B7ch	B—Q2
18 B—Kt8	B×Q
19 P—B8(Q)ch	K—K2

20 Q—Kt7ch K—B1

21 Q×R	B—Kt5ch		25 B—Kt6	Q—B8ch
22 K—B1	P—Kt4		26 K—B2	Q×R
23 B—B7ch	K—Kt2		27 B—B1	Q×P
24 Q×RP	Q—Kt7		Resigns	

38

In 1878 Paris and Marseilles played a game by correspondence with these curious conditions: Paris gave Marseilles Queen odds; in return for this advantage Marseilles undertook to *force* Paris to checkmate them!

39

In the Nuremberg Congress of 1906 there was no time-limit if a game took six hours or less. Afterwards the players were required to move at the rate of 15 moves an hour.

If they exceeded the time-limit, they were penalized at the rate of a mark a minute, for each minute of extra time. Under this ruling, Tarrasch not only lost his game to Salwe but had the unique privilege of paying the equivalent of $20.00 in fines for doing so!

40

Jacques Mieses was a participant in the almost legendary tournament at Hastings in 1895, where he drew with the then World Champion Emanuel Lasker. Fifty years later, Mieses played in the Hastings Christmas Tournament of 1945, where he drew with former World Champion Euwe and also won the Brilliancy Prize. Early in 1946, at the age of 82, Mieses played a match against Arturito Pomar, aged 14!

41

Frank Marshall once played in a tournament where he won 44 games in succession, without even permitting a draw. A mighty feat, and yet he won only third prize! Here is how it happened, as John Keeble tells it:

In its early days the British Chess Federation used to run a contest for congress competitors in which they might play in their spare time. All entrants were classified. A player received 7 points for a win against a player in his own class, 8 for a win against a player in a class above, 9 for a win against a player two classes above, and so on; correspondingly, 6 points for a win against a player one class below, and so on.

This went on until, at Richmond in 1912, Frank Marshall turned up too late to play in any of the ordinary tournaments, so entered this one. He won 44 games in succession, with no losses and no draws, and he took third prize! The reason was that he had been put in a class by himself!

42

Do you believe in reincarnation of chess ideas? The diagram shows a position which occurred in a game played in 1945 between Jorgensen and Sorensen. *This identical position* is described by al-Adli in an Arabian manuscript dating back to the *ninth century!*

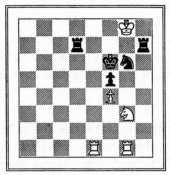

Jorgensen mated in three moves (thereby solving al-Adli's problem) by 1 Kt—R5ch, R×Kt; 2 R×Ktch, K×R; 3 R—K6 mate!

43

The greatest players have been known to blunder; that is not news. When five masters combine their talents as a team, and still overlook a simple combination—that *is* news.

In the diagram, the Allies conducting the black pieces (Bogolyubov, Gruenfeld, Kostich, Sterk and Abonyi) played 1 . . . R×R. No doubt they expected 2 B×R in reply; what they did get was a lesson in Knight forks! White played 2 Kt—R6ch, and Black must choose between 2 . . . K—R1 when 3 Kt×Pch wins the Queen, or 2 . . .

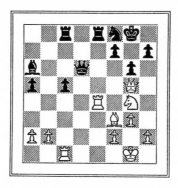

K—Kt2, when 3 Kt—B5ch wins the Queen. Note that after Black's Queen falls, the hungry Knight threatens both Rooks.

44

Rubinstein fell into an opening trap against Euwe at Bad Kissingen in 1928:

QUEEN'S GAMBIT DECLINED

WHITE	BLACK
Euwe	*Rubinstein*
1 P—Q4	P—Q4
2 P—QB4	P—K3
3 Kt—KB3	Kt—KB3
4 B—Kt5	QKt—Q2
5 P—K3	B—K2
6 Kt—B3	O—O
7 R—B1	P—B3
8 B—Q3	P—QR3
9 P×P	KP×P
10 O—O	R—K1
11 Q—Kt3	P—R3

12 B—KB4	Kt—R4
13 Kt×P!	

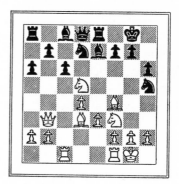

White wins a Pawn. If 13 . . . Kt×B; 14 Kt×Kt, and if 13 . . . P×Kt; 14 B—B7 wins the Queen.

Ordinarily, there is nothing unusual about a master stumbling into a pitfall, but Rubinstein fell into *the same trap* only two years later against Alekhine at San Remo!

45

How important is it to know the openings? In the Fifth American Championship tournament held at New York in 1880, Preston Ware played 1 . . . P—QR4 whenever he had the black pieces, against any opening chosen by his opponent! With this meaningless move Ware managed to win four out of nine games. As White, he began two games with 1 P—QR4, winning one and losing the other.

46

Many competent critics consider Emanuel Lasker to have been the greatest player that ever lived. Perhaps he was. It is curious, though, that he was beaten the first time he encountered each of the following players:

Van Vliet, Amsterdam 1889
Makovetz, Graz 1890
Tchigorin, Hastings 1895
Tarrasch, Hastings 1895
Charousek, Nuremberg 1896
Marshall, Paris 1900
Rubinstein, St. Petersburg 1909
Dus-Chotimirski, St. Petersburg 1909
Torre, Moscow 1925
Levenfish, Moscow 1925
Stahlberg, Zurich 1934
Fine, Nottingham 1936
Reshevsky, Nottingham 1936

47

The Russian master Ilyin-Genevski had to learn the moves twice! Shell shock in the first World War took away his memory, and the master player had to be told how the chess pieces move and capture!

48

Racing down the home stretch in a thrilling neck-and-neck tie for first place in the San Sebastian tournament of 1912 were Rubinstein and Nimzovich. Fittingly enough, they were scheduled to play each other in the last round. First prize would go to the winner of this one game!

In the opening, Rubinstein had a bit the better of it, and kept his advantage to the mid-game. Suddenly, Nimzovich, affected no doubt by the keen excitement of the occasion, blundered. He made a move which would allow his opponent to mate in two moves! An unbelievable error in a master of Nimzovich's ability, and sure to be pounced on by the eagle-eyed Rubinstein. This was the situation:

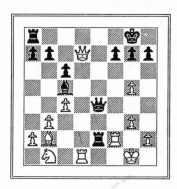

But, "curiouser and curiouser," eagle-eyed Rubinstein missed the mate by 1 Q×Pch, K—R1; 2 Q×P mate. Undoubtedly, this was one of the strangest double blunders in chess history!

49

The record for simultaneous chess is held by Gideon Stahlberg, Swedish master. He played 400 games at Buenos Aires, in an exhibition which started at 10:00 P.M., Friday, August 29, 1941, and ended at 10:00 A.M. on Sunday. He wound up with the remarkable score of 364 wins, 14 draws and only 22 losses!

50

Even the most confirmed problem solver would think twice before tackling this problem, which J. N. Babson composed for *Brentano's Chess Monthly* in 1882:

These were his terms: Mate on the 1220th move, after compelling Black to make three successive and complete Knight's tours!

51

In the Fifth American Championship tournament, held at New York in 1880, Congdon and Delmar reached a position which was "hopelessly won" for Delmar. He had a Queen and five passed Pawns (five potential Queens, if he needed them) against Congdon's lone Queen. Did he win? It was almost impossible not to, but this is what happened:

Delmar played 1 . . . Q—B6 (as the Tournament book says, "Almost any other move would have won") and Congdon saved his game by 2 Q—Kt8ch, K×Q, and White is stalemated.

52

Dr. Lasker made a clean sweep at the New York tournament of 1893. He won 13 games straight, without allowing a single draw!

But history repeats itself. In the New York tournament of 1913, Capablanca too faced 13 opponents and mowed them all down in quick succession, wihout allowing a single draw!

53

Do you sometimes wish your opponent would let you move the pieces around to help analyze a position?

In 1911, Spielmann and Alapin played a match at Munich, in which analysis by means of moving the pieces was permitted. Alapin used this privilege; Spielmann decided not to do so.

P.S. Spielmann won the match!

54

Steinitz and Capablanca had race horses named after them!

55

Steinitz was once misjudged to be a spy! Police authorities assumed that the moves made by him in playing his correspondence games with Tchigorin were part of a code by means of which important war secrets could be transmitted.

56

Rubinstein won only six games at Teplitz-Schönau in 1922. But of these six games, four were winners of brilliancy prizes!

57

G. A. MacDonnell was the winner of a tournament played at London in 1868. All the competitors began their games with the positions of their Knights and Bishops reversed. The reason? They wanted to avoid book play! (And this was way back in 1868!)

58

Alexandre Louis Honoré Lebreton Deschapelles was once acknowledged to be the best player in the world at both chess and whist. The Deschapelles Coup, his invention, is still used today by master bridge players.

59

The famous Bishop Ruy Lopez recommended as good chess tactics placing the board so that the light would shine in the opponent's eyes! (A valuable addition to the theory of the Ruy Lopez opening!)

60

The organist Sir Walter Parratt was able to play a Beethoven Sonata at the same time that he was conducting two games of chess blindfolded!

61

An extraordinary set of coincidences marked two problems submitted to the 8th Composing tourney of the "Brighton Society" in 1898. These were the positions:

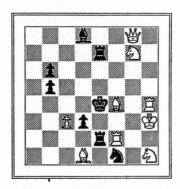

A. F. MACKENZIE
America
White mates in two
Key: Q—R2

H. W. LANE
England
White mates in two
Key: Q—R2

Not only were the positions almost alike, the key-moves matched, the resulting ideas duplicated each other, but strangest of all . . . both composers were blind!

62

In 1850, an old passion for chess awoke in Szechenyi (founder of the Magyar Academy) and took an insane character. It became necessary to pay a poor student to play with him for ten or twelve hours at a time. Szechenyi slowly regained his sanity, but the unfortunate student went mad!

63

What is the favorite recreation of a chess master? More chess! Pillsbury, in the course of the Hannover 1902 tournament, spent one of his precious days of rest in a record-breaking exhibition of simultaneous blindfold play! He took on 21 of the best players of Germany, offering prizes to those who scored against him (just to make things tougher!). He permitted consultation, as well as moving the pieces around to facilitate analysis. His final score of 3 wins, 11 draws and 7 losses is more impressive than might first appear, as his opponents were all budding masters.

64

One of the greatest chess teachers that ever lived was Dr. Siegbert Tarrasch. The one thing he harped on in his books, his teachings and his actual play was the importance of continual development of one's forces. "Bring all your pieces out! Give them scope! Occupy the central squares!" He stressed this, time and again, in his annotations. Rarely did he stray from the path he marked out. But once when he did . . .

It was in the important Ostend tournament of 1907, confined to six of the seven leading grandmasters. The winner of the tournament was to challenge Lasker for his world title. Tarrasch, playing White, reached this position against Marshall:

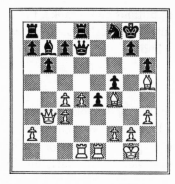

Play continued, 1 R—R1; Q—K2; 2 Q—Q1, Kt—K3; 3 B—B1, K—R2; 4 B—K2, R—KB1; 5 B—B1. After five retreating moves in a row, White's pieces all occupy the first rank! That Tarrasch eventually drew the game is a tribute to his great ability.

65

A ten-year-old once played in a master tournament! The prodigy, Sammy Reshevsky, subsequently won the United States Championship.

66

Before retiring from his throne, Paul Morphy, King of Chess, offered to play a match with anyone in the world at the odds of Pawn and move! The handicap was big, but no one accepted. They were convinced that he was invincible!

67

Even the greatest masters sometimes get bowled over with surprising speed. Capablanca, who was a wizard at simultaneous play, got a 13-move shock from Kevitz, then a youngster, in one of these sessions.

Arthur Dake, one of America's strongest players, once gave an exhibition of his skill at simultaneous chess at Baltimore. One of his opponents, an amateur, was evidently unimpressed by Dake's reputation, as he mated the Pacific Coast star in 9 moves! Here is the blow-by-blow description:

FRENCH DEFENSE

WHITE	BLACK
Dake	*Amateur*
1 P—Q4	P—K3
2 P—K4	P—Q4
3 Kt—QB3	B—Kt5
4 Kt—K2	P×P
5 P—QR3	B×Ktch
6 Kt×B	Kt—QB3
7 Q—Kt4	Kt×P
8 Q×KtP	Kt×Pch
9 K—K2	Q—Q6 mate

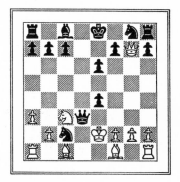

68

Dake's 9-move upset was speedy, but not the record for such debacles. On January 25, 1948, the European master Hans Kmoch met all comers in a simultaneous exhibition at Cleveland. One of his opponents did the unexpected. He made Kmoch surrender in only 8 moves! Here is the morsel:

FRENCH DEFENSE

WHITE	BLACK
Kmoch	*Ellison*
1 P—K4	P—K3
2 P—Q4	P—Q4
3 Kt—Q2	P—QB4
4 KKt—B3	BP×P
5 Kt×P	P×P
6 Kt(Q2)×P	Kt—KB3
7 B—KKt5	Q—R4ch
8 B—Q2	Q—K4

White resigns, as he must lose a piece.

69

A position was once sent to L. Hoffer for adjudication. He spent eight hours analyzing its possibilities, which was more time than both players had spent on the game themselves!

70

Can't solve problems? Here is a six-mover we guarantee you can do. Just move, and think later!

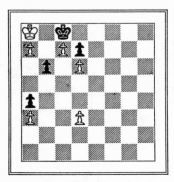

Ropke
White mates in six moves.

71

Steinitz's style is usually described as "sound, safe, dull and cautious." Morphy's play, on the other hand, is generally regarded as "daring, inspired, sparkling and brilliant."

In a book entitled *Quick Mate! 700 Short, Brilliant Games of Chess,* the player having the most examples to his credit is Steinitz! Next in order is Tarrasch, whose methods in the popular eye seemed to parallel those of Steinitz. The brilliant Morphy comes next— after these two "dull" players!

Curiously, Capablanca is not even in the book, while Lasker is represented by a lost game!

72

Paul Morphy once gave a simultaneous exhibition against five players. What's startling about that? All five were in the master class! He won from Arnous de Rivière and H. E. Bird, drew with S. S. Boden and J. J. Lowenthal, and lost to T. W. Barnes. Incidentally, Barnes, whose name may be completely unknown to present-generation chess players, won more games from Morphy than anyone else ever did!

73

Former United States Champion Sammy Reshevsky was asked whether he expected to win the Western Chess Association Championship tournament of 1933. His reply was, "Who is there to beat me?" Remarkably enough, he was right. Nobody did beat him; but he did not win the tournament!

74

In the eighth edition of a popular manual by Dufresne and Mieses, the following line of play is given:

WHITE	BLACK
1 P—Q4	P—Q4
2 P—QB4	P—K3
3 Kt—QB3	P—QB4
4 Kt—B3	BP×P
5 KKt×P	P—K4
6 Kt(Q4)—Kt5	P—Q5
7 Kt—Q5	Kt—QR3
8 Q—R4	B—Q2
9 P—K3	Kt—K2

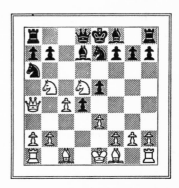

In this situation, the authors' comment is, "Black has the superior position." What the analysts seem to have overlooked is that White can mate on the move!

75

A book of Yates' games was published with the title, *One Hundred and One of My Best Games of Chess*. The reader gets a baker's dozen, as the book contains 109 games.

76

In the International tournament held at London in 1851, Mucklow won a grand total of two games, lost eight, forfeited the rest—and still won a prize!

77

In *Die Hypermoderne Schachpartie* Dr. Tartakover annotates a game between Spielmann and Tarrasch, played at Mährisch-Ostrau, 1923. To make sure that the student does not miss any of the fine points, he gives 11 columns of notes to *two moves* in the game! A lesser analyst would have filled up this space with 11 games, notes and all!

78

Schottlander needed only a draw to win first prize in the Leipzig tournament of 1888. Mieses offered him a draw in their last-round game, but he declined it! Schottlander lost the game, and with it first prize!

79

Perhaps the most fanatical devotee the game has ever known was Daniel Harrwitz. He wore stickpins shaped like chess pieces, chess ties, and had chess figures embroidered on his shirts. He played chess at the Café de la Régence morning, noon and night seven days a week! At one stage of his match with Morphy, Harrwitz pleaded illness, and failed to put in an appearance. His admirers found him resting up at the Café de la Régence, playing chess!

SOME FAMOUS FIRSTS

80

The first known historical document connected with chess is an inscription on a tablet in a pyramid at Gizeh, dating back to 3000 years before Christ!

81

The first chess problem, as far as can be ascertained, was composed by the Caliph Mutasim Billah during his reign in Baghdad from 834 to 842.

82

The first legal document in Europe dealing with chess was a testament of Armengo of Urgel in January 1010.

83

The first book dealing with chess was published in 1472, under the title *Dass Goldin Spil*, in the city of Augsburg.

84

The first International Chess tournament was played at Madrid in 1575, at the court of Philip the Second.

85

The first newspaper column on chess appeared in the *Liverpool Mercury*, July 9, 1813.

86

The first match to be played by correspondence was begun in April 1824 between the London and Edinburgh Chess Clubs. The match lasted two years, and was won by the Scotsmen. They scored two wins, lost one, and drew two games.

87

The first chess magazine appeared in Paris in 1836. It was called *La Palamède*, and its editors were Labourdonnais and Méry.

88

The first chess match by telegraph was played in 1844, the year in which the telegraph was invented. The players represented the cities of Baltimore and Washington, D. C.

89

The first problem-composing tournament was held at London in 1854. It was confined to Englishmen, and was won by Walter Grimshaw.

90

J. H. Blackburne, the great British master, once announced a forced mate in 16 moves in one of his games! This would be remarkable enough for over-the-board play, but in this case Blackburne was playing blindfold! This is the position, with White to move:

Scott

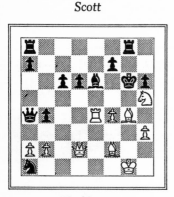

Blackburne

1 R×Bch	K—R2
2 Q—Q3ch	R—Kt3
3 Q×Rch	P×Q
4 R—K7ch	K—Kt1
5 B—K6ch	K—B1
6 R—B7ch	K—K1
7 Kt—B6ch	K—Q1
8 R—Q7ch	K—B1
9 R×RPch	K—Kt1
10 Kt—Q7ch	K—B1
11 Kt—B5ch	K—Q1
12 R—Q7ch	K—B1
13 R—KB7ch	K—Q1
14 Kt—Kt7ch	K—K1
15 Kt×Pch	K—Q1
16 B—Kt6 mate	

91

The *American Chess Bulletin* had this advertisement in its issue of February 1909:

"WANTED . . . A youth with the genius of Morphy, the memory of Pillsbury and the determination of Steinitz; of robust health which he values above rubies; full of a modest joy of living and possessor of habits of life that square with a sensible ideal—as adversary for the present and invincible champion of the world. Unto such an one will come support unlimited, friends by the legion, imperishable glory, and, possibly, Victory!"

They received a speedy reply to this advertisement (the terms of which seemed so difficult to fulfill) when their own pages recorded, a few months later, the decisive victory of Capablanca, the new chess star, over Frank Marshall, Champion of the United States. This was the beginning of Capablanca's meteoric chess career, which culminated in winning the World Championship from the mighty Lasker.

92

A book of Philidor's games, published in 1819, had illustrative diagrams showing the position of the pieces *after every move!* The editor, J. G. Pohlman, must therefore be given credit for being the originator of chess in "movie" form.

93

Dr. Milan Vidmar won more games than anyone else in the Budapest tournament of 1912, and yet he finished last! Marshall won the least games, and yet he tied for first! The point score explains:

	wins	draws	losses	point-total
Marshall	1	4	0	3
Schlechter	1	4	0	3
Duras	1	3	1	2½
Maroczy	1	3	1	2½
Teichmann	0	4	1	2
Vidmar	2	0	3	2

94

Arthur Dake took a 1500-mile airplane trip to play Alekhine, who was scheduled to give a simultaneous exhibition. He lost in 13 seconds!

Describing the game, the *American Chess Bulletin* says, "Shortly after play had started (on Alekhine's second round) all eyes were focused on Dake's board, where the two were moving the pieces at less than one second per move! Dake lasted thirteen seconds, when he blew a piece and the game."

95

One of the prizes donated for the winner of the match between Tarrasch and Mieses played in 1916, was a half pound of butter! The prize was more valuable than might first appear, as butter was a rarity in wartime Germany.

96

In the Bad Kissingen tournament of 1928, Spielmann won only one game—but that one game was from the almost invincible Capablanca!

97

At Monte Carlo in 1902, Tchigorin fought for 144 wearisome moves to defeat Mason, only to lose to Marshall in 8 moves!

98

On a wager, C. F. Burille solved 62 chess problems in one hour!

99

Conducting the chess and checker automaton *Ajeeb*, C. F. Burille played 900 chess games, of which he lost only three! Of the countless checker games he played, he never lost one!

100

In January of 1922, Frank Marshall played 155 games simultaneously at Montreal. He won 126, drew 21 and lost only 8 games, in the quick time of 7 hours and 15 minutes, an average of three minutes per game! More impressive than his speedy pace was the fact that he recalled all the moves that were made on 153 of the boards!

101

In the double-round tournament at Vienna in 1873, William **Steinitz** won 16 games in succession, without allowing even a single draw to be scored against him! The casualty list:

	Steinitz	2	Rosenthal	0
	"	2	Paulsen	0
	"	2	Anderssen	0
	"	2	Schwartz	0
	"	2	Gelbfuhs	0
	"	2	Bird	0
	"	2	Heral	0
	"	2	Blackburne	0
Grand Total:	Steinitz	16	Opponents	0

102

Games where the King meets his end by smothered mate are not un-common. Instances where the Queen gets this air-tight treatment are rare, as the Queen is a powerful fighting piece. . . .

In a game played at Ostend in 1907, Dr. Tarrasch forced a smoth-ered mate of Burn's Queen, although all of Burn's pieces were still on the board!

RUY LOPEZ

WHITE	BLACK
Tarrasch	*Burn*
1 P—K4	P—K4
2 Kt—KB3	Kt—QB3
3 B—Kt5	P—QR3
4 B—R4	Kt—B3
5 O—O	B—K2
6 R—K1	P—QKt4
7 B—Kt3	P—Q3
8 P—QR4	B—Kt5
9 P—B3	O—O
10 P—R3	B—Q2
11 P—Q4	Q—B1
12 B—Kt5	R—Kt1
13 RP×P	RP×P
14 QKt—Q2	R—K1
15 K—R2	B—Q1
16 Q—B2	P—R3
17 B—K3	B—K2
18 Kt—KKt1	P—Kt4
19 P—Kt3	B—B1
20 P—KB4	KtP×P

21 KtP×P	P×BP
22 B×P	Kt—Q1
23 R—KB1	Kt—K3
24 B—K3	B—Kt2
25 R—B2	Kt—R2
26 R(R1)—KB1	R—K2
27 Q—Q1	Q—B1
28 Kt(Kt1)—B3	B—K1
29 Kt—R4	Kt(K3)—Kt4
30 Kt—Kt6!	Resigns

103

In 1874, a tournament was conducted in Prague in which all the competitors played their games blindfold! The winner was the prob-lemist Jan Dobrusky, who scored a magnificent 13½ points out of a possible 14!

104

Possibly the most incongruous profession for a chess master was that of Max Harmonist, royal ballet dancer!

105

During the Cable Match between England and America in 1901, Bellingham (England) cabled his resignation at the same time that his opponent Voight cabled an offer of a draw! This was the final position, with Black (Voight) to move:

P.S. When time was called, the game was left as drawn.

106

In the match between Schlechter and Tarrasch played at Cologne in 1911, Schlechter won the ninth game after an exhausting, long-drawn-out 106-move battle, only to lose the very next game after an even more strenuous struggle—109 moves!

107

No astrologer, soothsayer or life-insurance actuary predicted in 1931 that the following year would be fatally dangerous to chess masters and chess problemists. In that year, there departed from this earth such distinguished chess personalities as these: F. D. Yates, Edgar Colle, Daniel Noteboom, Alexander Takacs, Herman Mattison, H. G. M. Weenink, L. van Vliet, Alexander Fritz, R. J. Loman, Bernhard Kagan, Friedrich M. Palitzsch, L. A. Issaeff and Will H. Lyons.

108

In 1891 a match was played at the Manhattan Chess Club between the bald-headed members and the hirsute ones (hirsute: one who removes his hat when he gets his hair cut). The baldheads won the match by 14 points to 11.

109

Playing simultaneously in Europe from June 1927 to March 1928, Geza Maroczy compiled the almost incredible score, from a total of 943 games, of 825 wins, 113 draws and only 5 losses!

110

One of Harry N. Pillsbury's favorite stunts in the realm of memory and imagination was to give a simultaneous display where he engaged ten chess players and ten checker players blindfolded, meanwhile taking a hand in a rubber of whist!

111

In ten years of tournament and match chess, from 1914 to 1924, Capablanca lost only one game!

112

Dr. Emanuel Lasker complimented Fred Reinfeld and Reuben Fine on their *Dr. Lasker's Chess Career*, but regretted the fact that none of his *lost* games were included in the book! (A modest chess master is a rare bird!)

113

Leonardo da Vinci may have been "perhaps the most resplendent figure in the human race," but Benjamin Franklin was a worthy runner-up. So many and varied were his interests that it should occasion little surprise that the man who was a printer, publisher, philosopher and Postmaster-General, the inventor of the lightning-rod, the rocking chair and bi-focal spectacles, should also have been the first player and writer on chess in America.

114

Are chess and checkers sister games?

In chess	In checkers
All 64 squares are used.	Only 32 squares are used.
White moves first.	Black moves first.
Captures are optional.	Captures are compulsory.
Only one piece may be taken at a time.	One or more pieces may be captured at one time.
The capturing piece replaces the one removed.	The capturing piece jumps over the one removed.
A stalemate is a draw.	A stalemate is a loss.
The pieces move in different ways.	The pieces all move the same way.
The Pawns promote to anything but a King.	The pieces promote only to a King.
Choice of openings is not restricted.	Openings are chosen by ballot.
The time limit specifies a certain number of moves per hour.	The time limit is five minutes on any one move.

115

Steinitz and Zukertort were once present at a dinner where a toast was proposed to the Chess Champion of the World. Both players stood up in response!

116

A grandmaster who has had forty years of tournament experience, and who has written more than twenty books of chess instruction, was once checkmated in 11 moves!

This is how he was polished off:

CARO-KANN DEFENSE
Vienna, 1910

WHITE	BLACK
Reti	*Tartakover*
1 P—K4	P—QB3
2 P—Q4	P—Q4
3 Kt—QB3	P×P
4 Kt×P	Kt—B3
5 Q—Q3	P—K4
6 P×P	Q—R4ch
7 B—Q2	Q×KP
8 O—O—O	Kt×Kt
9 Q—Q8ch!!	K×Q
10 B—Kt5ch	K—B2
11 B—Q8 mate	

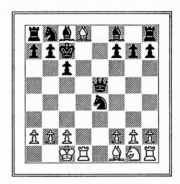

117

Blunders have been made by all classes of chess players—beginners, dubs, tyros, wood-pushers, amateurs, experts, masters, grandmasters and World Champions. Take heart, all of you! For here is an example of an almost incredible blunder made by the most brilliant player that ever lived! Alekhine, conqueror of Capablanca for the World Championship, profound analyst without peer, creator of dazzling combinations, makes a horrible mistake; overlooks a one-move Knight fork which would win his Queen!

In this position, Alekhine with the Black pieces played 1 . . . Q×P??, missing completely the devastating Knight fork by 2 Kt—R5ch, which would win his Queen.

Now comes the strangest part of it—Buerger (his opponent) moved his Knight, but not to R5! Instead, he captured the Bishop! That he won the game eventually is beside the point. In the meantime he had contributed to the greatest double-barreled blunder on record!

118

Mr. Edwin Anthony wrote an interesting article on the inexhaustibility of chess, from which we learn:

To estimate the actual number of ways of playing even a very few moves is beyond the power of calculation, but to get something of an approximation to that number is very simple. Taking an average variation of the opening as usually practiced, we find that the first player has 28, 30 and 33 ways of playing the second, third and fourth moves respectively; 29, 31 and 33 being corresponding numbers for the second player. Of course, both players, on their first move, have a choice of twenty moves. On the hypothesis that the number of replies open at each move is always the same, whatever the preceding moves may have been, and that the foregoing figures give those numbers, the number of possible ways of playing the first four moves only on each side would be 318,979,584,000. If, then, anyone were to play without cessation at the rate of one set a minute, it would take him more than six hundred thousand years to go through them all!

The number of possible ways of playing the first ten moves on each side in a game of chess is 169,518,829,100,544,000,000,000,000,000. On this basis, considering the population of the whole world to be 1483 millions, more than 217,000,000,000 years would be required to go through them all, even if every man, woman and child on the face of the globe played without cessation for that vast period at the rate of one game per minute, and no game ever repeated!

119

Dr. Threlkeld-Edwards of Bethlehem and Prof. Merriman of Lehigh University once tested Pillsbury's memory for things other than chess, by giving him this list of words to memorize:

Antiphlogistine, periosteum, takadiastase, plasmon, ambrosia, Threlkeld, streptococcus, staphylococcus, micrococcus, plasmodium, Mississippi, Freiheit, Philadelphia, Cincinnati, athletics, no war, Etchenberg, American, Russian, philosophy, Piet Potgelter's Rost, Salamagundi, Oomisillecootsi, Bangmamvate, Schlechter's Nek, Manzinyama, theosophy, catechism, Madjesoomalops.

Pillsbury looked at the list for a few minutes, repeated the words in the order given, and then backwards!

120

A brilliancy prize was awarded in 1933 to the winner of the following game:

QUEEN'S GAMBIT DECLINED

WHITE	BLACK
Mentges	Gitzen
1 P—Q4	P—Q4
2 P—QB4	P—K3
3 Kt—QB3	Kt—KB3
4 B—Kt5	B—K2
5 P—K3	O—O
6 Kt—B3	P—QKt3
7 B—Q3	B—Kt2
8 P×P	P×P
9 B×Kt	B×B
10 P—KR4	P—Kt3
11 P—R5	R—K1
12 P×P	RP×P
13 Q—B2	B—Kt2
14 B×P!	P×B

15 Q×P	Kt—Q2
16 Kt—KKt5	Q—B3
17 R—R8ch!	K×R
18 Q—R7 mate	

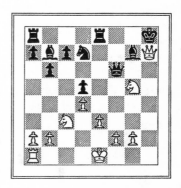

Very pretty, but the game is identical, *move for move*, with Marshall's classic brilliancy against Amos Burn in the Paris tournament of 1900!

121

A chess game where White and Black play perfectly theoretically should end in a draw. Theory should be strengthened when the players themselves are named White and Black! In the Nuremberg tournament of 1883, Weiss (which means White) met Schwartz (which means Black) in the fifth round. This is what happened:

FRENCH DEFENSE

	WHITE Weiss	BLACK Schwartz
1	P—K4	P—K3
2	P—Q4	P—Q4
3	P×P	P×P
4	Kt—KB3	Kt—KB3
5	B—Q3	B—Q3
6	O—O	O—O
7	B—KKt5	B—KKt5
8	P—B3	P—B3
9	QKt—Q2	QKt—Q2
10	Q—B2	Q—B2
11	KR—K1	KR—K1
12	P—KR3	B×Kt
13	Kt×B	P—KR3
14	B×Kt	Kt×B
15	Kt—R4	R×Rch
16	R×R	R—K1
17	R×Rch	Kt×R
18	Kt—B5	B—B1
19	Q—K2	Kt—Q3
20	Kt×Kt	Q×Kt
21	Q—K8	Q—K2
22	Q×Q	B×Q
23	B—B5	B—Kt4
24	B—B8	B—B8
25	B×P	B×P
26	B×P	B×P
27	B×P	B×P

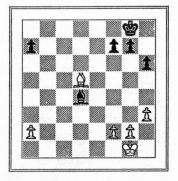

The game was called a draw at this point. Appropriately enough, the positions of White and Black (or Weiss and Schwartz) are completely identical!

Remarkable Games and Their Stories

THE most brilliant move ever seen on a chessboard was made by Frank J. Marshall, in a game against Levitzky. So electrifying was its effect on the spectators that they showered his board with gold pieces!

FRENCH DEFENSE
Breslau, 1912

WHITE	BLACK
Levitzky	*Marshall*
1 P—Q4	P—K3
2 P—K4	P—Q4
3 Kt—QB3	P—QB4
4 Kt—B3	Kt—QB3
5 KP×P	KP×P
6 B—K2	Kt—B3
7 O—O	B—K2
8 B—KKt5	O—O
9 P×P	B—K3
10 Kt—Q4	B×P
11 Kt×B	P×Kt
12 B—Kt4	Q—Q3
13 B—R3	QR—K1
14 Q—Q2	B—Kt5
15 B×Kt	R×B

16 QR—Q1	Q—B4
17 Q—K2	B×Kt
18 P×B	Q×P
19 R×P	Kt—Q5
20 Q—R5	R(1)—KB1
21 R—K5	R—R3
22 Q—Kt5	R×B

White cannot reply 23 P×R, as 23. . . . Kt—B6ch wins his Queen.

23 R—QB5

And now, Marshall played a move which has been called "fantastic," "extraordinary," "a stroke of genius," etc.

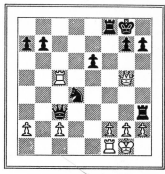

23 . . .   Q—KKt6!!

Thrusting his Queen into a nest of Pawns! Black's threat is *24 . . . Q×RP* mate. If *24 RP×Q*, *Kt—K7* mate, and on *24 BP×Q*, *Kt—K7ch*, and mate next move. Finally, if *24 Q×Q*, *Kt—K7ch*; *25 K—R1*, *Kt× Qch*; *26 K—Kt1*, *Kt×R*, with a piece ahead.

Levitzky did not play on; as soon as he recovered from the shock, he resigned!

Dus-Chotimirsky might not be the greatest player in the world, but he was a dangerous man. In the St. Petersburg tournament of 1909 he had scored a double upset; he beat Lasker and Rubinstein, the two men who shared first prize. Lasker was then World Champion, and Rubinstein his chief challenger.

When Marshall faced him to play their game in the great Karlsbad 1911 tournament, it was with the feeling that he might find Dus at his very best—in world-beating style—or just another player.

As it happened, Dus-Chotimirsky started what seemed to be a terrific attack. It looked as though Marshall would be on the wrong end of a brilliancy. Dus had already run into the next room, exclaiming excitedly in his broken German, "Poor Marshall dead! Must be mate!" One minute later (after Marshall's 13th move) he returned with "I am dead!" Here is the gamelet:

QUEEN'S GAMBIT
Karlsbad, 1911

WHITE	BLACK
Marshall	*Dus-Chotimirsky*
1 P—Q4	P—Q4
2 P—QB4	P—K3
3 Kt—KB3	P×P

4 P—K3	P—QR3
5 Kt—K5	Kt—Q2
6 Kt×Kt	B×Kt
7 B×P	B—B3
8 O—O	B—Q3
9 Kt—B3	Q—R5
10 P—B4	Kt—B3
11 B—Q2	Kt—Kt5
12 P—KR3	Q—Kt6

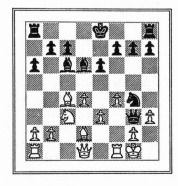

Seemingly an unanswerable move; Black's threats are *13 . . . Q—R7* mate, and *13 . . . Q×KtP* mate.

13 Q×Kt!   Resigns!

Arthur Dake began his game against Hans Mueller in the Folkestone Team tournament of 1933, with the English Opening. Unimpressed by the fact that his opponent was the author of an excellent treatise called *The English Opening*, Dake wound up the game in 21 snappy moves!

ENGLISH OPENING
Folkestone, 1933

WHITE	BLACK
Dake	*Mueller*
1 P—QB4	P—QB4
2 Kt—KB3	Kt—KB3

3 P—Q4	P×P
4 Kt×P	P—Q4
5 P×P	Kt×P
6 P—K4	Kt—Kt5

Does he think Dake will overlook the threatened 7 . . . Q×Kt?

7 Q—R4ch	QKt—B3
8 Kt×Kt	Kt×Kt
9 Kt—B3	B—Q2
10 B—K3	P—K3
11 R—B1	B—Q3
12 B—K2	B—K4
13 O—O	Kt—Q5
14 Q—Kt4	Kt×Bch
15 Kt×Kt	Q—Kt1
16 P—B4	B—Q3
17 B—B5	B×B
18 Q×B	P—QKt3
19 Q—Q4	P—K4
20 P×P	B—Kt4
21 Q—Q5!	Resigns

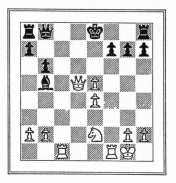

The double attack wins: if 21 . . . B×Kt; 22 Q×Pch, K—Q1; 23 KR—Q1ch, B×R, 24 R×Bch, K—B1; 25 Q—Q7 mate.

Dr. Tarrasch once beat Alapin in a tournament game in five moves! This would be an unbelievably short game for first-class masters to play, ordinarily. But this was *The Curious Incident of the Touched Piece.*

PETROFF DEFENSE
Breslau, 1889

WHITE	BLACK
Tarrasch	*Alapin*
1 P—K4	P—K4
2 Kt—KB3	Kt—KB3
3 Kt×P	P—Q3
4 Kt—KB3	Kt×P

At this point, Tarrasch moved 5 P—Q3. Alapin hardly looked at the board, as he expected 5 P—Q4, the customary move at that time. Almost automatically he touched his King Bishop, as he intended to answer 5 P—Q4 with 5 . . . B—K2. Imagine his horror when he looked at the board, and saw that his Knight was attacked, and that he could not move it! He had touched his Bishop, and regardless of the consequences, he had to move the Bishop!

There was nothing left but to resign at once; playing the game out with a piece minus, against a master like Tarrasch, was hopeless.

A strange double disaster occurred to Lasker and Capablanca in 1934. In that year, each lost a game (even that was rare!) to an opponent in 26 moves; each former World Champion was the victim of a brilliancy involving a Queen sacrifice by the winner!

QUEEN'S GAMBIT DECLINED
Zurich, 1934

WHITE	BLACK
Alekhine	Em. Lasker
1 P—Q4	P—Q4
2 P—QB4	P—K3
3 Kt—QB3	Kt—KB3
4 Kt—B3	B—K2
5 B—Kt5	QKt—Q2
6 P—K3	O—O
7 R—B1	P—B3
8 B—Q3	P×P
9 B×P	Kt—Q4
10 B×B	Q×B
11 Kt—K4	Kt(4)—B3
12 Kt—Kt3	P—K4
13 O—O	P×P
14 Kt—B5!	Q—Q1
15 Kt(3)×P	Kt—K4
16 B—Kt3	B×Kt
17 Kt×B	Q—Kt3

17 . . . P—KKt3! is correct.

18 Q—Q6	Kt(4)—Q2
19 KR—Q1	QR—Q1
20 Q—Kt3	P—Kt3
21 Q—Kt5	K—R1
22 Kt—Q6	K—Kt2
23 P—K4!	Kt—KKt1
24 R—Q3	P—B3
25 Kt—B5ch	K—R1
26 Q×KtP!	Resigns

Mate on the move is threatened. If 26 . . . P×Q; 27 R—R3ch, Kt—R3; 28 R×Kt mate.

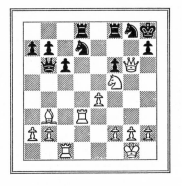

Lilienthal's brilliancy deserves more than casual mention. As Golombek says, "It is a game which becomes even a World Champion to lose."

NIMZOINDIAN DEFENSE
Hastings, 1934–35

WHITE	BLACK
Lilienthal	Capablanca
1 P—Q4	Kt—KB3
2 P—QB4	P—K3
3 Kt—QB3	B—Kt5
4 P—QR3	B×Ktch
5 P×B	P—QKt3
6 P—B3	P—Q4
7 B—Kt5	P—KR3
8 B—R4	B—R3
9 P—K4!	B×P
10 B×B	P×B
11 Q—R4ch	Q—Q2
12 Q×BP	Q—B3
13 Q—Q3	QKt—Q2
14 Kt—K2	R—Q1
15 O—O	P—QR4
16 Q—B2	Q—B5
17 P—B4	R—QB1
18 P—B5	P—K4
19 P×P	Q×KP

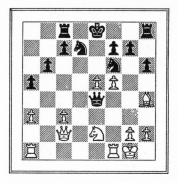

20 P×Kt!	Q×Q
21 P×P	R—KKt1
22 Kt—Q4	

Not only attacking the Queen, but also threatening quick mate beginning with 23 QR—K1ch. Black must give up his Queen, to begin with.

22 ...	Q—K5
23 QR—K1	Kt—B4
24 R×Qch	Kt×R
25 R—K1	R×P
26 R×Ktch	Resigns

Nimzovich was sensitive to the point of eccentricity. It was in the fifth round of the famous New York tournament of 1927 that he was paired with Milan Vidmar. As play began, Vidmar drew out a cigar, lit up, and began puffing on it. The smoke bothered Nimzovich. He appealed to the committee in charge of the players' comfort to ask Vidmar to hold off smoking for the duration of the game. The request was presented to Vidmar, and he good-naturedly complied by putting out his cigar. A few minutes passed, and again Nimzovich rushed off to protest to a committee member. That official was definitely puzzled. He glanced at Vidmar, and said to Nimzovich, "Your opponent isn't smoking." "Yes, yes, I know," was the reply, "but he looks as if he wants to!"

What sort of game did these disparate masters produce? Did it reflect Vidmar's calm, placid temperament? Were the pieces imbued with Nimzovich's nervous, volatile, high-strung nature? Curiously enough, an examination of Nimzovich's moves in his game with Vidmar would seem to show that they were made by a man with nerves of steel! It is precise, merciless chess, such as will no doubt be played by some automaton of the future!

QUEEN'S INDIAN DEFENSE
New York, 1927

WHITE	BLACK
Vidmar	Nimzovich
1 P—Q4	Kt—KB3
2 Kt—KB3	P—K3
3 P—B4	B—Kt5ch
4 B—Q2	Q—K2
5 Kt—B3	O—O
6 P—K3	P—Q3
7 B—K2	P—QKt3
8 O—O	B—Kt2
9 Q—B2	QKt—Q2
10 QR—Q1	B×Kt
11 B×B	Kt—K5
12 B—K1	P—KB4
13 Q—Kt3	P—B4
14 Kt—Q2	Kt×Kt
15 R×Kt	P—K4
16 P×KP	P×P
17 P—B3	P—KKt4!
18 B—B2	Kt—B3
19 KR—Q1	QR—K1!

Only a poor player, or a genius, would make this move. Black permits his opponent full control of the Queen's file!

20 Q—R4	B—R1

21 R—Q6   Q—KKt2
22 B—B1   P—K5
23 B—K1   P×P
24 B—B3   Q—K2!

A pretty trap; if 25 B×Kt, Q×Pch; 26 K—R1, P×Pch; 27 B×P, Q—K8ch; 28 R×Q, R×R mate.

25 R(6)—Q3   P×P
26 B×P   B×B
27 B×Kt   Q—K5!
28 R(1)—Q2   B—R6
29 B—B3   Q—Kt5ch

And Black mates in two moves.

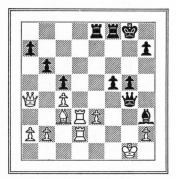

In 1909 at Paris, Janowski and Soldatenkov, as allies, beat the team of Lasker and Taubenhaus in a scintillating 24-mover.

Was their combination really inspired? Did they outplay the mighty Lasker? Or was it just coincidence that they played the whole game, move for move, exactly as it was published in the *British Chess Magazine*, in December 1900, nine years earlier?

Whatever the answer to this riddle may be, the game is undeniably pretty —perhaps the finest *Danish* ever played!

DANISH GAMBIT
Paris, 1909

WHITE	BLACK
Janowski	Em. Lasker
Soldatenkov	Taubenhaus

1 P—K4   P—K4
2 P—Q4   P×P
3 P—QB3   P×P
4 B—QB4   P×P
5 B×P   Kt—KB3
6 P—K5   B—Kt5ch
7 Kt—B3   Q—K2
8 Kt—K2   Kt—K5
9 O—O   Kt×Kt
10 B×Kt   B×B
11 Kt×B   O—O
12 Kt—Q5!   Q×P
13 R—K1   Q—Q3
14 Q—R5   P—QB3
15 Kt—B7!   P—KKt3

But not 15 . . . Q×Kt; 16 Q×BPch! and mate next move.

16 Q—R6   Q×Kt

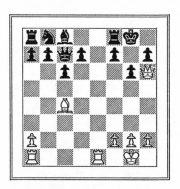

17 B×Pch!   K×B

Forced, as on 17 . . . R×B; 18 R—K8ch followed by mate.

18 Q×RPch	K—B3
19 Q—R4ch	K—Kt2
20 R—K7ch	R—B2
21 Q—Q4ch	K—B1
22 Q—R8ch!	K×R
23 R—K1ch	K—Q3
24 Q—Q4 mate	

At some time or other in a chess master's career, he plays the *game of his life*. Such a game may not be a masterpiece; the circumstances which produced it may be what gives it its aura.

Yates played the game of his life at Hamburg in 1910. It was the *only* game he won. But he won it from Dr. Tarrasch, the man who had objected to Yates' entry on the ground that he (Yates) was not a strong enough player for such a tournament!

QUEEN'S GAMBIT DECLINED
Hamburg, 1910

WHITE	BLACK
Tarrasch	Yates
1 P—Q4	P—Q4
2 Kt—KB3	Kt—KB3
3 P—B4	P—K3
4 P—K3	B—K2
5 Kt—B3	P—B4
6 B—Q3	Kt—B3
7 O—O	O—O
8 P—QKt3	P—QKt3
9 B—Kt2	B—Kt2
10 R—B1	R—B1
11 BP×P	KKt×P
12 Kt—K2	P×P
13 Kt(2)×P	Kt×Kt
14 Kt×Kt	R×R
15 Q×R	B—Q3
16 Kt—B3	Q—K2
17 Q—R1	P—B3

18 Kt—Q4	P—B4
19 R—B1	Kt×P!
20 P×Kt	Q—Kt4
21 K—B2	Q×KtPch
22 K—K1	B×P

Black has three Pawns for his piece, two passed Pawns, and the attack. What more could a man ask for?

23 B—K2	P—K4
24 Kt—K6	B—Kt6ch
25 K—Q1	B—B6
26 B×B	Q×Bch
27 K—B2	Q—K5ch
28 K—Q2	Q—Q4ch
29 Kt—Q4	P×Kt
30 B×P	P—B5
31 P—K4	Q×KP
32 R—B4	R—Q1
33 P—R4	B—B7
34 Resigns	

There are those who disparage the old-timers and their combinations. Given the same positions, the moderns would win just as brilliantly, they say. Here is a story from "real life."

QUEEN'S GAMBIT DECLINED
Prague, 1931

WHITE	BLACK
Mikenas	Kashdan
1 P—Q4	Kt—KB3
2 P—QB4	P—K3
3 Kt—QB3	P—Q4
4 B—Kt5	QKt—Q2
5 P—K3	B—K2
6 Kt—B3	P×P
7 B×P	P—QR3
8 O—O	P—QKt4
9 B—Q3	P—B4

10 Q—K2	B—Kt2
11 KR—Q1	Q—Kt3
12 QR—B1	O—O
13 Kt—K5	KR—K1
14 P×P	Kt×P
15 B×Kt	B×B
16 B×Pch	K×B
17 Q—R5ch	K—Kt1
18 Q×Pch	K—R2

In this position, Mikenas forced a draw by perpetual check at R5 and B7. In exactly the same position Janowski beat Chajes in their 1916 tournament game at New York, by a combination which was awarded the brilliancy prize!

19 Kt—Q7

Attacking the Queen, and threatening also 20 Kt×Bch.

19 . . .	Kt×Kt
20 R×Kt	

Now the threats are: 21 R×B and 21 Q×B.

20 . . .	B—B3
21 Kt—K4!	

A pretty move; if 21 . . . B×R; 22 Kt×Bch, K—R3 (or R1); 23 Q—

R5 mate, and if 21 . . . B×Kt; 22 Q×B, R—KKt1; 23 R(1)—B7 wins.

21 . . .	B×P
22 Kt—Kt5ch	K—R3
23 P—Kt4	P—Kt3

Not 23 . . . K×Kt; 24 Q—R5ch, K—B3; 25 R—B7 mate.

24 P—KR4	R—R1
25 Q—R7ch!	Resigns

Tarrasch needed only four minutes of thought to beat Marco in a tournament game!

Despite the short time consumed playing it, the game is an important one theoretically.

RUY LOPEZ
Dresden, 1892

WHITE	BLACK
Tarrasch	Marco
1 P—K4	P—K4
2 Kt—KB3	Kt—QB3
3 B—Kt5	P—Q3
4 P—Q4	B—Q2
5 O—O	Kt—B3
6 Kt—B3	B—K2
7 R—K1	

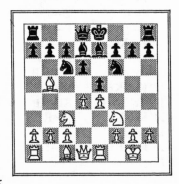

This position is the setting for what is now called "the Tarrasch Trap." The point of it is that Black must give up the center by 7 . . . P×P. It would take a genius to see any danger in castling!

7 . . .	O—O
8 B×Kt	B×B
9 P×P	P×P
10 Q×Q	QR×Q
11 Kt×P	B×P

If 11 . . . Kt×P?; 12 Kt×B wins a piece.

12 Kt×B	Kt×Kt
13 Kt—Q3!	P—KB4
14 P—KB3	B—B4ch
15 Kt×B	Kt×Kt
16 B—Kt5	R—Q4

If 16 . . . QR—K1; 17 B—K7 wins the exchange.

| 17 B—K7 | R—K1 |
| 18 P—QB4 | Resigns |

One chess club that the masters never cared to join was "The Vera Menchik Club." There were no dues to be paid, and no meetings to be attended in this strange club!

The roster consisted of masters who had lost a game in tournament or match play to the former Women's World Champion. Notable but unwilling members included such leading lights as former World Champion Max Euwe, former U. S. Champion Sammy Reshevsky, Edgar Colle, Lajos Steiner, Sultan Khan, Sir George Thomas, F. D. Yates, Albert Becker and William Winter.

This is how Sir George Thomas, Bart., was accepted for membership.

KING'S INDIAN DEFENSE
London, 1932

WHITE	BLACK
Menchik	Thomas
1 P—Q4	Kt—KB3
2 P—QB4	P—KKt3
3 Kt—QB3	B—Kt2
4 P—K4	P—Q3
5 P—B3	O—O
6 B—K3	P—K4
7 KKt—K2!	P—Kt3
8 Q—Q2	Kt—B3
9 P—Q5	Kt—K2
10 P—KKt4	Kt—Q2
11 R—KKt1	P—QR4
12 O—O—O	Kt—QB4
13 Kt—Kt3	B—Q2
14 P—KR4	P—R5
15 P—R5	Q—Kt1
16 B—R6	Q—R2
17 B×B	K×B
18 Kt—B5ch!	Kt×Kt
19 KtP×Kt	P—R6
20 P—B6ch!	K—R1
21 Q—R6	P×Pch
22 K—Kt1	R—KKt1
23 P×P	BP×P
24 Q×RPch!!	Resigns

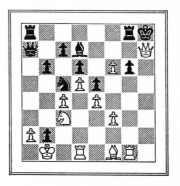

Frank Marshall once discovered an intricate line of play in the Ruy Lopez Opening. It was much too good to be used against ordinary masters (whom he might beat anyway). He saved it for ten years for the important game. His opportunity arose in the New York tournament of 1918, when the peerless Capablanca was his chief rival. They met, as it happened, in the first round. Marshall realized the importance of this game. Winning it might be the decisive factor in determining first prize. Here was the time, the place and the great opponent!

If there were any doubts in Marshall's mind, they must have been dispelled by the circumstance that Capablanca had the white pieces, and was known to favor opening the game with the Ruy Lopez—all in line with Marshall's plan, as the trappy play emanated from the black side!

The tournament director pushed Capa's clock, and the play began.

RUY LOPEZ

New York, 1918

WHITE	BLACK
Capablanca	Marshall
1 P—K4	P—K4
2 Kt—KB3	Kt—QB3

The first surprise for the Cuban. This was the first time in ten years that Marshall did not play the Petroff Defense to avoid the Ruy Lopez.

3 B—Kt5	P—QR3
4 B—R4	Kt—B3
5 O—O	B—K2
6 R—K1	P—QKt4
7 B—Kt3	O—O
8 P—B3	P—Q4
9 P×P	Kt×P
10 Kt×P	

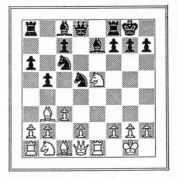

At this point, Capablanca says, "I thought for a while before playing this, knowing that I would be subjected to a terrific attack, all the lines of which would of necessity be familiar to my adversary. The lust of battle, however, had been aroused within me. I felt that my judgment and skill were being challenged by a player who had every reason to fear both (as shown by the records of our previous encounters), but who wanted to take advantage of the element of surprise and of the fact of my being unfamiliar with a thing to which he had devoted many a night of toil and hard work. I considered the position then and decided that I was in honor bound, so to speak, to take the Pawn and accept the challenge, as my knowledge and judgment told me that my position should then be defendable."

10 . . .	Kt×Kt
11 R×Kt	Kt—B3
12 R—K1	B—Q3
13 P—KR3	Kt—Kt5!
14 Q—B3	

Not 14 P×Kt, Q—R5; 15 P—Kt3, B(Q3)×P; 16 P×B, Q×Pch; 17 K—B1, B×P, and White must give up his Queen. White's actual move attacks and defends.

14 . . .	Q—R5
15 P—Q4	Kt×P

Setting a trap; if 16 Q×Kt, B—R7ch (not at once 16 . . . B—Kt6; 17 Q×Pch!, R×Q; 18 R—K8 mate); 17 K—B1, B—Kt6; 18 Q—K2, B×P; 19 P×B, QR—K1 and Black wins.

| 16 R—K2! | B—KKt5 |
| 17 P×B | |

Safer than 17 Q×Kt, B—Kt6, when a possibility could be 18 Q—B1, B×R; 19 Q×B, QR—K1 and Black wins.

17 . . .	B—R7ch
18 K—B1	B—Kt6
19 R×Kt	Q—R8ch
20 K—K2	B×R
21 B—Q2	B—R5
22 Q—R3	QR—K1ch

In order to avoid the exchange of Queens.

23 K—Q3	Q—B8ch
24 K—B2	B—B7
25 Q—B3	Q—Kt8

To release himself from the pin.

26 B—Q5	P—B4
27 P×P	B×P
28 P—Kt4	B—Q3
29 P—R4	

With the freeing of White's Queen-side pieces, the attack changes hands suddenly.

29 . . .	P—QR4
30 RP×P	P×P
31 R—R6	P×P
32 Kt×P	B—Kt5
33 P—Kt6	B×Kt
34 B×B	P—R3

Strangely enough, White's King is perfectly safe, although seemingly exposed; Black's King is in mortal danger, although apparently securely entrenched.

| 35 P—Kt7 | R—K6 |
| 36 B×Pch | |

White mates in five moves.

Golombek calls this game the *pièce de résistance* of this phase of Capablanca's career.

Combinations—the Heart of Chess

♛ WHEN chess fever first seized us, and we used to thumb through old works on the game, there was one section that invariably held us spellbound—the chapter on combination play. What was Keats' excitement "on first looking into Chapman's Homer" compared with ours on first seeing the wonders described by Mason? We had little patience then to play through what seemed to be dreary openings, and dull maneuvering for positional advantages.

Combinations, though, were another story! That was when exciting things happened! Pieces would be sacrificed recklessly, bewildering attacks would come into being magically, and mating nets would be woven out of thin air by the master hand of the champion. There was always a new thrill, a new surprise. The board might be cluttered up with pieces, the position fearfully complex, when suddenly all the pieces would fly off the board in a series of exchanges. The reason for the fireworks would be revealed when the smoke of battle cleared away. One Pawn might be left as survivor—just one Pawn, but enough to decide the game. There was endless variety and endless charm in the inspired brilliancies of combination play.

The combinations that follow have been carefully selected. Most of them are from modern times; the few that represent the older masters are not the usual hackneyed much-quoted specimens of play which one finds difficulty avoiding. You will find no Morphy—Duke of Brunswick, Anderssen—Kieseritzky, Anderssen—Dufresne, Zukertort—Blackburne positions. These have been reprinted again and again until the diagrams, as well as the readers' patience, have worn thin. Nor has the reputation of the players been the most important consideration. Some of the finest combinations have been created by almost unknown players. Guiding considerations have been originality of idea and brilliancy in execution.

But we are holding up the parade! Start with the first diagram, and discover for yourself the thrill of playing through the great combinations!

FROM a game played at Paris, in 1927:

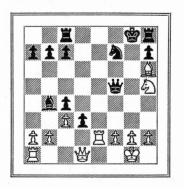

1 R—K8ch!!

White gives up his Rook, to clear the diagonal for his Queen.

1 . . .   R×R
2 Q—Kt4ch!!

And now his Queen, to lure Black's Queen away from an important square.

2 . . .   Q×Q
3 Kt—B6 mate

FROM a game played at Berlin in 1929; a pretty combination, but child's play for Richter:

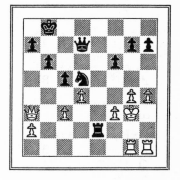

1 . . .	Q—Q3ch
2 K—R3	Kt—B5ch
3 K—Kt3	Kt—R4ch
4 K—R3	Q—Kt6ch!
5 R×Q	Kt—B5 mate

White's own Rook stands in the King's way. In the words of an old proverb, "Defend me from my friends; I can defend myself from my enemies."

MATING threats by Helling, playing White, keep his opponent on the run. Just as Black congratulates himself on having exchanged the menacing pieces, disaster in the form of a Rook faces him.

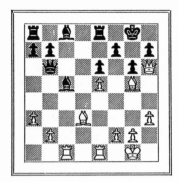

1 R×B!

Not at once 1 B—B6, as 1 . . . B—B1 would drive off the Queen.

1 . . .	Q×R
2 B—Kt5	Q—B1

Naturally, on 2 . . . Q×B; 3 B—B6 is conclusive.

3 B×R	Q×B
4 B—B6	Q—B1
5 Q×Qch	K×Q
6 R—Q1	

A quiet but unanswerable move. Black must give up his Bishop to stop mate.

A PRETTY finish by Opocensky.

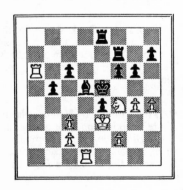

1 R×Bch!	P×R
2 Kt—Q3ch!	P×Kt
3 P—B4 mate	

Mate by a Pawn is always an attractive touch (and just as final, too).

WON by Bogolyubov in 1935, in a simultaneous exhibition.

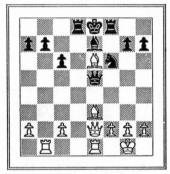

1 R×P!	Q×KB
2 B—QB5!	Q×Q

Of course not 2 . . . B×B, as his Queen is attacked.

Black hopes for 3 R×Q, when 3 . . . R—Q8ch forces mate; there is always a chance that the master, who is occupied with 40 other games at the same time, might make a monumental blunder.

3 R×Bch!	Q×R

The Queen is pulled all the way back!

4 R×Q mate

KASPARYAN won this in a simultaneous exhibition! The fact that he is one of the finest end-game composers in the world accounts for the imaginative splendor of this magnificent combination.

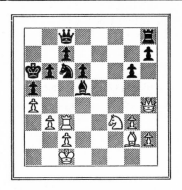

1	R×Kt!	B×R
2	Q—B4ch	K—Kt2
3	Q×Bch!!	K×Q
4	Kt—K5ch	K—B4
5	Kt—Q3ch	K—Q5
6	K—Q2!!	Q—K3
7	P—B3 mate	

Of what use are all Black's worldly goods?

SANZ *won this ending from Ortueta in Madrid, 1934. His play to create a passed Pawn, and the finesses with which he insures its irresistible forward advance, are truly artistic.*

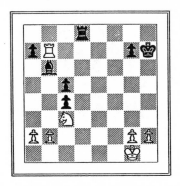

1 . . .   **R—Q7**

2 Kt—R4

Protecting the valuable Queen's Knight Pawn.

2 . . .   **R×P!!**

Unexpected, but Black wants a passed Pawn at any price!

3 Kt×R   **P—B6**

Black is prepared to answer 4 Kt—Q3 with 4 . . . P—B5ch; 5 R×B, P×Kt!, and the united Pawns laugh at the Rook.

4 R×B!

His best chance; if 4 . . . P×R; 5 Kt—Q3, P—B5; 6 Kt—B1.

4 . . .   **P—B5!**

Keeps the Knight out, and threatens 5 . . . P—B7.

5 R—Kt4

Again the best defense; if 5 . . . P×Kt; 6 R×KtP, or if 5 . . . P—B7; 6 R×P, winning in either case.

5 . . .   **P—R4!**

Presenting White with a dilemma; if 6 R—Kt5, P—B7 wins, or if 6 R×P, P×Kt does it.

6 Kt—R4

A last feeble hope; if 6 . . . P—B7 (Black might get over-anxious to queen his Pawn), then 7 R×P wins.

6 . . .   **P×R**

Black wins. Tartakover calls this "The prettiest ending of the year 1934." We might add, "Or any other year!"

IN SPITE of all the obstacles to the forward march of White's Queen Pawn, it still is a passed Pawn, and White thinks accordingly!

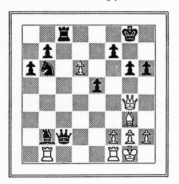

1 R×B!	Q×R
2 Q×Rch!!	Kt×Q
3 P—Q7	

Lo and behold! There are no obstacles! Engels won this from Maroczy at Dresden in 1936.

NO ONE knows whether Anderssen won this in actual play, or whether he composed this position. What can be said with certainty is that it has a genuine Anderssen flavor!

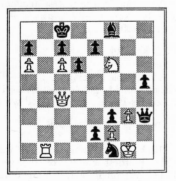

It is White's move; a lucky thing,

as he is threatened with 1 . . . Q—Kt7 mate and 1 . . . Q—R7 mate.

1 Q—K6ch!!

Giving up his Queen! But he does force Black's Queen to withdraw.

| 1 . . . | Q×Q |
| 2 Kt—Q7 | |

Now the Queen has no time to return, as White threatens mate by 3 R—Kt8.

| 2 . . . | Q×Kt |

"Oh, well," thinks Black, "after 3 P×Qch, K×P, I will still have two pieces against a Rook."

3 R—Kt8ch!!

The Rook in the ointment!

3 . . .	K×R
4 P×Q	Any
5 P—Q8(Q) mate	

WHAT greater praise can one give Denmark's Erik Andersen than to say that he won this in the brilliant style of his namesake Anderssen?

| 1 . . . | R×B! |

2 P×R   Kt—B6!!

Why these sacrifices?

3 P×Kt

The Knight must be taken; if White's Queen moves, then 3 . . . Q×Ktch; 4 K—Kt1, B—K5 wins.

3 . . .   B—K5

Pinning the Knight, which is now triply attacked. Black's first sacrifice is now accounted for, as without it, White would now interpose his Bishop at B5.

4 K—R3   Q×Ktch
5 Q×Q   R×Qch
6 K—Kt2   R—Kt6ch

The first of three double checks; and no one can survive the effects of three double checks!

7 K—R2   R—Kt7ch
8 K—R1   R—R7ch
9 K—Kt1   R—R8 mate!

VUKOVIC won this from an amateur, in 1937. Only two moves are made, but what a lot of action is crammed into those two moves!

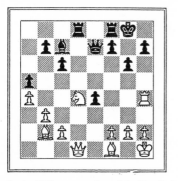

It is White to play; his Rook is

attacked, and his pinned Knight is a shining target.

1 Kt—B5!

Forcibly breaking loose from the pin. White does not fear 1 . . . R×Q, as he threatens 2 Kt×Q mate, as well as 2 Kt—R6 mate.

1 . . .   Q×R

Guards against both mates, and in turn threatens 2 . . . Q×P mate. Meanwhile, White's Queen and Knight are still *en prise*.

2 Q—R5!!

Brilliant—and unanswerable! Let us prove it: If 2 . . . P×Q; 3 Kt—R6 mate, or if 2 . . . Q×Q; Kt—K7 mate. Finally, if 2 . . . P×Kt; 3 Q×Q, and Black has no good counter against 4 Q—Kt5 mate, or 4 Q—B6. For example, if 3 . . . R—Q3; 4 Q—Kt3ch, R—Kt3; 5 Q×B wins another piece.

CAPABLANCA wins this by means of a unique Knight fork. His Knight attacks two important objects simultaneously; his opponent's Queen, and an empty square (Kt7)!

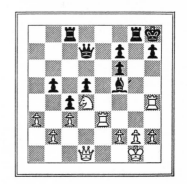

1 R—K7!!

An offer which Black dare not refuse. If his Queen moves away, then his Bishop will be unprotected.

| *1 ...* | Q×R |
| *2 Kt×B* | Resigns |

Black is convinced! The sequel would be: 2 . . . Q—B1; 3 R×Pch, K×R; 4 Q—R5ch, Q—R3; 5 Q×Q mate.

TARRASCH won this ending from his great rival Nimzovich in the 1911 San Sebastian tournament.

| *1 ...* | R—Kt4! |
| *2 K—Kt4* | |

Not at once 2 R×R, as after 2 . . . P×R, the passed Pawn could not be stopped.

| *2 ...* | R×R |
| *3 K×R* | |

But now he is near enough to catch the Pawn—he thinks!

| *3 ...* | P—R4 |
| *4 K—K4* | |

How will Black queen his Pawn?

4 . . .   P—B4ch!!

Tarrasch borrows a device from mythology! He throws a Pawn in the way of the runner. In the Greek legend, Milanion threw golden apples in the path of Atalanta. When she stopped to pick them up, he gained time to win the race. His reward was the fair Atalanta herself as his wife.

To get back to poor Nimzovich . . . If he picks up the golden apple by 5 K×P, then 5 . . . P—R5 wins, as his King has been lured a square further away. If he resists temptation, and plays 5 K—Q4, then 5 . . . P—B5 (to immobilize White's Knight Pawn) followed by 6 . . . K—Kt3 and 7 . . . K—R4. Black would then capture the King-side Pawns, and march his Bishop Pawn to the queening square.

RAGOZIN won this in 1945 by an exquisite combination.

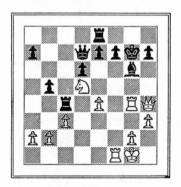

| *1 R×Bch!* | BP×R |

If *1* . . . K×R; 2 Q—Kt3ch, K—R3; *3* R—B4 followed by 4 R—R4 mate.

| *2 R—B7ch!* | K×R |

Of course not 2 . . . K—Kt1; 3 Q×P mate.

3 Q×RPch K—K3

On 3 . . . K—B1; 4 Kt—B4, R(K1)—B1; 5 Kt×Pch, K—K1; 6 Q—Kt8 mate.

4 Q×KtPch K—K4
5 Q—Kt7ch K×P

The lesser evil; if 5 . . . K—K3; 6 Kt—B4 mate.

6 Kt—B6ch!

A pretty blend of Knight fork and pin, which wins the Queen and the game.

TARTAKOVER'S Queen does some clever zigzagging to win an elegant ending.

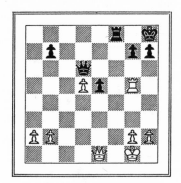

1 . . . Q—Kt3ch
2 K—R1 Q—Kt4!

Intending 3 . . . R—B8ch.

3 K—Kt1 Q—B4ch
4 K—R1 Q—B5

Same threat in another edition.

5 K—Kt1 Q—Q5ch
6 K—R1 Q—K5!

Not at once 6 . . . Q—K6; 7

Q×Q, R—B8ch; 8 Q—Kt1, **and** White wins.

7 Q—QB1

Of course not 7 Q×Q, R—B8 mate. On 7 Q—KKt1, Q—K7 wins, while 7 Q—Q1 is refuted by 7 . . . Q—KB5 attacking the Rook, and threatening mate in two. Finally, if White tries 7 Q—R1, Black plays 7 . . . Q—K7 (threatening 8 . . . R—B8ch) 8 K—Kt1, Q—K6ch winning the Rook.

7 . . . Q—Q6!
8 K—Kt1 Q—Q5ch
9 K—R1 Q—Q7!!

The final invasive maneuver. Black's Queen must not be touched. Meanwhile, White's Queen and Rook are under fire. White of course resigned, as his Rook falls at once.

A MIGHT-HAVE-BEEN combination. In the actual game Ed. Lasker— Moll in 1912, Lasker played 1 P—B4 and lost after 1 . . . P—B3. This is the win he discovered after the game was over:

1 P—B6! P×P

Forced, of course.

2 P—B4	K—Q5

Rushing to the rescue. If instead 2 . . . P—B4, then 3 P—Kt5, P×P; 4 P—R6 crashes through.

3 P—Kt5!	BP×P
4 P×P	K—K4

Naturally, not 4 . . . P×P; 5 P—R6. Black expects (after 4 . . . K—K4) 5 P×P, K—B3; 6 P—R7, K—Kt2.

5 P×P	K—B3
6 K—B2!	

A painful surprise (in our mythical game).

6 . . .	P—B6
7 K×P	

Black is in Zugzwang! His King must move, much against his will, and White's Pawn becomes a Queen.

A SPARKLING Morphy combination, from an offhand game against Schulten in 1857.

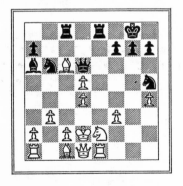

1 . . .	R×B!
2 P×R	B×Kt
3 R×B	Q×Pch
4 K—K1	Q—Kt8ch

5 K—Q2	R—Q1ch
6 K—B3	Q—B4ch
7 K—Kt2	

This is the position Morphy visualized when he played 1 . . . R×B, sacrificing the exchange. Now comes the coup de grâce.

7 . . .	Kt—R5ch!!

More subtle than might at first appear. If 8 P×Kt, Q—Kt5 mates neatly, and if 8 K—Kt1, Kt—B6ch; 9 K—Kt2, Kt×Qch; 10 K—Kt1, Kt—B6ch; 11 K—Kt2, Kt×R wins Queen and Rook by the hit-and-run trick.

PILLSBURY was rather proud of this pretty finale, which he brought off in a blindfold exhibition.

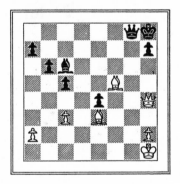

Pillsbury, as Black, is menaced with Q—B6ch, as well as B×KP. He moved:

1 . . .	Q—B2

His opponent, suspecting nothing, snatched at the King's Pawn.

2 B×KP	Q—B8ch

Pillsbury swoops down instantly.

3 B—Kt1   Q—B6ch!!

A delightful sacrifice.

4 B×Q   B×B mate

THE ALEKHINE touch is clearly evident in this magnificent combination. It is the conclusion of the game Alekhine—Tylor, Margate 1937.

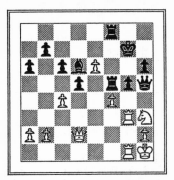

1 Kt×P!   B×P

If 1 . . . P×Kt; 2 R×Pch, R×R; 3 R×Rch wins the Queen. The move made by Black looks good as the Bishop attacks three pieces.

2 Q—B3ch!   R(1)—B3

On 2 . . . B—K4; 3 Kt—B3ch wins.

3 Kt—K4ch!   B×R
4 R×Bch   K—R1

Or 4 . . . K—B1; 5 Q—Kt4ch, K—K1; 6 Kt×Rch, R×Kt; 7 R—Kt8ch followed by mate.

5 Q×Rch!

The final point, reminiscent of some compositions by Greco and Stamma (Alekhine).

5 . . .   R×Q

6 R—Kt8ch!   Resigns

The continuation would be: 6 . . . K×R; 7 Kt×Rch, K—B1; 8 Kt×Q, P×P; 9 K—Kt2 with an easy win.

KROGIUS won this by a device rarely seen in over-the-board play—underpromotion. It is one of the most artistic themes in the repertoire.

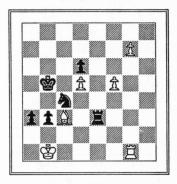

1 . . .   R×B!

What nonchalance!

2 P—Kt8(Q)   Kt—Q7ch
3 K—R1   R—B8ch!!

Brilliant play.

4 R×R   P—Kt7ch
5 K—R2   P×R(Kt)ch!

Promoting to a Queen only draws!

6 K×P

He could lose just as surely, but less artistically by 6 K—R1, Kt(7)—Kt6ch; 7 K—Kt1, P—R7ch; 8 K—B2, P—R8(Q), and Black wins.

6 . . .   Kt—B5 mate!

One of the loveliest mates produced in actual play.

A COMBINATION in the Alekhine style. But the great man himself is the victim! Petrov is the star, in this situation from the Margate tournament of 1938.

Queens are off the board, and yet White manages to generate a devastating attack against the King.

1 P—Kt4ch!   K×P

If 1 . . . K—Kt3; 2 R—Kt7ch, K—R3; 3 R—R1 mate.

2 R—Kt7ch   K—B6

Or 2 . . . K—B4; 3 R—Kt5 mate.

3 Kt—K4ch   K—B7

There is no retreat; if 3 . . . K—B5; 4 R—Q4 mate.

4 R(7)—Kt1!   Resigns

Nothing can delay the inevitable; White's next move will be 5 R(Q1)—B1 mate!

A COMBINATION in which the King is separated from home and family. Small wonder that White is able to work out the theme with such sadistic perfection: Black's King has no support.

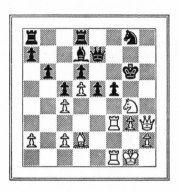

1 R×P!   B×R

There is no relief in 1 . . . R—KB1; 2 Kt×Pch, Q×Kt (. . . P×Kt; 3 Q—Kt4ch); 3 Q—R5ch, K—Kt2; 4 R—B7ch and mate next move.

2 R×B   K×R
3 Q—R5ch   K—K5
4 Q—Kt6ch   K—B6
5 Q—B5ch   K—K7

Drifting further and further, alone in a furious storm.

6 Q—B2ch   K—Q8
7 Kt—K3 mate

FINE won this from Dake in 1933 at Detroit. It is an expert blending of themes. Dake finds the combination irresistible!

[see diagram—next page]

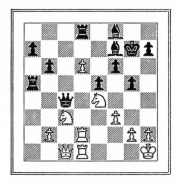

1 Kt×BP!   K×Kt
2 Kt—K4ch   K—Kt2

If 2 . . . K—B4; 3 R—QB2, Q—R5; 4 Q×Pch, K—K3; 5 Q—Kt4 mate.

3 R—QB2

Clearing the diagonal for the Queen.

3 . . .   Q—R5

Counter-attack on White's Rook, as his own is threatened by 4 Q×Pch.

4 Q×Pch   B—Kt3

If 4 . . . K—R1, White wins nicely by 5 Q×R, Q×R; 6 Q×Bch, B—Kt1; 7 Q—B6 mate.

5 R—B7ch   K—Kt1

If 5 . . . R—Q2, 6 Kt—B3 protects White's Rook at Q1, and drives Black's Queen away from the protection of his own (Black's) Rook.

6 Q×Bch!

This will hurt a bit!

6 . . .   P×Q
7 Kt—B6ch   K—R1
8 R—R7 mate

A fine specimen of attacking play.

THE PRETTIEST combination in the *Great Britain—America Cable* match of 1907 was this windup of the *Howell—Michell* game.

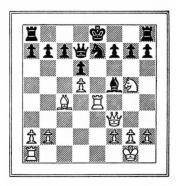

1 B—Kt5!   Q×B

Forced, as 1 . . . P—QB3; 2 P×P, P×P; 3 B×P, Q×B; 4 R×Ktch wins Black's Queen.

2 Q×B   P—KB3

No better is 2 . . . R—KB1; 3 R×Ktch, K×R; 4 R—K1ch, K—Q1; 5 Kt×Pch, R×Kt; 6 Q×R, and Black is curiously helpless against the threat 7 Q—B8ch, K—Q2; 8 R—K7 mate.

3 QR—K1   P×Kt
4 R×Ktch   K—Q1
5 Q×KtP   K—B1

Fleeing from a possible discovered check.

6 Q—Kt4ch   K—Q1

If 6 . . . K—Kt1, White continues in the same way, and Black is unable to stop R—K8ch followed by mate.

7 P—QR4!   Resigns

Black's Queen is driven off from the diagonal controlling Q2, where mate by White's Queen is threatened.

FROM a 1935 game; White has a powerful wedge at B6, indicating a quick finish. But how does he get at the King?

1 Kt—Kt5!

Beginning a delightful combination. The Knight must be taken, as White threatens mate on the move.

1 . . .	P×Kt
2 Q—Q2!	

Now he offers his Queen!

2 . . .	R—B1

Which Black of course refuses; taking it would have cleared the path for White's Rook to reach KR3, from where it would zoom up to R8.

3 Q×Pch	K—B1
4 Q—Kt7ch	K—K1
5 Q—Kt8ch	K—Q2
6 Q×Pch	K—B3
7 Q—Kt7 mate	

NIMZOVICH engineers a pretty break-through in this ending against Lund, played in 1921. This is perhaps the most beautiful of all the famous Nimzovich combinations.

1 . . .	P—Kt5!
2 P×P	R×Kt!

Which side does he intend to penetrate?

3 P×R	P—Kt6!

Knocking a prop out from under the Bishop. The Pawn must be taken, as otherwise 4 . . . P—Kt7 follows.

4 P×P	P—B6ch!

Every move deserves an exclamation mark.

5 P×P

There is no hope in 5 K×P, K×B.

5 . . .	P—R6!
6 Resigns	

White's hapless King cannot be everywhere at once.

FROM a game played by Tartakover at Paris in 1935. The combination is beautifully simple—and simply beautiful!

[see diagram—next page]

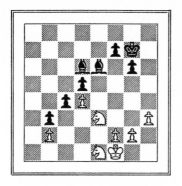

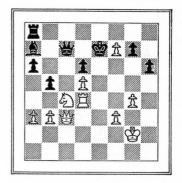

1 . . .   **B—R6!**

Blacks wants to remove the blockader of his furthest advanced Pawn. He does not fear 2 P×B, as then his Knight Pawn would have a clear road ahead.

  2 Kt—Q1   **B×KtP!**
  3 Kt×B   **P—B6**
  4 Kt(1)—Q3

If *4 Kt(2)—Q3, P—Kt7 wins.*

4 . . .   **B—B4!**

With this idea: 5 . . . B×Ktch; 6 Kt×B, P—Kt7 followed by . . . P—Kt8(Q).

  5 K—K2   **B×Ktch**
  6 K×B

Here too, 6 Kt×B permits 6 . . . P—Kt7.

6 . . .   **P×Kt**

White resigns, as his King cannot approach the Pawn at Kt7. So near and yet so far!

FROM a tournament game played in 1937; White sacrifices his Queen in order to promote a Pawn to a Knight!

  1 R—K4ch   **K—B1**

On 1 . . . K×P; 2 Kt—K5ch uncovers an attack on Black's Queen, while 1 . . . K—Q2 loses by 2 Q×P.

  2 Kt×P!   **Q×Kt**

If 2 . . . Q×Q; 3 R—K8ch, R×R; 4 P×R(Q) mate.

  3 R—K8ch   **R×R**
  4 Q×Pch!   **K×Q**

Refusing the Queen leads to 4 . . . K—K2; 5 P—B8(Q)ch, and mate in two more moves.

  5 P×R(Kt)ch!

An elegant Knight fork.

5 . . .   **K—B1**
  6 Kt×Q

White wins easily.

FROM a game Hoit—Amateur at New York in 1938. The winning combination is so elegant that it gives the impression of being a composed ending! Only unique and felicitous chance can produce such exquisite possibilities in practical play.

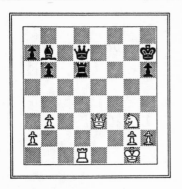

1 Q×Pch!!

An astonishing move, and an astonishingly beautiful one! The Queen is unprotected, and can be captured in two ways.

1 . . .   K×Q

If 1 . . . R×Q; 2 R×Qch followed by 3 R×B wins easily.

2 R×Rch   Q×R
3 Kt—B5ch

A striking Knight fork which wins the Queen and the game.

ATKINSON won this by one of the most attractive devices on the chessboard—the smothered mate.

1 R×B!

The first move of a charming combination.

1 . . .   Q×R
2 Kt—Kt5

There is a brutal Knight fork by 2 R×Pch, K×R; 3 Kt—Kt5ch which wins, but White wants the peculiar satisfaction which one can attain only by administering a smothered mate.

2 . . .   Q—Kt3

Defending against White's threat of 3 R×P mate.

3 R×Pch!   Q×R
4 Kt—B7 mate

GOSSIP won this beauty from Showalter in the New York 1889 tournament. The New York Herald ran the score with the heading Gossip's Brilliant Mate, and commented: "The following fine game elicited a hearty round of applause from the spectators when the winner announced a beautiful mate involving the sacrifice of the Queen and Rook." In spite of all the praise bestowed on it, the game failed to receive the brilliancy prize, to Mr. Gossip's eternal disappointment.

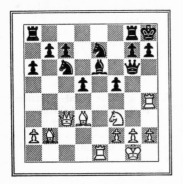

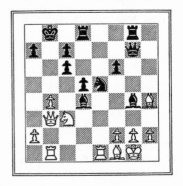

1 . . .	Kt—B6ch!
2 P×Kt	B(Kt5)×Pch
3 B—Kt3	Q×Bch!!
4 P×Q	R×Pch
5 K—R2	

On 5 B—Kt2, R×Bch; 6 K—B1, R—R7, and mate follows.

5 . . .	B×P

White is way ahead in material, but helpless to stop mate.

6 B—R3	R×Bch!

White resigns, for 7 K×R is answered by 7 . . . R—R1 mate!

Steinitz says, "One of the finest specimens of sacrificing play on record."

THE FINISH of one of Capablanca's greatest games, his sixth in the Marshall match, in 1909.

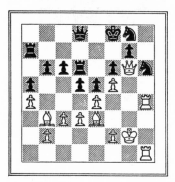

1 R×Kt!

A sacrifice of the exchange which smashes through the defensive barrier.

1 . . .	P×R

If 1 . . . Kt×R; 2 B×Kt, P×B; 3 R×P, and Black can safely resign (if 3 . . . R—KKt2, a spurious pin,

then 4 R—R8ch will convince him).

2 B×Pch	K—K2
3 Q—Kt7ch	K—K1
4 Q×Ktch	K—Q2
5 Q—R7ch!	

But not 5 Q—Kt7ch, as the Bishop must not be blocked; it has an important role to play!

5 . . .	Q—K2
6 B—B8!	

Pinned pieces must be attacked, again and again!

6 . . .	Q×Q
7 R×Qch	K—K1
8 R×R	Resigns

TARTAKOVER won this from Rubinstein in 1925; only the finest chess instinct would visualize the possibility of creating a passed Pawn in this position! It is this powerful Pawn that strikes the knockout blow.

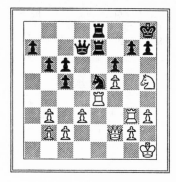

1 R×P!

Removing the support of the Bishop's Pawn.

1 . . .	R×R
2 Kt×P	

"Destroy the blockader!"

2 . . .   Q—K2
3 Kt×R   Q×Kt

White has only two Pawns for the piece he gave up. But he has other compensation in his pressure on the pinned Knight, and the potential power of his passed Pawn.

4 Q—B4!   R—K2
5 P—B6!   Kt—Kt3

If 5 . . . R—K3; 6 R×Kt!, R×R; 7 P—B7, and Black has too many questions to answer (8 Q—B6 mate, or 8 P×Qch, or 8 Q×Rch, Q×Q; 9 P—B8[Q] mate).

6 R×R   Kt×R
7 P—B7!   Resigns

For if 7 . . . Q—KB1; 8 Q—B6ch and mate in two more moves.

FROM a game played in 1926. So well does White realize the strength of a passed Pawn that he gives up a Bishop to obtain one. Once he has it, he gives up the exchange and then his Queen, to exploit it to the full.

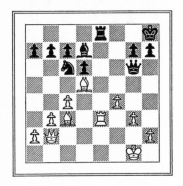

1 P—KB5!   Q—Kt4

The Pawn is taboo; if 1 . . .

Q×P; 2 B×P mate, or if 1 . . . B×P; 2 B×Pch, Q×B; 3 R×R mate.

2 B×Pch!   Q×B
3 P—B6   Q—Kt3

Unfortunately, Black cannot block the Pawn which threatens him with discovered check.

4 P—B7ch   Kt—K4
5 R×Kt!   P×R
6 Q×Pch!   Resigns

If 6 . . . R×Q; 7 P—B8(Q)ch, and mate next move, or if 6 . . . Q—Kt2; 7 Q×Rch and quick mate.

A MAGNIFICENT finish from an odds game by Teichmann, played at Zurich in 1920.

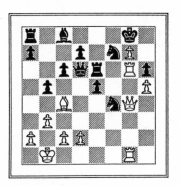

1 R×P!

With this continuation in mind: 2 R—R8ch, Kt×R; 3 P×Kt(Q)ch, K×Q; 4 Q—Kt7 mate.

1 . . .   Kt×R
2 Q—Kt5!

Now the threats are, 3 Q—Q8ch, and 3 Q×Kt(R6).

2 . . .   Kt—B2
3 Q—Q8ch!!

A gorgeous offer of the Queen!

3 . . .   Kt×Q
4 P—R6!

"Quiet desperation." A quiet move for White, and desperation for Black. The threat is 5 P—R7ch, followed by queening a Pawn. Black's Rook (which incidentally blocks his Queen) is pinned, and powerless to capture the Rook's Pawn. All of Black's numerous other pieces stand about helplessly—ineffectual spectators!

FROM an Anderssen game played in 1869 against Alexander; the great master of tactics gives a little lesson in assorted Knight fork threats.

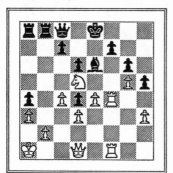

1 R×P!

Anderssen had no time for wins based on increasing the pressure, such as 1 Q—B3.

1 . . .   B×R
2 Q—B3!!

A tremendous move! Black cannot bring his Queen to the Bishop's defense as on 2 . . . Q—K3; 3 Kt× Pch wins the Queen, and if 2 . . . Q—Q2; 3 Kt—B6ch does likewise. Should the Bishop retreat by 2 . . . B—Kt1, then White plays 3 Q—

B8ch, K—Q2; 4 Q—Kt7ch, K—B3; 5 Kt—K7ch, once again catching the Queen. The three Knight forks on three different squares show the hand of the master!

2 . . .   B×Kt
3 BP×B!

Stronger than the obvious 3 Q—B8ch as now flight for Black's King (via QB3) is blocked. Black resigned.

NIMZOVICH'S teachings are so much taken for granted that one is apt to forget that he was also a very fine player. This example, from his game against Nielsen in 1930, is a good specimen of his tactical skill. White has the makings of a King-side attack: his Bishop is trained on the Knight Pawn, and his Queen and Rook can quickly bear down on that point. But how does he get rid of Black's Bishop without giving up his own in the process?

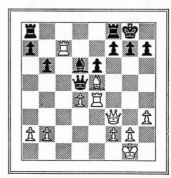

1 R—Q7!

The pin! Black cannot counter by 1 . . . P—B4 as 2 R×Pch, K—R1; 3 R×Pch forces mate.

1 . . .   QR—Q1
2 R×B!

At first glance, this will lead to an even exchange.

2 . . .   R×R

Now what? White has his Bishop, but 3 Q—Kt3 is meaningless after 3 . . . P—B3.

3 Q—B6!!

An unconventional way of stopping such moves as . . . P—B3!! Black resigned, as after 3 . . . P×Q; 4 R—Kt4ch, K—R1; 5 B×P is mate!

A MUCH-ADMIRED Mieses combination, dating away back to 1903. Black has his eye on a possible invasion of K6 by his Queen; just one check there would lead to mate—if only White's Queen were not on guard! With Mieses, to think is to act!

1 . . .   R—Kt6!!

Rarely does one see a move of such beauty in practical play.

2 Q×R

Naturally, 2 P×R shuts White's Queen off, and 2 . . . Q—K6ch follows with mate next move.

2 . . .   B—R5!

Pinning and winning the Queen; White can play 3 Q×B, but again the vital square would be unprotected, and mate in two would be the consequence.

In the actual game, White fought on a while, arguing with the inevitable.

FROM the famous Tarrasch—Tchigorin match, played in 1893. Two masters of such disparate styles and temperaments were bound to produce games that were classics; this was the decisive combination in a Tarrasch victory.

1 R×P!   K×R

If 1 . . . Q×R; 2 B—Kt5 wins the Queen.

2 B—Kt5ch   K—Kt2

On 2 . . . K—K4; 3 B—K7ch, K—B5; 4 Q—Kt5 is mate.

3 Q—R6ch   K—Kt1
4 R—KB1

Threatening mate on the move.

4 . . .   R—KB1
5 B—KB6

Now the threat is mate at **Kt7.**

5 . . .	Q×B

Trying to postpone the inevitable.

6 R×Q

Black resigns, as he realizes that he cannot stop the piquant continuation 7 R×Ktch, P×R; 8 Q×P mate (in epaulet style).

FROM the game Rubinstein—Grunfeld, Semmering 1926. White is a Pawn up, with what seems a long, weary fight on his hands. Rubinstein speeds up the win with some crisp, biting moves.

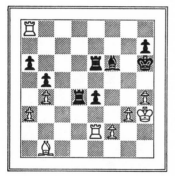

1 R—R7!

Intending to attack the King Pawn next move with 2 P—B3. Black could not then reply 2 . . . P—K6, as 3 R×P mate would follow.

1 . . .	B—Kt2
2 B×P!	

This must have startled Black!

2 . . .	R(5)×B

Has Rubinstein gone mad? He has lost a Bishop, with no apparent attack in sight.

3 R×R	R×R

4 R×Pch	K—R4
5 P—B3!	

The point! The mate threat by 6 P—Kt4ch will cost Black his Rook, leaving him the exchange down. Grunfeld of course resigned.

FROM an early Keres game; the young attacking genius treats us to a display of the art of combination.

1 . . .	Kt×Bch
2 Q×Kt	

If 2 R×Kt, Kt×Ktch; 3 P×Kt, Q—Kt4ch; 4 K—R1, B×P mate.

2 . . .	Kt×Ktch
3 P×Kt	

On 3 Q×Kt, R×Q; 4 R×Q, R×B, and Black wins a piece.

3 . . .	Q—Kt4ch
4 K—R1	R×P!

Threatening a painful discovered check.

5 R×R	Q—Kt5

A pin which cannot be broken. White resigned, as he saw no way to prevent loss of his Queen by 6 . . . B×Rch.

The student of combination play will note the force of Keres' moves; two exchanges which cut down considerably his opponent's choice of reply, a check to which there is only one answer, a threat of discovered check which is compelling, and finally the adding of pressure to a pinned piece—pressure which cannot be counterbalanced!

AN EUWE game, in which the former World Champion takes advantage neatly of Milner-Barry's unfavorably placed Rook.

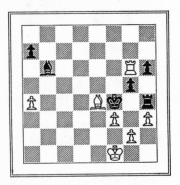

| 1 P—R5 | B×P |

Black snatches at the gift, without looking for hidden strings.

| 2 K—B2 | |

The reason for the gift: Euwe's King reaches this square, from which he can support his Knight's Pawn. White now threatens 3 P—Kt3ch winning the Rook.

| 2 . . . | K—K4 |

If instead 2 . . . B—Kt3ch; 3 R×B, P×R; 4 P—Kt3ch leaves White a piece up.

| 3 P—Kt3! | R×P |

| 4 K—Kt2 | R—R4 |
| 5 R—R6! | |

An attack on Black's unprotected Bishop which gains time—to attack the Rook!

| 5 . . . | B—Kt3 |
| 6 B—Kt6! | |

Winning the Rook and the game. Note how White's fifth move not only gained time but also vacated KKt6 for the Bishop's thrust.

SCHLECHTER weaves a mating net for Meitner's King.

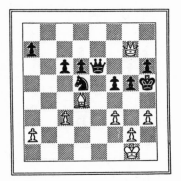

1 P—Kt4ch	P×P
2 RP×Pch	K—R5
3 Q×RPch!!	

One of the most remarkable moves ever seen in over-the-board play! White's offer must be accepted, as Black's own Queen is *en prise*.

| 3 . . . | Q×Q |
| 4 K—R2! | |

An astonishingly gentle sequel to a violent Queen sacrifice! Mate by the Bishop can be delayed, but only for one move. Black resigned.

FROM the game Tarrasch—Alapin, Dresden 1892; White menaces the Knight—to get at the King!

1 P—KR4!

Cutting off the Knight's retreat.

1 . . .   K—B2

Coming to the rescue.

| 2 R—B2 | K—K3 |
| 3 R—K2 | K—B4 |

The Knight seems well protected.

4 P—Kt4ch   K—B5

The King sticks close to the Knight; he refuses to be driven off! Who would suspect that this is all part of White's diabolical scheme? Believe it or not, mate is forced in three more moves!

5 K—Kt2!

A modest move, but White cannot be stopped from continuing with 6 R×Ktch!, B×R; 7 B—Q2 mate!

AN EARLY Capablanca; a good example of the way Capa was mowing them down at the Manhattan Chess Club, in his college years.

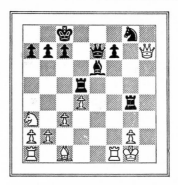

1 . . .   Kt—B3!

Black is a Pawn down, but far ahead in development.

2 Q—R8ch

Raubitschek thinks he can win a piece safely. Has the Cuban made a mistake?

| 2 . . . | R—Q1 |
| 3 Q×Kt | R(1)—Kt1! |

And now Black offers his Queen!

4 R—B2

Not 4 Q×Q, as after 4 . . . R×Pch; 5 K—R1, B—Q4, and White has no resource against the mating threats.

4 . . .   R×Pch
5 K—B1

He must not capture with his Rook, as his Queen would be unguarded.

5 . . .   B—B5ch!

Another elegant move.

6 Kt×B   R—Kt8 mate

FROM a game played by Dr. Tartakover at Paris, in 1933. The position, with four Queens on the board, is remarkable—even for such a lover of the unconventional as Tartakover.

1 . . .	Q—Q5ch
2 K—Kt3	

Naturally not 2 K—K2, Q(Kt8)—Q8 mate!

2 . . .	Q—Kt3ch
3 Q—Kt4	Q(Kt3)×Qch
4 P×Q	Q—K6ch

Driving White into a mating net.

5 K—R4

Now comes an extraordinary finish.

5 . . .	P—Kt4ch
6 K—R5	Q—K3
7 Q—B5ch	

Seemingly a winning check for White, as after the exchange of Queens he will be a Rook ahead.

7 . . .	Q—Kt3ch!
8 Q×Qch	P×Q mate!

FROM a game Rada—Kostal, Prague 1942:

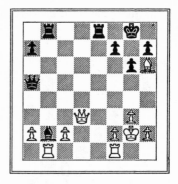

1 R×B!	R×R
2 Q—Q4	

An attack on the Rook, combined with a threat of mate at Kt7.

2 . . .	Q—K4

Guards the double menace, and apparently drives off White's Queen.

3 R—K1!

The Rook attacks! And his attack cannot be withstood! If 3 . . . Q×Q; 4 R×R mate, or if 3 . . . Q×R; 4 Q—Kt7 mate. The Queen must not move, and cannot stay!

FROM a game played in 1938; Black finds a subtle winning combination.

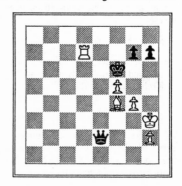

| 1 . . . | Q—B6ch |
| 2 B—Kt3 | P—Kt4! |

Threatening mate on the move.

3 P×P e.p.

On 3 R—Q6ch, Black forces the play with 3 . . . K—B2; 4 R—Q7ch, K—K1; 5 R—Q2, Q—B8ch; 6 R—Kt2, P—R4; 7 P×P, Q×P mate.

3 . . .	K—Kt4
4 R—Q2	P—R4!
5 P×P	Q—B8ch
6 R—Kt2	Q—B4 mate

FROM a game Moroni—Fletcher, London 1933; in an eight-move combination, White lets loose with a shower of sacrifices. He manages to give away both Rooks, a Knight and a Bishop!

1 R—Q7!	Q×R
2 R×Pch!	K×R
3 B—R6ch	K—R1
4 Kt—Kt6ch!	P×Kt

Refusing the Knight by 4 . . . K—Kt1 is hopeless after 5 Q—Kt4. But the text is also inadequate.

| 5 P×P | Q—B8ch |
| 6 K—R4 | Q—B6 |

Ready to counter a discovered check with 7 . . . Q×Qch.

7 B—Kt7ch!

But this is a *double* check!

| 7 . . . | K×B |
| 8 Q—R7 mate | |

A BRILLIANT combination from a game played in 1935.

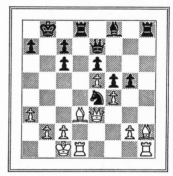

| 1 . . . | R(R1)×B!! |

Sacrificing a Rook at one end of the board in order to give up his Queen at the other end!

| 2 R×R | Q×P!! |
| 3 P×Q | |

If instead 3 K—Kt1, Kt—B6ch; 4 P×Kt, K—R1, and the coming Rook check at Kt1 will be decisive.

3 . . .	B×Pch
4 K—Kt1	Kt—B6ch
5 K—R1	B—Kt7ch!!
6 K×B	Kt×Rch
7 K—Kt3	Kt×Q

And Black wins. Now we see the reason for Black's first move; the protecting King Rook had to be lured away!

Adventures in the End Game

♛ "I HAVE met many who care little for the ordinary problem; I have never met any who were not overjoyed or bewitched by endings. . . . Endings are an inexhaustible source of entertainment, an endless feast of delight" (Reuben Fine).

What accounts for the peculiar fascination of endings? What charm is it which gives them such widespread popularity? Various reasons can be put forth:

The game-like, natural positions.

The absence of superfluous pieces, unnecessary for the solution.

The knowledge that a definite win or draw can be attained (depending on the terms), regardless of the apparent hopelessness of the situation.

The hairbreadth escapes.

The profusion of surprise moves in the solution.

These are plausible but not completely satisfying explanations. The chief delight of the end game is the infinite variety of ideas it offers, with a minimum of material.

GULAYEV

IN THIS delightful miniature, there occurs in the short space of five moves the offer of two Bishops and a Rook, underpromotion of a piece, and finally a pretty forced mate with meager material.

White to play and win

1 B—B6ch   K—K1

On 1 . . . K—B1; 2 B—R6ch forces the King to a black square when 3 B—K5ch wins the Rook and the game.

2 B—R5!   R×B

Otherwise 3 P—Kt7ch wins.

3 P—Kt7   R—Kt4!

Black knows some tricks, too.

4 B×R   B—B1!

So that if White makes a Queen, Black will be stalemated, or if 5 P×B(Q)ch, K×Q, and White cannot force mate with his lone remaining Bishop.

5 P—Kt8(B)!   B—Kt5

There is no salvation on the other diagonal. If 5 . . . B—Kt2; 6 B—B7ch, K—B1; 7 B—K7 mate.

6 B—B7ch   K—B1
7 B—R6 mate

HERBSTMANN

WHITE'S first problem is to dispose of the threat of 1 . . . Q—Kt7 mate. His combination to force the draw is a work of art.

White to play and draw

1 R×Pch!   Q×R

On 1 . . . K×R; 2 P—R8, queening his Pawn with check.

2 P—R8(Q)!

A Queen sacrifice which is brilliant —and compulsory! White was again threatened with mate in one.

2 . . .   Q×Q
3 R—R7ch!   Kt×R

If 3 . . . Q×R; 4 P×Q, Kt×P and the two Knights cannot force mate.

4 P—Kt7!!

A final resource, as elegant as it is modest.

4 . . .   Q×P

Drawn by stalemate!

MORAVEC

WITTY ideas can be concealed in the most innocuous-looking settings!

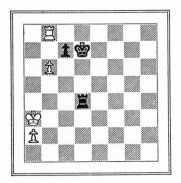

White to play and win

1 R—Q8ch!

Brilliant and brusque!

1 . . .   K×R
2 P—Kt7 R—QKt5!

The Pawn must be stopped. Black expects 3 K×R, P—B4ch; 4 K×P, K—B2. White would then lose his Knight's Pawn, and the subsequent position would be an easy draw.

3 K×R   P—B4ch
4 K—Kt5! K—B2
5 K—R6   K—Kt1

If instead 5 . . . P—B5; 6 K—R7, P—B6; 7 P—Kt8(Q) wins.

6 K—Kt6 P—B5
7 P—R4   P—B6
8 P—R5   P—B7
9 P—R6   P—B8(Q)
10 P—R7 mate

Once in every chess player's career he wins a game this way and gets the thrill of a lifetime!

SIMKOVICH

YES, WIN! At first glance, White seems hopelessly lost. Black threatens to exchange Rooks and zoom down with his Rook Pawn. White's King would be too far away and his Bishop pathetically helpless to stop the Pawn.

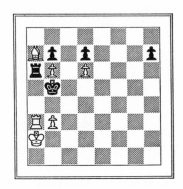

White to play and win

1 R×R   K×R

If 1 . . . P×R; 2 P—Kt7 wins at once.

2 K—Kt2 P—R4
3 K—B3   P—R5

Let's see. If 4 K—Q2, P—R6; 5 K—K2, P—R7 and Black wins. Clearly, chasing after the Pawn won't do.

4 K—Kt4!

What's this?

4 . . .   P—R6

Win or lose, there is no other move.

5 K—R4   P—R7
6 P—Kt4 P—R8(Q)
7 P—Kt5 mate!

SELESNIEV

THE PLOT: Black chases madly after a passed Pawn. Will he catch it in time? There is a surprise twist at the end of the story.

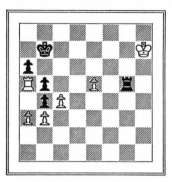

White to play and win

1 BP×P	K—Kt3

Of course not 1 . . . R×P; 2 P×Pch, and Black's Rook falls.

2 P×RP!	K×R
3 P—R7	R—R4ch
4 K—Kt7	

Not 4 K—Kt6 as Black gets to the first rank by 4 . . . R—R1.

4 . . .	R—Kt4ch
5 K—B7	R—B4ch
6 K—K7	R×Pch
7 K—Q7	R—Q4ch
8 K—B7	R—B4ch
9 K—Kt7	R—Kt4ch
10 K—B6!	

This time 10 K—B7 would not do, as the chase would begin all over again.

10 . . .	R—Kt3ch
11 K—B5	R—QR3

At last. With the passed Pawn ren-dered harmless, Black breathes a sigh of relief. But—

12 P×P mate!

A rude awakening.

NEWMAN

THAT White can win with his skimpy material against two healthy galloping Knights seems incredible!

White to play and win

1 K—Kt6	Kt—K4ch
2 K—B6	Kt(K4)—Kt5ch
3 K—K6	Kt×P
4 P—Kt6	Kt—B2!

To prevent 5 P—Kt7 which would now be answered by 5 . . . Kt—Q1ch.

5 K×Kt	Kt—B5

And now he threatens the Pawn directly, and intends on its advance to win it by 6 . . . Kt—Q3ch.

6 P—Kt7!	Kt—Q3ch
7 K—K7	Kt×P
8 P—Kt4!	

Paralyzing the Knight. White now walks over to the Knight with his King, captures it, and then simply steps aside to let the Pawn march up for the coronation.

MERKIN

WHEREIN a minor poet of the chess-board is gloriously inspired!

White to play and win

| 1 Kt—Q3ch | K—R7 |
| 2 Q—R2ch | K—Kt6 |

He must not return to the eighth rank, as 3 Q—Kt2 mate would follow.

| 3 Q—Kt2ch | K—B5 |

Here, if 3 . . . K—R5; 4 Q—R2 mate.

| 4 Q—Kt4ch | K—Q4 |

Up he must go; if 4 . . . K×Kt; 5 Q—Kt1ch costs the Queen.

| 5 Kt—B4ch | K—K4 |

If 5 . . . K—B3; 6 Q—Kt7ch, K—B4; 7 Q—Kt5ch wins the Queen.

6 Q—B3ch	K—K5
7 Q—Q3ch	K—K4
8 Q—Q5ch	K—B3

| 9 Kt—R5ch | K—Kt3 |

Forced, as his Queen was attacked.

| 10 Q—Kt8ch | K—R3 |

What if 10 . . . K×Kt? That question will be answered soon.

11 Q—Kt7ch	K×Kt
12 P—Kt4ch!	Q×P
13 Q×P mate!	

As exquisite as it was unexpected.

TROITZKY

IN HIS battle against the Bishop, the Knight leaps about with the grace and agility of a ballet dancer.

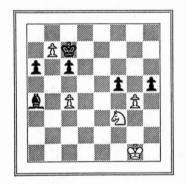

White to play and win

| 1 P×RP | B—B7 |

The dangerous Rook's Pawn must be stopped.

| 2 Kt—Q4 | B—Q6! |

His best chance. If instead, 2 . . . B—K5; 3 Kt—K6ch, K×P; 4 Kt—B4 followed by the advance of the passed Pawn.

| 3 Kt—K6ch | K—Kt1 |

If 3 . . . K×P; 4 Kt—B5ch wins.

| 4 Kt—B4! | B×P |
| 5 P—R6 | B—Kt1 |

Holding the Pawn at bay.

6 Kt—R5

Now White intends to play 7 Kt—B6 followed by Kt×B and P—R7.

6 . . .	B—R2
7 Kt—B6	B—Kt3
8 Kt—Q7ch	K×P
9 Kt—B8!	

The Bishop is cornered! White captures next move, pushes the Pawn and wins.

KAZANTSEV

IN THE course of the play, Black's pieces are as crowded as the Dormouse was at Alice's tea-party.

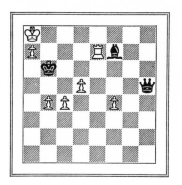

White to play and win

1 R—Kt7ch	K—R3
2 K—Kt8	Q—R1ch
3 K—B7	B×P

With the powerful threat 4 . . . Q—Kt2ch.

4 P—R8(Q)ch	Q×Q
5 R—Kt6ch	K—R2
6 P—Kt5	

Intending mate by 7 R—R6.

6 . . .   B—Kt2

Black just hopes for a breathing spell, so he can play . . . Q—Kt1ch.

| 7 R—R6ch! | B×R |
| 8 P—Kt6 mate! | |

KASPARYAN

FIENDISH ingenuity! Black is tied up and then given just enough moves to help complete his own destruction.

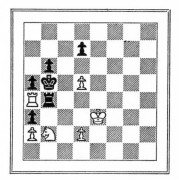

White to play and win

1 Kt—Q1   R×R

If 1 . . . K×R, 2 Kt—B3 is mate on the spot.

2 Kt—B3ch   K—Kt5

He must guard his Rook.

3 K—Q4   P—Kt4

If 3 . . . P—Q3; 4 Kt×R, K×Kt; 5 K—B4, P—Kt4ch; 6 K—B3, P—Kt5ch; 7 K—B4, P—Kt6; 8 P×P mate.

4 Kt—K4	P—Q3
5 Kt—B5!	P×Ktch
6 K—Q3	P—B5ch
7 K—Q4	P—B6
8 P×P mate!	

A lesson on the futility of mere material gain.

SELESNIEV

SELESNIEV could evolve the most charming conceptions from the most prosaic positions.

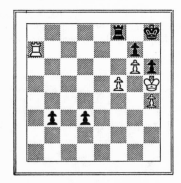

White to play and win

1 P—B6!

Threatening 2 P×Pch.

| 1 . . . | R—KKt1 |

Of course not 1 . . . R×P; 2 R—R8ch, nor 1 . . . P×P; 2 P—Kt7ch.

| 2 R—KB7 | P—Q7 |

And now 2 . . . P×P would permit 3 R—R7 mate.

| 3 P×Pch | R×P |
| 4 K×P | |

Posing a problem. If 4 . . . R×P; 5 P×R wins, or if 4 . . . R—Kt1; 5

R—R7 mate. Meanwhile Black is threatened with 5 R×R or worse!

4 . . .	P—Q8(Q)
5 R—B8ch!	R—Kt1
6 P—Kt7 mate	

HERBSTMANN

ANOTHER game-like position yields its secret possibilities to Herbstmann's artistry.

White to play and win

1 P—K6!

The plausible 1 K—B7 does not win after 1 . . . P—R3; 2 K—Kt6, R—Kt4ch; 3 K×P, R—Kt2.

| 1 . . . | P×P |

Forced, as 1 . . . R—R3 is a pin which doesn't pin.

2 K—B6!!	P—R3
3 R—R8ch	K—R2
4 R—R7ch	K—R1

If 4 . . . K—Kt1; 5 K—Kt6, R—Kt4ch; 6 K×P wins the Rook.

| 5 K—Kt6 | R—Kt4ch |

6 K×P   R—Kt1
7 R—R7 mate!

WHITE *wins this by a neat little trick.*

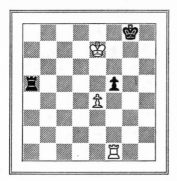

White to play and win

1 R—Kt1ch

The obvious 1 P×P or 1 R×P would only draw after 1 . . . R—R2ch.

1 . . .   K—R2
2 P—K5!

Unexpectedly giving up his important Pawn.

2 . . .   R×Pch

It would be hopeless to play 2 . . . R—R2ch, as White would reply 3 K—B6 followed by 4 P—K6.

3 K—B7

Threatening mate on the move.

3 . . .   K—R3
4 K—B6

Now the threat of mate wins the Rook, and of course the game.

BRON

A MASTERLY *composition in Bron's best style.*

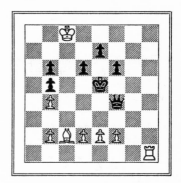

White to play and win

1 R—R5ch   K—K3

Naturally not 1 . . . P—B4; 2 R×Pch, nor 1 . . . K—Q5; 2 P—K3ch.

2 B—Kt3ch   P—Q4
3 R×P   Q×BP

Nowhere else can the Queen go to escape the dreadful threat of discovered check on the King, and simultaneous attack on the Queen. If 3 . . . Q×KtP, then 4 R×Pch wins the Queen.

4 P—Q4

Intending mate by 5 R—K5ch, K—Q3; 6 R—K6 mate.

4 . . .   P—B4
5 P—K4!

Now the threat is 6 R×BPch. White refutes 5 . . . P×P by 6 R—Q8ch, K—B3; 7 R—B8ch winning the Queen.

5 . . .   Q×KtP

How does White save his Bishop?

6 R—Q6ch!!   K×R
7 P—K5ch   K—B3
8 P—Q5 mate

TROITZKY

AN ENDING of classic simplicity. The number of Knight forks at White's disposal (first on black then on white squares) is amazing.

White to play and win

1 R—B8!   Q×R

Any attempt to escape by 1 . . . Q—Kt2, or 1 . . . Q—R3, or 1 . . . Q—K2 or 1 . . . Q—Q3 would be met by 2 Kt—B5ch winning the Queen.

2 Kt—B5ch

And now it is the King who is embarrassed. If 2 . . . K—B5 or 2 . . . K—K5, White wins by 3 Kt—Q6ch. Or if 2 . . . K—Q4, the Knight goes to K7 with a fatal double attack.

2 . . .   K—B4
3 P—Kt4ch!

Forcing the King to a white square. There are four such squares open to him, but any one permits a Knight fork which will win the Queen.

SELESNIEV

SELESNIEV himself was quite proud of this composition.

White to play and win

1 P—B5!   Kt—K3

On 1 . . . P×P; 2 R—Q7 will win, slowly but surely.

2 P×P!   Kt×R
3 P×P

Black seems lost already, but he has a little trick up his sleeve.

3 . . .   Kt—Kt2

So that if White makes a Queen, Black will be stalemated, and if he makes a Rook, then Kt×P looks drawish.

4 P—B8(R)   Kt×P

Black wins the Pawn. Actually, he was forced to take it, as any other move would have lost the Knight at once.

5 R—B5   Kt—Kt2

Where else could the poor Knight go?

6 R—B6 mate!

KAZANTSEV

BLACK is given his choice: he may be either the stalemater or the stalematee.

White to play and draw

1 Kt—K3   P—Q5
2 Kt—B5   P—R5
3 Kt—Kt3!

White is generous with the little that he owns.

3 . . .   P×Kt

On 3 . . . P—R6, White draws by 4 Kt×R, K×Kt; 5 K—B2.

4 K—K2!   P—Kt7

If 4 . . . K—Kt7, White has no moves.

5 K—K1

And now it is Black who is tied up!

LIBURKIN

WHO will be stalemated? Whatever your guess is, it is right!

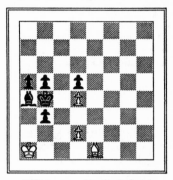

White to play and draw

1 P—Q3ch   K—R6
2 B—Kt4ch!   K×B
3 K—Kt2

Black is stalemated. If instead, 2 . . . P×B; 3 K—Kt1, P—Kt7 and now White is stalemated!

LAPIN

THE KNIGHT does some fancy stepping, but he is soon paralyzed.

White to play and win

1 P—Kt6   Kt—Q3!
2 P—Kt7   Kt—K1
3 P—Kt8(Q) Kt—B3ch
4 K—Kt5!   Kt×Q
5 P—Q6!

The Knight must look on helplessly while White queens his Pawn with check, with an easy win.

KUZNETSOV

THE TREASURE of beautiful combinations seems inexhaustible; here is one of the jewels:

White to play and draw

1 P—R7   Q—Kt7ch
2 K—R1   Q—R8

With the mating threat 3 . . . K—B7ch; 4 K×P, Q—Kt8ch etc.

3 P—R8(Q) Q×Q
4 R×Pch   K—B7
5 R—B7ch   K—Kt6
6 R—QR7!   Kt×R

No better is 6 . . . . Q×R; 7 P×Q, Kt×P; 8 R—K2, and the position is drawn.

7 P—Kt7!

Certainly a picturesque situation.

7 . . .   Q×P

Stalemate

SELESNIEV

RARELY did Selesniev clutter up the board; a handful of pieces was enough to illustrate a nice point. In this, Black is not only three Pawns ahead, but he also threatens mate by 1 . . . P—B3ch; 2 K—R5, B—Q8ch and mate next move.

White to play and draw

1 R—K8ch!

And not 1 R×P (hoping for 1 . . . K×R; 2 Kt—Q6ch) as 1 . . . P—R3ch would win.

1 . . .   B×R
2 Kt—K7ch   K—B1(or R1)
3 Kt—Kt6ch! BP(or RP)×Kt
        Stalemate

If Black refuses to take the Knight, then White draws by a perpetual check at K7 and Kt6!

BIRNOV

"DOMINATION" is always a pleasing theme. Here, White's King and Rook are sufficient to surround the Bishop.

White to play and win

1 R—Kt5ch   K—B1

Clearly forced, as moving to the Rook file would be met by 2 R—R5ch.

2 R—KR5   B—B2

Not 2 . . . B—Kt1; 3 R—R8ch. And if 2 . . . B—Kt6; 3 R—B5ch, K—K1; 4 R—KKt5, and the mating threat wins the Bishop.

3 K—Q7   B—Kt3

Again, if 3 . . . B—Kt6; 4 R—B5ch, K—Kt2; 5 R—Kt5ch catches the Bishop.

4 R—QKt5   B—R2
5 R—QR5   B—Kt3

Here if 5 . . . B—Kt1; 6 R—R8 does it.

6 R—R8ch   K—B2
7 K—B6

The King steps in and White wins.

SELESNIEV

LIKE RETI, Selesniev discovered that natural-looking positions could yield attractive ideas.

White to play and draw

1 K—Kt6   B—B5

He must be ready to stop White's Pawn.

2 B—B7!   K—Kt5

Unpinning his Pawn, and threatening to advance it.

3 B×P!   K×B
4 K—B5   B—Q3
5 K—K6   B—B1
6 K—B7   B—R3
7 K—Kt6

Around and around they go. White draws by perpetual chase!

RINCK

ONE COULD safely cast a vote for Rinck for the office of World's Greatest Composer, not only for the great number of his compositions but for his never-failing artistry.

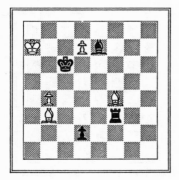

White to play and draw

1 B—R4ch

One Bishop gets away from the Rook's attack.

1 . . .   K—Q4

But now the other is still in danger, and White is threatened also with 2 . . . R—QR6.

2 B×P   R—QR6
3 K—Kt6   R×B

Now how does White draw? His Queen's Pawn seems useless, and he is a Rook down.

4 B—Kt5!   B×B

If 4 . . . R×Pch; 5 K—R5, and Black has more problems than he can solve.

5 P—Q8(Q)ch B×Qch
6 K—Kt5!

And now, no matter where the

Rook moves on the Rook file, White will still be stalemated!

HERBSTMANN

AS A compiler of endings, Herbstmann showed excellent taste; as a composer, he turned out some beauties on his own account.

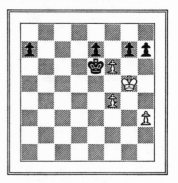

White to play and draw

1 P×KtP   K—B2

Stopping White's passed Pawn. But what does White do? If he chases after the Queen's Rook's Pawn, Black will capture all the King-side Pawns and win easily.

2 K—R6!

Threatening to win with 3 K×P.

2 . . .   K—Kt1
3 P—B5   P—R4
4 P—R4   P—R5
5 P—R5   P—R6
6 P—B6!   P×P
Stalemate!

GORGIEV

THIS brilliant ending won a high prize in a composing tourney.

White to play and win

| 1 B—B6ch | K—R2 |
| 2 R—Kt7ch | K—R3 |

On 2 . . . K—R1; 3 R×Ktch wins at once.

3 R—B7

Threatening 4 B×Kt. If Black tries to free himself from the pin by 3 . . . Kt—B3, then 4 B×B, Kt×B; 5 R—Q7 wins the Knight neatly.

| 3 . . . | K—Kt3 |
| 4 R—B8 | |

Black is in a Zugzwang position: if his King moves, then the Bishop is lost; if the Bishop moves, the Knight is lost.

4 . . .	Kt—B3
5 B×B	K—Kt2
6 R—K8	K—B2
7 R—R8	K—Kt2

What an annoying King!

8 B—B6ch!

The joker!

| 8 . . . | K×B |
| 9 R—R6ch | |

White wins the Knight and the game.

ANDREW

THE DREAD power of Zugzwang— against which even a Queen is helpless.

White to play and win

1 P—R5ch   K—Kt2

Naturally, he does not take the Pawn, as the Knight fork would win his Queen.

| 2 Kt—B6 | Q—R1 |
| 3 K—Kt7! | |

A strange position! Black's Queen must move, and in doing so give up its life!

157

GORGIEV

ONLY by delicate manipulation can White save himself.

White to play and draw

1 B—Q7	Kt—B4

Still menacing both of White's pieces.

2 Kt—B7ch	K—B3
3 Kt—Q6	Kt×B

The reply to 3 . . . K—K2 would be 4 Kt—B8ch followed by 5 Kt×B.

4 Kt—K4ch	K—K4
5 Kt×P	B—Q5

New troubles. How will White unpin his Knight?

6 K—Kt2	Kt—B4

Stopping the King from going to Kt3.

7 K—R3!

He loses the Knight, but . . .

7 . . .	B×Kt

. . . saves the King! Stalemate.

GUREVICH

AGILE stepping by the Knights in this!

White to play and win

1 Kt—Q5ch

Not at once 1 B×Kt on account of 1 . . . P—Kt7 in reply.

1 . . .	K—K5
2 B—B3ch!	K×B

If 2 . . . K—B4; 3 B×Kt(R1) and Black is lost.

3 Kt—Q2ch	K—Kt7
4 Kt—B4ch	K—Kt8(or R7)
5 Kt—B3 mate	

STULNIKOV

WHITE *is threatened with* . . .
B×R, . . . Q×Kt, *and* . . . Q—
Kt8 *mate. But in the most desperate
positions there is always a last-minute
hope—stalemate!*

NOVOTELNOV

CLEVER *finessing on both sides.*

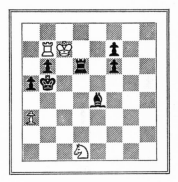

White to play and draw

1 Kt—B3ch	K—R3
2 Kt×B	R—K3

Bearing down on the Knight and
also threatening the Rook by 3 . . .
R—K2ch.

3 R—Kt8!	R—K2ch

. 3 . . . R×Kt would be answered
with 4 R×Pch, K—Kt2; 5 R—Kt7ch,
etc., drawing by perpetual check.

4 K—B6	K—R2

The Knight was immune, as mate
on the move would follow.

5 R—Kt7ch!	

Nobody expected this!

5 . . .	R×R
6 Kt—Q6	R—Kt1

The only other flight square K2
would permit 7 Kt—B8ch winning
the Rook.

7 Kt—Kt5ch	K—R3(or R1)
8 Kt—B7ch	

White draws by perpetual check.

White to play and draw

1 R—R2ch	K—K8

On *1* . . . Q×R; 2 R—B2ch wins
the Queen, or if *1* . . . B—B7;
R×Bch follows.

2 R—K3ch	K—B8

Not 2 . . . K—Q8, as 3 Kt—B2ch
and mate next move.

3 R—B2ch	K—Kt8
4 R—K1ch	Q×R

Stalemate!

Rinck

A FINE example of the famed Rinck craftsmanship.

White to play and win

1 Kt(Kt4)—B6ch   K—Kt3
2 R—Kt4ch   K—B4
3 Kt—Q7ch   K—Q3

If 3 . . . K×Kt; 4 R—Kt6ch wins the Queen, or if 3 . . . K—Q4; 4 Kt—K7ch does it.

4 Kt—K7!

Attacking the Queen, and also threatening 5 R—Kt6 mate.

4 . . .   Q—Kt8
5 R—B4

Now intending 6 R—B6 mate.

5 . . .   K—K3
6 K—K8!   Q—Q8
7 R—B6ch   Q—Q3

White can now take the Queen, but his remaining two Knights could not force mate.

8 Kt—B8ch   K—K4
9 Kt(B8)—Kt6ch   K—K3
10 Kt—B4ch   K—K4
11 Kt(K7)—Kt6ch

White wins, as Black's King can no longer protect his Queen.

Birnov

PROPOSITION: *to prove that the Bishop can be caught.*

White to play and win

1 R—Kt1ch   K—Q7
2 R—Kt2

The familiar pinning attack.

2 . . .   K—B8

On 2 . . . B—Q5; 3 R×Ktch, K—Q8 and White saves the Knight by moving his Rook to either R2.

3 R×Ktch   K—Kt8
4 R—B4!

In order to extricate his Knight by 5 Kt—B2.

4 . . .   B—B7ch

The only hope, as indifferent moves are answered by 5 Kt—B2, while 4 . . . K×Kt fails after 5 R—R4ch.

5 K—Kt4   K×Kt
6 K—B3!

White wins, as the Bishop has no

hiding place: if *6 . . . B—R2; 7 R—R4ch*, or if *6 . . . B—Kt3; 7 R—R4ch* followed by *8 R—Kt4ch*, or if *6 . . . B—Kt8 (or K8); 7 R—B1ch* wins the Bishop.

Q.E.D.

K2 wins. Or if in this *7 . . . Kt—B8; 8 K—K2, Kt—R7; 9 R—Kt2* wins.

| 6 . . . | Kt—Kt2 |

7 R—B8 mate!

GORGIEV

EVEN in the well-worked fields of "domination" Gorgiev manages to raise new crops.

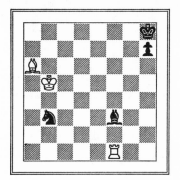

White to play and win

1 K—Kt4

Not at once *1 R×B*, as the Knight fork at Q5 would be painful.

1 . . .	Kt—Q5
2 K—B3	B—K7
3 B×B	Kt×Bch
4 K—Q3!	Kt—Kt6

The only square left.

| 5 R—B3 | Kt—R4 |

If *5 . . . Kt—R8; 6 K—K2* followed by *7 R—KR3* wins the Knight.

6 R—B5

The Knight is in trouble. If *6 . . . Kt—Kt6; 7 R—KKt5, Kt—R8; 8 K—*

KOROLIKOV

A DECEPTIVELY placid position, where the final stroke comes with surprising rapidity.

White to play and win

1 P—B7	R—QB1
2 P—Q7	R×P
3 P—Q8(Q)	

It looks as though it's all over, but Black has some powder left.

3 . . .	B—Kt3ch
4 K—Q3!	R—B6ch
5 K×R	B×Q
6 Kt—K6	

Attacking the Bishop who has only one refuge.

| 6 . . . | B—Kt3 |

7 B—K8 mate!

VEREZAGIN

WHITE'S object is to save the game by tying himself up in a stalemate knot. To do so requires a bit of finesse.

KUBBEL

THIS is the kind of ending Kubbel could probably dash off by the dozen; for a less gifted composer, it would rank as one of his masterpieces.

White to play and draw

1 P—Q6!	P×P

Otherwise, White's Pawn might even queen!

2 B×P	Q—K8

If 2 . . . K—Q5 (to avoid 3 B—B5ch) then 3 B—B5ch (anyway) K×B; 4 Kt—K4ch wins the Queen. Or if 2 . . . K—Q7; 3 Kt—K4ch.

3 B—B5ch	K—B5
4 B—Q6ch	K—Kt4
5 B—K7ch	P—B3

On 5 . . . K—R3; 6 B—B8ch with a perpetual check, or a return to the actual line of play.

6 B—B5!	

Threatening mate on the move.

6 . . .	Q—B6

A King move instead permits perpetual check by the Bishop.

7 B—K3ch	Q×B

Drawn by stalemate!

White to play and draw

1 B—B6	

Attacking the Queen, and also intending 2 Kt—Kt6ch, K×Kt; 3 B—K7 mate.

1 . . .	Q×B

If 1 . . . Q—K6; 2 Kt—Kt6ch, K×Kt; 3 B—Q4ch wins the Queen.

2 Kt—Q7!	B×Kt

Otherwise there follows 3 Kt(Q7)—Kt6 mate.

3 Kt—Kt6ch	K×P

Naturally, not 3 . . . K—B4; 4 Kt×Bch winning the Queen.

4 Kt—Q5ch!	P×Kt

Drawn by stalemate.

KURCHKIN

IT SEEMS almost incredible that the Rook's simple straight-line moves could lead to such complex maneuvers.

White to play and win

1 R—Kt1

With a mate-on-the-move threat.

1 . . .   R(R5)—Kt5

A pretty variation is *1* . . . R(B5)—QKt5; 2 Kt—Q4, R×R(Kt3); 3 R—Kt5ch! R×R; 4 Kt—B6 mate, and the powerful Rooks look foolish.

2 R—R1ch   R—R5
3 Kt—Q6

Now menacing no less than three one-move mates!

3 . . .   R—B2ch

If 3 . . . R×R; 4 Kt×Rch, K—R4; 5 R—R6ch winning the last Rook.

4 Kt—Kt7ch   R×Ktch
5 K×R   R×R
6 R—R6ch

White wins the Rook and the game.

BELENKIN

BEAU ideal of an ending!

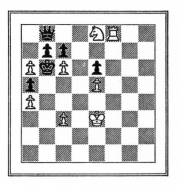

White to play and win

1 Kt—B6   Q—R2

Forced, as *1* . . . Q×R loses by 2 Kt—Q7ch.

2 R—QR8!   Q×R
3 RP×P!

The right way to capture; if 3 BP×P, Q—R2; 4 P—Kt8(Kt), Q—R1; 5 Kt(B6)—Q7ch, K—R2 and Black draws.

3 . . .   Q—R2
4 P—Kt8(Q)!

But not 4 P—Kt8(Q)ch, as the reply 4 . . . K×Pch; 5 Q×Q stalemates Black.

4 . . .   K—B4

Black was threatened with 5 Kt (B6)—Q7 mate. If instead 4 . . . Q×Kt; 5 Kt—Q7ch wins the Queen.

5 K—Q3   Q—R1
6 Kt(B6)—Q7ch K—Q4
7 P—B4 mate!

HORWITZ AND KLING

THE OLD composers knew a thing or two! In this beauty, White's first three moves are truly surprising. In order to win, the King tiptoes quietly away from the scene of action!

White to play and win

1 K—R6!	Q—KKt3ch
2 K—R7	Q—Kt8ch

Black's King cannot escape via 2 . . . K—Kt8 as the Bishop check wins the Queen.

| 3 K—R8 | Q—Kt8 |

And now if 3 . . . K—Kt8; 4 Q—R2ch, K—B8; 5 Q—R1ch wins the Queen.

4 Q—K5ch	Q—Kt7
5 Q—K1ch	Q—Kt8
6 Q—B3ch	Q—Kt7
7 Q—R5ch!	

White's first move is clear now: the King opened the way for the Queen to check at this square.

7 . . .	K—Kt8
8 B—K4ch	K—B8
9 Q—K1 mate	

KOZLOWSKI

ONLY a few moves, and Black is convinced that a Rook ahead is not always enough to win.

White to play and draw

1 R—B8ch	K—Q2
2 R—B7ch	K—K3!

The best chance, as returning to the first rank leads to perpetual check, or loss of a Rook. For example, if 2 . . . K—B1; 3 R—B8ch, K—Kt2; 4 R—B7ch, and the King must go back. After the move played, he does not fear 3 K×R as that would leave White's Rook unprotected.

3 R—B5!

Drawn! If Black moves his Rook from KR3 along the King's Rook file, then 4 R—B6ch wins the other Rook, and if Black's King moves, then the checks begin again.

BLATHY

IN THE light of Blathy's usual compositions (mate in 292 moves!) this must have been one of his short-short stories.

White to play and win

1 K—Q1   B—Kt7

Clearly, a King move by Black permits one of the Pawns to Queen.

2 K—K1   B—B8
3 K—B1   B—Q7
4 K—Kt1   B—K8

Black may vary his Bishop moves without affecting White's King moves —or the final result.

5 K—Kt2!

White gains a tempo.

5 . . .   B—Q7
6 K—B1   B—B8
7 K—K1   B—Kt7
8 K—Q1   B—R8
9 K—B1   B—Kt7ch
10 K—Kt1

White wins, as on 10 . . . K—Q2 (or Q1); 11 P—Kt7 follows, or if 10 . . . K—Kt2 (or 10 . . . K—Kt1); 11 P—Q7 ends it.

LOUNSBURY

AN AMUSING position. White has a tremendous material superiority, but how does he free Black from his stalemate position?

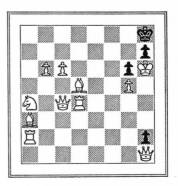

White to play and win

1 Q—R1   P—R8(Q)ch
2 R—R4ch   Q×Q

White must not recapture. How does he win?

3 B—Kt2ch   Q×B
4 Kt—B3!

Clearing the way for the Rook which now threatens mate.

4 . . .   Q×R
5 Q—Q4 mate

KARLINSKI

WHITE'S moves are timed with exquisite accuracy.

White to play and win

1 K—Q3

A mating threat to counter Black's dangerous queening threats.

1 . . .   K—K8

If 1 . . . K—B8; 2 Kt—K2ch, K—Kt8; 3 Kt—B3ch, K—B8; 4 R—B2 mate.

2 Kt—R1!

A pretty move, with a brutal follow-up in mind: 3 R—R1 mate.

2 . . .	P×Kt(Q)
3 R—R1ch	K—B7
4 R×Q	K—Kt7

And now it looks as though White might have trouble saving the game!

5 K—K2!	K×R
6 K—B1!	P—B4
7 P×P	P—K5
8 P—B6	P—K6
9 P—B7	P—K7ch
10 K×P	K—Kt7
11 P—B8(Q)	P—R8(Q)

12 Q—B2 mate

RETI

DESPITE the brevity of the solution this may be a tough nut to crack.

White to play and win in one move!

1 K—R1!!

After this quiet move, Black is in Zugzwang (the compulsion to move). A move by the Bishop permits a Knight fork winning the Bishop; a move by the King is answered by 2 P—R6 and the Pawn cannot be stopped from becoming a Queen.

Secret: the diagram is a shortened version of the original composition which had a much longer solution—two moves!

Gandolfi

THE WORD "wonderful" should be used sparingly; but surely no other word could describe so well Gandolfi's masterpiece.

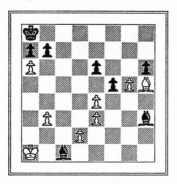

White to play and win

| 1 P—Kt6 | B×P |

To get on the long diagonal.

| 2 K—Kt2 | B×P |
| 3 K—B3 | B—B5 |

If 3 . . . B—Kt4; 4 P—K5, B—B5; 5 K—Q4, and the passed Pawn cannot be stopped.

4 K—Q4	B—B8
5 K—B5!	B—QKt7
6 K—Q6	

Threatening to shut out the Bishop with 7 P—K5.

| 6 . . . | BP×P |
| 7 K—B7 | |

Now White threatens 8 P×P mate.

| 7 . . . | B—K4ch |

Or 7 . . . P×P; 8 P—Kt7!, B×P; 9 B—K8, B—K4ch; 10 K—B8 and mate follows.

| 8 K—B8 | P×P |

| 9 P—Kt7! | B×P |
| 10 B—K8 | |

Intending mate next move.

10 . . .	P—K4ch
11 K—B7	Any
12 B—B6 mate	

Kasparyan

IN ALMOST any collection of composed endings, this bewitching beauty would qualify as the pièce de résistance. Its striking originality makes an impression not easily forgotten.

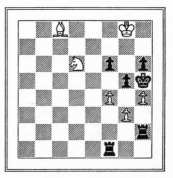

White to play and win

1 Kt—K8

Intending 2 Kt—Kt7ch, K—Kt3; 3 B—B5 mate.

| 1 . . . | K—Kt3 |

Or 1 . . . P—B4; 2 B×P and 3 Kt—Kt7 mate.

| 2 P—R5ch! | R×P |

On 2 . . . K×P, White carries out his originally planned mate in two.

| 3 P—B5ch | R×P |

Black has no choice.

4 P—Kt4

A pretty Pawn fork; threat: 5 B×R mate.

4 . . .   R—B4
5 B—B5ch!   R×B

The Rook's flight was futile; he is compelled to return. One would now expect White to capture one of the Rooks with his Pawn. Instead, he makes a gentle, unobtrusive move. And it is this modest move which completely paralyzes Black!

6 Kt—Kt7!!

Black must move one of his Rooks. When he does so, White takes the remaining one with his Pawn, announcing checkmate!

"Aha!"

Cartoon by George Price, by permission of the artist. Copyright 1939 The New Yorker Magazine, Inc.

The Problem Corner

♕ THERE are many ways of enjoying chess; so many, in fact, that the initiate quickly becomes an enthusiast of one particular branch of the game. There are those who apply their energies to its most practical aspect—they play chess! Their games may be friendly and leisurely— two or three of them providing a pleasant night's entertainment. There are those who prefer the split-second decisions required by "lightning" chess, when the player's time for thinking is limited to ten seconds a move! These speed demons can whiz through a whole tournament in one evening! Some there are who choose the variety offered by club chess—individual championships, team matches, handicap tournaments, or other forms of serious clock chess. A great many play chess by mail (not so cold-blooded a diversion as it sounds), conducting ten, twenty or thirty games at the same time. A few devote a good part of their lives to composing problems, for the delectation of the myriads who get their chess thrills from solving them.

It is hard to get the problem-solver to play a game of chess; he gets so much more fun from his problems. It is still harder to get the practical player to look at a problem; he cannot picture anything being more exciting than beating a flesh-and-blood opponent.

In this chapter, the problems have been selected with a view to satisfying the requirements of both species; the positions will please the player, as they have not, for the most part, the artificial appearance of most problems. They will appeal to the *aficionado* of problems, as they have the task-aspect which he requires—mate is to be forced in a specified number of moves.

Curiously enough, the casual reader need not fear the problems which stipulate mate in five, six, seven or eight moves, as they are easier than they sound. Generally, there is only one line of play; there are no bewildering variations to drive him frantic.

<table>
<tr>
<td>

BOSWELL

White mates in two moves

1 Q—R8!!

A quiet but powerful move. If Black plays 1 . . . P—Kt7; 2 K—Kt4 mates neatly. 1 . . . P—B6 yields to 2 K×P mate, and on 1 . . . P—Q5, White swoops down and mates by 2 Q—R1.

</td>
<td>

WORMALD

BLACK'S King is surrounded, but too well so! He must be released from his stalemate position. But how?

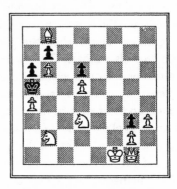

White mates in two moves

1 Q—R1!

The strongest piece on the board is stuck away in a corner!

1 . . .   K×P
2 Kt—B4 mate

</td>
</tr>
</table>

Van Eelde

THE KEY-MOVE is startling. White sacrifices his strongest piece!

White mates in two moves

1 Q—R6!   P×Q
2 B×P mate

If 1 . . . Kt×Q; 2 B×P mate
    1 . . . Kt—Q6ch; 2 B×Kt mate
    1 . . . Kt—B7ch; 2 B×Kt mate

Guarini

THE KEY is one of those silly-looking moves which give problems their peculiar charm.

White mates in two moves

1 R—Q4ch!

A five-fold sacrifice!

If 1 . . . B×R; 2 P—B4 mate
    1 . . . K×R; 2 Q—Q3 mate
    1 . . . Kt×R; 2 Kt×P mate
    1 . . . BP×R; 2 Kt—B6 mate
    1 . . . KP×R; 2 Q—B5 mate

Carpenter

EVEN more startling is this key-move which offers the Queen to seven pieces!

White mates in two moves

1 Q×P(Q4)ch!!

If 1 . . . K×Q; 2 R—QR4 mate
    1 . . . P×Q; 2 R—K6 mate
    1 . . . B×Q; 2 B×R mate
    1 . . . R×Q; 2 R×B mate
    1 . . . Q×Q; 2 B—Kt2 mate
    1 . . . Kt(4)×Q; 2 Kt—Q6 mate
    1 . . . Kt(6)×Q; 2 Kt—B5 mate

Cook

A *SIMPLE* but pretty old-timer.

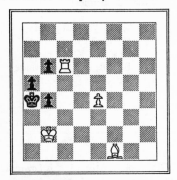

White mates in three moves

1 R—B4	P—Kt4
2 B—R3	P×R
3 B—Q7 mate	

If 1 . . .	K—Kt4
2 R—B1ch	K—R5
3 R—R1 mate	

White

BLACK'S King sits like a spider in the center of his web of Pawns. How does White break through?

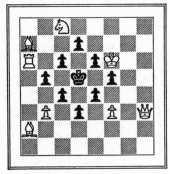

White mates in two moves

---

1 Q—Kt2!

If 1 . . . P—B5;	2 BP×P mate
1 . . . P—K4;	2 Q—Kt8 mate
1 . . . KP×P;	2 Q×P mate
1 . . . P—K6;	2 P—B4 mate
1 . . . P—Q3;	2 Kt—K7 mate
1 . . . P—Q7;	2 Q×P mate
1 . . . P—B4;	2 R—Q6 mate
1 . . . P—B6;	2 P—Kt4 mate
1 . . . BP×P;	2 B×P mate
1 . . . P—Kt5;	2 KtP×P mate

Tuxen

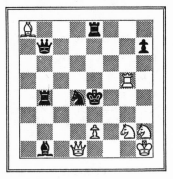

White mates in two moves

1 Kt—B3

Threatens 2 Kt—Q2 mate. Black can only defend by moving his Knight, to give his King freedom. Each Knight move (and there are eight of them) serves that purpose, but opens up a new mating possibility for White.

If 1 . . . Kt—B3;	2 Q—Q5 mate
1 . . . Kt—Kt4;	2 B×Q mate
1 . . . Kt—Kt6;	2 Q×B mate
1 . . . Kt—B7;	2 Q—Q3 mate
1 . . . Kt×P;	2 Q×Kt mate
1 . . . Kt×Kt;	2 P×Kt mate
1 . . . Kt—B4;	2 R—Kt4 mate
1 . . . Kt—K3;	2 R—K5 mate

MEISNER

WHITE wins by giving away his strongest pieces!

White mates in three moves

1 R—KR8!

Threatening 2 R—Kt1 mate.

1 . . .   B×R
2 R—Kt7!   B×R
3 Kt—Kt3 mate

WARTON

THE POWERFUL 1 K—B5 would not do at all, as Black would be stalemated. White spins his mating net in a roundabout way.

White mates in three moves

1 Q—QKt3!   P×Q
2 K—B5   P—Kt7
3 P—Kt4 mate

If 1 . . .   K moves
2 Q—Kt8ch etc.

KOERS

THE QUEEN makes two delightful moves!

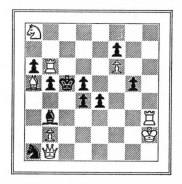

White mates in three moves

1 Q—Q3

Threatening 2 R—R8 followed by 3 R—B8 mate.

1 . . .   P—KKt5

In order (after 2 R—R8) to check at Kt6, making it impossible to mate in three moves.

If 1 . . . P×Q; 2 R—R8, K—B5; 3 R—B8 mate.

2 Q—B4ch!!   QP×Q
3 R—R5 mate

If 2 . . . KtP×Q; 3 B—Kt4 mate
   2 . . . B×Q; 3 P—Kt4 mate
   2 . . . K×Q; 3 R—B6 mate

173

KIPPING

WHITE has a great many mating ideas, but first he must give Black, who is stalemated, a move!

White mates in three moves

```
1 Q—QR1!      P×Q(Q)ch
2 B×Q         P—Kt7
3 Kt—B6 mate
```

ZANGGER

BLACK'S King is hemmed in by his own men.

White mates in three moves

```
1 K—B6        P×P
```

```
2 K—K7        P×Kt
3 Kt—B6 mate
```

A pretty final position.

LATZEL

IT SEEMS incredible, but in the main line of play the Rook at R1 breaks through the entire row of Black pieces to mate at R8 in four moves!

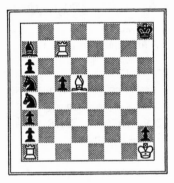

White mates in four moves

```
1 R×RP
```

Threatening 2 R×RP mate.

```
1 . . .       Kt—Kt7
2 R×RP
```

Now intending 3 R—R3 mate.

```
2 . . .       Kt—Kt6
3 R×RP
```

To follow with 4 R—R6 mate.

```
3 . . .       B—Kt3
4 R—R8 mate
```

GERBEC

WHITE plots a long-range mate.

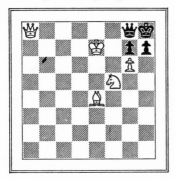

White mates in three moves

1 Kt—R6   P×Kt
2 P—Kt7ch   K×P
3 Q—R1 mate

If 1 . . .   Q×Q
2 Kt—B7ch   K—Kt1
3 P×P mate

VALLEJO

THE KNIGHTS spurn the help of the Queen, and arrange a remarkable mate in the center of the board.

White mates in three moves

1 Kt—K6   Kt—Q4

On other moves of this Knight, mate would follow by 2 Q—Q3 mate. Should the other Knight move, the reply would be 2 Q—K5 mate.

2 Q—K5ch!!   Kt×Q
3 Kt—Q6 mate!

If 1 . . .   K—B4
2 Kt—Q4ch   K—K5
3 Kt—Kt5 mate

RICHTER

IN WHICH the variations are as pretty as the main-play.

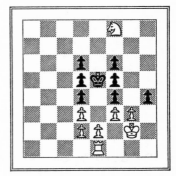

White mates in four moves

1 R—KR1   RP×P
2 Kt—K6!   K×Kt
3 R—R7   K—K4
4 R—K7 mate

If 1 . . .   P—R6ch
2 R×P   P×P
3 R—R5   K—B5
4 Kt—Kt6 mate

If 1 . . .   BP×P
2 R×P   P—B5
3 R—R6   P—B4
(Or 3 . . . K—B4; 4 R—R5 mate)
4 Kt—Q7 mate

ANDERSSEN

THE MASTER player could turn out a cute problem, too.

White mates in four moves

1 Kt—K8	K×Kt
2 Kt—Kt7ch	K—R5
3 K—B4	P—R4
4 Kt—B5 mate	

VON HOMMA

AN UNEXPECTED gift does the trick.

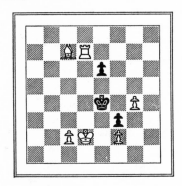

White mates in four moves

1 K—B3	P—K4

2 R—Q4ch!	P×Rch
3 K—B4	P—Q6
4 P×P mate	

KOHTZ AND KOCKELKORN

THAT old devil Zugzwang (the necessity for making a move—most especially when you don't want to!)

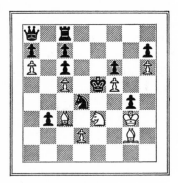

White mates in four moves

1 P—Q3

Threatening 2 B—K4 followed by 3 Kt×P mate, or 3 Kt—B4 mate

1 . . .	R—R1!
2 B—K4	Q—KKt1
3 B—QKt2!	

Zugzwang! Black's Queen must move, and cannot continue to guard both vital squares.

3 . . .	Q moves
4 Kt mates	

GILBERG

THE TIMING of the Pawn's moves is a pleasure to watch.

White mates in five moves

1 P—B4	P—K4
2 P—B5	P—K5
3 P—B6	P—K6
4 P—B7	P—K7
5 Q—B6 mate	

PALATZ

THIS has a family resemblance to the Gilberg.

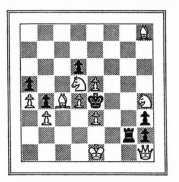

White mates in five moves

1 K—Q1	P×P
2 K—B1	P×P
3 K—Kt1	P×P (or P—Q6)
4 K—R1	P—K7(or Q7)
5 Q—QKt1 mate	

ZEPLER

THE KING goes to and fro in pendulum style in this clever little problem.

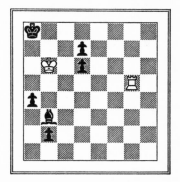

White mates in five moves

1 K—B7

Threatening 2 R—R5 mate.

1 . . .   P—Q4

Shuts off the Rook, but now—

2 K—Kt6

Intending 3 R—Kt8 mate.

2 . . .   P—Q5

Guards the mate.

3 K—B7

Back to the first threat.

3 . . .   P—Q4
4 K—Kt6!   Any
5 R mates

HENDEL

EVERYTHING just clicks in this masterly miniature.

White mates in five moves

1 P—Kt4	K—Q2
2 P—Kt5	K—B1
3 P—Kt6	K—Q2
4 P—Kt7	K—B3
5 P—Kt8(Kt!) mate	

KOHNLEIN

WHITE'S cute little mating plan is countered by Black's threat to stalemate himself. Ingenious, but White "has a trick worth two of that."

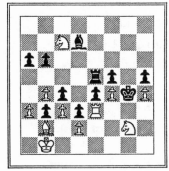

White mates in five moves

---

1 K—B1

He means to bring the King over to KB2, and then play 5 R—Kt3 mate.

| 1 ... | B—R5! |
| 2 K—Q1 | R—R4 |

In order to continue with 3 ... P—Kt4, burying his pieces alive, and stalemating the Black King.

| 3 P—Kt5! | R×P |

Capturing with the Bishop or the Pawn would permit 4 Kt—Q5 followed by 5 Kt—B6 mate.

| 4 Kt—K8 | Any |
| 5 Kt—B6 mate | |

FAHRNI

A MODERN composer turns one out in the style of the Old School.

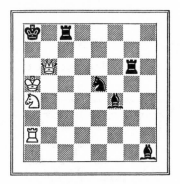

White mates in six moves

1 Kt—B5!

With two strong threats: 2 Q—Kt7 mate, and 2 K—Kt4 mate.

| 1 ... | R×Q |
| 2 K×Rch | K—Kt1 |

3 Kt—R6ch	K—R1
4 Kt—B7ch	K—Kt1
5 R—R8ch!	B×R
6 Kt—R6 mate	

An epaulet mate by the Knight.

THE RULES say that capturing a Pawn en passant is a privilege, but here Black has as little choice as a man hypnotized.

White mates in six moves

1 P—Kt4

Threatens 2 Kt—B7 mate.

1 . . .	P×P e.p.
2 P—B4ch	P×P e.p.
3 P—Q4	P×P e.p.
4 P—K4ch	P×P e.p.
5 P—B4	P×P e.p.
6 R—Kt5 mate	

CURNOCK

THE KING takes a stroll!

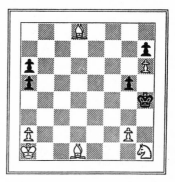

White mates in seven moves

1 K—Kt2	P—R5
2 K—B3	P—R6
3 K—Q4	P—R4
4 K—K5	P—R5
5 K—B6!	P—Kt5
6 K—Kt7ch	K—R4
7 Kt—Kt3 mate	

WAINWRIGHT

GENTLY but firmly the Knight pushes the King to his doom.

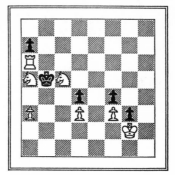

White mates in eight moves

1 Kt—B4	K×Kt
2 Kt—Q6	K—Q4
3 Kt—K4	K—K4
4 Kt—B6	K—B4
5 Kt—Kt4	K—Kt4
6 Kt—R6	K—R4
7 Kt—B7	K—R5
8 R—R6 mate	

4 Kt—B6ch	K—K5
5 Kt—Q6ch	K—B6
6 Kt—K5ch	K—Kt6
7 Kt—B5ch	K—R7
8 Kt—B3ch	K—R8
9 Kt—Kt3 mate	

BORDERS

THE KNIGHTS gallop joyously all over the chessboard.

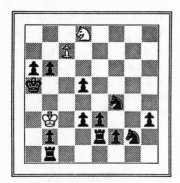

White mates in nine moves

1 P—B8(Kt)

Already threatening 2 Kt—Kt7ch, K—Kt4; 3 Kt—R7 mate.

1 . . .	K—Kt4
2 Kt—R7ch	K—B4
3 Kt—Kt7ch	K—Q5

BARRY

HINT: *Some great players thought the Ruy Lopez opening a sure way to force a win for White!*

White mates in three moves

1 P—K4	P—K4
2 Kt—KB3	Kt—QB3
3 B—Kt5 mate!	

Many a player has started with the Ruy Lopez opening, but how many have finished their games with it?

What's the Right Move?

1

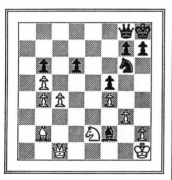

Black to play and mate on the move

2

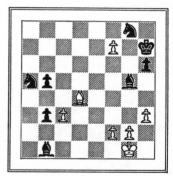

White to play and mate on the move

3

White to play and mate on the
move

4

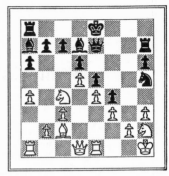

Black to play and mate on the
move

5

White to play and mate in two
moves

6

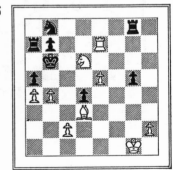

White to play and mate in two
moves

7

Black to play and mate in two moves

8

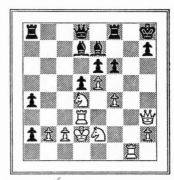

White to play and mate in two moves

9

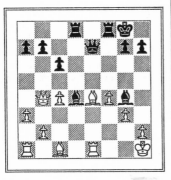

Black to play and mate in two moves

10

White to play and mate in two moves

11

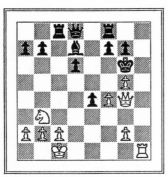

White to play and mate in two
moves

12

Black to play and mate in two
moves

13

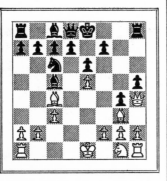

Black to play and win White's
Queen

14

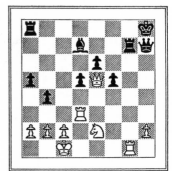

White to play and win Black's
Queen

15

White to play and win Black's Queen

16

White to play and win Black's Queen

"Don't look now, old man, but I think your opponent is setting a nifty trap for you!"

From Chess Magazine, by courtesy of the publisher, B. H. Wood, Sutton Coldfield, England.

"These guys who play chess by mail give me a pain in the neck!"

Part Three

CHESS AS IT IS PLAYED

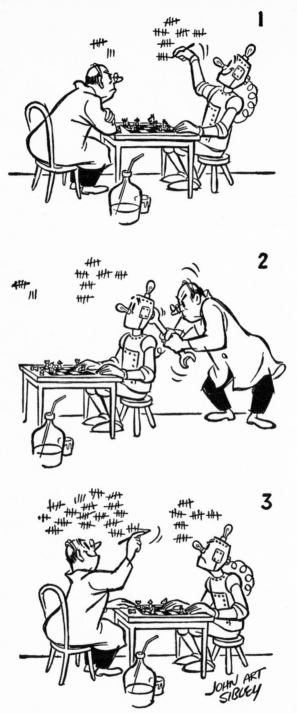

Cartoon by John A. Sibley, reprinted by special permission of *The Saturday Evening Post*. Copyright 1946 The Curtis Publishing Co.

Quickies

♛ CONCERT recitalists always begin with heavy fare and leave the frivolous encore pieces for the end of their performance. We have often wondered whether reversing the procedure might not immediately put an end to those restive fits of coughing and throat-clearing which invariably turn up about halfway through the playing, for example, of Bach's *Chaconne*.

Hence our first games are of the lightest imaginable sort, running to 21 moves or less. The play is delightfully lively, drastic and brilliant. Mistakes are punished at once in sparkling fashion. World champions forget their portentous problems and give us games that are just as playful as those of the most lighthearted amateur.

Brief as these games are, some of them have been greatly admired as classics of attacking play. Although they are offered for their sheer value as entertainment, their witty tactical devices will help you to improve your game even while they amuse you.

DEVELOPMENT *is not enough: it must be effective and efficient. The following game is one of the most drastic instances on record of the proper way to exploit faulty development.*

FRENCH DEFENSE
Odense, 1934

WHITE	BLACK
Blom	Jensen
1 P—K4	P—K3
2 P—Q4	P—Q4
3 Kt—QB3	P×P

This gives a cramped defense even with best play.

4 Kt×P	B—Q3?
5 B—Q3	Kt—K2?
6 B—Kt5	O—O?

Losing at once! White has developed in exemplary fashion and he now unleashes a crushing attack.

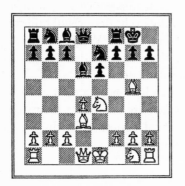

7 Kt—B6ch!!	P×Kt

If 7 . . . K—R1; 8 Q—R5, P—KR3; 9 B×P, P×Kt; 10 B—Kt5ch, K—Kt2; 11 Q—R7 mate.

8 B×P	Q—Q2

In order to be able to answer 9 Q—Kt4ch with 9 . . . Kt—Kt3. Too late!

9 B×Pch!!	Resigns

For after 9 . . . K×B there follows 10 Q—R5ch, K—Kt1; 11 Q—R8 mate. White forced through his attack in beautiful style.

ABRAHAMS *is a wayward player who likes unconventional openings. He discovers here that improvisation is a two-edged weapon.*

POLISH DEFENSE
Bournemouth, 1939

WHITE	BLACK
Euwe	Abrahams
1 P—Q4	P—QKt4?

A move with definite drawbacks and no positive values. It weakens the Queen-side and allows White to establish a powerful center.

2 P—K4	B—Kt2
3 P—KB3	P—QR3
4 P—QB4	P×P
5 B×P	

Threatening to win a piece by 6 Q—Kt3!

5 . . .	P—K3
6 Kt—B3	P—Q4

Losing at least a Pawn; but he has no good moves.

7 Q—Kt3!	

So that if 7 . . . P×B; 8 Q×B, Kt—Q2; 9 Q—B6 and Black loses a Pawn without compensation.

7 . . .	Kt—QB3?!

His game is so deeply compromised that he sees nothing left but sheer swindle. The idea is that if 8 Q×B??, Kt—R4; 9 B—Kt5ch (the only move left to save the Queen), K—K2!; 10 Kt×Pch, P×Kt and Black comes out a piece ahead!

8 P×P!   Kt×P?!

If 8 . . . Kt—R4; 9 Q—R4ch, P—B3; 10 P×KP and Black's game is in ruins.

9 Q×B!

For if 9 . . . Kt—B7ch; 10 K—B1, Kt×R; 11 P×P, P×P; 12 Q—B6ch and Black can resign.

9 . . .   R—Kt1

9 . . . B—B4 is a good try (threat: 10 . . . R—R2 winning the Queen!); 10 P×P! (so as to retreat the Queen to K4), Kt—KB3 (preventing the retreat); 11 Kt—Q5! If now 11 . . . R—R2; 12 Kt×Ktch and the Queen escapes; or 11 . . . Kt—B7ch; 12 K—B1, Kt×R; 13 Q—B6ch wins.

10 Q×RP   R—R1
11 B—Kt5ch   K—K2
12 P—Q6ch!   Resigns

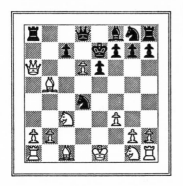

If 12 . . . P×P; 13 B—Kt5ch, P—B3 (or 13 . . . Kt—B3); 14 Q—

Kt7ch and mate next move! If 12 . . . K—B3; 13 P×P wins easily. If 12 . . . Q×P; 13 Q×R, Kt—B7ch; 14 K—B1, Kt×R; 15 B—Kt5ch! followed by 16 Q—K8 mate! Such games are rare in tournaments nowadays!

BLACK's cramped development makes a bad impression, but who would imagine that his resignation will come after six moves?

KING'S FIANCHETTO DEFENSE
Vienna, 1899

WHITE	BLACK
Hamlisch	*Amateur*
1 P—K4	P—Q3
2 P—Q4	Kt—Q2
3 B—QB4	P—KKt3
4 Kt—KB3	B—Kt2?

Natural—and fatal!

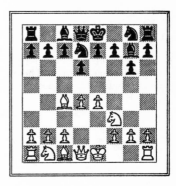

5 B×Pch!!   K×B

5 . . . K—B1 would drag out the game a bit.

6 Kt—Kt5ch   Resigns

If 6 . . . K—B3; 7 Q—B3 mate.

If 6 . . . K—K1; 7 Kt—K6 traps the Queen! And if 6 . . . K—B1; 7 Kt—K6ch wins the Queen.

As LONG as chess is played, this delightful game will continue to give pleasure to millions of readers.

DUTCH DEFENSE
London, 1912

WHITE	BLACK
Ed. Lasker	Thomas
1 P—Q4	P—KB4
2 Kt—KB3	P—K3
3 Kt—B3?	Kt—KB3

3 . . . P—Q4! makes it impossible for White to free himself with P—K4.

4 B—Kt5	B—K2
5 B×Kt	B×B
6 P—K4	P×P
7 Kt×P	P—QKt3
8 B—Q3	B—Kt2
9 Kt—K5	O—O
10 Q—R5!?	Q—K2?

Who can blame him for failing to see White's luscious sacrifice? The correct defense was 10 . . . B×Kt!; 11 P×B, R—B4!

11 Q×Pch!!!	K×Q
12 Kt×Bch	K—R3

If 12 . . . K—R1; 13 Kt—Kt6 mate! But now Black's King will be mated at KKt8!

13 Kt(5)—Kt4ch	K—Kt4
14 P—R4ch	

14 P—B4ch mates a move sooner.

14 . . .	K—B5
15 P—Kt3ch	K—B6
16 B—K2ch	K—Kt7
17 R—R2ch	K—Kt8
18 K—Q2 mate	

Or 18 O—O—O mate! This game is in the best tradition of skittles play.

THIS is what is known as "a typical Mieses game"—bright, short, deft, with several sacrifices; and all in eleven moves!

VIENNA GAME
Liverpool, 1900
(Simultaneous Exhibition)

WHITE	BLACK
Mieses	Amateur
1 P—K4	P—K4
2 Kt—QB3	Kt—KB3
3 B—B4	Kt×P
4 Q—R5	

Naturally 4 Kt×Kt, P—Q4 is too simple for his taste.

4 . . .	Kt—Q3
5 B—Kt3	B—K2
6 P—Q3	O—O?

Premature. 6 . . . Kt—B3; 7 Kt—B3, P—KKt3 is safer.

| 7 Kt—B3 | Kt—B3 |

8 Kt—KKt5!   P—KR3

If *8 . . . B×Kt; 9 B×B, Q—K1; 10 Kt—Q5* with the decisive double threat of *11 Kt×P* and *11 Kt—B6ch!*

9 P—KR4!

Mieses is in his element. He threatens *10 Q—Kt6!* (note the pin!), *P×Kt; 11 P×P, R—K1; 12 Q—R7ch, K—B1; 13 Q—R8* mate.

If Black tries *9 . . . P×Kt* now, then *10 P×P* followed by *11 Q—R8* mate.

9 . . .   Kt—K1
10 Kt—Q5!   Kt—B3

At last his King-side seems adequately protected. But now comes one of those lightning strokes for which Mieses is famous:

11 Q—Kt6!!!   Resigns

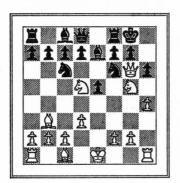

The threat is *12 Kt×Ktch, B×Kt; 13 Q—R7* mate.

If Black tries *11 . . . P×Kt;* then *12 Kt×Ktch, B×Kt; 13 P×P, R—K1; 14 Q×BP* mate.

But why not capture the Queen? In that case White answers *11 . . . P×Q* with *12 Kt×Bch, K—R1; 13 Kt×P* mate!

This game was played simultaneously with 20 other games!

THIS bright little game is a far cry from the usual run of tournament encounters.

BISHOP'S OPENING
Hamburg, 1905

WHITE	BLACK
Leonhardt	Schwarz

1	P—K4	P—K4
2	B—B4	Kt—KB3
3	P—Q3	B—K2?

3 . . . P—B3 (intending *. . . P—Q4*) is much better.

4	P—B4	P×P?
5	P—K5!	Kt—Kt1
6	Kt—QB3	P—Q3
7	B×P	P×P
8	Q—R5!	

With his huge lead in development, White can take liberties. If now *8 . . . P×B; 9 Q×Pch, K—Q2; 10 B—K6ch, K—B3; 11 B×B* winning easily.

8	. . .	P—KKt3
9	Q×KP	Kt—KB3
10	Kt—Q5	QKt—Q2
11	Kt×Pch	Resigns

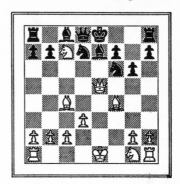

If *11 . . . K—B1* there is a pretty finish with *12 B—R6ch, K—Kt1; 13 B×Pch!, K×B; 14 Q—K6* mate!

THE moral of this game is: always watch out for the unexpected!

SICILIAN DEFENSE
Antwerp, 1932

WHITE	BLACK
Thomas	Sapira
1 P—K4	P—QB4
2 Kt—KB3	Kt—KB3
3 Kt—B3	P—Q4
4 P×P	Kt×P
5 B—Kt5ch	B—Q2
6 Kt—K5!	

This seems to lose a piece by 6 . . . Kt×Kt; 7 B×Bch, Kt×B etc.

6 . . .   Kt×Kt?

If Black had looked more deeply into the position, he would doubtless have played the safer 6 . . . Kt—KB3!

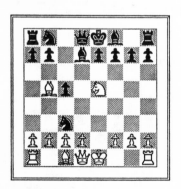

7 Q—B3!!

Threatens 8 Q×P mate.

7 . . .   P—B3

Realizing that after 7 . . . Q—B2; 8 B×Bch, Kt×B; 9 Q×Pch, K—Q1; 10 Kt×Kt he would have a hopeless game.

8 Q—R5ch   P—Kt3
9 Kt×P   K—B2

Avoiding the tragi-comic finish 9 . . . P×Kt; 10 Q×P mate!

10 Kt—K5ch!!   Resigns

If 10 . . . K—Kt2; 11 Q—B7ch, K—R3; 12 QP×Kt mate!
Or 10 . . . K—K3; 11 B—B4ch, Kt—Q4 (or 11 . . . K—Q3; 12 Kt—B7ch winning the Queen); 12 B× Ktch, K×B; 13 Kt—B7ch winning the Queen! A very attractive gamelet.

WHO said that close openings don't lead to brilliant games?

QUEEN'S GAMBIT DECLINED
Berlin, 1931

WHITE	BLACK
Nadel	Amateur
1 P—Q4	P—Q4
2 P—QB4	P—QB3
3 Kt—KB3	Kt—B3
4 Kt—B3	P×P
5 P—QR4	B—B4
6 Kt—K5	P—B4?

Apparently Black has forgotten the book line, which gives 6 . . . QKt—Q2 or 6 . . . P—K3.

7 P—K4!!

If Black disregards this inspired move and counterattacks with 7 . . . P×P? there follows 8 P×B, P×Kt; 9 Q×Qch, K×Q; 10 Kt×Pch winning a Rook.

7 . . .   Kt×P

The consequences of this move are grisly, but 7 . . . B×P loses by 8 Kt×B, Kt×Kt; 9 Q—B3!, Kt—Q3 (what else?); 10 B×P! (threatens 11

Q×Pch!), P—K3; *11* B—Kt5ch!, K—
K2; *12* P×P and the miserable Knight
cannot move!

8 Q—B3!   P×P

If *8* . . . Kt×Kt (or *8* . . . Kt—
Q3; 9 P×P winning a piece); 9 Q×B,
P—B3; *10* B×P!, P×Kt; *11* B—B7
mate!

9 Q×B   Kt—Q3

How should White answer this attack on his Queen?

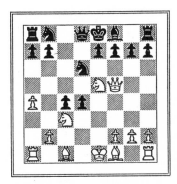

10 B×P!   P—K3

If he captures the Queen or the
Bishop, it is mate on the move.

11 B—Kt5ch   K—K2

If *11* . . . Kt—Q2 White simply
remains a piece ahead, by playing *12*
B×Ktch, Q×B; *13* Q—B4.

12 Kt—Kt6ch!!   RP×Kt
13 Kt—Q5ch!   P×Kt
14 Q—K5 mate!

SURPRISE *is still a deadly weapon in
chess. All the study in the world
cannot save a master from occa-
sional defeats like this one.*

DUTCH DEFENSE
Baden-Baden, 1925

WHITE	BLACK
Tartakover	Mieses
1 P—Q4	P—KB4
2 P—K4	P×P
3 Kt—QB3	Kt—KB3
4 P—KKt4!?	

This novel "bayonet attack" is a
departure from the more customary **4
B—KKt5**, as in Anderssen—Dufresne,
p. 308. *4* . . . P—KR3 is perhaps the
safest reply.

4 ...	P—Q4
5 P—Kt5	Kt—Kt1
6 P—B3!	P×P

Developing White's game, but after
6 . . . B—B4; 7 P×P, P×P; 8 B—
QB4 White has an attractive attacking game.

| 7 Q×P | P—K3 |
| 8 B—Q3 | P—KKt3 |

9 Q—R5ch was threatened. White
develops rapidly with an eye to crushing pressure on the King's Bishop file.

9 KKt—K2	Q—K2
10 B—KB4!	P—B3
11 B—K5!	B—Kt2
12 Q—Kt3!	Kt—QR3
13 O—O	B—Q2

The pressure is irresistible. Thus if
13 . . . Q—Q2; 14 R—B2, P—Kt3;
15 QR—KB1, B—Kt2; 16 R—B7,
Q×R; *17* R×Q, K×R; *18* B×B,
K×B; *19* Q—K5ch wins.

14 B—Q6   Q—Q1
15 Q—B4!   Resigns

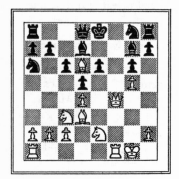

Black must lose at least a piece to parry the double threat of *16* Q—B7 mate or *16* Q—B8ch!, B×Q; *17* R×B mate. Many a King's Gambit does not yield so devastating an attack along the King's Bishop file!

EVADING *the book lines is always enjoyable; the consequences, as in this snappy little game, may be quite unpleasant.*

BISHOP'S OPENING
Team Match, 1925

WHITE	BLACK
Prokes	Zander
(Prague)	(Berlin)
1 P—K4	P—K4
2 B—B4	Kt—KB3
3 P—Q4	P×P
4 Kt—KB3	

A Pawn sacrifice for rapid development.

4 . . .   Kt×P
5 Q×P   Kt—Q3?

5 . . . Kt—KB3 is normal and good. The text is abnormal and bad.

6 O—O   Kt—B3

If *6 . . . Kt×B; 7* R—K1ch, B—K2; *8* Q×KtP, R—B1; *9* B—R6 forces the game.

Or if *6 . . .* Q—B3; *7* R—K1ch, B—K2 (not *7 . . .* K—Q1??; *8* B—KKt5 winning the Queen); *8* Q—Q3! (not *8* B—KKt5, Q×Q; *9* R×Bch, K—B1; *10* Kt×Q, P—KB3!), P—KR3; *10* Kt—B3, P—B3; *11* B—K3 (threatens B—Q4) and Black's game is untenable.

7 R—K1ch   Kt—K2
8 B—Kt3   P—KB3

The weakening of the diagonal is very disagreeable, but something must be done about the threat of *9* Kt—Kt5 and *10* Q×Kt!

9 Q—Q5   P—KKt4

Another ugly weakness, but White was threatening *10* B—KB4 and *11* B×Kt.

10 Kt×P!

Threatens *11* Q—B7ch!

10 . . .   P×Kt
11 B×P

196

Still threatening B—KB4 followed by B×Kt (or by Q—R5ch etc.).

11 . . .   P—KR3

So that if *12* B—KB4, R—R2.

12 Kt—B3!!   R—R2

If *12* . . . P×B; *13* Kt—K4!!, Kt×Q; *14* Kt×Kt mate!

13 Q—Kt8   P×B

If *13* . . . R—Kt2; *14* Kt—Q5!!, R×Q; *15* Kt—B6 mate!

14 Q×R   Resigns

He has no satisfactory way of parrying the threat of *15* Q—Kt6 mate. Grrr!

STEINITZ *made a point of insisting that the King is a fighting piece. But there are also times when the King is as helpless as a babe.*

RUY LOPEZ
Vienna, 1895?

WHITE	BLACK
Meitner	*Schlechter*
1 P—K4	P—K4
2 Kt—KB3	Kt—QB3
3 B—Kt5	P—QR3
4 B—R4	Kt—B3
5 Kt—B3	B—B4
6 O—O	

6 Kt×P!, Kt×Kt; 7 P—Q4 is the continuation which leaves White with the initiative.

6 . . .   P—QKt4
7 B—Kt3   P—Q3
8 P—Q3   B—KKt5
9 Kt—K2?

9 B—K3 is a better way to rule out

the dangers resulting from the threatened . . . Kt—Q5.

9 . . .   Q—Q2!
10 P—B3   B×Kt!
11 P×B   Q—R6!

Immediately exploiting the smashed-up state of White's King-side Pawns. Critical as White's position appears, who would imagine that his resignation will come in five moves?

12 Kt—Kt3   P—KR4!

With the fearful threat of *13* . . . Kt—KKt5!; *14* P×Kt, P×P (threatens mate); *15* R—K1, Q×Pch; *16* K—B1, Q×P mate.
White therefore protects his King's Bishop Pawn.

13 B—K3   P—R5!
14 Kt—R1

In a game Teichmann—Tarrasch, San Sebastian, 1912, Black now played *14* . . . B×B; *15* P×B, R—R3 and won on the 37th move. Yet an immediate decision is possible!

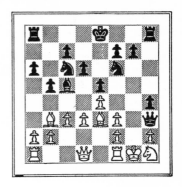

14 . . .   R—R3!!

One of those moves of pure genius which look obvious—after you see them! The text threatens *15* . . . R—Kt3ch winning at once.

15 B×R	P×B
Resigns	

Why? Because there is nothing to be done against the threatened 16 . . . K—K2! (so much venom in such a quiet move!) followed by 17 . . . R—Kt1ch and *finis*.

A SPARKLING *skittles game in which a mating idea leads to a series of brilliant sacrifices.*

RUY LOPEZ
Vienna, 1911

WHITE	BLACK
Wolf	Haas
1 P—K4	P—K4
2 Kt—KB3	Kt—QB3
3 B—Kt5	Kt—B3
4 O—O	Kt×P
5 P—Q4	Kt—Q3
6 B×Kt	KtP×B
7 P×P	Kt—Kt2
8 Kt—B3	B—K2
9 Kt—Q4	O—O
10 B—K3	P—QB4?

Very bad: he prevents his wretchedly stranded Knight from coming into play *via* QB4 and at the same time he lets in White's Knights.

11 Kt—B5	P—Q3
12 Kt×Bch	Q×Kt
13 Kt—Q5!	Q—Q1

After 13 . . . Q×P White gets a powerful game with 14 B—B4!

| 14 Q—R5 | R—K1 |
| 15 B—Kt5!!? | |

The simple 15 P×P etc. would have given him an overwhelming positional advantage, whereas the text,

brilliant as it is, allows Black an ingenious defensive resource.

| 15 . . . | R×P |
| 16 KR—K1! | |

Now we see why White permitted the pin: if 16 . . . R×B?; 17 Q×R!, Q×Q; 18 R—K8 mate.

| 16 . . . | P—KB3? |

Having noticed the variation just given, Black should have guarded his first rank with 16 . . . B—Kt5!; 17 Q×B, Q×B; 18 Q×Q, R×Q. Then, after 19 Kt×P Black could still put up a fight.

17 P—KB4!!

With two pieces attacked, this is the only way to keep the initiative (if 17 . . . R×Kt; 18 R—K8ch forces mate).

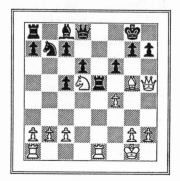

| 17 . . . | P—Kt3 |

Loses quickly; but if 17 . . . R—K3; 18 Kt×Pch!, P×Kt; 19 B—R6! and Black is helpless: 19 . . . R×Rch; 20 R×R, B—Q2; 21 Q—Q5ch; or 19 . . . P—B4; 20 R×R, B×R; 21 Q—B3!, P—Q4; 22 Q—Kt3ch; or 19 . . . Q—Q2; 20 Q—Kt4ch, K—R1 (if 20 . . . K—B2 White mates in two); 21 R×R and wins.

18 Q—R6   R×Kt
19 B×P!   Q—B1

19 . . . Q×B; 20 R—K8ch leads to mate next move.

20 R—K8!   Resigns

WHITE's *play shows some beautiful imaginative touches.*

PHILIDOR'S DEFENSE
(in effect)
Norway, 1928

WHITE	BLACK
Christoffersen	Loven
1 P—K4	P—K4
2 Kt—QB3	Kt—KB3
3 Kt—B3	P—Q3
4 P—Q4	B—Kt5?
5 P×P	B×Kt
6 Q×B	P×P
7 B—Kt5	B—Kt5
8 R—Q1	Q—K2
9 B—QB4	QKt—Q2
10 O—O	

Black has played the opening poorly, and no matter how he continues, he will be under severe pressure. At this point he must do something about White's intended Kt—Q5.

10 . . .   B×Kt

Anticipating 11 P×B (11 Q×B is obviously unsatisfactory) after which Black has at least succeeded in weakening his opponent's Pawn structure.

11 Q×B!

Difference of opinion makes horse races . . . and chess games. The text may *look* "obviously unsatisfactory," but there is a deep plan behind it.

11 . . .   Kt×P?

Expecting 12 B×Q, Kt×Q; 13 P×Kt, K×B; 14 B×P when White has equality at best.

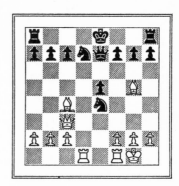

12 R×Kt!!

A move as beautiful as it is unexpected. The first point is that if 12 . . . Kt×Q; 13 R×Qch followed by 14 R×BPch and 15 P×Kt with an easy win. Or if 12 . . . Q×R; 13 Q×Pch, K—B1; 14 Q×Kt, again with an easy win. Finally, if 12 . . . K×R?; 13 Q—R3ch! wins the Queen!

12 . . .   Q×B
13 Q—Q3!   Kt—Q3

The Knight fork 13 . . . Kt—B4 fails because of 14 B×Pch, K—B1; 15 Q—QR3, P—QKt3; 16 R×P winning quickly.

14 R×QBP	R—Q1
15 P—B4!	P×P
16 R—K1ch	K—B1
17 Q×Ktch!!	Resigns

If 17 . . . R×Q; 18 R×Pch, K—Kt1; 19 R—K8 mate. The White Queen has done everything but turn somersaults!

WHITE develops complacently—and carelessly. An unexpected Knight fork shatters his illusions.

KING'S INDIAN DEFENSE

Hastings Christmas Tournament,
1925–1926

WHITE	BLACK
Norman	Vidmar
1 P—Q4	Kt—KB3
2 P—QB4	P—KKt3
3 Kt—QB3	B—Kt2
4 Kt—B3	O—O
5 P—K4	P—Q3
6 B—Q3?	

The Bishop is misplaced here.

6 . . .	B—Kt5
7 P—KR3	B×Kt
8 Q×B	Kt—B3
9 B—K3	Kt—Q2!
10 Kt—K2?	

10 P—Q5 was absolutely essential, but White is reluctant to open up the fianchettoed Bishop's diagonal. He is thinking about strategy and forgets all about tactics.

10 . . .	Kt(3)—K4!!

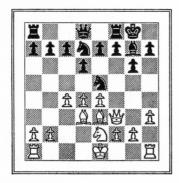

11 P×Kt	Kt×P

12 Q—Kt3	Kt×Bch
13 K—B1	P—QB4
14 P—KR4	

In the realization that he has a lost game, White begins an attacking gesture which Black turns to his own advantage.

14 . . .	Q—Q2
15 P—R5	Q—K3!
16 R—R4	Q×BP
17 P×P	BP×P!
18 Q—R3?	Kt×BP!
19 B×Kt	B—Q5
Resigns	

An instructive position. White's Bishop and Knight are pinned, and 20 R—B4? simply loses the Rook.

MARSHALL's dashing play often fails to impress us on sober second thought. But refuting his flashy moves over the board is something else again!

GIUOCO PIANO

Ostend, 1905
(Second Brilliancy Prize)

WHITE	BLACK
Marshall	Burn
1 P—K4	P—K4
2 Kt—KB3	Kt—QB3
3 B—B4	B—B4
4 P—B3	Kt—B3
5 P—Q4	P×P
6 P×P	B—Kt5ch
7 K—B1?!	

Typical Marshall. The move looks bad enough (loss of the castling privilege) to tempt the usually stolid Burn to grab a Pawn, instead of getting the better game with 7 . . . P—Q4!

7 . . .	Kt×KP?
8 P—Q5	Kt—K2
9 Q—Q4	Kt—KB3
10 B—KKt5	Kt—Kt3
11 QKt—Q2	P—KR3?

Attempting to shake off the pressure, he runs into a catastrophe.

12 R—K1ch	K—B1

If 12 . . . B—K2; 13 B×Kt, P×B; 14 P—Q6!, P×P; 15 Q×BP, R—B1; 16 Kt—K4!! and wins.

13 B—Q3!	B—K2
14 B(Q3)×Kt	RP×B

No better is 14 . . . BP×B; 15 Kt—K5!, Q—K1; 16 Q—Q3! etc.

15 Kt—K5!!

A beautiful move which forces Black's reply.

15 . . .	P×B
16 Kt×KtPch	K—B2
17 R×Bch	K×Kt

Giving up the Queen loses a bit more slowly.

18 Q—Q3ch	K—R3

Now Black seems safe. If 18 . . . K—R4; 19 R×KtP wins right off.

19 P—KR4!!	P—Kt5

Or 19 . . . Q×R; 20 P×Pch, K×P; 21 Kt—B3ch, K—Kt5 (if 21 . . . K—B5; 22 P—Kt3ch, K—Kt5; 23 Q—Kt6ch, K×Kt; 24 Q—B5 mate); 22 Q—Kt6ch, K—B5; 23 P—Kt3ch, K×Kt; 24 Q—B5 mate!

20 P—R5!!	Kt×P
21 Q—B5	Resigns

The only move is 21 . . . P—Kt3, allowing 22 R×Ktch!, P×R; 23 Q—B6 mate! A real Marshall game!

PAWN-GRABBING, *like sin, cannot be abolished by fiat.*

FRENCH DEFENSE
Riga, 1913

WHITE	BLACK
Nimzovich	Alapin
1 P—K4	P—K3
2 P—Q4	P—Q4
3 Kt—QB3	Kt—KB3
4 P×P	Kt×P
5 Kt—B3	P—QB4
6 Kt×Kt	Q×Kt
7 B—K3!	

The emphasis of Nimzovich's play is on development.

7 . . .	P×P
8 Kt×P	P—QR3
9 B—K2!	Q×KtP?
10 B—B3	Q—Kt3
11 Q—Q2	

Nimzovich just keeps developing—something must come of it!

11 . . .	P—K4

Black cannot form a constructive plan. To play for King-side castling is out of the question, in view of the open King's Knight file.

12 O—O—O!! P×Kt
13 B×QP Kt—B3

Else White plays 14 B×KKtP! threatening 15 Q—Q8 mate.

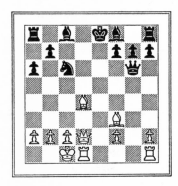

14 B—B6!! Q×B

There is no salvation for Black, 14 ... P×B or 14 ... B—K3 or 14 ... B—K2 being answered by 15 B×Ktch with mate to follow.

15 KR—K1ch B—K2

If 15 ... Kt—K4; 16 R×Ktch! or 15 ... B—K3; 16 Q—Q7 mate.

16 B×Ktch K—B1

The position is a nest of mating possibilities. If 16 ... B—Q2 (on 16 ... Q×B or 16 ... P×B; 17 Q—Q8 mate); 17 Q×Bch, K—B1; 18 Q—Q8ch! leads to mate.

17 Q—Q8ch!! B×Q
18 R—K8 mate

This sparkling game compares favorably with any played by Morphy!

As a youngster, Alekhine worshiped the games of his great forerunner Tchigorin. One of the most obvious links between these immortals is their uncanny skill in handling the Knight.

SICILIAN DEFENSE
St. Petersburg, 1912

WHITE	BLACK
Potemkin	Alekhine
1 P—K4	P—QB4
2 P—KKt3	P—KKt3
3 B—Kt2	B—Kt2
4 Kt—K2	Kt—QB3
5 P—QB3	Kt—B3
6 Kt—R3?	

Badly timed. The opening is worth comparison with that of Tartakover—Broadbent, p. 307. There Tartakover succeeds brilliantly; here Potemkin fails miserably.

6 ...	P—Q4!
7 P×P	Kt×P
8 Kt—B2	O—O
9 P—Q4	P×P
10 P×P	B—Kt5
11 P—B3	B—B4

Playing with his customary energy, Alekhine has a clear initiative. He now threatens to win the isolated Queen's Pawn by 12 ... B×Kt etc.

12 Kt—K3 Q—R4ch!
13 K—B2

If 13 B—Q2? (or 13 Q—Q2?), Kt×Kt! wins a piece!

13 ... Kt(4)—Kt5!

With troublesome threats of ... Kt—Q6ch or ... B—Q6.

14 Kt×B Q×Kt

15 P—Kt4

An ingenious idea: if now 15 . . . Kt—Q6ch; 16 K—Kt3, Q—QKt4; 17 Kt—B3 followed by 18 B—B1 and Black's exposed Knight will go lost.

15 . . .   Kt—Q6ch!!

A blunder in appearance, this move is actually the prelude to a charming combination.

16 K—Kt3

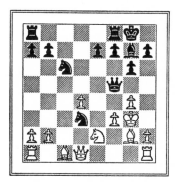

16 . . .   Kt×QP!!
17 P×Q

"Better" is 17 Kt×Kt, Q—K4ch and Black is bound to win in a few moves.

17 . . .   Kt×Pch

Alekhine announced mate in two: 18 K—Kt4 (if 18 K—R3, Kt—B7 mate—a pure mate!), P—R4ch; 19 K—R3, Kt—B7 mate or 19 K—Kt5, B—R3 mate (or 19 . . . B—B3 mate).

Is IT not a tribute to the inexhaustibility of chess that such a stunning combination is possible as early as the eighth move?

CENTER GAME
Leipzig, 1903

WHITE	BLACK
Amateur	Swiderski
1 P—K4	P—K4
2 P—Q4	P×P
3 Q×P	Kt—QB3
4 Q—K3	Kt—B3
5 B—B4	Kt—K4
6 B—Kt3	B—Kt5ch
7 P—B3	

Always develop when possible! 7 Kt—B3 or 7 B—Q2 was in order.

7 . . .   B—B4!

This sets two traps, one of which is 8 Q×B??, Kt—Q6ch winning the Queen. White sees this, but misses the other trap:

8 Q—Kt3??   B×Pch!!
Resigns

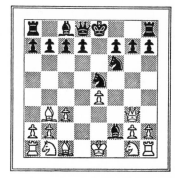

If 9 Q×B, Kt—Q6ch; if 9 K×B, Kt×Pch. White must capture the Bishop, but loses the Queen in either case!

In UNORTHODOX positions, a bold leap into the unknown is often safer than routine "secure" moves.

KING'S INDIAN DEFENSE
London Team Tournament, 1927

WHITE	BLACK
Palau	Te Kolste
(Argentina)	(Holland)

1	Kt—KB3	Kt—KB3
2	P—Q4	P—KKt3
3	Kt—B3	P—Q4
4	B—B4	Kt—KR4
5	B—K5!	P—KB3
6	B—Kt3	Kt×B
7	RP×Kt	B—Kt2

Black has the two Bishops, but in return he has had to weaken his Pawn position and allow White some attacking chances on the King's Rook file.

8	P—K3	P—B3
9	B—Q3	P—K4?!

Apparently played without any thought of White's dashing reply.

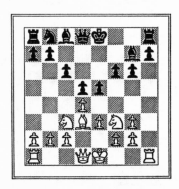

10	R×P!	K—B2?

Correct was 10 . . . P—K5!; 11 R×Rch (stronger than 11 R×B, P×B when Black threatens . . . R—R8

ch), B×R; 12 Kt×KP, P×Kt; 13 B×P, P—KB4; 14 B—Q3 with about even chances.

11	B×Pch!!	K×B
12	Kt×Pch!!	P×Kt

If 12 . . . K×R; 13 Q—R5ch, K—Kt1 (or 13 . . . B—R3; 14 Q—Kt6 mate); 14 Q—B7ch, K—R2; 15 O—O—O and mate follows.

13	Q—R5ch	K—B3
14	Q×Pch	K—B2

Or 14 . . . K—Kt3; 15 Q×Bch, K—B4; 16 P—Kt4ch, K—K3; 17 Q—K5 mate.

15	Q×Bch	K—K3
16	Q—K5 mate	

THE old, old story: slow development in an open game leads to disaster.

KING'S GAMBIT
(in effect)
Oslo, 1928

WHITE	BLACK
Hansen	Lundin

1	P—K4	P—K4
2	Kt—QB3	Kt—QB3
3	P—B4	P×P
4	Kt—B3	Kt—B3
5	P—Q4	P—Q4
6	P×P	KKt×P
7	Kt×Kt	Q×Kt
8	B×P?	

White rushes to recover the gambit Pawn, realizing that if 8 . . . Q—K5ch; 9 Q—K2 saves the menaced Bishop. But 8 P—B4!, driving away the Queen from her dominating centralized position, is far better.

| 8 . . . | B—Kt5! |
| 9 B—K2 | O—O—O |

Threatening to win the Queen's Pawn.

| 10 P—B3 | Q—K5! |

A troublesome move: if *11 B—Kt3, R—K1; 12 K—B2* (trying to castle), *Q—K6ch* and White will have difficulty disentangling himself.

11 Q—Q2

This promises to be satisfactory, as *11 . . . R—K1* is to be answered by *12 K—B2* and *13 KR—K1.*

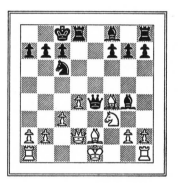

| 11 . . . | R×P!! |

Beautiful play! If now *12 P×R, B—Kt5* wins the Queen.

| 12 Kt×R | Kt×Kt |

Threatening . . . *Kt—B7ch* in addition to . . . *Kt×B.*

| 13 P×Kt | B—Kt5! |

Winning the Queen after all!

14 K—B2	B×Q
15 B×Bch	P—B4
16 B×B	P×B
17 KR—K1	Q×QPch

18 B—K3	Q×Pch
19 K—B1	R—K1
Resigns	

WE ARE accustomed to appraising opening variations for their strategical values. It is easy to forget that the slightest inexactitude will often transform an acceptable line into a tempest of tactical complications.

QUEEN'S GAMBIT DECLINED
Dallas, 1942

WHITE	BLACK
H. Steiner	Thompson
1 Kt—KB3	P—Q4
2 P—Q4	Kt—KB3
3 P—B4	P—K3
4 Kt—B3	P—B4
5 BP×P	Kt×P
6 P—K4	Kt×Kt
7 P×Kt	

Black should now simplify further with *7 . . . P×P; 8 P×P, B—Kt5ch; 9 B—Q2, B×Bch* which leaves him with a comfortable game.

| 7 . . . | Kt—B3? |
| 8 P—Q5! | Kt—K2? |

Even *8 . . . P×P; 9 P×P, Kt—K2* leaves him with an inferior position; but the text is disastrous.

| 9 B—Kt5ch! | B—Q2 |
| 10 B×Bch | Q×B |

If *10 . . . K×B; 11 Kt—K5ch, K—K1; 12 Q—R4ch* wins a piece.

| 11 Kt—K5! | Q—Kt4 |

There is no good move: if *11 . . . Q—B2; 12 P—Q6* wins; or if *11 . . .*

Q—B1; *12* Q—R4ch or *12* P—Q6 etc.

12 P×P!   P×P

Amusing would be *12* . . . R—Q1; *13* P×P mate! If *12* . . . P—B3 White wins as in the text.

13 QR—Kt1!   Resigns

Black's Queen has no moves, and if *13* . . . R—Q1; *14* Q×Rch etc. All very instructive!

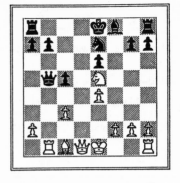

The Hand Is Quicker Than
the Mind

♛ WHEN you see how quickly and incisively oversights are exploited in these games, you may say to yourself: "Why do they blunder? The refutations are so obvious. Why do they overlook them?" Why, indeed?

Every player has at some time or other reflected with wonderment on the remarkable co-ordination of brain, eye and hand. The player studies the position—visually and mentally. He decides on a move; his brain sends a message to his hand, which accordingly plays the indicated move.

The automatic perfection of this process fills us with awe. Suppose the process were to fail someday? Excitement, fatigue, nervousness, time pressure—all these are possible reasons for breakdown in the functioning of the automatic mechanism.

There are, of course, other reasons for oversights. Sometimes a player becomes so deeply absorbed in a certain possibility that he quite overlooks something else which is all too obvious (to his opponent!). Sometimes he calculates accurately just what he wants to do, and yet, as he reaches out his hand to move, he capriciously decides on some other, totally unexplored move. This second choice may even be fatal; yet it is so insidiously attractive that he cannot control himself long enough to take a second look. Finally, there is the case of a player who sees that a given move is bad, forgets why it is bad, and eventually plays it. Of course, no sooner does he play the move than he immediately recollects why it is inferior! Many an important game has been decided in this unfortunate manner.

But in all these cases, the hand cannot evaluate the moves; it can only make them as instructed—be they good, bad, or indifferent.

It took two players to lose this gamelet!

FROM GAMBIT
Hastings, 1897

WHITE	BLACK
Bird	Gunsberg
Dobell	Locock

1 P—KB4	P—K4
2 P×P	P—Q3
3 P×P	B×P
4 Kt—KB3	P—KKt4
5 P—B3?	

5 P—Q4 is the move.

5 . . .	P—Kt5
6 Q—R4ch	Kt—B3

If 6 . . . B—Q2; 7 Q—Q4.

7 Kt—Q4	Q—R5ch
8 K—Q1	P—Kt6
9 P—Kt3??	Q×P!

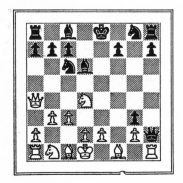

White resigns, for if 10 R×Q, P×R; 11 Kt×Kt, P—R8(Q). Black is the exchange ahead and must win a piece, for example 12 K—K1, B—Kt6ch; or 12 Kt—Q4ch, B—Q2; or 12 Kt—K5ch, K—B1; 13 Q—KB4, B×Kt.

Chess traps are particularly fascinating when they raise the problem of who is to laugh last!

NIMZOINDIAN DEFENSE
Antwerp, 1934

WHITE	BLACK
Dyner	Walter

1 P—Q4	Kt—KB3
2 P—QB4	P—K3
3 Kt—QB3	B—Kt5
4 Q—Kt3	P—B4
5 P—QR3	Q—R4

Taking advantage of the fact that White is momentarily unable to play 6 P×B.

However, Black would have been better off with 5 . . . B×Ktch or 5 . . . P×P.

6 B—Q2	Kt—B3
7 Q—Q1!	

Refutes Black's idea, as there is nothing better than 7 . . . B×Kt; 8 B×B, Q—Q1; 9 P—Q5 with a splendid game for White.

7 . . .	Kt×P?

Setting a trap: if 8 P×B?, Q×R!; 9 Q×Q, Kt—B7ch and Black comes out the exchange ahead.

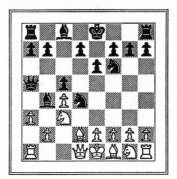

8 P—K3!   Resigns

He must lose a piece, for if the attacked Knight retreats, then 9 P×B is feasible. If, however, 8 . . . B×Kt; 9 B×B attacking Queen and Knight and still winning a piece!

THIS defense has fine points which even Nimzovich didn't suspect!

NIMZOINDIAN DEFENSE

Correspondence, 1935

WHITE	BLACK
Hansen	Jensen
1 P—Q4	P—K3
2 P—QB4	Kt—KB3
3 Kt—QB3	B—Kt5
4 Q—Kt3	P—B4
5 P×P	Kt—B3
6 Kt—B3	Kt—K5
7 B—Q2	Kt×B
8 Kt×Kt	

So far all according to Hoyle and Nimzovich. But here Black deviates:

8 . . .   Q—R4

This can be satisfactorily answered by 9 P—K3 or 9 Kt(2)—K4, but it does have one tricky feature—and it is just this feature which White overlooks.

9 O—O—O?   Kt—Q5!
Resigns

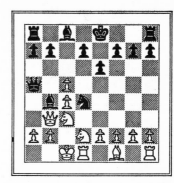

White's Queen has only one flight square: to R4. But after 10 Q—R4, B×Kt! Black wins a piece!

THIS really happened in a tournament game!

BUDAPEST DEFENSE

Philadelphia, 1936

WHITE	BLACK
Arnold	Hanauer
1 P—Q4	Kt—KB3
2 P—QB4	P—K4
3 P—Q5	

This gives Black a fine square for his King's Bishop at B4. The obvious move 3 P×P is best.

3 . . .   B—B4
4 B—Kt5??   Kt—K5!!

If now 5 B—K3, B×B; 6 P×B,

Q—R5ch and wins. But White prefers to end it all.

5 B×Q   B×P mate

PAWN-GRABBING *is expected and normal in skittles games. In tournament play, however, it comes as a surprise.*

CARO-KANN DEFENSE

U. S. Open Championship, 1946

WHITE	BLACK
Adams	Kramer
1 P—K4	P—QB3
2 P—Q4	P—Q4
3 P—K5	B—B4
4 B—Q3	B×B
5 Q×B	P—K3

Black has an easy game and can develop without difficulty.

6 Kt—K2	P—QB4
7 P—QB3	Kt—K2

7 . . . Q—Kt3 is simple and safe, but the text sets an amusing trap.

8 Q—Kt5ch?	Q—Q2
9 Q×BP??	Kt—B4

White has only one move: 10 Q—R5—but then 10 . . . P—QKt3! and the trap snaps shut. White resigned.

How many moves does it take to lose a game of chess?

FRENCH DEFENSE

Hastings, 1947

WHITE	BLACK
Van Steenis	Wechsler
1 P—K4	P—K3
2 P—Q4	P—Q4
3 Kt—QB3	B—Kt5
4 P×P	Q×P

4 . . . P×P gives a much easier game.

5 Q—Kt4

An awkward move to meet; Black decides on a Pawn sacrifice.

5 . . .	Kt—K2
6 Q×KtP	Q—K5ch??
7 K—Q1!!	Resigns

Black must lose a Rook: 7 . . . R—Kt1; 8 Q×Rch or 7 . . . B×Kt; 8 Q×Rch etc.

Blindfold Games

♛ BLINDFOLD chess requires a combination of several remarkable qualities. The most obvious is a vivid imagination: right at the start, a player must be able to visualize the 32 pieces as they are placed on the board of 64 squares. From then on he must keep track of the changes, some of them far-reaching, that occur from move to move.

The blindfold player must of course have a tenacious, infallible memory. If one little detail is "blacked out," the whole mental picture of the game is spoiled. He must have the ability to concentrate: let his attention wander for a while, and God knows what may come into his mind instead of that chessboard with its numerous pieces jumbled haphazardly in every sector.

How much does a blindfold player have to "see"? If he "sees" all the board and chessmen as one composite image at any given stage, and the game goes 35 moves, that means that while the game is in progress, he must "see"—and remember perfectly!—70 such images! Now, if he plays 30 games simultaneously, and we again assume 35 moves to be the average length, we find that he has to deal with 2100 such images during an exhibition. And at any given moment he must keep 30 images in mind at the same time. Of course, as the number of games gradually tapers off, he has less to think about; but on the other hand, fatigue begins to tell on him.

So expert are the geniuses of blindfold play that at the end of a performance they are able to rattle off all the moves of every game, in their exact order, with the most astonishing glibness! It sometimes happens during an exhibition that there is a dispute as to the correct position in one of the games. In such cases, the blindfold player will settle the matter conclusively by calling out all the previous moves; it will be found that he is right, and that his opponent, moving the men on the board, is wrong!

How do they do it? So far we have had no wholly satisfactory explanation: the blindfold artist, like the magician, keeps his trade secrets to himself.

Most of us would be happy indeed to play this well over the board!

FRENCH DEFENSE
Tarnopol, 1916

WHITE	BLACK
Alekhine	*Feldt*
1 P—K4	P—K3
2 P—Q4	P—Q4
3 Kt—QB3	Kt—KB3
4 P×P	Kt×P
5 Kt—K4	P—KB4?

A typical inexperienced player's blunder: he leaves a permanently backward Pawn at K3 and a hole at K4.

6 Kt—Kt5	B—K2
7 Kt(5)—B3	P—B3?
8 Kt—K5	O—O
9 KKt—B3	P—QKt3
10 B—Q3	B—Kt2
11 O—O	R—K1

Black's development is necessarily limited to very conservative moves. White, on the other hand, has the makings of an overwhelming position.

12 P—B4	Kt—B3
13 B—B4	QKt—Q2
14 Q—K2	P—B4

This perfectly natural move allows a superb finish; but after *14 . . . Kt—B1; 15 QR—Q1* Black would certainly have had nothing to hope for.

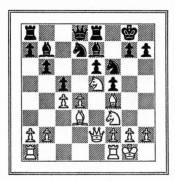

15 Kt—B7!!	K×Kt

Or *15 . . . Q—B1; 16 Q×P, B—B1; 17 Kt—R6ch, K—R1; 18 Q—Kt8ch!, Kt×Q; 19 Kt—B7 mate!*

16 Q×Pch!!!

The even more electrifying sequel to the first sacrifice! If *16 . . . K×Q; 17 Kt—Kt5 mate* (!). If *16 . . . K—B1; 17 Kt—Kt5* is decisive.

16 . . .	K—Kt3
17 P—KKt4!	B—K5
18 Kt—R4 mate	

This beautiful game, played in an exhibition at a military hospital, calls to mind Sergeant's description of a famous Morphy game: a Damascus blade cutting a silken cushion.

It is a far cry from Philidor's timid essays in blindfold play to Naidorf's superb feat in playing forty-five blindfold games simultaneously. The following game was contested in that record-smashing exhibition.

ENGLISH OPENING
São Paulo, 1947

WHITE	BLACK
Naidorf	Allies
1 P—QB4	P—K4
2 Kt—QB3	Kt—QB3
3 Kt—B3	P—Q3
4 P—Q4	P×P
5 Kt×P	Kt×Kt?
6 Q×Kt	P—QR3?

Naidorf has been presented with almost complete control of the center—an advantage which he proceeds to augment with his customary assured technique.

7 P—KKt3	Kt—B3
8 B—Kt2	P—KKt3
9 P—Kt3	B—Kt2
10 B—Kt2	O—O
11 P—KR4!	

White has all the play and does not yield a single option. Instead of automatically playing 11 O—O, he prepares to open the King's Rook file.

| 11 . . . | Kt—Q2 |
| 12 Q—Q2 | Kt—B4 |

He should prevent, or at least post-pone, the opening of the file by playing 12 . . . P—KR4.

13 P—R5	P—R4
14 P×P	BP×P
15 B—Q5ch	Kt—K3
16 Kt—K4!	

The removal of Black's guardian Bishop at Kt2 will strengthen White's attack.

| 16 . . . | B×B |
| 17 Q×B | P—B3 |

His desire to drive off the annoying Bishop is quite natural, but careful defense is now called for.

| 18 B×Ktch | B×B |
| 19 O—O—O | Q—Kt3? |

Missing the point. 19 . . . P—Q4 was better.

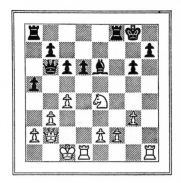

20 R×RP!!

Considering the magnitude of Naidorf's task, one can only marvel at the rapidity with which he observes that the absence of the Queen makes a mating combination possible!

20 . . .	K×R
21 R—R1ch	K—Kt1
22 R—R8ch	K—B2
23 Q—B6ch	

Now we see why Black's Queen move was bad.

23 . . .	K—K1
24 R×Rch	K—Q2
25 Q—Kt7ch	B—B2
26 Q×B mate	

Duration of the game: fourteen and a half hours! This may explain why Naidorf missed the quicker 24 Q×R ch, K—Q2; 25 Q×P mate.

"IN DIFFICULT positions," we read in the Book of the Hastings, 1895, Tournament, "Tchigorin gets very excited, and at times seems quite fierce, sitting at the board with his black hair brushed back, splendid black eyes, and flushed face looking as if he could see right through the table. When calm, however, he is decidedly handsome, and calculated to beget confidence."

TWO KNIGHTS' DEFENSE
St. Petersburg, 1885

WHITE	BLACK
Arnold	Tchigorin
1 P—K4	P—K4
2 Kt—KB3	Kt—QB3
3 B—B4	Kt—B3
4 Kt—Kt5	P—Q4
5 P×P	Kt—QR4

Himself a master of attack, Tchigorin does not find the "Fried Liver" (5 . . . Kt×P; 6 Kt×BP?!) a palatable dish.

6 B—Kt5ch	P—B3
7 P×P	P×P
8 B—K2	P—KR3

9 Kt—KB3	P—K5
10 Kt—K5	Q—B2
11 P—KB4	B—Q3
12 P—Q4	O—O
13 O—O	P—B4!

Just the kind of position that Tchigorin loved: he is a Pawn down, but he has a fine development, and open lines are a dime a dozen.

| 14 P—B3 | R—Kt1! |

So that if 15 Kt—Q2, P×P; 16 P×P, R—Kt5; 17 Kt—Kt3, Kt×Kt; 18 P×Kt, R×QP!

| 15 Kt—R3 | P×P |
| 16 Kt—Kt5 | |

Avoiding 16 P×P, B×QKt; 17 P×B, Q—B6! etc. But now he runs into a typical Tchigorin attack.

| 16 . . . | R×Kt! |
| 17 B×R | Q—Kt3 |

Now the attacked Bishop must not move, because of 18 . . . P×Pch followed by 19 . . . P×P.

18 P—QR4	P—Q6ch
19 K—R1	P—R3!
20 Kt—B4	Kt×Kt
21 B×Kt	B—KKt5
22 P—R5	Q—R2

23 Q—R4	B—K7
24 R—K1	Kt—Kt5
25 P—R3	Q—B7!

The rapid succession of threats is typical of Tchigorin's aggressive style.

| 26 B—Q2 | B—B4! |

Threatening to win at once with 27 . . . Q—Kt6! White's desperate reply is refuted in the most elegant manner.

27 B×Pch?!	R×B!
28 Q—K8ch	K—R2!
29 Q×R	Q×Pch!!

Black announces mate in two: 30 K×Q, B—B6ch; 31 K—Kt3, B—B7 mate or 31 K—B1, Kt—R7 mate! This was played simultaneously with nine other games. Tchigorin did not see through the table, but he saw through his opponent!

In this brilliant little game there are no less than four Queen sacrifices!—three declined, one accepted.

BISHOP'S OPENING
Odessa, 1918

WHITE	BLACK
Gonssiorovsky	*Alekhine*
1 P—K4	P—K4
2 B—B4	Kt—KB3
3 P—Q3	P—B3!
4 Q—K2	B—K2
5 P—B4	P—Q4!

Energetic play.

6 KP×P	KP×P
7 B×P	O—O
8 Kt—Q2	

With his King and Queen on the same open line, White does not care to win a Pawn with 8 P×P.

8 . . .	P×P
9 B—QKt3	P—QR4!
10 P—B3?	P—R5
11 B—B2	P—R6!
12 P—QKt3	R—K1!

This wins at least a Pawn because of the threatened . . . B—Q3.

13 O—O—O	B—QKt5
14 Q—B2	B×P
15 B—Kt5	Kt—B3
16 KKt—B3	P—Q5!

The weakness of White's black squares gives Alekhine an idea: he senses the mating possibilities!

| 17 KR—K1 | B—Kt7ch |
| 18 K—Kt1 | Kt—Q4!! |

Threatens . . . Kt—B6 mate!

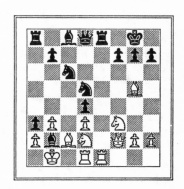

19 R×Rch

If 19 Kt—K4, R×Kt!

| 19 . . . | Q×R |
| 20 Kt—K4 | Q×Kt!! |

Still harping on the idea of . . . Kt—B6 mate.

21 B—Q2   Q—K6!!

More of the same.

22 R—K1?!

It's contagious!

22 . . .   B—B4!

But not 22 . . . Q×Q??; 23 R—K8 mate.

23 R×Q   P×R

If now 24 Q×P, Kt×Q and White is a Rook down; or 24 B×P, Kt—B6 mate as usual. Alekhine is pitiless in exploiting the black squares.

24 Q—B1

Alekhine announced mate in three: 24 . . . P×B; 25 B—Q1, Kt(3)—Kt5! followed by 26 . . . Kt—B6 mate. This game was one of a set of six, played simultaneously.

THE RULING PASSION

"Eureka!"

From *Chess* Magazine, by courtesy of the publisher, B. H. Wood, Sutton Coldfield, England.

Odds Games

♛ ODDS-GIVING *is* an art. There is something about removing the Queen's Knight or Queen's Rook or . . . even the Queen (!) from the board that fills most players with horror. This antipathy toward odds-giving doubtless arises instinctively: the lopsided material relationship is such a radical negation of the justice and equality that prevail at the beginning of the game. In ordinary games, both players start off on even terms, and may the best man win: therein lies the great charm of chess as a sporting encounter.

Yet all this is exaggeration: for the lopsidedness which prevails in the material realm of odds-giving is but an attempt to redress a different kind of inequality: that between the *stronger* and the *weaker* player. But if the odds are extended on a rational basis and if the odds-giver is truly the stronger player, his skill will more than compensate for the missing material. If, on the other hand, the odds-giver is merely a boastful bully, the odds will cut him down to size.

Why do we say that odds-giving is an art? Because it calls for specific abilities; for self-confidence; for self-knowledge. The odds-giver must be a master of the "calculated risk." He must know just how far he can go with his opponent; he must be a gambler, but a dispassionate one; he must be a fatalist who knows infallibly that the weaker player will inevitably blunder, yet he must be active enough to push his opponent into the blunder. The highest art of all is to play creatively, undismayed by the lacking material.

THE low level of defensive technique which was prevalent in their day gave the great nineteenth-century masters many opportunities for brilliant odds play. To Zukertort goes the honor of producing the finest finish in this type of contest.

ODDS OF QUEEN'S KNIGHT *
Berlin, 1874

WHITE	BLACK
Zukertort	Epoureano
1 P—KB4	P—K3
2 Kt—B3	Kt—KB3
3 P—QKt3	P—Q4
4 B—Kt2	P—B4
5 P—K3	Kt—B3
6 P—QR3	P—QR3
7 B—Q3	B—Q3
8 Q—K2	O—O
9 P—KKt4	Kt×P?

Black has played with commendable caution and achieved a fair development. All the more surprising, therefore, is this imprudent capture, which gives White the open line he needs so badly for attacking purposes.

10 Q—Kt2	Kt—B3
11 P—KR4	P—R3
12 P—R5	K—R1
13 O—O—O	Kt—K1?
14 QR—Kt1	KR—Kt1
15 B—R7!!	

A characteristic Zukertort blitz!

15 . . .   P—B3

And not 15 . . . K×B; 16 Q—Kt6ch!!, P×Q; 17 P×Pch, K—R1; 18 R×P mate!

* Remove White's Queen's Knight.

| 16 B×R | K×B |
| 17 Q—Kt6 | K—R1? |

Failing to realize how serious the situation is, Black misses his best chance: 17 . . . K—B1, which holds out possibilities of fleeing from the King-side.

18 Kt—Kt5!   RP×Kt

Likewise after 18 . . . BP×Kt White has a winning attack.

19 P×P   Kt—K2

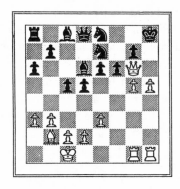

20 P×P!!!	Kt×Q
21 P×Ktch	K—Kt1
22 R—R8ch!!	K×R
23 P—B7!!	Resigns

With a Queen, Bishop and Knight to the good, Black is at a loss for a move! If 23 . . . B—K2; 24 R—R1ch, B—R5; 25 P—B8(Q) mate. Or 23 . . . Q—R5; 24 P×Kt(Q)ch and mate next move.

THE varied charm of Tarrasch's intricate concluding combination lifts this game far above the usual run of odds encounters.

ODDS OF QUEEN'S KNIGHT *
Nuremberg, 1890

WHITE	BLACK
Tarrasch	Meiser
1 P—K4	P—Q4
2 P—K5	P—Q5?

Pointless. Development with 2 . . . B—B4 was indicated.

3 P—KB4	P—QB4
4 B—B4	Kt—QB3
5 Kt—B3	B—Kt5?
6 B×Pch!	K×B
7 Kt—Kt5ch	K—K1
8 Q×B	Kt—R3
9 Q—R3	Q—Q2
10 Q—QKt3!	

10 P—K6 is premature (10 . . . Q—Q4!).

10 . . .	Kt—R4
11 P—K6!	Q—B3
12 Q—KR3	R—Q1

Too slow; better . . . P—KKt3 and . . . B—Kt2 directly.

13 O—O	P—KKt3
14 P—B5!	B—Kt2

The attack has started: Black has no time for 14 . . . Kt×P?; 15 R×Kt!, P×R; 16 Q—R5 mate!

15 P×P	R—Q4

If 15 . . . P×P; 16 Q—Q3!, Kt—B4; 17 R×Kt! etc.

16 Kt—B7	Kt×Kt

* Remove White's Queen's Knight.

17 KtP×Ktch	K—B1

If instead 17 . . . K—Q1; 18 Q—KKt3!, B—B1; 19 Q—Kt8.

18 P—Q3	P—KR3
19 B—Q2	P—Kt3
20 Q—Kt3!	Kt—Kt2

White threatened mate beginning with 21 Q—Kt8ch.

21 QR—K1	Kt—Q1
22 R—K4!	R—Q3

Or 22 . . . Kt×KP; 23 R×Kt!, Q×R; 24 Q—Kt8ch etc. White's passed Pawn is certainly obnoxious!

23 R—Kt4!

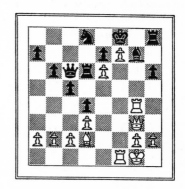

23 . . .	Kt×KP

Tarrasch had it all figured out after 23 . . . R—R2: 24 R×B!, R×R; 25 Q×Rch, K×Q; 26 P—B8(Q)ch, K—R2; 27 Q×RPch, K—Kt1; 28 R—B8 mate.

24 R×B!!	Kt×R
25 B×P!	R(1)×B

Or 25 . . . R(3)×B; 26 Q—Kt8ch etc.

26 Q×Ktch!	K×Q

27 P—B8(Q)ch	K—Kt3
28 Q—B7ch	K—Kt4
29 Q—B5ch	K—R5
30 P—Kt3 mate	

30 R—B4ch is also mate—but not a pure mate! There is real artistry in this game.

KOLISCH *was famous for his brilliancies, but his greatest combinations were played on the stock exchange. When Master Kolisch became Baron Kolisch, chess lost a potential World Champion.*

ODDS OF QUEEN'S ROOK AND MOVE *
Paris, 1859

WHITE	BLACK
Mandolfo	Kolisch
1 P—K4	P—K4
2 B—B4	Kt—KB3
3 Kt—QB3	P—B3
4 P—Q3	P—QKt4
5 B—Kt3	P—QR4
6 P—QR4	P—Kt5
7 Kt—R2?	

Now the Knight will be out of play for the balance of the game; 7 QKt—K2 was correct.

7 . . .	P—Q4
8 P×P	P×P
9 Kt—KB3	Kt—B3
10 Q—K2	B—Kt5
11 O—O	B—QB4
12 B—Kt5	P—R3

White has played poorly, but the odds minimize his shortcomings.

* Remove Black's Queen's Rook.

13 P—R3?

Objectively this is wrong, as Black could now win a piece by 13 . . . B×Kt; but since Kolisch wants to maintain the attack, he ignores this possibility.

13 . . .	P—R4?!
14 P×B	P×P
15 Kt×KP?	

Much too greedy! With a Rook and Bishop ahead, White can afford to return some of his booty. 15 P—B3! was the proper move, to prevent a possible . . . Kt—Q5. White would be reasonably safe, with little to fear from the open King's Rook file.

| 15 . . . | Kt—Q5! |

If now 16 Kt—B6ch, Kt×Q mate! Or if 16 Q—Q2, Kt—K5!; 17 P×Kt, Q×B! and wins.

16 Q—K1	Kt—K5!!
17 B×Q	Kt—Kt6!!
Resigns	

18 . . . R—R8 mate is threatened. If 18 P×Kt, Kt—B6 mate or 18 . . . Kt—K7 mate. Any discovered check by White's Knight at move 18 is answered by . . . Kt—K7ch (either

Knight will do) and mate next move. The finish is pure poetry!

CHESS writers strongly recommend castling, but none of them hit on the idea used here by Morphy.

ODDS OF QUEEN'S ROOK *
New Orleans, 1858

WHITE	BLACK
Morphy	Amateur
1 P—K4	P—K4
2 Kt—KB3	Kt—QB3
3 B—B4	Kt—B3
4 Kt—Kt5	P—Q4
5 P×P	Kt×P
6 Kt×BP?!	K×Kt
7 Q—B3ch	K—K3

The "Fried Liver" Attack adopted here by Morphy is unsound even when the players are on even terms; but Morphy confidently anticipates his opponent's coming blunders.

| 8 Kt—B3 | Kt—Q5 |

8 . . . Kt—K2 is safer, but even the text will do.

| 9 B×Ktch | K—Q3 |
| 10 Q—B7 | B—K3? |

10 . . . Q—K2! repulses the attack.

* Remove White's Queen's Rook.

11 B×B	Kt×B
12 Kt—K4ch	K—Q4
13 P—B4ch!	K×Kt

If 13 . . . K—B3; 14 Q×Ktch with a winning attack.

| 14 Q×Kt | Q—Q5? |

Missing his last chance (14 . . . K—Q5!). But who can blame Black for failing to fathom what follows?

15 Q—Kt4ch	K—Q6
16 Q—K2ch	K—B7
17 P—Q3ch!	K×B
18 O—O mate!	

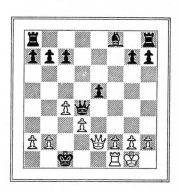

Odds-giving with a smile!
Note that if Black had tried 17 . . . K—Kt8 Morphy would have played 18 O—O, K×P; 19 Q—B2! leading to mate.

Simultaneous Exhibitions

♛ THE simultaneous exhibition is a test of skill, a social occasion and as a rule the only way in which an amateur gets a chance to play against the masters. To the latter, simultaneous play is an important source of income.

Most exhibitions yield the master a batting average of .900 if not better. He has on his side years of experience and training, phenomenally developed technique, and the ability to appraise positions at an instant's notice. On the other hand, he generally arrives at an exhibition after a tiring trip; and the continual walking which is required during the course of the play intensifies his fatigue.

At every session there are generally two or three strong players who require special attention. In most cases the master spots these players quickly and makes it his business to play his best against them. Failure to detect formidable opponents leads to such defeats as the one suffered by Mieses (p. 223)—although there are not many amateurs capable of producing the exceptionally brilliant chess that led to Mieses' downfall.

Another and more difficult type of exhibition is played against from five to ten players who are nearly of master strength. Both the master and his opponents use clocks, so that the master is forced to give an enormous time handicap. Alekhine and Capablanca were particularly successful in such exhibitions.

To the amateur, there is something miraculous in the master's ability to play so many games simultaneously. Ask any master what he considers the most taxing feature of a simultaneous exhibition, and you will always get the same reply: "Walking!"

In an exhibition on 20, 30, 40 or 50 boards, the master's imagination must of necessity operate on a routine level. And yet, even this handicap cannot prevent the poets of the chessboard from achieving dazzling effects!

KING'S GAMBIT
Pisek, 1912

WHITE	BLACK
Duras	*St. Jes*
1 P—K4	P—K4
2 P—KB4	P×P
3 Kt—KB3	P—Q4
4 P×P	Q×P
5 Kt—B3	Q—KR4
6 P—Q4	B—KKt5
7 B×P	B×Kt
8 Q×B	Q×Q
9 P×Q	Kt—QB3
10 B×P	Kt×P

Black has achieved his heart's desire, the early exchange of Queens. There are two disquieting factors: he is behind in development, and White has two powerful Bishops.

But who would expect Black to be mated in three moves?

11 O—O—O

If now 11 . . . Kt×KBP?; 12 B—Kt2, Kt—Kt4; 13 B×P winning a whole Rook! If 11 . . . Kt—QB3; 12 B—Kt5 (or 12 B—R3) followed by 13 KR—K1ch with a decisive attack.

11 . . .   Kt—K3?

12 B—Kt5ch   K—K2
13 Kt—Q5 mate!

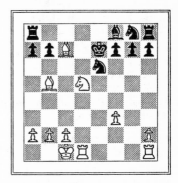

As we study this picturesque mate, produced in a 31-board exhibition, we are not surprised to learn that Duras was famous for the elegance of his endgame compositions.

This is the kind of game that the master dreads to encounter in a simultaneous exhibition. Even the smallest hamlet contains some unknown who has one masterpiece in him!

SCOTCH GAME
Vienna, 1923

WHITE	BLACK
Mieses	*Fuchs*
1 P—K4	P—K4
2 Kt—KB3	Kt—QB3
3 P—Q4	P×P
4 Kt×P	

223

As a master who first made his mark in the '80s, Mieses continued to play this old-fashioned opening long after its heyday had passed.

4 ...	Kt—B3
5 Kt×Kt	KtP×Kt
6 B—Q3	P—Q4
7 P—K5?	Kt—Kt5
8 B—KB4	B—QB4
9 O—O	P—Kt4!
10 B—Q2	Q—K2
11 B—B3	B—K3
12 P—KR3?	

As usual, development is in order! 12 Q—K2 was better.

12 ...	P—KR4!
13 P×Kt?	

Why not? He expects to outplay his opponent in the ensuing complications.

13 ...	P×P
14 P—KKt3	Q—B1!

Threatening 15 . . . Q—R3 followed by mate along the open file.

15 K—Kt2

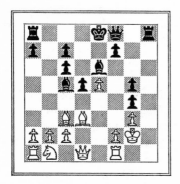

This seems quite safe (if 15 . . . Q—R3; 16 R—R1). 15 R—K1, Q—R3; 16 K—B1 is inadequate: 16 . . . Q—R7!; 17 R—K3 (17 Q—Q2 allows mate in three), B×R; 18 P×B, Q—R8ch and mate next move.

15 ...	R—R7ch!!
16 K×R	Q—R3ch
17 K—Kt1	Q—R6

Threatening 18 . . . Q×Pch; 19 K—R1, Q—R6ch; 20 K—Kt1, P—Kt6 and White is helpless. By this time Mieses realizes that he has caught a Tartar, but the knowledge comes too late in the day.

18 B—Q4   O—O—O!!

Another beautiful move, robbing White of the resource 18 . . . B×B; 19 B—K4!, Q×Pch; 20 B—Kt2! After the text, 19 . . . R—R1 is threatened.

19 B—R7	R—R1
20 Q—Q3	B×B
21 Kt—Q2	R×B
22 Q×R	Q×Q
23 P—B3	B—Kt3
24 Kt—Kt3	B—KB4
Resigns	

White has been magnificently outplayed!

As A youngster Capablanca was famous for the lightning rapidity of his simultaneous play. Even in the following game, played toward the end of his career, there is no indication that he suffers from the severe time handicap.

CARO-KANN DEFENSE
Barcelona, 1935
(Simultaneous Exhibition with clocks)

WHITE	BLACK
Capablanca	Ribera
1 P—K4	P—QB3
2 Kt—QB3	P—Q4
3 Kt—B3	P×P
4 Kt×P	Kt—Q2
5 P—Q4	KKt—B3
6 Kt—Kt3	P—K3
7 B—Q3	B—K2
8 O—O	O—O
9 Q—K2	P—B4

Black's development has been rather slow and he still has to find a good square for his Queen's Bishop. Capablanca has much the freer game with overtones of King-side attacking possibilities.

10 R—Q1	Q—B2
11 B—KKt5	P—QKt3

Such is the furious tempo of the following play that Black's Bishop never gets to Kt2!

12 P—Q5!

Beginning a combination in the grand manner. If now 12 . . . P×P; 13 Q×B, R—K1; 14 B×Kt!, R×Q; 15 B×R with a winning superiority of material.

12 . . .	Kt×P

13 B×B	Kt×B

Anticipating 14 Q—K4, Kt—KB3; 15 Q×R, B—Kt2; 16 Q×P, R—R1; 17 Q×Rch, B×Q with equality. But a surprise awaits him!

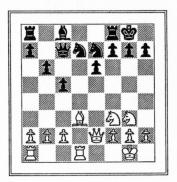

14 B×Pch!	K×B
15 Kt—Kt5ch	K—Kt1

Forced: if 15 . . . K—Kt3??; 16 Q—R5ch, K—B3; 17 Kt(5)—K4 mate.

16 R×Kt!

This forceful coup leaves White a Rook down—but with a won game! 16 Q—R5? is harmless because of 16 . . . Kt—B3.

16 . . .	Q×R

Or 16 . . . B×R; 17 Q—R5, KR—K1; 18 Q×Pch, K—R1; 19 Kt—R5, R—KKt1(. . . Kt—B4; 20 Q—Kt6, K—Kt1; 21 Kt—B6ch and mate next move); 20 Kt—B6, Kt—B4; 21 Q—R5ch, Kt—R3; 22 Kt—B7 mate.

17 Q—R5	R—Q1
18 Q×Pch	K—R1

Many a player would now snap at 19 Kt—R5??, allowing 19 . . . Q—Q8ch!

19 P—KR4!	Q—K1

20 Kt—R5!　　　Q—B1

His only chance to prolong the game was 20 . . . Q×Q; 21 Kt×Q ch, K—Kt1; 22 Kt×R, B—Q2; 23 Kt—Kt7 leaving White a Pawn ahead with an easy end-game win.

21 Kt—B6!!　　　Kt—Kt1

If *21* . . . Q×Q; 22 Kt×Q mate! Or *21* . . . P×Kt; 22 Q—R7 mate.

22 Q—R5ch　　　Resigns

If *22* . . . Kt—R3; 23 Q—Kt6! is decisive. Obviously Capablanca has not been troubled by the time handicap.

Beating a Grandmaster

♛ "THEY laughed when I sat down at the chessboard, but their laughter changed to amazement when I defeated the champion." So runs the daydream of the humble chess player. And why not? If David managed to slay Goliath, who will doubt that it would have been even easier to defeat the giant at chess?

For an ordinary player to defeat a grandmaster is one of the most exciting rarities in chess. The great player has everything on his side: genius, technique, patience, intimidating reputation. Therefore we rightly admire anyone who can overcome these tremendous odds to defeat one of Caissa's immortals.

What is ironic about many of these games is that victory is generally achieved in the style for which the loser is famous! Thus Showalter plays with Pillsbury's typical blend of energy and inspiration (p. 228); Hasenfuss attacks on both wings (p. 229)—a favorite device of Bogolyubov's; Pirc outmaneuvers Nimzovich (p. 232) and finally works up a surprise attack in the manner of the master; Van den Bosch finds many a move which is full of hidden and startling aggressiveness—just the quality that often delights us in Spielmann's masterpieces (p. 234); Steiner plays a "typical Tartakover game" (p. 231)—except that Tartakover happens to be on the losing side! And so it goes.

Sometimes the great man's defeats are even more drastic, as when Lasker loses in 14 moves (p. 228) and Euwe (p. 232) loses in 13!

Such games are unexcelled for human interest—they reveal the grandmaster in those rare moments when his play is less than perfection itself, when he becomes, after all, an ordinary mortal, "even as you and I," struggling with baffling difficulties.

WANTED: *a defense to the Queen's Gambit!*

QUEEN'S GAMBIT DECLINED
Berlin, 1890

WHITE	BLACK
Caro	Em. Lasker
1 Kt—KB3	P—Q4
2 P—Q4	B—B4
3 P—B4	P—QB3
4 Q—Kt3	Q—B1?

4 . . . Q—Kt3 is absolutely essential.

5 P×P	P×P
6 Kt—B3	P—K3
7 B—B4	P—QR3
8 Kt—QR4!	R—R2

Even at this stage, resignation would not be premature! If 8 . . . Kt—Q2; 9 R—B1 etc.

9 Kt—Kt6	Q—Q1
10 B×Kt	Q×B
11 Q—R4ch	K—K2
12 R—B1	P—Kt4
13 Kt—K5	

White disdains Kt—B8ch. He threatens 14 Q—Q7ch, K—B3; 15 Q×BP mate. Who else can boast of having had the great Lasker in such a predicament?

13 . . .   Kt—R3

13 . . . Kt—B3 leads to the quaint finish 14 Kt—B8ch, K—Q1; 15 Kt×P mate.

14 Kt—B8ch   Resigns

The Queen is lost.

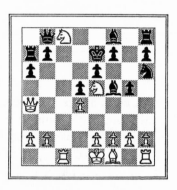

JINXES *are not uncommon in master play. Although Showalter consistently succumbed to the great Pillsbury in tournament play, their matches were decided by close scores. It was in one of these contests that Showalter played his most brilliant game.*

RUY LOPEZ
Match, 1897

WHITE	BLACK
Showalter	Pillsbury
1 P—K4	P—K4
2 Kt—KB3	Kt—QB3
3 B—Kt5	Kt—B3
4 O—O	Kt×P
5 P—Q4	Kt—Q3
6 B—R4!?	

A Pawn sacrifice which is best declined.

6 . . .	P×P
7 P—B3!	P×P
8 Kt×P	B—K2
9 Kt—Q5	O—O
10 R—K1	

Already threatening to win a piece by 11 B×Kt etc. The acceptance of the Pawn sacrifice has given White a tremendous initiative which is augmented by the fact that Black cannot get his pieces out properly.

10 . . .	B—B3
11 B—B4!	

Threatening 12 Kt×P!

11 . . .	Kt—K1
12 R×Kt!	Q×R

If 12 . . . R×R?; 13 B×P wins the Queen!

13 Kt×P	Q—K5
14 B—Q6	R—Kt1
15 B—B2	Q—KKt5

As will be seen, White has his sinister reasons for driving the Queen off the King file.

16 B×R	K×B
17 Q—Q6ch	B—K2
18 R—K1!	

Bringing the Rook into the attack without loss of time (if 18 . . . B×Q?; 19 R—K8 mate).

18 . . .	P—KKt3
19 Q—Q2	Q—R4

White was threatening 20 Q—R6ch, K—Kt1; 21 Kt—Q5, B—B1; 22 Kt—B6ch and mate next move.

20 Kt—Q5	B—Q1

This time the threat was 21 Kt×B, Kt×Kt; 22 Q—Q6 and wins.

21 Q—B3	

And now he threatens 22 Q—R8 mate!

21 . . .	P—B3
22 Kt×P	B—R4

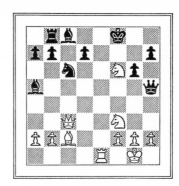

Showalter announced mate in five moves, beginning with 23 Kt×QPch!, B×Kt (if 23 . . . K—B2; 24 B—Kt3ch etc.); 24 Q—B6ch etc. A breezy game!

IN THIS game, says The British Chess Magazine, *"Bogolyubov's optimism meets with very much the same treatment as Voltaire's Candide."*

DUTCH DEFENSE
Kemeri-Riga, 1939

WHITE	BLACK
Bogolyubov	*Hasenfuss*
1 P—Q4	P—K3
2 Kt—KB3	P—KB4
3 P—KKt4?	

Too much of a good thing. Moving the Pawn one square is far better.

3 . . .	P×P
4 Kt—K5	Q—R5!
5 P—K4?	

Curiously enough, this repeats the previous mistake. 5 P—K3 was in order.

5 . . .	P—Kt6!

Alert exploitation. White must surrender a second Pawn, for 6 BP×P??, Q×KPch wins a Rook for Black.

6 B—Kt2	P×Pch

Depending on one's taste in metaphors, this Pawn is a thorn in White's side, a rusty nail in his knee or a bone in his throat.

7 K—B1	Kt—QB3
8 Kt×Kt	KtP×Kt

Threatening to decide the game at once with . . . B—R3ch.

9 P—B4	Kt—B3
10 P—K5	Kt—Q4!

The Knight is strongly centralized, and quite safe (11 P×Kt??, B—R3ch).

11 B—B3	B—R3
12 P—Kt3	

On 12 Q—R4, Kt—Kt5 is too strong.

12 . . .	B—K2
13 K—Kt2	

Threatening to capture the Knight.

13 . . .	O—O!!

So that if 14 P×Kt, P—B8(Q)ch; 15 R×Q, B×Rch; 16 Q×B (if 16 K×B, R×Bch), Q×P winning White's remaining Rook.

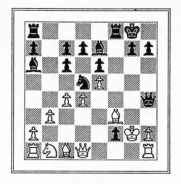

14 R—B1	R×B!
15 Q×R	

If 15 K×R, R—B1ch; 16 K—K2 (or 16 K—Kt2, Q—K5ch), Q—K5ch; 17 K—Q2, B—Kt4 mate.

15 . . .	R—KB1

15 . . . Q×P also wins.

16 Q—Q3	Q—Kt5ch
17 K—R1	Kt—Kt5!
18 Q—Kt3	

If 18 Q—K3, Kt—B7; 19 Q—Q3, Kt—K8! wins at once.

18 . . .	Q×P
19 Kt—B3	B—R5!
20 Q—K3	P—B4!
21 Q×Q	P×Q
Resigns	

His Knight is *en prise*, and . . . B—Kt2ch is threatened with devastating effect. A fascinating game because of the succession of tactical threats.

FAMOUS for his whimsical opening play and original treatment of the middle game, Tartakover finds himself outgeneraled on both counts in this masterpiece!

FRENCH DEFENSE
Budapest, 1929

WHITE	BLACK
A. Steiner	Tartakover
1 P—K4	P—K3
2 P—QB4!?	P—Q4
3 BP×P	P×P
4 Q—R4ch	B—Q2

Possibly taken aback by Steiner's unusual second move, Tartakover misses the safe and sane 4 . . . Q—Q2 and soon finds himself enmeshed in unpleasant complications.

5 Q—Kt3	B—B3
6 P—Q4!	Kt—B3

He does not like the looks of 6 . . . P×P; 7 B—QB4, Q—K2; 7 Kt—QB3, P—QKt3; 8 Kt—R3.

7 P—K5	KKt—Q2
8 Q—Kt3!	

With Black's best defensive piece driven away from KB3, White avoids shutting his Queen out of the attack with an immediate 8 B—Q3.

8 . . .	P—B3
9 B—Q3	B—Kt5ch
10 Kt—B3	O—O
11 Q—R3!	P—KKt3
12 B—KR6	R—K1
13 P—B4	Kt—B1
14 Kt—B3	Q—Q2
15 Q—R4!	P×P
16 BP×P	

White has built up a powerful attacking formation.

16 . . .	B—Kt4
17 B×B	Q×B
18 Q—B6!	Kt—K3
19 Kt—Kt5!	

Black has removed one of the mighty Bishops, but the attack rolls on.

19 . . .	Q—Q2
20 O—O	Kt×Kt
21 Q×Kt	Kt—B3
22 R—B6!	Kt×QP

If 22 . . . B—K2; 23 R×Pch! and Black can resign.

23 Kt×P!	Kt—K3

23 . . . Q×Kt or 23 . . . B—K2 is refuted by 24 R×Pch!

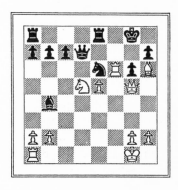

24 R×Pch!!	P×R
25 Q×Pch	K—R1

If 25 . . . Kt—Kt2; 26 Kt—B6ch wins the Queen.

26 Kt—B6	R—KKt1

If 26 . . . Q—K2; 27 B—Kt7ch! and mate in two; or 26 . . . Q—Q5ch; 27 K—R1, R—K2; 28 B—Kt7ch! etc.

27 Q—R5!	R×Pch

Air!

| 28 K×R | Q—B3ch |

Or 28 . . . R—Kt1ch; 29 B—Kt5ch!, K—Kt2; 30 Q—R7ch and mate follows.

29 K—R3!	Kt—Kt2
30 B×Ktch	K×B
31 R—Kt1ch	K—B1
32 R—Kt8ch	K—K2
33 R×R	Q—K3ch
34 Q—Kt4	Resigns

A FORMER World Champion loses in 13 moves!

RETI OPENING
Hilversum, 1947

WHITE	BLACK
Euwe	Muhring
1 Kt—KB3	P—KB4
2 P—KKt3	P—K3
3 B—Kt2	Kt—KB3
4 O—O	B—K2
5 P—Kt3	O—O
6 B—Kt2	Kt—B3
7 P—B4	P—Q3
8 Kt—B3	Q—K1
9 P—Q3?	

Correct is 9 P—Q4, with a favorable variation of the Dutch Defense at White's disposal. But Euwe wants to prevent . . . Kt—K5, and therefore advances the Queen's Pawn only one square. The flaw is that Black is given too much scope in the center.

9 . . .	B—Q1
10 Q—Q2	Q—R4
11 P—K4?	P—K4
12 QR—K1?	P—B5!

A difficult move to meet, the threat being 13 . . . B—Kt5! In order to provide a retreat for his King's Knight, Euwe plays:

13 K—R1?

Loses quickly—not that there were any good moves.

| 13 . . . | B—Kt5! |
| Resigns | |

Euwe has overlooked that if 14 Kt—KKt1, P—B6 wins a piece. Of course, if 14 Q—K2 or 14 Q—Q1, Kt—Q5 wins.

By DINT of much labor and effort, Nimzovich manages to obtain the inferior position.

QUEEN'S GAMBIT DECLINED
(in effect)
Bled, 1931

WHITE	BLACK
Nimzovich	Pirc
1 Kt—KB3	Kt—KB3
2 P—B4	P—B3
3 P—QKt3	P—Q4
4 B—Kt2	P—K3
5 Q—B2	B—Q3

6 Kt—B3	O—O
7 P—K3	P—QR3
8 P—Q4	

After a spell of portentous maneuvering, Nimzovich finds himself in a variation of the semi-Slav Defense in which Black has fair prospects.

8 . . .	QKt—Q2
9 B—K2	Q—K2
10 O—O	R—K1
11 QR—Q1	P×P
12 B×P	P—QKt4
13 B—Q3	B—Kt2
14 Kt—K4	Kt×Kt
15 B×Kt	P—KB4

Now *16 B×QBP?* is refuted by *16 . . . QR—B1; 17 P—Q5, P×P; 18 Kt—Q4, Kt—K4 etc.*

| 16 B—Q3 | P—B4 |
| 17 P—K4? | |

Strange as it may seem, this is suicidal. *17 Kt—K5* still leaves White with a tenable game.

17 . . .	P×QP
18 B×QP	P—K4
19 B—Kt2	Kt—B4!
20 Kt—Q2	QR—Q1!

Pirc has a winning attack. His im-mediate threat is *21 . . . Kt×B; 22 Q×Kt, B—R6; 23 Q—Kt1 (or 23 B×B, R×Q; 24 B×Q, R×B and Black wins a Pawn because of the threat of . . . KR—Q2), B—Kt5!; 24 Kt—B3, B×P; 25 Q—R1, B—Q6 etc.*

21 P×P

If *21 P—B3??, Kt×B; 22 Q×Kt, B—B4ch wins the Queen.*

| 21 . . . | P—K5! |
| 22 P—B6 | |

Closing the Queen's diagonal; but this does not help for long.

| 22 . . . | P×P |
| 23 B—K2 | |

If *23 KR—K1?, P×B etc.*

| 23 . . . | Kt—Q6 |
| 24 B×Kt | |

Or *24 P—Kt3* (to prevent the terrible *. . . Kt—B5), Kt×B; 25 Q× Kt, P—K6 winning.*

| 24 . . . | P×B |
| 25 Q—Kt1 | Q—Kt2! |

If now *26 P—B3, R—K7!; 27 P— Kt3, B×KtP wins.*

| 26 P—Kt3 | Q—Kt3! |

Not *26 . . . R—K7; 27 Q×P.*

27 B—Q4

White is helpless: if *27 KR—K1, R—K7; 28 R×R, P×R; 29 R—K1, B—Kt5 wins.*

27 . . .	R—K7
28 B—Kt6	B×P!
Resigns	

If *29 RP×B (29 BP×B, R— Kt7ch), Q—R3* soon forces mate.

A DISCOVERED check, no matter how wildly improbable, is always worth a second look. Nobody knew this better than the great tactician Spielmann; yet even he occasionally missed the point.

FRENCH DEFENSE
Match, 1935

WHITE	BLACK
Spielmann	Van den Bosch
1 P—K4	P—K3
2 P—Q4	P—Q4
3 Kt—QB3	Kt—KB3
4 B—Kt5	B—K2
5 P—K5	Kt—K5
6 B×B	Q×B
7 Kt×Kt	P×Kt
8 Q—K2	Kt—Q2

Ignoring the possibility of 9 Q×P, when he will recover the Pawn with 9 . . . Q—Kt5ch.

9 O—O—O	P—KB4
10 P×P e.p.	Kt×P
11 P—KKt3	

Paradoxically, the successful attempt to capture the weak Pawn is not White's best course! 11 P—KB3!, P×P; 12 Kt×P leaves White with strong pressure in the center.

11 . . .	O—O
12 B—Kt2	P—K4!

Opening up the game favorably.

13 B×P	Kt×B

But not 13 . . . P×P??; 14 B×Pch winning the Queen (14 . . . K—B2; 15 B—Kt6ch).

14 Q×Kt	R×P!

Black has seen farther ahead than his great opponent, for if 15 Q×KP?,

Q×Q!; 16 P×Q, B—B4; 17 R—Q2, R×R; 18 K×R, B—K5! wins—or 15 P×P, B—B4; 16 Q—B4ch, K—R1 and White is very much on the defensive.

15 Kt—B3	Q—B2!

A clever surprise move, threatening . . . Q×Kt as well as . . . Q×P. If now 16 Kt×P??, Q×P and he has no defense to the coming 17 . . . Q—R8ch (mate). If 16 KR—B1?, B—B4! wins as in the text.

16 Kt—Kt5?

This looks strong, but there is a crushing refutation. 16 Kt—Q2 was the only chance.

16 . . .	B—B4!

If now 17 Kt×Q, B×Q; 18 KR—K1, R×Pch; 19 K—Kt1, R—Q7ch!; 20 K—B1, R×Rch; 21 K×R, B—B6ch; 22 K—Q2, K×Kt; 23 R—KB1, P—K5 and Black keeps the extra piece.

17 Q×KtP	R×Pch
18 K—Kt1	

With his Queen and Rook attacked, it would seem that Black is lost: 18 . . . R—B7ch; 19 K—R1, Q—B1; 20 Q—Q5ch, K—R1; 21 Kt—B7ch, K—Kt1; 22 Kt×Pch etc.

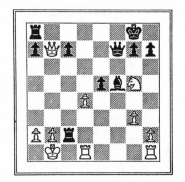

18 . . .	R—B8ch!!	22 K—B1	R—KB1!

This miracle move wins.

19 K×R	Q—B5ch

This explains everything.

20 K—Q2	Q—Q6ch
21 K—K1	Q—K6ch

22 K—B1   R—KB1!
    Resigns

Spielmann doesn't care for any discovered checks! The threat is 23 . . . B—R6 mate. If 23 Q—Kt3ch, B—K3ch mates in two. If 23 K—Kt2, Q—K7ch; 24 K—Kt1, B—K3! etc.

Surprise Attack

HAVING been selected for their sprightly qualities, the games in this book are studded with surprise moves. "Surprise," as we put it in *Winning Chess*, "is nothing but logic that packs a wallop." In this case we are more interested in the wallop than in the logic. Moves that give the game an unexpected turn not only upset the balance of power on the chessboard; they also upset one's opponent.

Some surprise moves come at so early a stage that they bring about a quick decision. Thus Alekhine's 13 P—QKt4!! shoves aside whatever plans Chajes may have had (p. 249) and Black is left in a helpless state. Similarly, Landau's 15 R×Kt!! (p. 251) practically winds up the game before either player has completed his development! Most amazing of all is Spielmann's incandescent attack (p. 247) even before the opening stage has been completed.

No less entertaining are surprise attacks which emerge in unlikely settings. Thus, from a defense (the Caro-Kann) which is notorious for its stodgy qualities, Fine evolves a series of sparkling threats against Monticelli (p. 252). Similarly, Capablanca manages to produce a problem-like finish against Steiner (p. 237) from one of the most colorless of all the openings.

For Black to win by a deep Queen sacrifice in 19 moves in a Queen's Gambit Declined is equally unheard of; but that is just what Lasker accomplishes against Steadman (p. 250). Just as Kolski has obtained what seems to be a promising middle-game position, Kremer strikes one hammer blow after another (p. 244) to work out a brilliant win. Equally ingenious, although with a delayed action which makes it even more deadly, is Treybal's 26 R—K8!! (p. 248), which spares no expense to snuff out Black's resistance.

In the games Bernstein—Znosko-Borovsky (p. 245) and Janowski—Jaffe (p. 241), the early, fairly placid phase is succeeded by brilliant, sustained attacks remarkable for their resourceful and unflagging inventiveness.

Then there are games in which a plan for sacrificial attack is apparent in the opening stage. To commit oneself to such an attacking policy, and to carry it out consistently, requires a knack for bright play and for determination as well. Flohr is called upon to sacrifice piece after piece (p. 246) in order to justify what at first has all the earmarks of a premature attack. Naidorf's great win against Sapiro (p. 243) is one of the most brilliant games of all time—a game that Anderssen would have admired wholeheartedly. Even this masterpiece is dwarfed by Saemisch's fireworks against Herzog (p. 240). Baker—Chernev (p. 238) is rewarding because of Black's ingenuity in maintaining the initiative by means of one surprise move after another.

But enough of superlatives! These beautiful games will bear replaying long after all their surprise value has been lost.

A GAME with "living pieces" calls for lively play. Capablanca obliges with a brilliant Rook sacrifice and then gives up his remaining Rook for a problem mate.

FOUR KNIGHTS' GAME
Los Angeles, 1933

WHITE	BLACK
Capablanca	H. Steiner
1 P—K4	P—K4
2 Kt—KB3	Kt—QB3
3 Kt—B3	Kt—B3
4 B—Kt5	B—Kt5
5 O—O	O—O
6 P—Q3	P—Q3

7 B—Kt5	B×Kt
8 P×B	Kt—K2
9 Kt—R4	P—B3
10 B—QB4	B—K3

The opening play is very similar to that of Tarrasch's pretty game with Janowski (p. 283).

11 B×Kt	P×B
12 B×B	P×B
13 Q—Kt4ch	K—B2
14 P—KB4!	

Energetic play against Black's broken-up King-side. Black's best chance now was 14 . . . Kt—Kt3, after which he would still be exposed to attack without being exposed to the pretty sacrifice that follows.

14 . . .	KR—Kt1
15 Q—R5ch	K—Kt2
16 P×P	QP×P

16 . . . BP×P?? allows mate in two.

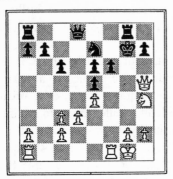

17 R×P!!	K×R
18 R—B1ch	Kt—B4

Forced. White can now win with 19 P×Kt, but Capablanca plays a far less obvious move which leaves him a whole Rook down:

19 Kt×Kt!!	P×Kt
20 R×Pch	K—K2
21 Q—B7ch	K—Q3
22 R—B6ch	K—B4

22 . . . Q×R was the only way to prolong the game; but the extra Pawns would give White an easy win.

23 Q×KtP!

So that if 23 . . . Q×R; 24 Q—Kt4 mate!

23 . . .   Q—Kt3

Seems to defend everything . . . but not quite.

24 R×Pch!!   Q×R

25 Q—Kt4 mate

A problem-like finish!

THERE is always something appealing about games in which Black gains the initiative quickly. Perhaps they contain an element of poetic justice which is richly satisfying.

QUEEN'S INDIAN DEFENSE
United States Championship, 1942

WHITE	BLACK
Baker	Chernev
1 P—Q4	Kt—KB3
2 P—QB4	P—K3
3 Kt—KB3	P—QKt3
4 P—KKt3	B—Kt2
5 B—Kt2	B—K2
6 O—O	O—O
7 Q—B2	B—K5
8 Q—Kt3	Kt—B3

With this simple developing move Black seizes the initiative. He threatens to win a Pawn by 9 . . . B×KKt and 10 . . . Kt×P.

9 R—Q1   P—Q4

Now he threatens to win a Pawn by 10 . . . Kt—QR4.

10 Q—R4   Kt—QKt5

More threats: 11 . . . B—B7 or 11 . . . Kt—B7.

11 Kt—K1	P×P
12 P—QR3	

The interpolation of 12 P—B3?? would be disastrous because of 12 . . . B—B3; 13 Q—R3, Kt—B7 etc.

12 . . .	B×B
13 Kt×B	P—QKt4!

An important gain of time which allows Black to retain the initiative.

14 Q×KtP   Kt—B7

15 R—R2   Kt×QP
16 Q—R4

He must protect his King's Rook:
if 16 Q×P?, Kt—B6ch wins.

16 . . .   Kt×Pch
17 K—B1   Kt—Q5
18 Q×BP   P—B4

Black does not fear 19 P—QKt4,
which can be answered satisfactorily
with 19 . . . QR—B1 and if 20
P×P, R×P!; 21 Q×Kt, Q×Q; 22
R×Q, R×Bch followed by . . .
R×Kt with a piece to the good.

19 B—K3   Q—Kt3!

White must not try to regain the
Pawn: 20 B×Kt, P×B; 21 R×P??,
QR—B1; 22 Q—Q3, R—B8ch; 23
Kt—K1, R×Kt! or 21 Q×QP??, Q—
Kt6!; 22 Kt—B3, QR—Q1 again win-
ning a piece.

20 P—QKt4   KR—Q1
21 Kt—B3

Threatening 22 Kt—QR4. At last
Black seems to be in real trouble.

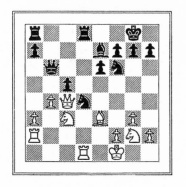

21 . . .   Kt—Kt5!

A convincing reply, for if 22 Kt—
QR4, Kt×Pch; 23 K—K1 (on 23 K—
Kt1??, Kt[5]—B6ch followed by . . .

R×Rch decides at once), Q—B3; 24
Kt×P, Q×KKt; 25 B×Kt, P—K4!
wins. Or 24 B×Kt, Q×QKt and wins!

22 P×P   Kt×Pch
23 K—Kt1   Kt(5)—B6ch
24 K—R1   R×Rch
25 Kt×R   Q—Kt8
26 Q—B2

If 26 Q—K2?, R—Q1 wins at once.

26 . . .   Q—Kt4

Threatens . . . Q—B8 mate!

27 Q—K2   Q—B3
28 R—Kt2   R—Q1
29 Kt—B3   B—B3!

So that if 30 Q—Kt5?, Q×Q wins
a piece.

30 R—Kt3   P—Kt4!

A very useful move: it creates a
mating net in the following variation:
31 Q—Kt5, B×Kt!!; 32 Q×Q, R—
Q8ch; 33 Kt—K1, R×Ktch; 34 K—
Kt2, R—Kt8ch; 35 K—R3, P—Kt5
mate!

In addition, Black plans to bring his
Queen to KR6—so that it is vital to
prevent a possible Kt—B4 in reply.

31 Kt—Kt5

Black was threatening 31 . . .
B×Kt; 32 R×B, Q—Q4 with men-
aces of . . . Q—Q8ch or . . . Q—
B4—R6.

31 . . .   Q—Q4
32 R—Kt1   Q—B4!
Resigns

The double threat of 33 . . .
Q×Rch etc. as well as 33 . . . Q—
R6 and 34 . . . Kt—B8 mate cannot
be answered.

THIS *beautiful game has many remarkable features—not the least remarkable being that this unknown masterpiece appears now in book form for the very first time!*

FRENCH DEFENSE

Gablonz, 1924

WHITE	BLACK
Saemisch	Herzog
1 P—Q4	P—K3
2 P—K4	P—Q4
3 Kt—QB3	P—QB3??

This leaves Black with a cramped game from which he never recovers.

4 Kt—B3	Kt—Q2
5 B—Q3	B—K2
6 O—O	P×P
7 Kt×P	KKt—B3
8 Q—K2	Kt×Kt
9 Q×Kt	Kt—B3
10 Q—K2	O—O
11 P—B4	P—KR3?

Black's severely limited terrain was already enough of a handicap, but this gratuitous weakening of his King's position will expose him to a devastating attack.

12 B—Q2	R—K1
13 B—B3	P—QKt3
14 Kt—K5	B—Kt2
15 QR—K1!	

Black's weakening 11th move begins to have noticeable effects. The threat is *16 Kt×KBP!, K×Kt; 17 Q×Pch, K—B1; 18 B—Kt6* forcing mate.

15 . . .	B—KB1
16 Q—B3!	Q—B2
17 Q—R3!	QR—Q1
18 R—K3!	R—K2

19 R—Kt3!

Threatening *20 Q×RP*. Note how cleverly White has maneuvered to concentrate his forces against Black's King. White is now ready for a magnificent break-through, primarily based on the weakness created by *11 . . . P—KR3?*

19 . . .	K—R1
20 P—Q5!!	KP×P
21 Kt—Q7!!!	

This exquisite sacrifice, perfectly sound in all its numerous possible consequences, is the key to the attack.

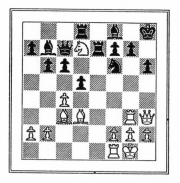

21 . . .   R(1)×Kt

Relatively best. If *21 . . . Q×Kt* (not *21 . . . Kt×Kt?; 22 Q×Pch, K—Kt1; 23 Q—R7 mate*); *22 Q×Pch!!, P×Q; 23 B×Ktch, B—Kt2; 24 B×Bch, K—Kt1; 25 B—B6ch, K—B1; 26 B—R7* and despite his huge material advantage, Black is helpless against the coming *R—Kt8 mate!*

If *21 . . . R(2)×Kt; 22 Q×Pch!!, P×Q; 23 B×Ktch, B—Kt2; 24 R×B!* and there is nothing to be done about *25 R—R7ch* and *26 R—R8 mate!*

22 Q×Pch!!!

Another, but less elegant, winning process was *22 B×Kt, P×B; 23 Q—*

B5, R—K5; 24 B×R, P×B; 25 Q—Kt4 forcing . . . Q×R.

22 . . .	P×Q
23 B×Ktch	B—Kt2
24 R×B!	

Black has a Queen for a Bishop, but he cannot save the game. The immediate threat is 25 R—R7ch, K—Kt1; 26 R—R8 mate; hence Black's next move.

24 . . .   R—K5

Expecting 25 P—B3?, which can be refuted by 25 . . . Q—B5!

25 R—Kt4ch!	K—R2
26 P—B3	P—KR4
27 R—Kt7ch	K—R3
28 P×R	P×BP
29 B—Kt1!	

The Bishop is kept on the attacking diagonal. White is still behind in material, but his attack continues to flourish.

| 29 . . . | P—Kt4 |
| 30 P—K5! | R—Q6 |

Forced, in view of the threatened 31 R—R7 mate.

| 31 P—K6! | Q—Kt3ch |
| 32 K—R1 | |

If now 32 . . . Q—B7; 33 B×R! wins a whole Rook!

32 . . .   P×P

Black seems to have extricated himself nicely.

33 B×R	P×B
34 R—Q7!!	P—B4
35 B—Q8!!	

Attacking the Queen, and at the same time threatening 36 R—B6ch, K—Kt4; 37 R—Kt7ch, K—R5; 38 R—B4 mate.

35 . . .   B×Pch?!

The Bishop is free at last. Black expects 36 K×B?, which he will answer with 36 . . . Q—B3ch.

36 K—Kt1!!   Resigns

For if 36 . . . Q—Kt1; 37 R—B6ch, K—Kt4; 38 R—Kt7ch, K—R5; 39 R—B4 DOUBLE CHECK, K—R6; 40 R—Kt3 mate. One of the most beautiful games on record!

EVERY book of chess instruction stresses the dangers of moving the Queen far afield to capture distant Pawns. Yet the Old Adam continues to succumb to temptation, so that we get extraordinary games like this one:

QUEEN'S PAWN OPENING
Match, 1918

WHITE	BLACK
Janowski	Jaffe
1 P—Q4	P—Q4
2 B—B4	P—K3
3 P—K3	B—Q3
4 B—Kt3	P—QB4
5 P—QB3	Kt—QB3
6 P—KB4	P—B4

With both sides firmly barricaded in the center, the position may be considered about even.

7 Kt—B3	Kt—B3
8 QKt—Q2	Kt—K5
9 Kt×Kt	BP×Kt
10 Kt—K5	O—O
11 Q—R5	P—B5
12 B—K2	Kt×Kt

13 BP×Kt   B—K2

In the event of *14* O—O—O Black will play *14* . . . P—QKt4 intending a Pawn storming advance. Janowski therefore prefers to castle on the safe side.

14 B—B4   P—QKt4
15 O—O   B—Q2
16 R—B2   P—Kt5

It would be stronger to preface this advance with . . . P—R4.

17 P×P   B×P

Now this Bishop has been lured away from the defense of the King-side.

18 QR—KB1!   Q—R4?

Threatening to win the exchange by *19* . . . B—K8.

19 P—KKt3   Q×P??

This allows Janowski to win by means of an attack which is colorful, precisely timed and full of picturesque surprises.

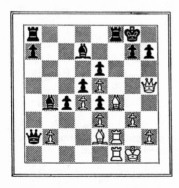

20 B—R6!!   R—B4

Capture of the Bishop leads to quick defeat: *20* . . . P×B; *21* R—B7!, R×R (else *22* Q—Kt4ch forces

mate); *22* Q×Rch, K—R1; *23* Q—B6ch, K—Kt1; *24* B—R5! etc.

Or if *20* . . . B—K1; *21* Q—Kt4, B—Kt3; *22* Q×Pch, K—R1; *23* Q×P, P×B; *24* B×P, Q—R5; *25* R×Rch, R×R; *26* R×Rch, B×R; *27* Q—Kt8 mate.

21 R×R   P×R
22 B×KtP!!   K×B
23 Q—Kt5ch   K—R1

23 . . . K—B1 leads to the same position, for after *24* Q—B6ch, K—K1? allows *25* B—R5 mate!

24 Q—B6ch   K—Kt1
25 Q—Kt5ch   K—R1
26 P—K6!   B—K1

If *26* . . . B×P; *27* Q—B6ch, K—Kt1; *28* Q×Bch and Black can resign.

27 R×P   B—Kt3
28 B—R5   Q—Kt8ch

28 . . . B×R allows mate in five: *29* Q—B6ch, K—Kt1; *30* B—B7ch, K—B1; *31* B—Kt6ch etc.
If *28* . . . B×B; *29* R—B7!!, B×R; *30* P×B and Black cannot stop mate!

29 R—B1   Q—Q6
30 B×B   R—KKt1

If *30* . . . P×B; *31* Q—R6ch, K—Kt1; *32* Q×Pch, K—R1; *33* R—B7 with a mating attack.

31 R—B7!

More elegant than *31* Q—K5ch, which also wins.

31 . . .   Q—Q8ch
32 K—Kt2   Q—B6ch

Realizing that if *32* . . . R×B; *33* Q—K5ch, K—Kt1; *34* Q—Kt8ch and mate next move.

33 R×Q	P×Rch
34 K×P	R×B
35 Q—K5ch	R—Kt2
36 Q—Kt8ch	Resigns

The Bishop is lost—the final comment on Black's faulty moves 16–19.

EVEN the masters sometimes show surprisingly poor taste when they are invited to select their best game. Naidorf was, however, assured of universal agreement when he chose this masterpiece as his best effort.

FRENCH DEFENSE
Lodz, 1929

WHITE	BLACK
Naidorf	Sapiro
1 P—K4	P—K3
2 P—Q4	P—Q4
3 Kt—QB3	P×P
4 Kt×P	Kt—Q2
5 Kt—KB3	KKt—B3
6 B—Q3	B—K2
7 O—O	P—QKt3

Black's third move has left him with a cramped and lifeless game; but here he would do better to castle.

8 Kt—K5!	B—Kt2
9 Kt×Ktch	P×Kt?

He wants to drive the Knight away, but he provokes an amazing reply.

10 Kt×P!!	K×Kt
11 Q—R5ch	K—Kt1

On 11 . . . K—Kt2 (or 11 . . . K—B1) there is a forced mate: 12 B—R6ch, K—Kt1; 13 Q—Kt4ch, K—B2; 14 Q—Kt7ch, K—K1; 15 Q—Kt6ch! etc.

12 R—K1!	Kt—B1

He has no great choice: if 12 . . . Q—K1; 13 Q—Kt4ch mates, or wins the Queen; or if 12 . . . B—Q4; 13 R—K3! and Black is helpless against the coming R—Kt3ch.

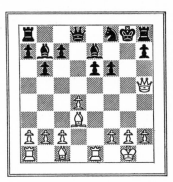

13 R×P!!

Beautiful play. The threat is 14 R×B!, Q×R; 15 B—B4ch, Kt—K3; 16 B—KR6 followed by R—K1 etc.

13 . . .	Kt×R
14 B—QB4	Q—Q3
15 B—KR6	B—KB1

White was threatening 16 Q—Kt4ch, K—B2; 17 Q—Kt7ch etc.

16 R—K1	B—B1

Or 16 . . . B×B; 17 B×Ktch, K—Kt2; 18 Q—B7 mate! Naidorf has augmented the attack with breathtaking rapidity.

17 Q—K8!!	B—Q2

Black is desperate: if 17 . . . B—Kt2; 18 Q×Ktch, Q×Q; 19 B×Q mate.

18 R×Kt!!	R×Q
19 R×Rch!	B—K3

Mate is now forced.

20 B×Bch   Q×B
21 R×B mate!

Allegro con brio!

WHITE'S snappy tactical play sparkles and crackles with bright combinative ideas.

QUEEN'S GAMBIT DECLINED
Polish Championship, 1935

WHITE	BLACK
Kremer	Kolski

1 P—Q4	Kt—KB3
2 P—QB4	P—K3
3 Kt—QB3	P—Q4
4 B—Kt5	B—K2
5 P—K3	QKt—Q2
6 Kt—B3	O—O
7 R—B1	P—B3
8 B—Q3	P—QKt3

Weak. The standard Capablanca
simplifying maneuver 8 . . . P×P;
9 B×P, Kt—Q4 is much more likely
to give Black an easy game.

9 P×P	KP×P
10 O—O	B—Kt2
11 Kt—KR4!	P—Kt3
12 Kt—B3	R—K1
13 Kt—K5	Kt×Kt

Else White plays P—B4 in order to
recapture even more strongly with the
Bishop Pawn.

14 P×Kt	Kt—Q2
15 B×B	Q×B
16 P—B4	P—B3?

The most natural-looking move in
the world—but it provides White
with the opportunity to unleash a remarkable surprise attack.

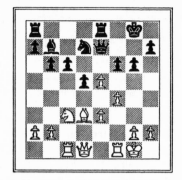

17 Kt×P!!	P×Kt
18 R—B7	Q—Q1

This is not the refutation that Black
fancies it to be; however, if 18 . . .
B—B1; 19 B×P!, P×B; 20 Q×Pch,
K—R1; 21 Q×R, B—R3; 22 Q×P,
B×R; 23 R×Kt and wins. Or 18 . . .
QR—Kt1; 19 B—Kt5, KR—Q1; 20
R×B!, R×R; 21 Q×Pch etc.

19 R×B	Kt—B4
20 R×KRP!!	Kt×B

If 20 . . . K×R; 21 Q—R5ch, K
—Kt2; 22 Q×Pch, K—B1; 23 Q—
R6ch, K—Kt1 (if 23 . . . K—B2 or
. . . K—K2; 24 Q—R7ch, K—K3;
25 B—B5 mate or 24 . . . K—B1;
25 B—Kt6, Q—Q2; 26 Q—R8ch,
K—K2; 27 Q×P mate); 24 Q—R7ch,
K—B1; 25 B—Kt6 etc.

21 R—R3!	Kt—B4

Or 21 . . . Kt×KP; 22 P×Kt,
R×P; 23 R—B4 and wins.

22 Q—Kt4!	K—Kt2
23 P—B5	P—KKt4
24 Q—R5!	KR—Kt1
25 P—K6!	Kt×P

White threatened 26 Q—B7 mate
or 26 Q—R6 mate!

26 P×Kt	Resigns

BERNSTEIN was famous for his quick sight of the board. This bright game is a good example of his tactical prowess.

FRENCH DEFENSE
St. Petersburg, 1909

WHITE	BLACK
Bernstein	Znosko-Borovsky
1 P—K4	P—K3
2 P—Q4	P—Q4
3 Kt—QB3	Kt—KB3
4 B—Kt5	B—Kt5

The McCutcheon Defense, which almost invariably leads to interesting chess, was still something of a novelty at the time this game was played.

5 P×P	Q×P
6 B×Kt	B×Ktch
7 P×B	P×B
8 Kt—B3	P—Kt3
9 P—Kt3	B—Kt2
10 B—Kt2	Q—KR4
11 O—O	Kt—Q2
12 Q—K2	QR—B1
13 Q—K3	P—QB4

The position is about even: White's game is freer, Black has pressure on the Queen's Bishop file.

14 Kt—R4	B×B
15 Kt×B	P×P
16 P×P!	O—O!

Discreet. After 16 . . . R×P?; 17 Q—R3! Black would be unable to castle and White would soon take over the open file with QR—B1.

17 Q—K4!	R—B2
18 Kt—B4	Q—Kt5
19 P—KB3!	Q—Kt4
20 R—B2	R—Q1

The move is pointless, and has the direct disadvantage of depriving Black's Rooks of mutual protection. 20 . . . KR—B1 was in order.

21 P—KR4!	Q—R3
22 P—Kt4!	Q×P

22 . . . K—R1 was safer.

23 R—R2	Q—Kt4

Allowing a pretty combination, but if 23 . . . Q—Kt6ch; 24 K—R1, R—B6; 25 R—KB1 and Black is helpless against 26 R—R3!

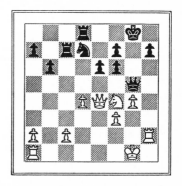

24 Kt×P!!	P×Kt
25 Q×KPch	K—R1

If 25 . . . K—Kt2; 26 Q—K7ch, K—Kt1; 27 Q×Rch wins outright. If 25 . . . K—B1; 26 Q—Q6ch wins the other unguarded Rook!

26 Q—K7!	Q—Kt1
27 R×Pch!	Q×R
28 Q×Rch	Kt—B1

The only way to save the unguarded Rook!

29 Q×Ktch	Q—Kt1
30 Q×Pch	Resigns

Too many White Pawns!

FLOHR has been described as a dull dog, but every dog has his day!

ENGLISH OPENING
Zwickau, 1930

WHITE	BLACK
Blechschmidt	*Flohr*
1 P—QB4	Kt—KB3
2 P—KKt3	P—B4
3 B—Kt2	P—KKt3
4 Kt—QB3	B—Kt2
5 Kt—B3	Kt—B3
6 O—O	P—Q3
7 P—KR3?	B—Q2
8 P—K3	Q—B1
9 K—R2	P—KR4!

White has avoided an exchange by . . . B—R6 etc.—but in order to do it he has badly weakened his King-side. The consequences will be devastating!

| 10 P—Q4 | P—R5! |

If now 11 Kt×P, P—KKt4; 12 Kt —B3, B×P wins.

| 11 KtP×P | P—KKt4! |

So that if 12 RP×P, B×P! and wins. Or 12 Kt×P, R×P with a strong attack.

12 R—R1	P—Kt5!
13 RP×P	B×P
14 K—Kt1	Q—B4
15 P—Q5	

In view of the rapid concentration of Black's forces on the King-side, White must do something drastic before Black plays . . . O—O—O and . . . QR—Kt1.

15 . . .	Kt—K4
16 Q—R4ch	KKt—Q2
17 Kt×Kt	B×Kt
18 P—K4	Q—Kt3

| 19 K—B1 | B×Kt |

White has prevented . . . B—B6; but Flohr snatches the attack anyway.

20 P×B	B—K7ch!
21 K×B	Q×B
22 B—K3	Q×P
23 QR—QKt1	P—Kt4!!

Begins a charming combination.

| 24 Q×KtP | QR—Kt1! |
| 25 Q—B6! | |

Rightly rejecting as insufficient 25 Q×Rch, Kt×R; 26 R×Ktch, K—Q2; 27 R×R, Q×Pch!! and Black will *still* win a Rook!

| 25 . . . | Q×Pch |
| 26 K—B3 | |

If 26 K—Q2, O—O!; 27 Q×Kt, Q×RPch; 28 K—Q3, Q×Pch! and wins. Note that White now threatens 27 R×R mate!

| 26 . . . | P—B4!! |

This devilish move creates a much needed loophole for Black's King and also threatens 27 . . . Q—Kt5 mate!

27 R×Rch

If 27 QR—Kt1, Q—K5ch and

Black has a decisive attack.

| 27 . . . | K—B2 |
| 28 B—Q4 | |

With his Knight unpinned, Flohr threatens not only mate but . . . Kt —K4ch as well. If 28 K—Kt2, Q— Kt5ch; 29 K—B1, R×R etc.

| 28 . . . | Kt—K4ch |
| 29 B×Kt | |

Also hopeless is 29 K—Kt2, Kt×Q; 30 R×R, Q×Pch etc.

| 29 . . . | Q—K5ch! |
| Resigns | |

Black mates in two.

RUDOLPH SPIELMANN *was a bald, short, pudgy, timid, good-natured man who liked a glass of good beer. Yet this quiet little man could make brilliant combinations blaze up out of the most harmless-looking positions.*

FRENCH DEFENSE
Vienna, 1926

WHITE	BLACK
Spielmann	Wahle
1 P—K4	P—K3
2 P—Q4	P—Q4
3 Kt—QB3	Kt—KB3
4 P×P	P×P
5 B—Kt5	B—K2
6 B—Q3	Kt—B3
7 KKt—K2	Kt—QKt5
8 Kt—Kt3	Kt×Bch
9 Q×Kt	

The variation selected by Spielmann (4 P×P) aids Black's development and is therefore rarely adopted. Fur-

thermore, Black has removed the "all-important" attacking Bishop.

Yet in only three more moves Spielmann begins one of his prettiest combinations!

| 9 . . . | P—KKt3? |

A serious weakening of the black squares.

| 10 O—O | P—B3 |
| 11 QR—K1 | O—O? |

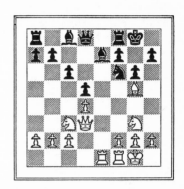

| 12 R×B!! | |

This sacrifice is made in order to create a pin.

| 12 . . . | Q×R |
| 13 Q—B3 | K—Kt2 |

If 13 . . . B—B4; 14 Kt×B, P× Kt; 15 Q—Kt3!!, K—Kt2 (if either 15 . . . P—B5 or . . . K—R1; 16 Q—R4 wins); 16 B×Ktch!, K×B; 17 Q—R4ch, K—K3; 18 R—K1ch and wins.

| 14 QKt—K4!! | P×Kt |
| 15 Kt×P | Q—K3 |

An exquisite point: if 15 . . . Q× Kt; 16 Q×Ktch, K—Kt1; 17 B—R6 etc.

| 16 B×Ktch | K—Kt1 |

If *16* . . . K—R3; *17* Q—B4ch and mate next move.

17 Q—B4   Resigns

There is no good way of preventing *18* Q—R6.

TREYBAL *was one of those natural attacking players who gladden our hearts with their beautiful combinations. The following game is one of the most enjoyable examples of Treybal's flair for elegant sacrificial play.*

CARO-KANN DEFENSE
Prague, 1938

WHITE	BLACK
Treybal	Petkevich
1 P—K4	P—QB3
2 P—Q4	P—Q4
3 Kt—QB3	P×P
4 Kt×P	Kt—B3
5 Kt—Kt3	P—K3
6 Kt—B3	P—B4
7 B—Kt5	P×P
8 Q×P	Q—R4ch

He would have been wiser to exchange Queens, despite White's endgame advantage of the Queen-side majority of Pawns.

9 P—B3	Kt—B3
10 Q—Q2	B—K2
11 B—QB4	P—QKt4
12 B—Q3	B—Kt2
13 O—O	P—Kt5
14 P×P	B×P
15 Q—K2	O—O?

Truly a case of "castling into it." *15* . . . B—K2 should have been

played in order to avoid the following smash-up of his King-side Pawns.

16 B×Kt	P×B
17 Q—K4	P—B4
18 Q—R4	B—K2

Treybal was threatening *19* Kt—Kt5 etc. *18* . . . P—B3 is refuted by *19* B—B4! winning at least a Pawn.

19 Kt—Kt5	B×Kt
20 Q×Bch	K—R1
21 Q—B6ch	K—Kt1

Black's King-side is ruined, his King has no more than hand-to-mouth protection. The position is made to order for Treybal.

22 KR—K1!

Preventing *22* . . . Q—K4, which would be the reply to *22* Kt—R5.

22 . . .   Q—Q1
23 Q—R6

Still threatening Kt—R5.

23 . . .   K—R1

In order to meet *24* Kt—R5 with *24* . . . KR—Kt1.

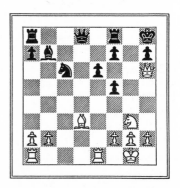

| 24 B×P! | P×B |
| 25 Kt×P | KR—Kt1 |

So far, so good.

26 R—K8!!   Resigns

A delightful finishing touch. If
26 . . . R×R; 27 Q—Kt7 mate. If
26 . . . Q×R; 27 Q—B6ch and
mate next move.

WHAT lends this sprightly game its
superlative interest is the way
Black's weakening of the black
squares is exploited by a series of
brilliant surprise moves.

ENGLISH OPENING
Karlsbad, 1911

WHITE	BLACK
Alekhine	*Chajes*

1	P—QB4	P—K3
2	P—K4	P—QB4
3	Kt—QB3	Kt—QB3
4	Kt—B3	P—KKt3?

The combination of Black's first
and fourth moves weakens his black
squares irretrievably. 4 . . . Kt—Q5
was quite playable.

5	P—Q4	P×P
6	Kt×P	B—Kt2
7	KKt—Kt5!	B—K4
8	P—B4	P—QR3

Black has little choice; the weakened black squares give his game a very
uninviting appearance.

9	P×B	P×Kt
10	B—B4	P×P
11	B×P	R—R4!?

The only chance for counter-play:
he attacks the King's Pawn and prevents 12 Kt—Kt5? because of 12 . . .
R×Kt!; 13 B×R, Q—R4ch.

12 O—O!

So that if 12 . . . Kt×P; 13 B×Kt,
R×B; 14 Q—Q6, R—QR4; 15 P—
QKt4!, R—R1; 16 Kt—Kt5 and Black
can resign.

12 . . .   P—QKt4

Now he hopes for 13 Kt×P, R×Kt;
14 B×R, Q—Kt3ch etc. But Alekhine
has a witty reply.

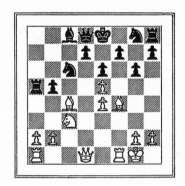

13 P—QKt4!!   Q—Kt3ch

If the Rook retreats, 14 Kt×P is
devastating. 13 . . . Kt×KtP; 14 Kt
×P transposes into the text.

14	K—R1	Kt×KtP
15	B×KtP!	R×B
16	Kt×R	Q×Kt
17	QR—Kt1!	

Now we see the point of Alekhine's
clever 13th move. He has set up a pin
which is not easily disposed of: if
17 . . . Q—R4; 18 B—Q2; or
17 . . . Q—B5; 18 Q—R4; or
17 . . . Q—B4; 18 R—B1—very entertaining!

17 . . .   B—R3

Threatening . . . Q×Rch.

18 Q—Q6!   P—B3

Black is helpless: 18 . . . Kt—K2

is refuted by *19 Q×Kt!, Q×Q; 20 R×Q, B×R; 21 R—Kt8ch* coming out a Rook ahead.

| 19 KR—B1 | Q—Q6 |
| 20 R×Kt | P—Kt4 |

Or *20 . . . Q×Q; 21 P×Q* and White's material and positional advantage assures him a quick win.

21 R—Q4!	Q—Kt4
22 P—QR4	Q—Kt2
23 R—B7	Q—Kt8ch
24 R—Q1	Resigns

A pleasant little game.

Was Black's 17th move calculated right down to the last detail, or was it played intuitively? Whatever the answer, this move remains one of the prettiest and most startling Queen sacrifices on record.

QUEEN'S GAMBIT DECLINED
London, 1913

WHITE	BLACK
Steadman	Ed. Lasker
1 P—Q4	P—Q4
2 P—QB4	P—K3
3 Kt—QB3	P—QB4
4 Kt—B3	BP×P
5 KKt×P	P—K4
6 Kt—B3	P—Q5
7 Kt—Q5	Kt—KB3
8 Kt×Ktch?	

This easygoing move gives Black the initiative. Preferable was *8 B—Kt5, B—K2; 9 Kt×B, Q×Kt* with about even chances.

| 8 . . . | Q×Kt |

9 B—Kt5	B—Kt5ch!
10 B—Q2	Kt—B3
11 P—K3	O—O!

Note the rapidity with which Black strives to complete his development.

12 P×P	P×P
13 B×B	Kt×B
14 P—QR3	

If *14 B—K2, B—B4!* with the crushing threat of . . . *P—Q6.*

| 14 . . . . | R—K1ch |
| 15 B—K2 | |

If *15 K—Q2?, Q—B5 mate!*

15 . . .	P—Q6
16 P×Kt	R×Bch
17 K—B1	Q×Kt!!

Absolutely sound!

18 P×Q	B—R6ch
19 K—Kt1	QR—K1
	Resigns!

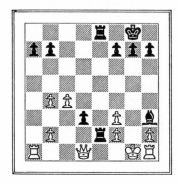

White has Queen for Bishop, yet he is quite lost! Why? Because his King is badly boxed in, and because his pieces are useless for defensive purposes. Black threatens *20 . . . R(1) —K3* and *21 . . . R—Kt3 mate.*

If *20 Q×P, R—K8ch; 21 Q—B1,*

R×Qch!; 22 R×R, R—K3 followed by 23 . . . R—Kt3 mate!

If 20 Q—KB1, B×Q; 21 K×B, P—Q7; 22 K—Kt2, R—K8; 23 R—Q1, R×KR; 24 R×R, R—K8 wins.

The prettiest line is 20 P—B4, R(1)—K3; 21 P—B5, R(3)—K5; 22 P—B3, R—Kt7ch; 23 K—B1, R×KtPch; 24 K—Kt1 and now there are two winning procedures:

A. 24 . . . R(5)—K7 (threatens mate in four!); 25 Q×R, R×Q; 26 R—Q1, R—Kt7ch; 27 K—B1, R—Q7ch; 28 K—K1, R—K7 mate!

B. 24 . . . R—Kt7ch; 25 K—B1, R(5)—K7 (threatens mate in one!); 26 Q×R, R×Qch; 27 K—Kt1, R—Kt7ch; 28 K—B1, R—R7ch winning both Rooks!

The exquisite winning process deserves careful study.

An ORTHODOX *Defense is refuted in unorthodox fashion!*

QUEEN'S GAMBIT DECLINED
Hilversum, 1940

WHITE	BLACK
Landau	Van Doesburgh
1 P—Q4	P—Q4
2 P—QB4	P—K3
3 Kt—QB3	Kt—KB3
4 Kt—B3	B—K2
5 B—Kt5	O—O
6 P—K3	QKt—Q2
7 R—B1	P—B3
8 B—Q3	P—KR3
9 B—B4	P×P

Beginning the familiar freeing maneuver.

10 B×BP	P—QKt4
11 B—Q3	P—R3
12 O—O	P—B4

13 Kt—K4	Q—Kt3
14 P×P!	Kt×P?

Relatively better was 14 . . . B×P —although after 15 Kt×B, Kt×Kt; 16 B—Kt1 White would have the better game.

15 R×Kt!!	B×R

15 . . . Kt×Kt; 16 B×Kt leaves Black a piece down.

16 Kt×Ktch	P×Kt
17 Kt—K5!!	

This pretty sacrifice exploits the break-up of the King-side which was made possible by the previous sacrifice. The immediate threat is 18 Q—Kt4ch, K—R1; 19 B×RP, KR—Kt1; 20 Kt×P mate.

17 . . .	P×Kt

17 . . . P—B4 holds out longer, but after 18 B×RP White has too many threats.

18 Q—Kt4ch	K—R1
19 Q—R5!	Resigns

If 19 . . . P—B4 (19 . . . P×B allows mate in two); 20 Q×Pch, K—Kt1; 21 Q—Kt6ch, K—R1; 22 B×Pch and mate next move.

A DULL opening turns into a lively attacking game!

CARO-KANN DEFENSE
Syracuse, 1934

WHITE	BLACK
Monticelli	*Fine*
1 P—K4	P—QB3
2 P—Q4	P—Q4
3 Kt—QB3	P×P
4 Kt×P	B—B4
5 Kt—Kt3	B—Kt3
6 Kt—B3	P—K3
7 B—QB4	

The Bishop is not very useful here; it would be preferable to exchange it by B—Q3 etc.

7 . . .	Kt—B3
8 Q—K2	QKt—Q2
9 Kt—K5	Kt×Kt
10 P×Kt	Kt—Q2
11 P—B4?	

A better way to meet the threat of . . . Q—R4ch was 11 O—O.

11 . . .	B—QB4!

If now 12 B—K3, Q—Kt3! and White has nothing better than 12 B—B1 (12 B×B?, Q×P!)

12 B—Kt3	P—QR4!
13 P—QR4	

Black's last is very difficult to meet: if 13 B—Q2, P—R5 wins a Pawn.

13 . . .	Q—Kt3!
14 B—Q2	O—O—O
15 Kt—B1	

Not 15 O—O—O, B—Q5! followed by . . . Kt—B4! leaving White without resource.

15 . . .	B—Kt5!
16 O—O—O	

If 16 P—B3?, B×P! The alternative 16 B×B, Q×Bch; 17 Q—Q2, Kt—B4 leads to a bad ending for White.

16 . . .	Kt—B4!

So that if 17 B×B, R×Rch; 18 Q×R, Kt×Bch; 19 P×Kt, Q×B and wins.

17 Q—K3	R—Q6!!

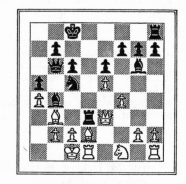

18 P×R	Kt×Bch
19 K—B2	

Or 19 K—Kt1, Kt×Bch; 20 K—R2 (if 20 R×Kt, Q×Q), Q×Q; 21 Kt×Q, B×P winning.

19 . . .	B—QB4
20 Q—R3	

If 20 Q—K1, Kt—Q5ch; 21 K—B1, Q—Kt6; 22 Kt—K3, Q×QP and mate follows.

20 . . .	Kt—Q5ch
21 K—B1	

If 21 K—Kt1, Q—Kt6 wins quickly.

21 . . .	Q—Kt6
	Resigns

For if 22 Kt—K3, Q×QP followed by mate in two.

The Brilliancy Prize

♕ Just as the Pulitzer Prizes honor American writing of distinction, brilliancy prizes serve to perpetuate some of the most memorable and fascinating games produced in great international tournaments. As a rule, the award of a brilliancy prize is a key to chess immortality.

It is natural to expect that a notable attacking game will feature the element of surprise. Thus the encounter between Forgacs and Tartakover (p. 256) is still remembered for Forgacs' smashing breakthrough in a manner which astounds us no matter how often we examine the game. As a complement to the surprise attack, we have a series of relentless forcing moves which leave even the volatile Tartakover at a loss. Alekhine's opening play against Wolf (p. 260) is perhaps even more impressive in the unforeseeable quality of its successive surprises. We can readily sense the dejection of Alekhine's opponent as he tries to brace himself against the onslaught while Alekhine's imagination runs riot over the chessboard.

A brilliancy prize game is nothing if not colorful; yet simplicity and lack of ostentation are also qualities which evoke our admiration. Thus Reti, in his celebrated victory over Bogolyubov (p. 261), uses methods which are almost transparent in their directness; yet he reduces a great master to utter helplessness. The famous final move gives the effect of a powerful fortissimo played by a great symphony orchestra after a quiet opening phrase. Capablanca's play against Janowski (p. 263) is also simple; but it is the simplicity of sophistication—the ability to make the difficult look easy. How many other players could imitate Capa's telling maneuver involving seven moves with the same Knight, with each move contributing to a weakening of the opponent's position? To conduct a brilliancy prize game after an early exchange of Queens, and against a great master at that, seems the most taxing assignment of all; but that is precisely what Takacs accomplishes against Rubinstein (p. 264).

Few games are as enjoyable as those in which the loser fights back with ingenuity and determination. Duras—Cohn (p. 265) is such a game, and the double Rook sacrifice at the end winds up a superb contest in fitting fashion. If one could take the score of only one game to a desert island, this might well be the game!

The thrill of a great game is sometimes enhanced by our knowledge of the circumstances under which it was played. Picture two famous masters tied for first place in one of the great tournaments of chess history, with each player determined to dislodge his adversary from his commanding position. The result of their grim struggle is one of the deepest combinations in chess history. The cold-blooded will to win, coupled with almost superhuman subtlety, enables Teichmann to outrank Schlechter (p. 267).

Something like 70 per cent of all brilliancy prize games are won by White. This high percentage is natural enough, for as a rule the second player can hardly hope to gain so thoroughgoing an initiative that he can win brilliantly. In our group of fifteen brilliancy prize games, only four were won by Black. One of them is particularly enjoyable, for in it Wolf, generally an also-ran, convincingly smashes the great Reti (p. 275) with an attack of remarkably sustained virulence. Alekhine's victory over Gruenfeld (p. 268) is in a way even more sensational, for it has been described by competent judges as the finest game ever played. We cannot help being dazzled by the ease with which Alekhine bowls over the famous theoretician. In his game with Tarrasch (p. 258), Alekhine gives the great teacher a sharp lesson in the importance of center Pawns—a subject on which Tarrasch was himself an authority! The game is a particularly attractive one to play over because of Alekhine's skill in conjuring up one threat after the other. As in the two following games, some of the best ideas never reached the chessboard! Fortunately, the notes tell us what might have happened.

The remaining game won by Black, Johner—Nimzovich (p. 274), richly deserves the title of the Evergreen Game of modern times. Though Johner defends tenaciously, he proves helpless against Nimzovich's scintillating blend of strategy and tactics. Perhaps the best tribute of all to Nimzovich's masterly play is the realization that he succeeded in winning despite the fact that Johner foiled some of the most charming of his intended combinations!

Capablanca—Schroeder (p. 270) is another game, quite simple in appearance, in which the most striking idea of all does not achieve the recognition which comes to moves that are actually played. When such games are published, it is always with the risk that the master's finest ideas will be neglected.

Many players have a strong conviction that most brilliant games begin with 1 P—K4. But this is often not the case, as we see for example in Denker—Feit (p. 257), in which White skillfully switches from a sedate positional game to a fresh, resourceful attack in which a whole series of sacrifices spells Black's doom.

Perfection is one of the attributes we assign by definition to a brilliancy prize game; yet there are exceptions that prove the rule. Cohn was modest and honest enough to admit that he had miscalculated in the opening against Tchigorin (p. 271). Yet Cohn's mishap proved Tchigorin's undoing. Few games have been as entertaining as this one, in which an artless oversight was the prelude to a murderous attack! Alekhine's defeat of Sterk (p. 273) is another instance of a magnificent recovery; anyone could have played the opening as inexactly as Alekhine does; but only Alekhine could have found the inspired sacrificial combination which dashes Black's hopes to smithereens.

Thus we see that brilliancy prize games live up to the high hopes of prize donors: the play is varied, dramatic and full of surprise turns. These games are a feast for your imagination!

SOME games retain their capacity to thrill us no matter how often we play them over. Forgacs' 17 P—B5!! and 18 P—Kt4!! will be remembered long after many other brilliant combinations have been forgotten.

FRENCH DEFENSE
St. Petersburg, 1909
(Second Brilliancy Prize)

WHITE	BLACK
Forgacs	Tartakover
1 P—K4	P—K3
2 P—Q4	P—Q4
3 Kt—QB3	Kt—KB3
4 B—Kt5	B—K2
5 P—K5	Kt—K5
6 Kt×Kt	B×B

6 . . . P×Kt might very well lead to the kind of play seen in the game Spielmann—Van den Bosch (p. 234).

7 Kt×B	Q×Kt
8 P—KKt3	P—QB4
9 P—QB3	Kt—B3
10 P—KB4	Q—K2
11 Kt—B3	B—Q2
12 Q—Q2	O—O
13 B—Q3	

With his strong center Pawn formation and aggressively posted Bishop, White has the makings of an attack. A timid opponent would now try 13 . . . P×P; 14 P×P, Q—Kt5 exchanging Queens. But Tartakover, as usual, is perfectly willing to brave the storm.

13 . . .   P—B5

As will be seen, the advance of Black's Queen-side Pawns is nowhere near as formidable as White's attack on the King-side. Here or on the next

three moves, Black should have tried to make himself secure against assault by means of . . . P—B4!

14 B—B2

The Bishop is still doing business on the same diagonal.

14 . . .	P—QKt4
15 O—O	P—QR4
16 QR—K1	P—Kt5?

Missing the last chance for . . . P —B4! But who can blame him for not seeing what follows?

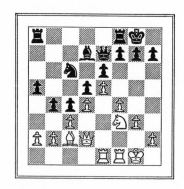

17 P—B5!!

Tartakover was expecting 17 P—Kt4, intending 17 . . . P—B4 in reply. But now his plans are shattered by White's brusque advance, which threatens 18 P—B6!, KKtP×P; 19 B×Pch! and wins (19 . . . K×B; 20 KP×P, Q×P; 21 Kt—Kt5ch winning the Queen; or 20 . . . Q—Q1; 21 Q—Kt5 and the mate threat decides).

17 . . .   KP×P

There is little choice: if 17 . . . P—B3; 18 P×KP, B×P; 19 KP×P, R×P (if 19 . . . Q×P; 20 Kt—Kt5 wins); 20 B×Pch! winning a Pawn: 20 . . . K×B; 21 Kt—Kt5ch followed by 22 R×R and 23 R×B.

18 P—Kt4!!   BP×P
19 Kt—Kt5   P—Kt3

White's brilliant Pawn moves have given him open lines for attack. Successful defense is impossible, for example 19 . . . P—R3; 20 Kt—R7, KR—Q1; 21 Kt—B6ch!, P×Kt (21 . . . K—R1; 22 Kt×QP is much in White's favor); 22 Q×P, P—B4; 23 B×P, B×B; 24 R×B and wins.

20 R—B6!   K—Kt2

Black is condemned to observe how White prepares a powerful finish. If 20 . . . P—R3; 21 B×P!, P×B; 22 R×Pch, K—R1; 23 R×Pch, K—Kt1; 24 R—Kt6ch, K—R1; 25 P—K6, B—K1; 26 Kt—B7ch wins.

21 QR—KB1   B—K1

If 21 . . . B—K3; 22 Kt×Bch, P×Kt; 23 Q—Kt5! and Black is helpless.

22 Q—B4!

He sees even more in the position than the win of the exchange by 22 Kt—K6ch etc.

22 . . .   Kt—Q1
23 P—K6!!   R—R3
24 Q—K5!

Threatens 25 R×KtP mate!!

24 . . .   K—R3

This hardly inspires confidence, but the more natural 24 . . . K—Kt1 loses a whole Rook! (25 P×Pch).

25 R(1)—B5!   BP×P

Now comes a picturesque finish.

26 Kt—B7ch!!   Q×Kt

26 . . . K—Kt2 permits the exquisite 27 R×KtPch!, K×R; 28 R—B1 mate!

27 R—R5ch   K—Kt2
28 R×KtP mate!

The double check motif has created some delightful effects, all made possible by the masterly Pawn sacrifices.

THIS is how a future champion wins his games!

DUTCH DEFENSE
New York, 1929
(Brilliancy Prize)

WHITE	BLACK
Denker	*Feit*

1 P—Q4   P—KB4
2 Kt—KB3   P—K3
3 P—KKt3   P—QKt3?

The counter-fianchetto is not good in this form of the opening (see White's 8th and 9th moves).

4 B—Kt2   B—Kt2
5 O—O   Kt—KB3
6 P—B4   B—K2
7 Kt—B3   P—Q3
8 P—Q5!   P—K4
9 Kt—KKt5!   B—QB1
10 P—K4!   O—O
11 P—B4!

White's vigorous play is bound to open up new lines for his aggressively posted pieces.

11 . . .   KP×P
12 B×P   P×P
13 QKt×P   Kt×Kt
14 B×Kt!!

The first sacrifice in a brilliantly sustained attack.

14 . . .   B×Kt

Why not? If *14 . . .* P—Kt3; *15* Kt×P! etc.

15 Q—R5

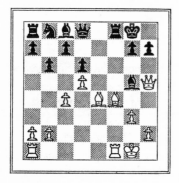

15 . . R×B

As Denker points out, the alternatives lead to quick mates: if *15 . . .* P—KR3 (or *15 . . .* B×B; *16* Q× Pch etc.); *16* B×B, Q×B; *17* R×Rch, K×R, *18* R—B1ch, K—K2; *19* Q— B7ch and mate in three.

Or *15 . . .* B—KR3; *16* B×B, P× B; *17* Q×P, R×Rch; *18* R×R, Q— K2; *19* R—B8ch!, Q×R; *20* Q×P mate!

16 Q×Pch	K—B2
17 B—Kt6ch	K—B3
18 R×Rch!	

More elegant than *18* P×R, which, however, also wins.

18 . . .	B×R
19 Q—R4ch!	B—Kt4
20 Q—K4!!	B—K6ch
21 K—R1	B—R6

To prevent *22* R—B1ch.

22 R—B1ch!	K—Kt4

Or *22 . . .* B×R; *23* Q—B5ch, K —K2; *24* Q—B7 mate.

23 B—R7!!	Resigns

He cannot defend himself against the threat of *24* Q—R4 mate or *24* Q—Kt6 mate.

Denker was fifteen when this game was played.

WHOEVER awarded this game a brilliancy prize showed good taste: the attack may not be "brilliant" in the conventional sense, but it is sustained, inventive and full of fine points.

BLUMENFELD COUNTER GAMBIT
Pistyan, 1922
(Brilliancy Prize)

WHITE	BLACK
Tarrasch	Alekhine
1 P—Q4	Kt—KB3
2 Kt—KB3	P—K3
3 P—B4	P—B4
4 P—Q5	P—QKt4
5 P×KP?	

This and his next move are part of a big blunder which violates one of Tarrasch's own fanatically defended rules: *don't give up the center!* Correct is the developing move *5* B— Kt5!

5 . . .	BP×P
6 P×P?	P—Q4
7 P—K3	B—Q3
8 Kt—B3	O—O
9 B—K2	B—Kt2
10 P—QKt3	QKt—Q2
11 B—Kt2	Q—K2
12 O—O	QR—Q1
13 Q—B2	P—K4
14 KR—K1	P—K5

15 Kt—Q2   Kt—K4

The result of Tarrasch's faulty captures is that Black, after monopolizing the center, has built up a terrific attacking position. White's extra Pawn plays no role whatever in the coming play.

16 Kt—Q1   Kt(3)—Kt5
17 KB×Kt

If 17 Kt—B1 directly, then 17 . . . Kt—B6ch!; 18 P×Kt, P×P; 19 B—Q3, Q—R5 and White is helpless against the coming . . . Q—R6 and . . . Q—Kt7 mate! As we shall see, the congestion of White's forces is an important factor in the success of Black's attack.

17 . . .   Kt×B
18 Kt—B1   Q—Kt4!

Taking advantage of the absence of White's best defender: a Knight at KB3. Alekhine now intends the maneuver . . . Kt—R3—B4—R5 forcing the ghastly weakening move P—Kt3. To avoid this, Tarrasch makes KR—Kt1 possible; but he weakens himself all the same.

19 P—KR3   Kt—R3
20 K—R1   Kt—B4
21 Kt—R2   P—Q5!!

Instead of the anticipated . . . Kt—R5, he hits at KKt7 in a finer and subtler way: if now 22 P×P, P—K6! (Black's long-range Bishop comes to life!); 23 Kt×P (if 23 KR—Kt1, Q—Kt6!! forces mate), Kt×Kt; 24 P×Kt, Q—Kt6! is crushing.

22 B—B1   P—Q6
23 Q—B4ch   K—R1

Threatening . . . P—Q7!

24 B—Kt2

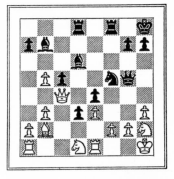

24 . . .   Kt—Kt6ch!

The Knight is immune, for if 25 P×Kt?, Q×KtP; 26 Kt—B1, R×Ktch and mate next move.

25 K—Kt1   B—Q4!

It takes iron nerves to avoid 25 . . . P—Q7; but the win of the exchange is deferred to a more advantageous time.

26 Q—R4   Kt—K7ch
27 K—R1   R—B2
28 Q—R6   P—R4!

Anticipating the sacrifice on move 34 and the related variations!

29 P—Kt6   Kt—Kt6ch!

If 29 . . . P×P; 30 R×Kt gives White some defensive chances.

30 K—Kt1   P×P
31 Q×KtP   P—Q7!
32 KR—B1   Kt×R
33 Kt×Kt   B—K3!!

Planning an exquisite "staircase" mate: 34 Q—B6, R—B6!; 35 Q×KP, B—Q4; 36 Q—QR4, Q×Pch!!; 37 K×Q, R—Kt6ch; 38 K—R2, R—Kt7ch; 39 K—R1, R—R7ch; 40 K—Kt1, R—R8 mate!

34 K—R1	B×RP!
35 P×B	R—B6
36 Kt—Kt3	P—R5!

Now we see the point of 28 . . . P—KR4!

37 B—B6	Q×B
38 Kt×P	R×Pch
Resigns	

If *39* K—Kt2, Q—B6ch and mate follows; if *39* K—Kt1, B—R7ch wins the Queen! Bravo!

FAMOUS as Alekhine was for the dazzling originality of his play, he resented any confusion of the surprising with the outlandish. The more logical his moves were, the more surprising they seemed!

QUEEN'S PAWN OPENING

Pistyan, 1922

(Brilliancy Prize)

WHITE	BLACK
Alekhine	*Wolf*
1 P—Q4	P—Q4
2 Kt—KB3	P—QB4
3 P—B4	BP×P
4 P×P	Kt—KB3
5 Kt×P	P—QR3?

Black's object in playing this variation is to create a symmetrical position in which White can make little or nothing of the advantage of the first move. *5* . . . Kt×P was therefore the logical continuation; but Black fears the continuation *6* P—K4 followed by *7* B—Kt5ch. What follows now is, however, much worse!

| 6 P—K4!! | Kt×KP |
| 7 Q—R4ch! | B—Q2 |

If *7* . . . Q—Q2; *8* B—QKt5 wins the exchange.

| 8 Q—Kt3! | Kt—B4 |
| 9 Q—K3! | P—KKt3 |

Alekhine has violated orthodox opening rules (three Queen moves in a row!) but Black's development is partly bad, partly hampered.

10 Kt—KB3!

Again he moves an already developed piece—this time in order to spoil Black's intended fianchetto.

10 . . .	Q—B2
11 Q—B3	R—Kt1
12 B—K3	

Not *12* P—QKt4 because of *12* . . . B—Kt2; *13* Kt—Q4, Q—K4ch; *14* B—K3, Kt—R5 and Black has a fair game.

12 . . .   P—Kt3

And now if *13* P—QKt4 Black saves the piece with *13* . . . B—Kt2; *14* Kt—Q4, Q—R2!; *15* P×Kt, P×P etc.

13 QKt—Q2	B—Kt2
14 B—Q4	B×B
15 Q×B	

Black's game has been kept in such

a turbulent state that all prospect of sensible development has been dashed irrevocably. Thus if *15 . . . B—B4; 16 B—K2, QKt—Q2; 17 P—KKt4* wins a piece.

15 . . .	B—Kt4
16 B×Bch	P×B
17 O—O	R—R5
18 P—QKt4	Q—Q1
19 P—QR3	QKt—Q2
20 KR—K1	K—B1
21 P—Q6!	Kt—K3

What can he do? If *21 . . . P—K3; 22 Q—K3, Kt—Kt2; 23 Q—Q3* with an easy win.

22 R×Kt!	P×R
23 Kt—Kt5	Q—Kt1

On *23 . . . P—K4* there is a neat forced win: *24 Q—Q5, Q—K1; 25 Kt—K6ch, K—B2; 26 Kt—B7ch, P—K3; 27 Q—B3ch* winning the Queen!

24 Kt×KPch	K—B2

Or *24 . . . K—K1; 25 Kt—K4!* and Black is tied hand and foot.

25 Kt—Kt5ch	K—B1

If *25 . . . K—K1; 26 R—K1, P—K4; 27 R×Pch!*

26 Q—Q5!	R—Kt2
27 Kt—K6ch	K—Kt1
28 Kt×Rch	K×Kt
29 P×P	Kt—B3
30 Q×P	R—R2
31 R—K1	Q—Q3
32 P—K8(Kt)ch	

Simplifying into a position in which White gets a mating attack in addition to his material advantage.

32 . . .	Kt×Kt
33 Q×Kt	Q×Kt

34 Q—K5ch	K—B2
35 P—KR4	R×P?!
36 Q—K8ch	K—Kt2
37 R—K7ch	K—R3
38 Q—B8ch	K—R4
39 R—K5ch	K—Kt5

Hoping for *40 P—B3ch, K—Kt6; 41 R—Kt5ch??, Q×R!; 42 P×Q, R—R8* mate.

40 R—Kt5ch!	Resigns

A game that sparkles with original ideas.

As a rule, brilliancy prize games are quite flashy. To obtain such a prize for a game in which utter simplicity is the keynote means that every move of the winner's play reaches unsurpassable heights of artistry. Such games achieve a happy effect, as they can be appreciated by the great master and the mere tyro.

RETI OPENING
New York, 1924
(First Brilliancy Prize)

WHITE	BLACK
Reti	Bogolyubov
1 Kt—KB3	P—Q4
2 P—B4	P—K3

With the apparently harmless combination of his first two moves, Black has committed the mistake of hemming in his Queen's Bishop. The resulting lack of mobility will prove disastrous.

3 P—KKt3	Kt—KB3
4 B—Kt2	B—Q3

5 O—O	O—O
6 P—Kt3	R—K1
7 B—Kt2	QKt—Q2
8 P—Q4	P—B3
9 QKt—Q2	Kt—K5

Black despairs of solving the problem of how to develop his Queen's Bishop. If 9 . . . P—QKt3; 10 Kt—K5!, B—Kt2; 11 P—K4! with tremendous pressure. Or 9 . . . P—K4; 10 BP×P, BP×P (not 10 . . . Kt×P?; 11 Kt—B4! and White wins a Pawn); 11 P×P and Black's isolated Pawn will be a serious weakness.

10 Kt×Kt!	P×Kt
11 Kt—K5	P—KB4
12 P—B3!	

Opening up the game for his pieces and uncovering weaknesses in Black's game.

12 . . .	P×P
13 B×P	Q—B2

Instructive is 13 . . . Kt×Kt; 14 P×Kt, B—B4ch; 15 K—Kt2, Q×Q; 16 QR×Q and the Black Queen's Bishop is paralyzed!

14 Kt×Kt!	B×Kt
15 P—K4!	P—K4

Apparently freeing himself. Reti must now play very exactly to demonstrate his advantage.

16 P—B5	B—KB1
17 Q—B2!	

Attacks two Pawns and therefore forces Black's reply (if 17 . . . BP×P?; 18 B×P wins a Pawn).

17 . . .	KP×P
18 P×P!	QR—Q1

The plausible 18 . . . R—K4 is met by 19 Q—B4ch, K—R1; 20 P—B6! with a winning game.

19 B—R5!	R—K4
20 B×P	R×KBP

He sees that 20 . . . R—Q4 will not do because of 21 Q—B4!, K—R1; 22 B—Kt4 maintaining the Pawn (if 22 . . . B×KBP?; 23 R×B, R×B; 24 Q×R! and wins).

21 R×R	B×R
22 Q×B	R×B

One would think that Black has simplified very cleverly. Actually White wins by force!

23 R—KB1!	R—Q1

Or 23 . . . Q—K2; 24 B—B7ch, K—R1; 25 B—Q5! (threatens 26 Q×Bch and prevents 26 . . . R—Q1), Q—B3; 26 Q—B8 and Black is helpless!

24 B—B7ch	K—R1

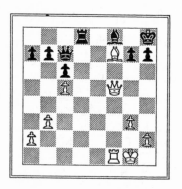

25 B—K8!!	Resigns

A very beautiful finish! If 25 . . . R×B; 26 Q×Bch and mate next move.

THIS flawless game is played by Capablanca with all the slick technique for which he was famous. A delightful feature is the sure-footed maneuvering of the Queen's Knight: Q2—QB4—Q6—K4—Q2—B3—Q4!

QUEEN'S GAMBIT DECLINED
New York, 1918
(Second Brilliancy Prize)

WHITE	BLACK
Capablanca	*Janowski*
1 P—Q4	P—Q4
2 Kt—KB3	Kt—KB3
3 P—B4	P—K3
4 B—Kt5	QKt—Q2
5 P—K3	P—B3
6 QKt—Q2	B—K2
7 B—Q3	P×P?

One of those minor mistakes which often have catastrophic results in modern chess. The right course was 7 . . . P—B4 followed by . . . P—QKt3 and . . . B—Kt2, whereby Black completes his development satisfactorily without conceding White's Queen's Knight an active role.

8 Kt×P	O—O
9 O—O	P—B4
10 R—B1	P—QKt3
11 Q—K2	B—Kt2

Janowski has carried out the recommended procedure, but White's Queen's Knight is poised for action!

| 12 KR—Q1 | Kt—Q4 |

The routine simplifying move; but Capablanca's reply is anything but routine!

| 13 Kt—Q6! | B—QB3 |

If 13 . . . B×B; 14 QKt×B, Q—K2; 15 Kt×B, Q×Kt; 16 P×P with a Pawn to the good.

14 Kt—K4	P—B4?
15 B×B	Q×B
16 Kt(4)—Q2	

Home again! But no time has been lost, for the Knight has provoked weaknesses in the hostile position.

16 . . .	P—K4
17 P×KP	QKt×P
18 Kt×Kt	Q×Kt
19 Kt—B3	Q—K2

Or 19 . . . Q—B3; 20 B—B4, QR—Q1; 21 P—K4, P×P; 22 Q×P and the pin is decisive.

20 Kt—Q4!

The Knight surrenders his life in order to assure White a won game. If the "sacrifice" is declined by 20 . . . B—Q2, then 21 B—B4! will be decisive.

| 20 . . . | P×Kt |
| 21 R×B | Kt—Kt5 |

If 21 . . . P×P?; 22 B—B4 wins. Or if 21 . . . K—R1; 22 P×P, Q×Q; 23 B×Q, Kt—Kt5; 24 R—B4, Kt×P?; 25 R—R4 and the Knight is trapped.

| 22 B—B4ch | K—R1 |

23 R—K6	P—Q6
24 R×QP	Q—B4
25 R—Q4	P—QKt4
26 B×P	Kt×P
27 B—B4	Kt—Kt5
28 Q—R5	P—Kt3

If 28 . . . QR—Q1; 29 R×R, R×R; 30 R—K8ch wins. If 28 . . . KR—Q1; 29 Q×Pch!!, K×Q; 30 R—R4ch, K—Kt1; 31 R—K8 mate! On other moves, 29 R—R4, P—KR3; 30 R×Pch! leads to mate.

29 R×P	QR—Q1
30 R—Kt7!!	Resigns

A charming finish. If 30 . . . K×R; 31 Q—Kt5ch, K—R1; 32 R×R, R×R; 33 Q—B6 mate!

To PLAY a glorious combination and at the same time to defeat one of the greatest masters of the game—what more could any chess player ask?

ENGLISH OPENING
Rogaska-Slatina, 1929
(First Brilliancy Prize)

WHITE	BLACK
Takacs	Rubinstein
1 P—QB4	Kt—KB3
2 Kt—KB3	P—B4
3 Kt—B3	P—Q4
4 P×P	Kt×P
5 P—K4!	Kt—Kt5?

5 . . . Kt×Kt; 6 KtP×Kt, P—KKt3!; 7 P—Q4, B—Kt2 leads into an excellent variation of the Gruenfeld Defense.

6 B—B4	Kt—Q6ch
7 K—K2	Kt×Bch

8 R×Kt	P—QR3
9 P—Q4!	P×P
10 Q×P	Q×Q
11 Kt×Q	P—K3

White has an enormous lead in development. Yet Rubinstein hopes that the exchange of Queens has given him time to neutralize this advantage. Takacs disagrees!

12 Kt—R4!!	Kt—Q2

If 12 . . . P—QKt4; 13 Kt—Kt6, R—R2; 14 Kt×B, R—B2; 15 B×Pch winning easily.

13 KR—Q1!!	P—QKt4

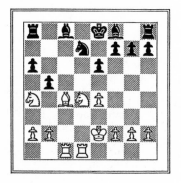

14 Kt×KP!!

The first point of White's deeply calculated combination. Note that three of his pieces are *en prise!*

14 . . .   BP×Kt

If 14 . . . QR—Kt1; 15 Kt—B7ch, K—K2; 16 Kt×KtP!, P×Kt; 17 B×KtP!, R×B; 18 R×B with the winning threat of 19 R—B7. Or 15 . . . K—Q1; 16 B×BP, P×Kt; 17 P—K5!, R×Pch; 18 K—B1 followed by 19 P—K6 and wins.

15 B×KP	P×Kt

If instead *15 . . . K—K2; 16 B×Kt, B×B; 17 R×Bch!, K×R; 18 Kt—Kt6ch* followed by *19 Kt×R* wins. Or if *15 . . . Kt—B3; 16 B×B!, P×Kt; 17 P—K5!, Kt—Kt1* (forced!); *18 B—Q7ch, K—B2; 19 B×P* followed by *20 R—B7ch* with an easy win.

16 R×Bch!	R×R
17 B×Ktch	K—Q1
18 B—Kt4ch!	

Rubinstein must have overlooked this discovered check, reckoning only on *18* B×Rch?, which leaves Black a piece ahead.

18 . . .	B—Q3

If *18 . . . K—B2; 19 R—B1ch* crushes Black.

19 B×R!

Not *19* R×Bch?, *K—B2!* and Black remains the exchange ahead!

19 . . .	K—K2
20 B×P	R—QKt1
21 R—QKt1	P—Kt4
22 P—QKt3	P—R4
23 B—Q3	P—R6
24 B—B4	P—R5

With three Pawns down, Rubinstein has nothing left to salvage but his dignity. Hence he plays on a bit.

25 P—R3	R—KB1
26 R—Q1	R—B5
27 P—B3	R—B1
28 R—Q5	B—B5
29 K—Q3	B—B8
30 P—QKt4	R—QKt1
31 K—B3	K—B3
32 P—Kt5	Resigns

It verges almost on the miraculous that an attack conducted without the Queen could receive a first brilliancy prize!

THIS *game wears well. As one of the greatest fighting contests on record, it thrills us with its large-scale struggle over the whole board. Both players are out to win: they spare neither effort nor ingenuity to achieve their purpose.*

RUY LOPEZ
Karlsbad, 1911
(Brilliancy Prize)

WHITE	BLACK
Duras	Cohn
1 P—K4	P—K4
2 Kt—KB3	Kt—QB3
3 B—Kt5	P—QR3
4 B—R4	Kt—B3
5 P—Q3	P—Q3
6 P—B4	P—KKt3
7 P—Q4	

White's last three moves are part of a variation for which Duras had a great fondness despite the fact that it loses time and gives Black's fianchettoed Bishop considerable power.

7 . . .	P×P
8 Kt×P	B—Q2
9 Kt×Kt	P×Kt
10 O—O	B—Kt2
11 P—B5!	O—O
12 Kt—B3	Q—K2
13 P×P	P×P
14 P—B3	P—Q4!

As Black's center Pawns are weak, he forms an ingenious plan to use them as attacking instruments.

15 R—K1	P—Q5!

16 Kt—K2

If *16* Q×P?, Kt—Kt5 followed by . . . Q—B4ch or . . . Q—R5 depending on where White's Queen retreats.

16 . . .	P—B4
17 Kt—B4!	B—K3
18 P—QKt3!	KR—Q1
19 Kt—Q3!	

Blockade!

19 . . .	B—Q2
20 B×B	Kt×B
21 B—R3!	QR—B1
22 QR—B1!	B—B1
23 Q—Q2!	Q—R5!

The beginning of a magnificent plan: if now 24 Q—R5, B—Q3; 25 P—K5, B—B2; 26 Q×RP, R—R1; 27 Q—Kt7, R×B; 28 Q×B, R×P and Black stands well.

24 P—Kt3	Q—R4
25 K—Kt2	P—B5!
26 Kt—B4	Q—K4
27 B×B	P—B6!
28 Q—Q3	Kt×B
29 Kt—Q5!	R×Kt!

White was threatening 30 P—B4 with decisive effect. Hence Black, relying on his two passed Pawns, gives up the exchange.

| 30 P×R | Q×P |
| 31 KR—Q1 | Kt—K3! |

If now 32 R×P?, R×R!; 33 Q×R, P×Q; 34 R×Q, P—B7 and the Pawn must queen!

| 32 Q×RP | R—R1 |
| 33 Q—K2 | P—Q6! |

Ruthlessly sacrificing the passed Pawns in order to get his Rook on the seventh rank!

| 34 R×QP | Q—KKt4! |

Threatening . . . Kt—B5ch **and** also . . . Q×R.

35 Q—K3!	R×Pch
36 K—Kt1	Q—KR4
37 P—R4	Q—KB4!

Black is endlessly inventive. He plans to answer 38 P—KKt4 with 38 . . . Q—B5!; 39 Q×Q (39 R—Q8ch, K—Kt2; 40 Q×Pch?, K—R3 loses for White), Kt×Q followed by . . . Kt—K7ch and draws.

38 R(3)×P	Q—R6
39 R—B8ch	K—Kt2
40 Q—K5ch!	P—B3!

If *40* . . . K—R3; 41 R(8)—B2 beats off the attack.

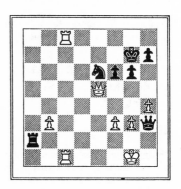

41 R(1)—B7ch!! K—R3!

If *41* . . . Kt×R?; 42 R×Ktch, K—R3; 43 Q—B4ch and mate in two more moves.

| 42 Q—K3ch | P—Kt4 |
| 43 P×Pch | Kt×P? |

Too bad! He had a draw with 43 . . . P×P!; 44 Q×Ktch!, Q×Q; 45 R—B6, R—R8ch! with perpetual check! Now Duras wins with an immortal combination:

44 R×Pch!!	K×R
45 Q—K7ch	K—Kt3
46 R—Kt8ch	K—B4
47 R×Ktch!!	K×R

Or 47 . . . P×R; 48 Q—Q7ch winning the Queen!

48 Q—Kt7ch	Resigns

He loses the Queen after 48 . . . K—R4; 49 Q—R7ch or 48 . . . K—B4; 49 Q—Q7ch. An exciting affair!

THIS crucial game was played toward the end of one of the most celebrated tournaments of chess history. When the game started, these great masters were tied for first place; when the game ended, Teichmann had first place all to himself. He went on to win the tournament.

RUY LOPEZ
Karlsbad, 1911
(Brilliancy Prize)

WHITE	BLACK
Teichmann	*Schlechter*
1 P—K4	P—K4
2 Kt—KB3	Kt—QB3
3 B—Kt5	P—QR3
4 B—R4	Kt—B3
5 O—O	B—K2
6 R—K1	P—QKt4
7 B—Kt3	P—Q3
8 P—B3	O—O
9 P—Q3	Kt—QR4
10 B—B2	P—B4
11 QKt—Q2	Q—B2
12 Kt—B1	Kt—B3

Preparing to free himself with . . . P—Q4, which Teichmann immediately prevents.

13 Kt—K3!	B—Kt2?

Such errors of judgment were rare with Schlechter. The Bishop should guard Black's KB4, say by 13 . . . B—K3 (still aiming for . . . P—Q4).

14 Kt—B5!	KR—K1
15 B—Kt5!	Kt—Q2
16 B—Kt3!	Kt—B1
17 B—Q5!	

White's forces have been converging in a menacing way on the Kingside, and now he actually threatens to win material by 18 B×Kt, B(K2)×B; 19 B×R etc.

17 . . .	Kt—Kt3
18 B×B	Kt(Kt3)×B

If 18 . . . Kt(B3)×B; 19 B×B, Q×B; 20 Kt×QP winning a Pawn and the exchange.

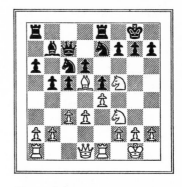

19 B×Pch!!

A bombshell! What is remarkable about this sacrifice is the quiet play that leads up to it and the quiet play that follows it. The violence simmers below the surface.

19 . . .   K×B
20 Kt—Kt5ch   K—Kt1

If 20 . . . K—B1; 21 Kt—K6ch wins the Queen.

If 20 . . . K—Kt3; 21 Kt×KtP! wins quickly, for example 21 . . . R—R1 (capture of either Knight allows the deadly fork 22 Kt—K6ch); 22 Q—R5ch!, K×Kt; 23 Q—B7ch, K—R3; 24 Kt—K6 and White wins as he pleases.

Even more interesting is 20 . . . K—B3; 21 Kt×Pch, K—B2; 22 Q—R5ch, P—Kt3 (if 22 . . . K—Kt1; 23 Kt—Kt5 transposes into the game); 23 Kt—Kt5ch, K—B3; 24 Q—R7!!, P×Kt (if 24 . . . K×Kt; 25 Q—R4 mate; or 24 . . . R—KB1; 25 Q—Kt7ch leads to mate); 25 Q—B7ch!, K×Kt; 26 Q—Kt7ch forcing mate or winning the Queen!

21 Q—R5   Kt×Kt

White menaced mate in two.

22 Q×Pch   K—B1
23 Q×Ktch   K—Kt1

Or 23 . . . K—K2; 24 Q—K6ch, K—Q1 (if 24 . . . K—B1; 25 Kt—R7 mate!); 25 Kt—B7ch wins the Queen.

24 Q—Kt6!

This wonderfully "quiet" move prevents . . . P—Kt3 and leaves Black helpless against R—K3—B3.

24 . . .   Q—Q2

If 24 . . . R—KB1; 25 Q—R7 mate. If 24 . . . Kt—K2; 25 Q—B7 ch, K—R1; 26 R—K3 etc. If 24 . . . Kt—Q1; 25 Q×R mate.

25 R—K3!   Resigns

White simply threatens 26 R—B3 followed by 27 Q—R7 mate. A great game worthy of a memorable occasion!

YATES and Winter describe this game as the finest ever played. To which we may add that winning a brilliancy prize on the Black side of the Orthodox Defense, without one's opponent making any serious mistake, is in itself a memorable feat!

QUEEN'S GAMBIT DECLINED
Karlsbad, 1923
(First Brilliancy Prize)

WHITE	BLACK
Gruenfeld	Alekhine
1 P—Q4	Kt—KB3
2 P—QB4	P—K3
3 Kt—KB3	P—Q4
4 Kt—B3	B—K2
5 B—Kt5	QKt—Q2
6 P—K3	O—O
7 R—B1	P—B3

This defense was fashionable in the Karlsbad tournament.

8 Q—B2	P—QR3
9 P—QR3	P—R3
10 B—R4	R—K1
11 B—Q3	P×P
12 B×P	P—QKt4
13 B—R2	P—B4
14 R—Q1	P×P
15 KKt×P	Q—Kt3
16 B—Kt1	

A tricky move, the idea being to prevent 16 . . . B—Kt2, which would be answered by 17 KKt×KtP, P×Kt; 18 R×Kt!, when Black must not recapture.

16 . . .   B—Kt2!

Alekhine has seen further ahead: if 17 KKt×KtP, Q—B3!; 18 Kt—Q4,

Q×P with a fine game.

17 O—O	QR—B1

Black has completed his development in exemplary fashion and already threatens the annoying moves 18 . . . B—K5 or 18 . . . Kt—K5.

18 Q—Q2	Kt—K4!

This Knight will be beautifully posted at QB5.

19 B×Kt	B×B
20 Q—B2	P—Kt3
21 Q—K2	Kt—B5
22 B—K4!	B—Kt2!

And not 22 . . . Kt×RP?; 23 Q—B3!, B×B; 24 Kt×B, B×Kt; 25 P×B, Kt—B5; 26 Kt—B6ch winning the exchange.

23 B×B	Q×B
24 R—B1	P—K4!

Now that White's King's Bishop is gone, Black's Knight will go to an even stronger post at Q6.

25 Kt—Kt3	P—K5

Again threatening . . . Kt×RP.

26 Kt—Q4	KR—Q1!
27 KR—Q1	Kt—K4
28 Kt—R2?	

28 P—B3 holds out longer.

28 . . .	Kt—Q6
29 R×R	Q×R
30 P—B3	

Now this move comes too late, but getting the off-side Knight back into the game is likewise futile: 30 Kt—QB3, P—B4; 31 P—B3, R×Kt!; 32 P×R, B×Pch; 33 K—B1, Kt—B5!;

34 Q—Q2, Q—B5ch; 35 Kt—K2, P—K6!; 36 Q—K1, B×P with an easy win.

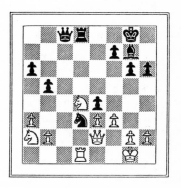

30 . . .	R×Kt!

In the last analysis, this striking combination is based on the unfortunate position of the Knight at R2.

31 P×P

Apparently a clever way out of his troubles. Against 31 P×R Alekhine intended 31 . . . B×Pch; 32 K—B1, Kt—B5!; 33 Q×P (if 33 Q—Q2, Q—B5ch; 34 K—K1, P—K6! winning), Q—B5ch; 34 K—K1, Kt×Pch; 35 K—Q2, B—K6ch and it is all over.

31 . . .	Kt—B5!
32 P×Kt	Q—B5!!
33 Q×Q	

Else he comes out a piece down.

33 . . .	R×Rch
34 Q—B1	B—Q5ch
Resigns	

It is mate next move.

CAPABLANCA received a special prize for this game, even though the best variations never happened!

QUEEN'S GAMBIT DECLINED
New York, 1916
(Second Brilliancy Prize)

WHITE	BLACK
Capablanca	Schroeder
1 P—Q4	P—Q4
2 Kt—KB3	P—K3
3 P—B4	Kt—KB3
4 Kt—B3	QKt—Q2
5 B—Kt5	B—K2
6 P—K3	O—O
7 R—B1	P—QR3

Planning . . . P×P followed by . . . P—QKt4, . . . B—Kt2 and . . . P—B4 completely solving his opening problems.

8 Q—B2!	R—K1
9 B—Q3	P×P
10 B×P	P—Kt4
11 B—Q3	B—Kt2
12 P—QR4!	

He hopes to prevent . . . P—B4, in which case Black will have a backward Pawn on a vital open line.

12 . . .	P—Kt5
13 B×Kt!	Kt×B
14 Kt—K4	Kt×Kt
15 B×Kt	B×B

After 15 . . . P—Kt6; 16 B×Pch!, K—R1; 17 Q—Q3, P—Kt3; 18 B×P, P×B; 19 Q×KKtP White wins without much trouble.

16 Q×B	P—QB4!?

An ingenious bid for freedom.

17 P×P	Q—R4
18 P—QKt3	B×P

19 Kt—Kt5	P—R3

On 19 . . . P—Kt3; 20 Q—B3! leaves White with a powerful attack.

20 Q—R7ch	K—B1
21 Q—R8ch!	

Beginning a combination out of the ordinary. It nets two Pawns in return for the sacrificed piece, to begin with, and, after hounding Black's King to QKt3, leads to virtual Zugzwang.

21 . . .	K—K2
22 Q×KtP	P×Kt
23 Q×KtPch	K—Q3

Forced!

24 K—K2!	QR—B1

If 24 . . . P—K4; 25 KR—Q1ch, K—B3; 26 Q—B6ch wins easily.

25 R—B4!	K—B3
26 KR—QB1!	K—Kt3
27 P—R4!	

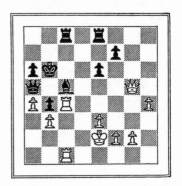

27 . . .	P—B4

Capablanca expected 27 . . . R—B2, for which he had prepared the following variation: 28 P—R5, KR—QB1; 29 P—R6, B—Q3; 30 Q×Qch,

K×Q; 31 R×R, R×R; 32 R×R, B×R; 33 P—B4!, B—Q1; 34 P—Kt4, B—B3; 35 P—Kt5, B—R1; 36 P—K4, K—Kt3; 37 P—B5, P×P; 38 P×P, K—B4; 39 P—Kt6! and a Pawn must queen!

28 Q—Kt7!	R—K2
29 Q—K5!	R—B3
30 R×B!	Resigns

If 30 . . . R×R; 31 Q—Q6ch is murderous.

HUMAN *nature being what it is, even chess masters succumb to the almost irresistible temptation of explaining away mistakes which turn out well. In this game, however, Cohn freely confessed that his loss of a Pawn in the opening was a blunder. Despite this fact, he conducted the rest of the game so masterfully that he won a brilliancy prize in a tournament that was studded with beautiful games.*

OLD-INDIAN DEFENSE
Karlsbad, 1907
(Second Brilliancy Prize)

WHITE	BLACK
Cohn	Tchigorin
1 P—Q4	Kt—KB3
2 P—QB4	P—Q3
3 Kt—QB3	QKt—Q2
4 P—K4	P—K4
5 KKt—K2	B—K2

Tchigorin pioneered in popularizing this defense in master play. Later on it became customary to fianchetto the King's Bishop (2 . . . P—KKt3 and 3 . . . B—Kt2).

| 6 P—KKt3 | O—O |

7 B—Kt2	R—K1
8 O—O	B—B1
9 P—KR3	P×P
10 Q×P?!	

This is subjectively a mistake, objectively a good move. 10 Kt×P was safe and good.

| 10 . . . | Kt—K4 |

Threatening to win a Pawn by 11 . . . P—B4 or by 11 . . . B×P (12 B×B??, Kt—B6ch winning the Queen). White cannot parry both threats.

11 P—B4	P—B4
12 Q—B2	Kt×BP
13 P—Kt3	Kt—QR4
14 B—Kt2	Kt—B3
15 QR—Q1	

White is fortunate: he has a good game in consequence of his mistake! His Bishops are powerful, his Kingside Pawns threaten to advance menacingly, he hopes to occupy Q5; Black is badly off, as his Queen's Pawn is backward, his development lags and his pieces have little scope.

| 15 . . . | Q—R4 |

Else P—K5 is annoying.

| 16 P—KKt4! | Kt—Q5?! |
| 17 Kt×Kt | P×Kt |

Tchigorin yearns for a bit of freedom. If 18 Q×P or 18 R×P, he plays 18 . . . P—Q4! threatening 19 . . . B—QB4! and thus improves his position considerably. But Cohn prefers to remain a Pawn down:

18 P—Kt4!!	Q×KtP
19 R×P	Q—R4
20 P—Kt5!	Kt—Q2
21 Kt—Q5!	Q—Q1

22 P—KR4	Kt—Kt3
23 P—B5	Kt×Kt

Black is stifling: he must remove the powerful Knight.

24 R×Kt	B—Q2
25 P—K5!	B—B3

If 25 . . . P×P; 26 P—B6! (not 26 KR—Q1, Q—B1!!; 27 R×B, B—B4! coming out at least the exchange ahead), P—KKt3 (else 27 P×P wins); 27 B—KR3! and Black has nothing better than 27 . . . B×B giving up his Queen.

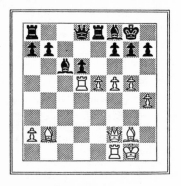

26 P—K6!!

The first of a series of magnificent moves. If now 26 . . . B×R; 27 B×B, P×P; 28 P×P, Q—K2; 29 Q—Q4! and there is no defense against the coming 30 R—B7.

26 . . .	P×P
27 P×P	Q—K2

If 27 . . . B×R; 28 Q—B7ch, K—R1; 29 B×B (threatens 30 P—K7!), R—K2; 30 Q—B5 (threatens 31 B—K4 followed by mate), K—Kt1; 31 B—K4, P—KKt3; 32 Q—B7ch!, R×Q; 33 P×R mate!

28 Q—B7ch!	K—R1
29 R(5)—KB5!	Q×Q

30 P×Q!	R—K7

As Tchigorin will soon discover to his sorrow, the exchange of Queens does not diminish the fury of White's threats.

31 R(1)—B2	R×R
32 R×R	P—Q4
33 B—Q4!	

Stopping . . . B—B4. With Black's King cooped up in the corner, all sorts of mating menaces appear, and White's advanced Pawn at B7 plays a decisive role. The immediate threat is 34 P—R5 and 35 P—R6 followed by 37 P×Pch, B×P; 38 P—B8(Q)ch and mate next move!

33 . . .	P—KR4
34 P—Kt6!	

Threatens 35 R—B5 and 36 R×P mate!

34 . . .	B—Q2
35 R—K2!	

This time threatening 36 R—K5 and 37 R×P mate!

35 . . .	B—Q3
36 B—R3!	B—Kt4

If 36 . . . B×B; 37 R—K8ch wins at once.

37 R—K6	Resigns

For if 37 . . . B—B2; 38 B—QB5!, B—Kt3; 39 B×B, P×B; 40 R—K5 still forcing mate!

A very beautiful game. Notice the career of White's King Pawn, which goes to K4, then K5, then K6, then KB7. It is really the secret of White's success!

ALEKHINE's *pluck and ingenuity overcome the effects of a poor opening in a spectacular effort that few players could equal. Picture Black's astonishment at the electrifying 23 B—B6!!*

QUEEN'S GAMBIT DECLINED
Budapest, 1921
(First Brilliancy Prize)

WHITE	BLACK
Alekhine	Sterk

1	P—Q4	P—Q4
2	Kt—KB3	Kt—KB3
3	P—B4	P—K3
4	Kt—B3	QKt—Q2
5	P—K3	B—Q3?
6	Kt—QKt5?	

Instead of this loss of time, 6 P—B5!, B—K2; 7 P—QKt4 should have been played.

6	. . .	B—K2
7	Q—B2	P—B3
8	Kt—B3	O—O
9	B—Q3	P×P
10	B×P	P—B4!
11	P×P	B×P
12	O—O	P—QKt3

As a result of Alekhine's lapse, Black has an excellent game. But Alekhine tries to force the pace just the same.

13	P—K4!?	B—Kt2
14	B—KKt5	Q—B1!
15	Q—K2	B—Kt5!
16	B—Q3	B×Kt
17	KR—B1!	Kt×P?

Too risky; best was 17 . . . Kt—B4!; 18 R×B, B×P; 19 B×Kt, B×B; 20 Q—K3!, P×B; 21 P—QKt4, B—Kt3! and Black remains a Pawn ahead,

although he has to stay on the defensive.

18	B×Kt	B×B
19	Q×B	Kt—B4
20	Q—K2!	

Even stronger than 20 Q—Kt1, B—Kt5; 21 P—QR3, Q—Kt2! etc. when Black can put up a much longer resistance than after the text.

20	. . .	B—R4
21	QR—Kt1	Q—R3
22	R—B4!!	

Keeping the threat of P—QKt4 alive and also planning a little surprise.

22	. . .	Kt—R5?!

So that if 23 P—QKt4, Kt—B6! But this is picayune in comparison to what Alekhine has in mind.

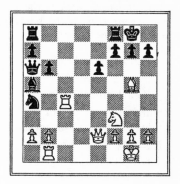

23	B—B6!!	KR—B1

If 23 . . . P×B; 24 R—Kt4ch wins the Queen! If 23 . . . P—R4; 24 R—KKt4!!, Q×Q; 25 R×Pch, K—R1; 26 Kt—Kt5! followed by 27 R—R7ch and 28 R—R8 mate!

24	Q—K5!!	R—B4

Or 24 . . . Q×R (if 24 . . . P×B; 25 R—Kt4ch and mate in two!); 25 Q—KKt5, K—B1; 26

Q×Pch, K—K1; 27 Q—Kt8ch, K—
Q2; 28 Kt—K5ch, K—B2; 29 Q×Pch
followed by 30 Kt×Q.

If 24 . . . R×R; 25 Q—KKt5,
R—KKt5; 26 Q×R, P—Kt3; 27
Q×Kt with a piece to the good.

25 Q—Kt3!	P—Kt3
26 R×Kt	Q—Q6
27 R—KB1	Q—B4
28 Q—B4	Q—B7
29 Q—R6	Resigns

Black's lineup on the Queen's Rook
file cried aloud for refutation; but who
but Alekhine would have hit on the
text method?

THIS is the Evergreen Game of
modern times. Note how the opposition has improved: the brilliancies are now in the notes instead of in the moves!

NIMZOINDIAN DEFENSE
Dresden, 1926
(First Brilliancy Prize)

WHITE	BLACK
Johner	Nimzovich
1 P—Q4	Kt—KB3
2 P—QB4	P—K3
3 Kt—QB3	B—Kt5
4 P—K3	O—O
5 B—Q3	P—B4
6 Kt—B3	Kt—B3
7 O—O	B×Kt

The thematic idea of this defense:
he gives White the "doubled Pawn
complex."

8 P×B	P—Q3
9 Kt—Q2!	P—QKt3
10 Kt—Kt3?	

Bad timing: correct was 10 P—B4!,
P—K4; 11 BP×P, QP×P; 12 P—Q5
with a good game.

10 . . .	P—K4

If now 11 P—Q5, P—K5! Thus
White is unable to op n the Bishop
file.

11 P—B4	P—K5!
12 B—K2	Q—Q2!!
13 P—KR3	Kt—K2
14 Q—K1	P—KR4!

This blockade of White's King-side
Pawns is an important factor in Nimzovich's plans. If now 15 Q—R4, Kt
—B4; 16 Q—Kt5, Kt—R2! wins the
exchange.

15 B—Q2	Q—B4!
16 K—R2	Q—R2!!

The whole idea of bringing the
Queen from Q1 to KR2 is typical
Nimzovich: original, profound and
powerful.

17 P—QR4	Kt—B4!

Threatens 18 . . . Kt—Kt5ch!; 19
P×Kt, P×Pch; 20 K—Kt1, P—Kt6
winning.

18 P—Kt3	P—R4!
19 KR—Kt1	Kt—R3
20 B—KB1	B—Q2
21 B—B1	QR—B1!

He wants to block the center (if
necessary, by . . . B—K3) before
starting a King-side attack.

22 P—Q5	K—R1!
23 Kt—Q2	KR—Kt1!
24 B—KKt2	P—KKt4!
25 Kt—B1	R—Kt2
26 R—R2	Kt—B4
27 B—R1	QR—KKt1
28 Q—Q1	P×P

29 KP×P	B—B1!
30 Q—Kt3	B—R3

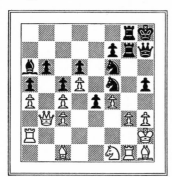

Nimzovich has built up a mighty attack on the King's Knight file according to plan. If now 31 Q×P, B×P wins quickly. Or if 31 R(2)—KKt2?, Kt—Kt5ch; 32 P×Kt, P×P mate!

Most entertaining of all is the following line given by Nimzovich: 31 B—Q2 (to support the King-side), R—Kt3!; 32 B—K1, Kt—Kt5ch!; 33 P×Kt (or 33 K—Kt2, B×P!), P×Pch; 34 K—Kt2, B×P!; 35 Q×B, P—K6!! (threatens . . . Q—R6 mate); 36 Kt×P (what else?), Kt×Ktch winning the Queen. Diabolical!

31 R—K2	Kt—R5
32 R—K3	

If 32 Kt—Q2, B—B1!; 33 Kt×P (if 33 Q—Q1, B×P!; 34 K×B, Q—B4ch wins), Q—B4; 34 Kt—B2, Q×Pch!!; 35 Kt×Q, Kt—Kt5 mate! (Nimzovich).

32 . . .	B—B1!
33 Q—B2	B×P!

So that if 34 K×B, Q—B4ch; 35 K—R2, Kt—Kt5ch; 36 K—R3, Kt—B7ch; 37 K—R2, Q—R6 mate!

34 B×P	B—B4
35 B×B	Kt×B
36 R—K2	P—R5!

The decisive smash.

37 R(1)—Kt2	P×Pch
38 K—Kt1	Q—R6
39 Kt—K3	Kt—R5
40 K—B1	R—K1!
Resigns	

If 41 K—K1, Kt—B6ch followed by 42 . . . Q—R8ch and a quick mate. A very beautiful game.

Black's *inventiveness in maintaining the attack is really exhilarating. Rarely has a grandmaster been pelted with so many sacrifices in so few moves!*

QUEEN'S GAMBIT DECLINED
Teplitz-Schönau, 1922
(First Brilliancy Prize)

WHITE	BLACK
Reti	Wolf
1 P—Q4	P—Q4
2 P—QB4	P—K3
3 Kt—QB3	Kt—KB3
4 B—Kt5	B—K2
5 P—K3	O—O
6 Kt—B3	QKt—Q2
7 R—B1	P—B3
8 Q—B2	P—QR3

So far the game has followed familiar patterns of the Orthodox Defense. But now Reti tries to restrict Black's game, and Wolf reacts energetically:

9 P—B5?!	P—K4!
10 P×P	Kt—Kt5
11 B×B	Q×B
12 Kt—QR4	R—K1
13 B—Q3	P—R3

13 . . . Kt—B1 is interestingly refuted by *14 Kt—Kt6, R—Kt1; 15 Kt×B, R×Kt; 16 B—B5* and Black loses the exchange.

| 14 Kt—Q4 | Kt(2)×KP |
| 15 Kt—Kt6? | Kt×BP!! |

The first point of this astounding move is that if *16 Kt×R, Kt(4)×Bch* with a winning attack.

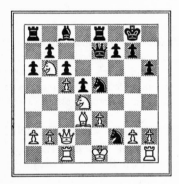

16 B—R7ch

Releasing his Bishop from the double attack.

If instead *16 K×Kt, Kt—Kt5ch; 17 K—K1* (or *17 K—Kt3, Q×Pch; 18 K—R4, Q—Kt4ch; 19 K—R3, Kt—B7 mate*), *Q×Pch; 18 Kt—K2* (if *18 B—K2, Q—B7ch* and *19 . . . Q×Ktch*), *B—B4!; 19 B×B* (if *19 R—Q1, Q—B7ch; 20 K—Q2, R×Ktch!*), *Q—B7ch; 20 K—Q2, R×Ktch* and wins.

16 . . .	K—R1
17 O—O	Kt(7)—Kt5!!
18 Kt×R	Kt×KP
19 Q—K2	

If *19 Q—Kt1* (to guard the Bishop), *Kt×R; 20 K×Kt, P—KKt3* or *20 R×Kt, Q×P* and Black wins.

| 19 . . . | Kt×R |

So that if White captures the Knight at KB1, Black can reply *20 . . . K×B* with two Pawns to the good.

| 20 B—Kt1 | Kt×P! |

Also good is *20 . . . B—Kt5* or *20 . . . Q—R5.*

| 21 Kt—Kt6 | Kt(4)—B6ch! |

If now *22 K—R1, Kt—B8!!* (perhaps White will play *23 Q×Q?* allowing *23 . . . Kt—Kt6 mate*); *23 Q×Kt(B3), Q—R5ch; 24 K—Kt1, Kt—Kt6; 25 R—Q1, B—Kt5; 26 Q—Q3, P—B4; 27 Kt—B3, B×Kt; 28 Q×B, R—K7* wins.

| 22 P×Kt | Q—Kt4ch |

The point!

23 K×Kt	R×Qch
24 Kt×R	Q—K4ch
25 Kt—Kt3	Q×Pch
26 R—B2	Q×B
27 R—K2	B—K3

Black has come out of the complications with an easy win.

28 P—B4	P—Kt3
29 Kt—R1	P—KR4
30 Kt—B2	P—R5
31 Kt—R1	Q—Q6
32 R—KB2	B—B4
Resigns	

Wolf's crisp timing has created some very enjoyable effects.

The Pawns Decide

♛ CHESS writing abounds in clichés about the "humble Pawn" and the "measly Pawn." For all that, chess literature is rich in examples of the Pawn's power. The general course, and even the outcome, of most games is determined in large measure by the Pawn position. Countless games are decided by Pawn captures, Pawn promotions, Pawn forks and other tactical play with the Pawn.

The games in this section are good examples of the many-sided usefulness of the Pawns. In the games Capablanca—Allies (p. 278) and Freymann—Alekhine (p. 281) we see how the queening of a passed Pawn provides the crowning touch to a brilliantly conducted attack.

Such aggressive exploitation of a passed Pawn is a familiar motif; what is less common, and hence even more attractive, is the advance of a passed Pawn as a weapon of *counterattack*. There are fascinating examples of this in Winawer—Lasker (p. 286) and Bruckner—Rubinstein (p. 282).

The storming of a castled position by Pawns is a device which goes back to the days of Philidor. Venerable as this procedure is, we get a thrill out of the way that the "lowly" Pawns sweep away every obstacle in the games between Albin and Winawer (p. 280) and between Tarrasch and Janowski (p. 283).

Sacrificing a piece for a couple of Pawns is another way of emphasizing the power of the Pawns. When several of them are passed and the hostile King is exposed to attack, as in the game Pillsbury—Wolf (p. 288), the Pawns invariably prove irresistible.

The Queen-side majority has decided many a famous game. Few players have illustrated this theme as ably as has Saemisch in his game with Gottschall (p. 285). "Masterly" is the word that must inevitably be applied to the way in which Saemisch establishes his Bishops in positions of power, acquires a Queen-side majority of Pawns, transforms it into a passed Pawn, and finally ensures the promotion of this Pawn. Everything else in the game is subordinate to the fate of this Pawn!

And so we see, again and again, how powerful the Pawn is, how versatile, how patient, how crafty! These are but a handful of the many master games that have been decided, in one way or another, by Pawn moves.

THE great Capablanca generally preferred simple positions in which he could display his wonderfully polished technique with moves of an unsurpassed crystal clarity. But there were times, as in the following game, when he launched farsighted speculative attacks which thrill us with their superb mastery of the whole board.

KING'S GAMBIT DECLINED
Buenos Aires, 1914

WHITE	BLACK
Capablanca	Allies
1 P—K4	P—K4
2 P—KB4	B—B4
3 Kt—KB3	P—Q3
4 Kt—B3	Kt—QB3

5 Kt—QR4	B—Kt3
6 B—Kt5	B—Q2
7 Kt×B	RP×Kt

Capablanca has acquired the Bishop-pair, and in the play that follows he makes good use of his Bishops.

8 P—Q3	KKt—K2
9 O—O	O—O
10 P—B5!	

This advance has two virtues: it cramps Black's game, and it is the introduction to a powerful attack.

10 . . .	P—B3
11 B—B4ch!	K—R1
12 P—QR3	B—K1
13 B—K6	B—R4
14 Q—K1	Q—K1
15 Q—R4	

White's attack is gradually becoming formidable.

15 . . .	Kt—Q1
16 B—R2	B—B2
17 P—B4!?	

Rather than exchange, he prefers to bury his Bishop alive! Only a player supremely sure of himself could dare to play such a move.

17 . . .	P—B4
18 P—KKt4	Kt—Kt1
19 B—Q2	P—QKt4
20 P—Kt5!	BP×P

He must capture, in view of the deadly threat of 21 P—Kt6.

21 Kt×KtP

White's advance of the King's Knight Pawn has briskly stepped up the tempo of his attack: his Knight has become very menacing, and the King's Knight file has been opened.

21 . . .	Kt—KB3
22 R—B3	P×P
23 Kt×P!	

The beginning of a combination which is remarkable for its sustained imaginative brilliance.

23 . . .	Kt×Kt
24 R—R3	B—Kt1
25 B×P	

The buried Bishop is resurrected; White threatens to win at once with 26 B×B.

| 25 . . . | R—B2 |

Bitter necessity: if 25 . . . Kt—B2; 26 P—B6!, P—KKt4 (if 26 . . . P×P??; 27 Q×P mate!); 27 Q—R5, Kt—Q1 (else 28 Q—Kt6 forces mate!); 28 Q—R6, R—B2; 29 B×P, Q—B1; 30 K—R1!, Q×Q; 31 B×Q,

R×BP; 32 R—KKt1! and Black is helpless.

26 K—R1!	P—QKt4
27 B—Q5	R(1)—R2
28 R—KKt1	R—B3
29 B—Kt5	R(2)—KB2

Black's position seems very solid, and there does not appear to be any way of breaking through. Brutal attempts would fail; but Capablanca has a method which is deliciously "quiet."

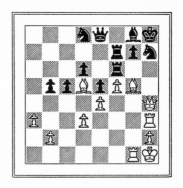

30 P—Kt3!!

One of the finest attacking moves ever played!

| 30 . . . | Q—B1 |

If 30 . . . R—B1?; 31 B×B wins at once. Or 30 . . . R—R2?; 31 B×R and Black cannot recapture. Throughout, of course, Black's Bishop is tied to Kt1 in order to guard the Knight at KR2.

31 P—R4!

Now everything becomes clear: White gets a passed Pawn which has fair chances of queening!!

| 31 . . . | P×P |
| 32 P×P | Q—K1 |

It is futile to take steps against the passed Pawn: if 32 . . . Kt—Kt2; 33 QB×R, P×B; 34 B×R, Q×B; 35 R(3)—Kt3 and wins. Or 32 . . . R—R2; 33 B×B, Q×B; 34 B×R and wins!

| 33 P—R5 | Kt—B3 |
| 34 P—R6 | Kt—Kt5 |

Note that all this time White has been a piece down! But the passed Pawn is worth more than a piece.

| 35 QB×R | Kt×B |

Pretty is 35 . . . P×B; 36 R×B ch!!, Q×R; 37 B×R, Q×B; 38 Q×Ktch!, Q×Q; 39 R×Qch, K×R; 40 P—R7 and the terrible Pawn queens!
Or try 35 . . . R×B; 36 Q×R!!, P×Q; 37 R×Bch, Q×R; 38 B×Q, K×B; 39 P—R7 with the same result.

36 B×Pch!!	R×B
37 R×R	K×R
38 Q—R6ch	K—R1

38 . . . K—B2 leads to a series of fatal exchanges: 39 R—Kt3, K—K2; 40 R—Kt7ch, B—B2; 41 Q—K6ch, K—B1; 42 R×Bch, Q×R; 43 Q×Qch, K×Q; 44 P×Kt and again the Pawn queens!

| 39 Q×P! | Resigns |

What to do? If 39 . . . Q—K2; 40 Q×Q, Kt×Q; 41 P—R7 etc.
If 39 . . . Kt moves; 40 Q—B6 mate!
If 39 . . . Q—B2; 40 Q×Pch, Kt—B3; 41 Q—R1!!, K—Kt2; 42 P—R7 or 41 . . . Q—R2; 42 Q×Ktch and wins. Thus the passed Pawn continues to play a vital role.
Capablanca's marvelously sustained combination has provided superb entertainment!

Something of Winawer's sly humor often spilled over into his games!

GIUOCO PIANO
Nuremberg, 1896

WHITE	BLACK
Albin	Winawer
1 P—K4	P—K4
2 Kt—KB3	Kt—QB3
3 B—B4	B—B4
4 P—B3	Kt—B3
5 O—O	

This lackadaisical line is inferior to the customary 5 P—Q4.

5 . . .	Kt×P
6 B—Q5	Kt×KBP!?
7 R×Kt	B×Rch
8 K×B	Kt—K2

Black has Rook and two Pawns for two minor pieces. Material is about equal, but the advantage will go to White if he develops rapidly, or to Black if his Pawns can become formidable.

| 9 Q—Kt3? | |

Too slow; 9 B—Kt3 is better.

| 9 . . . | O—O! |

So that if 10 Kt×P, Kt×B; 11 Q×Kt, Q—R5ch with a promising game. But White's feeble continuation enables Winawer to do even better.

10 B—K4?	P—Q4
11 B—B2	P—K5
12 Kt—K1	Kt—Kt3
13 P—B4	

In order to reinforce the King-side with his next move.

| 13 . . . | P—Q5! |

For if *14 B×P?, Q—R5ch* wins a piece.

14 Q—Kt3   P—KB4
15 K—Kt1   P—B4
16 P—Q3   P—B5
17 Q—B2   P—K6

With the hostile Pawns seeping into his position like a swarm of black ants, Albin is at his wit's end!

18 Q—B3   Q—R5

If now *19 P—KKt3, P×P; 20 Q×KKtP, Q—B3; 21 Q—Kt2, B—R6* and wins. Or *19 Q—K2, B—Kt5; 20 Kt—B3, Q—R4* and White's position is bound to collapse, as his Queenside pieces are hopelessly bottled up.

19 Q—Q5ch   K—R1
20 Kt—B3   Q—B7ch
21 K—R1   Kt—R5!

Heads straight for mate.

22 Q—Kt5   B—R6!
    Resigns

If *23 P×B, Kt×Kt; 24 Q—Kt2, Q—K8ch* and mate follows. *23 Q×Kt* or *23 Kt×Kt* allows mate on the move.

Experienced players devote years of study to the task of finding a good defense to the Queen's Gambit. Young Alekhine succeeds with no effort!

QUEEN'S GAMBIT DECLINED
St. Petersburg, 1913

WHITE	BLACK
Freymann	Alekhine

1 P—Q4   P—Q4
2 Kt—KB3   Kt—KB3
3 P—B4   P—K3
4 B—Kt5   P—KR3
5 B—R4   P×P
6 Q—R4ch   QKt—Q2
7 Q×BP   P—B4
8 Kt—B3   P—R3

Black is on the point of getting an excellent development with . . . P—QKt4 and . . . B—Kt2. Naturally Freymann stops this with:

9 P—R4   P—QKt4!

This "impossible" move is based on the fact that *10 RP×P??, RP×P!* costs White a Rook!

10 Q—Q3   P—B5
11 Q—Kt1   B—Kt2!

Now he really loses a Pawn; but he gets ample compensation in the form of development plus pressure.

12 P×P   P×P
13 Kt×P   B—Kt5ch
14 Kt—B3   P—Kt4!
15 B—Kt3   Kt—K5
16 Q—B1   Kt—Kt3

In order to strengthen the pin with . . . Kt—R5 or . . . Kt—Q4. White gets out of this pin, running into another one even more disastrous!

17	R×R	Q×R
18	Kt—Q2	Kt×KKt
19	K×Kt	Q—R7!

Adding another pin, and threatening to reinforce both pins murderously with . . . Kt—R5!

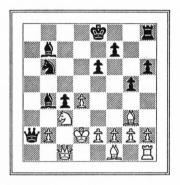

20	K—Q1	Q—Kt6ch
21	Q—B2	

Out of one pin, into another!

21	. . .	B×Kt!
22	P×B	B—K5!
23	Q×Q	P×Q
24	P—K3	

24 K—B1, Kt—B5! results in a quick mate!

24	. . .	P—Kt7
	Resigns	

Alekhine's reliance on Pawn moves at the critical stages has led to interesting play.

WHAT's in a name? Here S. Rubinstein produces a masterpiece of which the great Akiba would have been proud.

RETI OPENING
Vienna, 1937

WHITE	BLACK
Bruckner	S. Rubinstein
1 Kt—KB3	P—Q4
2 P—B4	P×P
3 Q—R4ch	Kt—B3
4 Q×BP	P—K4
5 P—Q3	B—K2
6 P—KKt3	Kt—B3
7 B—Kt2	O—O
8 O—O	Kt—Q2!

The Knight is brought to the more centralized square K3, while at the same time Black prepares for attack by means of . . . P—B4—5.

9 Q—B2	Kt—B4
10 B—K3	Kt—K3
11 R—B1	P—B4
12 Q—Kt3	

As he cannot stop the attack, White prepares an interesting combination based on the long-range striking power of his fianchettoed Bishop.

12 . . .	P—B5
13 R×Kt?!	P×R
14 Kt×P?!	P×B!
15 Kt×P	P×Pch
16 K—B1	Q—K1
17 Kt×Bch	

All this has been cleverly played by White. The idea is 17 . . . Q×Kt; 18 B×R, K—R1; 19 B—B3, Kt—Q5; 20 Q—Q1, B—R6ch; 21 K×P, B—Kt5; 22 Kt—Q2 and White should be able to weather the storm.

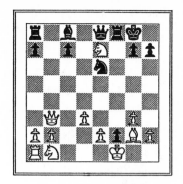

17 . . .   K—R1!!

Beautiful play! If now 18 B×R, Kt—Q5; 19 Q—Q1, B—R6ch; 20 B—Kt2, B×Bch; 21 K×B, P—B8(Q) ch and wins!

18 Q—Kt4   P—B4!
19 Q—KR4   QR—Kt1
20 B—K4!

The mating threat seems to leave White with an excellent game, as neither 20 . . . P—Kt3 nor 20 . . . P—KR3 is a satisfactory reply.

20 . . .   Kt—Kt4!!

Parries the mate threat and in turn menaces 21 . . . B—R6ch with deadly effect.

21 Kt—Kt6ch   Q×Kt!!
22 B×Q   B—R6ch
23 Q×B   Kt×Q
24 B—K4   R×P

Despite the fact that Black is a clear exchange ahead, the remaining play is quite interesting. His far-advanced Pawn continues to be the decisive factor.

25 Kt—B3   Kt—Kt4
26 P—KR4   Kt—K3!
27 P—K3   P—Kt4!

28 B—Q5   Kt—Kt2!
29 P—Kt4

If 29 P×P, Kt—B4! wins at once!

29 . . .   P—KR4!

And now if 30 KtP×P, Kt—B4! wins, while if 30 RP×P, P×P etc.

30 P—K4   RP×P
31 Kt—Q1   R—Q7
32 Kt—K3   Kt—R4!
33 Kt—B5

A last flimsy barricade (if 33 K—Kt2?, P—B8[Q]ch).

33 . . .   R×Kt!
     Resigns

For if 34 P×R, Kt—Kt6ch forcing 35 K—Kt2, P—B8(Q)ch after all. A very attractive game!

WHEN *Tarrasch wrote that "chess has the power to make men happy," he must have been thinking of games like this one.*

FOUR KNIGHTS' GAME
Ostend, 1907

WHITE	BLACK
Tarrasch	*Janowski*
1 P—K4	P—K4
2 Kt—KB3	Kt—QB3
3 Kt—B3	Kt—B3
4 B—Kt5	B—Kt5
5 O—O	O—O
6 P—Q3	P—Q3
7 B—Kt5	Kt—K2

The usual move here is 7 . . . B×Kt, in order to prevent the threatened Kt—Q5. But Janowski was never the man to part readily with a Bishop; he prefers, instead, to run the risk of

getting a broken-up King-side Pawn
formation.

   8 Kt—KR4   P—B3
   9 B—QB4   B—Kt5

This brings trouble in its train. 9
. . . P—Q4; 10 B—Kt3, Q—Q3 is
the more palatable alternative.

  10 P—B3   B—K3
  11 B×Kt   P×B

Forced (*11* . . . B×B??; *12* B×Kt!
winning a piece).

  12 B×B   P×B
  13 P—B4!   Kt—Kt3

Trying to shield his King from the
coming attack; but now the loss of a
Pawn is inevitable.

  14 Kt×Kt   P×Kt
  15 Q—Kt4   Q—K1
  16 P—B5!   P×P
  17 P×P   B×Kt

Now he consents to the exchange,
hoping that simplification will slow
down the coming attack.

  18 P×B   K—Kt2

On *18* . . . P—KKt4; *19* P—KR4
wins a Pawn.

  19 R—B3   R—R1
  20 P×P   Q—K2

He realizes that if *20* . . . R—R3
(on *20* . . . Q×P; *21* Q—Q7ch
wins) White can crash through with
21 R×P!!, K×R; *22* R—B1ch, K—
Kt2; *23* R—B7ch, Q×R (if *23* . . .
K—Kt1; *24* Q—Kt5 followed by *25*
Q—B6 is decisive); *24* P×Qch, K×P;
25 Q—Q7ch etc.

  21 P—KR4   P—Q4
  22 QR—KB1 QR—KB1
  23 P—R5   R—R3

The blockade! In order to smash
through Black's barricade, White must
play P—Kt4—5.

  24 R(1)—B2   R(3)—R1
  25 Q—B5   Q—Q3
  26 P—Kt4!   Q—K2

If *26* . . . R—R3?; *27* P—Kt5!
wins. Or if *26* . . . K—R3?; *27* P—
Kt7!, K×P; *28* Q—Kt6 mate!

  27 P—Kt5!   P×P
  28 Q×Rch!   R×Q
  29 R×R

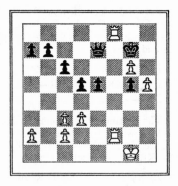

Black is helpless. *29* . . . Q—Q3?
is refuted by *30* R(2)—B7ch, K—R3;
31 R—R7 mate or *31* R—R8 mate.
29 . . . Q—B4 will not do because
of the insidious unpinning Pawn move
30 P—Q4!

  29 . . .   Q×R

Hoping for *30* R×Q?, which gives
a drawn King and Pawn ending.

  30 P—R6ch!   Resigns

For if *30* . . . K—Kt1; *31* P—
R7ch, K—Kt2; *32* R×Q etc. Tarrasch's pretty Pawn play has created
some charming effects.

For decades, Steinitz's contemporaries laughed at him when he stressed the power of the two Bishops. To the modern master, however, this is a familiar theme, illustrated in countless games. Saemisch shows us here how technique can rise to the level of great art.

SICILIAN DEFENSE
Hannover, 1926

WHITE	BLACK
Von Gottschall	Saemisch
1 P—K4	P—QB4
2 Kt—KB3	Kt—QB3
3 P—Q4	P×P
4 Kt×P	Kt—B3
5 Kt—QB3	P—Q3
6 B—K2	P—K3
7 O—O	B—K2
8 B—K3	O—O
9 Q—Q2	P—QR3
10 QR—Q1	Q—B2
11 P—B4	B—Q2
12 Kt×Kt	B×Kt

Saemisch has played the Scheveningen Variation, on which he is a leading authority. It is a tough, sinewy defense, with considerable scope for patient maneuvering. Von Gottschall, whose playing career dates back to the '80s, does not hold with this newfangled line, and yet he is at a loss for a promising policy. He drifts imperceptibly toward disaster.

13 B—B3	QR—B1
14 Q—B2	P—QKt4
15 P—QR3	Kt—Q2
16 Q—Q2	KR—Q1
17 Kt—K2	Q—Kt2
18 Q—Q3?	Kt—B4!
19 B×Kt	P×B

20 Q—K3	R×R
21 R×R	R—Q1
22 R×Rch	B×R

Of course White must not play 23 Q×P?? because of . . . B—Kt3. Following the exchange on move 19, Saemisch has courted simplification as the best way of enabling him to assert the power of the Bishops.

23 Kt—Kt3	B—Kt3
24 K—B1	K—B1
25 Q—B3	Q—Q2
26 Q—Q3?	Q×Qch
27 P×Q	P—K4!!

Very powerful, and the key to the ending. If White replies 28 P×P, then 28 . . . B—B2—after which Black regains the Pawn and wins one of the Queen-side Pawns as well.

28 P—B5	K—K2
29 Kt—K2	P—Kt5!

Keeping the Knight out of QB3.

30 Kt—B1	P—QR4!
31 K—K2	P—R5
32 K—Q1	B—Kt4

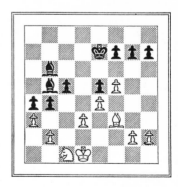

White's Bishop is ineffectual, being limited to defense; his Knight has hardly any scope. The following exchange, which has the drawback of giving Black a clear wing majority, seems unavoidable. Thus if 33 B—K2, P—Kt6!; 34 P—Kt3, K—Q3; 35 P—Kt4, P—B5!; 36 P×P, B—B3; 37 B—B3 (or 37 B—Q3, B—Q5), K—B4 winning easily.

33 P×P	P×P
34 Kt—R2	B—R4
35 B—K2	P—Kt6!

The winning move: if now 36 Kt—B1, P—R6!; 37 Kt×P, B—R5!; 38 K—B2, P—R7 and the Pawn queens!

36 Kt—B3	B×Kt
37 P×B	P—R6
38 K—B1	K—Q3

With two connected, well-advanced passed Pawns Black must win; but the finish is quite interesting.

39 K—Kt1	K—B3
40 K—R1	K—Kt3
41 K—Kt1	K—R4
42 K—R1	K—R5
43 K—Kt1	P—R7ch!
44 K—Kt2	P—R8(Q)ch!
45 K×Q	K—R6
46 K—Kt1	P—Kt7!
Resigns	

Now we see the point of the Pawn sacrifice: Black is bound to queen the remaining passed Pawn by . . . B—R5—Kt6—R7ch etc. This is chess of a very high order!

WHITE plays energetically for attack; yet a mere Pawn exercises an irresistible gravitational pull on White's attacking forces, so that they must ultimately scurry back to the defense.

RUY LOPEZ

Nuremberg, 1896

WHITE	BLACK
Winawer	Em. Lasker
1 P—K4	P—K4
2 Kt—KB3	Kt—QB3
3 B—Kt5	Kt—B3

Now generally discredited, this ("Berlin") Defense was a great favorite with Lasker for many years.

4 O—O	Kt×P
5 P—Q4	B—K2
6 Q—K2	Kt—Q3
7 B×Kt	KtP×B
8 P×P	Kt—Kt2
9 Kt—Q4!	O—O
10 Kt—QB3	B—B4
11 Kt—B5	

For all its aggressive appearance, this move relaxes the pressure which 11 R—Q1 would have maintained.

11 . . .	P—Q4
12 Q—Kt4	B×Kt
13 Q×B	R—K1
14 B—B4	B—Q5

Threatening to win a Pawn by . . . P—Kt3.

15 KR—K1	Kt—B4

White should now prevent the doubling of his Queen's Bishop Pawn by 16 B—Q2—but not 16 Kt—Q1, Kt—K5!; 17 P—B3, P—Kt3; 18 Q—Kt4, B×KP; 19 B×B, R×B; 20 P—

B3, Kt—B3! and Black has safely won a Pawn.

16 QR—Q1?	B×Kt
17 P×B	Q—B1
18 Q—R5	

Now that his Pawn position has been weakened, Winawer plays resolutely for attack.

| 18 . . . | Q—R3 |
| 19 R—K3 | Q×P! |

This is more than mere Pawn-grabbing. Lasker is confident that he can get his Queen back into the game before White's attack gains too much momentum. Even though the defense will be far from easy, the advance of his passed Pawn will provide the necessary diversion to slow down the attack.

20 R—QB1	Q—B5
21 R—B3	Kt—K3
22 B—Q2	R—K2
23 R—R3	Q—K5!

The seemingly formidable 24 P—KB4 will be answered by 24 . . . Q—Kt3!

| 24 P—B3 | Q—Kt3 |
| 25 Q—R4 | R—Q2 |

| 26 P—KB4 | Q—K5 |
| 27 P—Kt4 | Kt—B1! |

Preventing P—B5, which White can now force only at the price of taking his pieces off the King's Rook file.

| 28 Q—B2 | P—QR4! |

The relief expedition!

| 29 R—K3 | Q—B5 |
| 30 P—B5 | P—R5! |

30 . . . Q×Pch? would give White a new attacking line (31 R—Kt3).

| 31 R—B1 | |

If 31 P—K6, P×P; 32 P×P, Kt×P!; 33 R×Kt, Q×Pch picking up the Rook.

31 . . .	P—R6!
32 R(3)—K1	P—R7!
33 P—R3	P—B4!

If now 34 P—K6, P×P; 35 P×P, Kt×P!; 36 R×Kt, P—R8(Q) and wins!

| 34 K—R2 | P—Q5 |
| 35 Q—B3 | P—QB3! |

In order to double Rooks on the Rook file. 36 Q×P will not do because of 36 . . . R(2)—R2; 37 R—QR1, Q—K7ch etc.

36 P—K6	P×P
37 P×P	Kt×P
38 Q×P	R(2)—R2!
39 R—QR1	R—KB1!

Most instructive: a quick switch wins for Black on the *King-side!*

40 KR—K1	Kt—Q1
41 Q—QKt6	R(2)—KB2
42 B—Kt5	R—B7ch
43 K—Kt3	

On *43* K—Kt1, Q—Q4 is crushing.

43 . . .   Q×Pch
          Resigns

For *44* K—R4 allows mate in three
(*44* . . . Q×Pch! etc.). An absorbing game, played by Lasker with all
the assurance of a World Champion.

*It is difficult to select a good Pills-
bury game—he played so many of
them!*

QUEEN'S INDIAN DEFENSE
Monte Carlo, 1902

WHITE	BLACK
Pillsbury	*Wolf*

1 P—Q4	Kt—KB3
2 P—QB4	P—K3
3 Kt—QB3	P—QKt3?

This move, quite acceptable after *3*
Kt—KB3, is a blunder here; White
secures a lasting monopoly of the
center.

4 P—K4	B—Kt2
5 B—Q3	P—Q4
6 BP×P	P×P
7 P—K5	Kt—K5
8 Kt—B3	B—K2
9 O—O	O—O
10 Q—B2!	Kt×Kt

He cannot resort to *10* . . . P—
KB4 because of *11* P×P e.p., Kt×P
(*3*); *12* Kt—KKt5! winning at least
a Pawn.

11 B×Pch!	K—R1
12 P×Kt	P—Kt3
13 B×P	P×B
14 Q×P	

White has three Pawns for the
piece, four connected passed Pawns, a
lead in development and attacking
chances. What more could Pillsbury
want?

14 . . .	Q—K1
15 Q—R6ch	K—Kt1
16 Kt—Kt5	B×Kt
17 Q×Bch	K—B2
18 P—KB4	K—K3

The threat was *19* P—B5 and *20*
P—K6ch.

19 P—B5ch	K—Q2

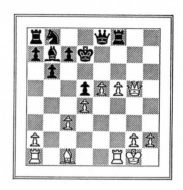

20 Q—Kt7ch!

A nice Pillsbury touch: If *20* . . .
Q—K2 (interposition at B2 loses after
21 P—K6ch); *21* P—K6ch wins the
Queen! (*21* . . . K—Q1; *22* B—Kt5
or *21* . . . K—Q3; *22* B—B4ch).

20 . . .	K—B1

How will Black get out his bottled-
up Queen-side pieces?

21 P—K6	R—Kt1
22 Q—R7	R—R1
23 Q—Kt6!	B—R3

If *23* . . . Q×Q; *24* P×Q, R—
Kt1; *25* P—Kt7! wins.

24 Q×Qch	R×Q

25 R—K1	Kt—B3
26 B—Kt5!	Kt—Q1
27 B×Kt!	

The Knight is removed to make P—B6 possible. Pillsbury's remorseless swapping down is a notable feature of this game.

27 . . .	K×B
28 P—B6	R—R1

Else 29 P—B7 wins right off.

29 R—K5!	P—B3
30 QR—K1	QR—B1
31 R—Kt5!	B—Q6

Best under the circumstances. If 31 . . . R—B2; 32 P—K7ch, K—Q2; 33 P—B7 or 32 . . . K—K1; 33 R—Kt7 etc.

32 R(1)—K5!

If 32 P—K7ch, K—K1; 33 R—Kt7, B—K5.

32 . . .	R—R3

He is helpless against the Pawns: if 32 . . . K—K1; 33 R—Kt7, R—B1; 34 P—K7 (34 R—K7ch is another way), R—KB2; 35 R—Kt8ch wins.

33 R—Kt8ch	K—B2
34 R×Rch	K×R
35 P—K7	B—Kt3
36 P—K8(Q)ch	Resigns

After 36 . . . B×Q; 37 R×Bch, K—Q2; 38 P—B7 and Black must give up his Rook. Smooth technique!

"You know Bill, I had to give up Tournament Chess— my nerves couldn't stand it!"

From Chess Magazine, by courtesy of the publisher, B. H. Wood, Sutton Coldfield, England.

Women in Chess

♛ EVERY radio comedian and night-club wit has several entries in his card-index file about the possibility of a woman's becoming President of the United States. The idea that a woman might become our chess champion seems equally "comical."

Yet both of these possibilities are less remote than they were in, say, 1930. As far as chess is concerned, many of us have had to revise our estimate of feminine ability since Vera Menchik earned the right to be considered a full-fledged chess master. Her game against Sir George Thomas, which appears on p. 117, speaks well for her great capabilities. Miss Menchik was also a fine analyst and annotator, and many a grateful pupil has paid tribute to her qualities as a teacher.

At the time these lines are written, no other woman player has quite approached Miss Menchik's playing strength; but, as more and more women turn to chess, her pioneering achievements are bound to be surpassed. The chief obstacle to further popularization of chess among women is, paradoxically enough, the nature of the male ego. There cannot be many men who are capable of losing a game to a woman without turning purple with rage. We venture to predict that as soon as men learn to accept defeat more gracefully, more women will play chess, and play it better. But when are men likely to start accepting defeat more gracefully?

HIMSELF a great master of combinative play, Spielmann was lavish in his praise of Miss Menchik's startling sacrifice.

QUEEN'S GAMBIT DECLINED
Match, 1937

WHITE	BLACK
Miss Menchik	Miss Graf
1 P—QB4	P—K3
2 Kt—QB3	P—Q4
3 P—Q4	Kt—KB3
4 Kt—B3	QKt—Q2
5 P—K3	P—B3

5 . . . P—B4 gives an easier game.

6 B—Q3	B—K2
7 O—O	O—O
8 P—K4	P×KP
9 Kt×P	Kt×Kt

This leaves White with a much freer game and good attacking chances. 9 . . . P—QKt3 as in the game Mikenas—Weenink (p. 339) is preferable.

10 B×Kt	Kt—B3
11 B—B2	P—B4
12 P×P	Q—R4

Black does not care to allow the exchange of Queens, for White would have distinctly better chances with the Queen-side majority of Pawns and more favorable development.

13 B—K3	B×P
14 B—Q2	Q—B2?

After 14 . . . B—Kt5; 15 B—Kt5 White would also have the better game; but after the text, which allows both White Bishops to combine ominously against Black's King-side, defense is difficult if not impossible.

15 B—B3!	B—K2

16 Q—K2   P—QKt3

Black does not fear 17 B×Kt, B×B; 18 Q—K4, P—Kt3; 19 Q×R, B—QKt2; 20 Q×P, R—R1; 21 Q×Rch, B×Q for the Black Bishops would then be very powerful.

17 Kt—Kt5!   P—Kt3

After 17 . . . P—KR3; 18 B×Kt, B×B (not 18 . . . P×Kt??; 19 Q—R5, P—Kt3; 20 Q—R8 mate); 19 Kt—R7, R—Q1; 20 Kt×Bch, P×Kt Black's exposed King would be subjected to a lasting attack.

18 Q—B3!   B—Kt2
19 Q—R3   P—KR4

If she prevents the threatened B× Kt by 19 . . . P—K4; 20 P—B4! is crushing.

20 QR—Q1   Kt—Kt5

Somewhat better was 20 . . . QR —Q1; but then 21 Kt×KP!, P×Kt; 22 B×P should be decisive.

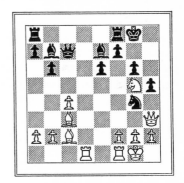

21 R—Q7!!

Not 21 Q×P, Q×Pch! and Black is safe.

21 . . .   Resigns

For if *21 . . . Q×R; 22 Q×P!!, P×Q; 23 B—R7 mate!*

THE war between the sexes ends in an airplane checkmate!

FRENCH DEFENSE
Berlin, 1937

WHITE	BLACK
Miss Karff	*Lugatsch*
1 P—K4	P—K3
2 P—Q4	P—Q4
3 P—K5	P—QB4
4 Q—Kt4	P×P
5 Kt—KB3	P—B4
6 Q—Kt3	Kt—QB3
7 B—K2	B—Q2?

7 . . . Q—B2 is better.

8 Kt×P!!   Kt×Kt?

The Knight should be declined in favor of some such move as *8 . . . K—B2* or *8 . . . KKt—K2.*

9 B—R5ch   K—K2

Or if *9 . . . P—Kt3; 10 Q×Pch!!, P×Q; 11 B×Pch, K—K2; 12 B—Kt5ch* and mate next move.

10 Q—R3 mate!!

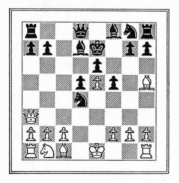

MISS GRAF plays a cut-and-thrust attack with a brilliant verve that reminds us of Spielmann's combinative skill in his palmiest days.

RUY LOPEZ
Margate, 1939
(Premier Reserves)

WHITE	BLACK
Solomon	*Miss Graf*
1 P—K4	P—K4
2 Kt—KB3	Kt—QB3
3 B—Kt5	P—QR3
4 B—R4	Kt—B3
5 Q—K2	P—QKt4
6 B—Kt3	B—B4
7 P—QR4	QR—Kt1
8 P×P	P×P
9 Kt—B3	O—O

Black plans an enterprising sacrificial attack.

10 Kt×KtP	Kt×P!?
11 Q×Kt	R×Kt
12 Q—QB4	R×B

If White declines this forced sacrifice of the exchange, there follows *13 Q×B, R×Kt!; 14 P×R, Kt—Q5* with a winning attack.

13 Q×R

Or *13 P×R, Q—K2* followed by *. . . P—Q4* with a tremendous attack.

13 . . .	P—K5
14 P—Q4	

The position is very difficult: if *14 Kt—Kt1, Q—B3; 15 Kt—R3, Kt—Q5* and the position gets too hot for White.

14 . . .	P×Kt
15 P×B	R—K1ch

16 K—B1

Or *16* B—K3, Kt—Q5; *17* Q—Q3, P×P; *18* KR—Kt1, Kt—B6ch and wins.

16 . . .   Kt—Q5!
17 Q—Q5

Or *17* Q—Q3, P×Pch; *18* K×P, B—Kt2ch and wins.

17 . . .   Kt×P

Threatens mate!

18 B—Kt5

Stops the mate and seems to kill Black's attack, as *18 . . .* R—K2 is indicated. But what player of spirit would want to make such a miserable move?

18 . . .   Kt×R!!

For if *19* B×Q?, B—R3ch leads to mate!

19 P×P   B—Kt2!
20 B×Q   B×Q
21 K—Kt2

Or *21* B×P, B×P; *22* R—Kt1, Kt —B7 wins quickly.

21 . . .   R×B
       Resigns

White has no compensation for the lost piece. An entertaining little game!

ᵔ*Decisive Games*

♛ CHESS is generally regarded as a searching test of skill. It is that, and it is something else as well: a war of nerves, all the more tense because lacking in physical action. In the higher reaches of master play, all the skill in the world will not avail a player if he is not a fighter.

This is a proposition with which Emanuel Lasker was thoroughly familiar, and it explains how he managed to hold the World Championship for a quarter of a century. Time and again, Lasker remained in the running by sheer will power and superb fighting spirit.

A case in point: the early rounds of the great international tournament at St. Petersburg in 1914 were a walkover for the great Capablanca. One opponent after another toppled with incredible rapidity, and the famous Cuban soon had what seemed an impregnable lead. Lasker was playing well, too, but he was trailing his younger rival. Finally, toward the end of the contest, Lasker had his chance in an individual encounter with Capa (p. 296).

How does such a crucial game proceed? Capablanca, confidently relying on his substantial lead, is content with a draw. Lasker *has* to win. The natural course is to seek complications, take risks, try to set the pace. But Lasker's approach is far more subtle: he plays for the early exchange of Queens. Capablanca wonders: Is it to be a quick draw after all?! He feels quite relieved—but not for long! Soon problems present themselves. With diabolical skill Lasker begins to offer his opponent difficult choices. Capablanca's mood changes to one of nagging uncertainty: every possibility seems to have a slight but dangerous flaw. First he fancies that every move is bad, and after a while every move *is* bad. Lasker reduces him to helplessness and winds up the game in brilliant fashion.

In Lasker's game with Reti (p. 298), we see a different kind of decisive game. Here Lasker, a man of fifty-five who has lost his title, is trying to make a comeback. He is an old-timer; his ideas are old-fashioned; the gossip is that he is a has-been. Reti is young, confident, ingenious, a leader of the dazzling Hypermodern School. Perhaps— who knows?—he has contempt for his elderly opponent. Yet he cannot help himself: his attitude toward Lasker is compounded of that instinctive respect and reluctant admiration that we have for a stern father or schoolmaster; and in the end Lasker beats him—in Marshall's immortal phrase—"like a child."

Alekhine was the only player in the history of the game who ranked with Lasker as a fighter. Alekhine's loss of the title in 1935 came as a shock to the whole chess world. When he lost the first game of the return match in 1937, it seemed that he was through. It was a situation much like that of a great boxing champion's failure to hold his own in the ring. While his admirers were overwhelmed by the pathos of Alekhine's decline, he himself had by no means lost hope. This he proved in the famous game (p. 299) in which he took a headlong gamble with such fabulously successful results that Euwe's spirit was broken for the rest of the match. Of Alekhine's famous sixth move it might be said: "This is the move that won a title."

Precisely that same term can be applied to Denker's almost equally famous seventh move against Fine (p. 301). Chess technique has been perfected to such an extent among the masters that for many of them the sacrifice of a precious Pawn is unthinkable. Not only did Denker sacrifice a Pawn: he sacrificed it on "spec." The tactical power of the sacrifice was great, but its psychological value was incomparably greater. Fine found himself in one of those disagreeable situations ("to take or not to take") where whatever one ultimately decides to do seems wrong. We can sense that he was plagued first by indecision, then by regret. Denker, on the other hand, was savoring that feeling of optimism which comes from dictating the course of events. While in this ebullient mood, he rained crushing blows on his opponent's position. The result is history: Denker won the game and the United States Championship.

Chess is a war of nerves. Who can doubt it after playing over these games?

The end of the great tournament nears; Lasker is a full point behind his great rival; only a win will keep him in the running. How does Lasker go about winning? He allows the exchange of Queens on the sixth move!!

RUY LÓPEZ
St. Petersburg, 1914

WHITE	BLACK
Em. Lasker	Capablanca
1 P—K4	P—K4
2 Kt—KB3	Kt—QB3
3 B—Kt5	P—QR3
4 B×Kt	QP×B
5 P—Q4	P×P
6 Q×P	Q×Q
7 Kt×Q	B—Q3
8 Kt—QB3	Kt—K2
9 O—O	O—O

Despite the exchange of Queens, there is plenty of fight in this position. White has a clear, unimpeded Pawn majority on the King-side; Black's corresponding Pawn majority on the other wing is practically worthless because of the doubled Pawn, but he has two Bishops. So Lasker has what he wants: a position full of tension, uncertainty and complex possibilities.

10 P—B4!	R—K1
11 Kt—Kt3	P—B3?

This creates a weakness at K3 which will later become disastrous. 11 . . . B—K3 was simple and good (if then 12 P—B5, B×Kt or 12 Kt—Q4, B—QB4).

12 P—B5!

Very daring: he means to attack later with P—KKt4—5, disregarding the weakening of his King's Pawn and the fact that Black gets a strong square for his pieces at K4.

12 . . .   P—QKt3?

Beginning a bad plan. The best chance was 12 . . . B—Q2; 13 B—B4, B×B; 14 R×B, P—QKt3!; 15 P—KKt4, Kt—B1 and it is still a fight.

13 B—B4!	B—Kt2

And here he could still try 13 . . . B×B; 14 R×B, B—Q2.

14 B×B!!	P×B

From here on the game may be considered lost for Black. His Queen's Pawn is weak, his pieces are in each other's way.

15 Kt—Q4	QR—Q1
16 Kt—K6	R—Q2
17 QR—Q1	Kt—B1
18 R—B2	P—QKt4
19 R(2)—Q2	R(2)—K2

Lasker is now in his element, and it is very instructive to see how he builds up a won game. Black can do nothing constructive, and even . . . R×Kt does not appeal to him: it would give him a more comfortable game, but with only a Pawn for the exchange, he would be sure to lose in due course.

20 P—QKt4!

A preparation for the ultimate opening of the Queen's Rook file.

20 . . .	K—B2
21 P—QR3	B—R1
22 K—B2	R—R2
23 P—Kt4	P—R3
24 R—Q3	P—QR4
25 P—KR4!	P×P
26 P×P	R(2)—K2

As Black has no mobility, the open file is useless to him.

27 K—B3	R—Kt1
28 K—B4	P—Kt3
29 R—Kt3	P—Kt4ch
30 K—B3!	Kt—Kt3

A little trap: if 31 R×P, Kt—B5 followed by . . . Kt—K4ch and . . . P×P with a game of sorts. But Lasker is too busy completing his plans for the final breakthrough:

31 P×P	RP×P
32 R—R3!	R—Q2
33 K—Kt3!	

Preparing for his 35th move, when his King must be off the diagonal.

33 . . .	K—K1
34 QR—KR1	B—Kt2

He is helpless about what is coming: if 34 . . . R—QR2; 35 R—R8 wins a Rook; if 34 . . . Kt—B5; 35 R—R8 wins a piece; if 34 . . . P—Q4; 35 P×P, Kt×P; 36 Kt—K4 followed by 37 R—R8 wins.

35 P—K5!!

Now the stored-up power of White's formidable position explodes with terrific effect.

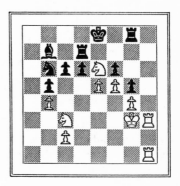

35 . . .	QP×P

If 35 . . . P—Q4; 36 Kt—B5, R—K2; 37 R—R8, R×R; 38 R×Rch, K—B2; 39 R—R7ch, K—K1; 40 R×Rch, K×R; 41 P×Pch, K×P; 42 Kt×B and wins.

Or if 35 . . . BP×P; 36 Kt—K4, Kt—Q4; 37 R—R8, R×R; 38 R×Rch, K—K2; 39 Kt(6)×P, Kt—B3; 40 Kt×Kt, K×Kt; 41 R—R6ch!, K—K2; 42 P—B6ch, K—Q1; 43 P—B7 and wins.

36 Kt—K4	Kt—Q4
37 Kt(6)—B5	

37 R—R7 is another way.

37 . . .	B—B1

If 37 . . . R—K2 (or 37 . . . R—QB2); 38 Kt×B, R×Kt; 39 Kt—Q6ch wins a Rook.

38 Kt×R	B×Kt
39 R—R7	R—B1

Black is helpless.

40 R—R1	K—Q1
41 R—R8ch	B—B1
42 Kt—B5	Resigns

Lasker: "The spectators had followed the final moves breathlessly. That Black's position was in ruins was obvious to the veriest tyro. And now Capablanca turned over his King. From the several hundred spectators, there came such applause as I have never experienced in all my life as a chess player. It was like the wholly spontaneous applause which thunders forth in the theater, of which the individual is almost unconscious."

In this game both players were out for blood. A few months earlier, Lasker had made some very disparaging remarks about the Hypermoderns, and tempers had flared in arguments over the relative merits of the Old and New Schools.

FRENCH DEFENSE
New York, 1924

WHITE	BLACK
Em. Lasker	Reti
1 P—K4	P—K3
2 P—Q4	P—Q4
3 Kt—QB3	Kt—KB3
4 B—Kt5	B—Kt5
5 Kt—K2	P×P
6 P—QR3	B—K2
7 B×Kt	P×B
8 Kt×P	P—KB4

This is premature because it exposes the Pawn to attack and because in some cases it permits White to advance effectively with P—Q5. 8 . . . P—Kt3 followed by . . . B—Kt2 is best.

9 Kt(4)—B3	B—Q2
10 Q—Q2	B—Q3
11 O—O—O	Q—K2

12 Kt—Kt3

Lasker has developed very rapidly and already threatens 13 Kt×P, P×Kt; 14 R—K1, B—K3; 15 P—Q5 with considerable advantage.

12 . . .	Q—R5

13 Q—K1!

Guarding against the threatened . . . B—B5 and in turn menacing 14 Kt×P.

13 . . .	Kt—B3
14 Kt×P	Q—B5ch
15 Kt—K3	Kt×P
16 P—KKt3!	Q—K4
17 B—Kt2	

A strongly posted Bishop!

17 . . .	Kt—B3?

Natural as this move looks, it proves disastrous. 17 . . . O—O—O! was necessary.

18 P—B4!

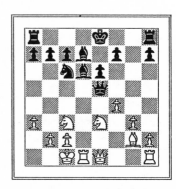

Black must lose at least a Pawn, for example 18 . . . Q—B3; 19 Kt—Kt5, Q—K2 (if 19 . . . K—K2??; 20 Kt—Q5ch); 20 Kt—B4 etc.
Or 18 . . . Q—QB4; 19 Kt—K4, Q—Kt3; 20 Kt—B4, Q—R3; 21 B—B1, Q—R5; 22 Kt—B3 winning the

Queen; while if *21 . . . P—Kt4; 22
Kt(B4)×Bch, P×Kt; 23 B×P, Q—
Kt3; 24 Kt×Pch, K—K2; 25 Kt—
B5ch, K—K1; 26 Q—B3* with a quick
win.

```
18 . . .          Q—Kt2
19 Kt—Kt5!        O—O
```

He must lose the Pawn (if *19 . . .
Q—B1; 20 Kt—B5!*) but *19 . . .
O—O—O* holds out longer.

```
20 Kt×B           P×Kt
21 R×P            KR—Q1
22 Q—Q2           B—K1
23 R—Q1           KR—B1
24 P—B5!
```

Every move of Lasker's is vigorous
and to the point. If now *24 . . .
P×P; 25 Kt×P, Q—K4; 26 Q—
Kt5ch, K—B1; 27 R—B6* and wins.
Or *25 . . . Q—B1; 26 Q—Kt5ch,
K—R1; 27 Q—B6ch* winning the
Queen. Finally, if *25 . . . Q—R1; 26
Q—Kt5ch, K—B1; 27 Q—R6ch, K—
Kt1; 28 R×Kt!* etc.

```
24 . . .          P—K4
25 P—B6!          Q—B1
```

If *25 . . . Q—Kt3; 26 B—R3* is
very powerful.

```
26 Kt—B5          K—R1
27 Q—Kt5          R—B2
```

This loses a Rook, but the position
had become untenable: if *27 . . .
Q—Kt1; 28 Q×Qch, K×Q; 29 B×Kt,
P×B; 30 Kt—K7ch, K—B1; 31
Kt×R, R×Kt; 32 R—Q8, R×R; 33
R×R* and Black has an acute case of
Zugzwang!
Another impressive tie-up results
from *27 . . . R—Q1; 28 Kt—K7,
R×R; 29 R×R* and there is nothing
to be done against *B—K4* and *Q—B5.*

```
28 B×Kt           R×B
```

Or *28 . . . B×B; 29 R—Q8!*

```
29 R—Q8!          R(3)—B1
30 Q—Kt7ch!       Q×Q
31 P×Qch          K—Kt1
32 Kt—K7ch        Resigns
```

This is truly "common sense in
chess."

LESSER *men are fond of saying that
the World Champions are lucky.
It would be more accurate to say
that the titans of the chessboard
know how to play for intensely
difficult positions in which their
less gifted opponents are bound
to go astray.*

QUEEN'S GAMBIT DECLINED
World Championship Match, 1937

WHITE	BLACK
Alekhine	*Euwe*

```
1 P—Q4            P—Q4
2 P—QB4           P—QB3
3 Kt—QB3          P×P
4 P—K4            P—K4
```

Hoping for *5 P×P, Q×Qch; 6
Kt×Q, B—K3* and Black has a very
promising game.
White's indicated course, however,
is *5 Kt—B3, P×P; 6 Q×P, Q×Q;
7 Kt×Q* with excellent end-game
chances, as the gambit Pawn cannot
be maintained.
Instead, Alekhine springs one of his
famous surprises:

```
5 B×P?!           P×P
```

If *5 . . . Q×P; 6 Q—Kt3, Q—Q2;
7 B—KKt5* with the terrible threat of
8 R—Q1.

```
6 Kt—B3?!
```

Logical . . . and yet unbelievable!

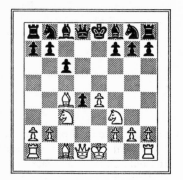

| 6 . . . | P—QKt4?? |

Euwe falters—and who can blame him? There are innumerable variations, all of them complicated and all of them dangerous-looking, to be plowed through. Such a task becomes a crushing burden under a time limit and the terrifying knowledge that the sacrifice is offered by the greatest attacking player in the history of chess.

Black could have obtained the better game, as Alekhine later admitted, with 6 . . . P×Kt!; 7 B×Pch, K—K2; 8 Q—Kt3, P×P!; 9 B×P, Q—Kt3!; 10 B×Kt, R×B; 11 Q×R, Q—Kt5ch; 12 Kt—Q2, Q×B etc.

7 Kt×KtP!

Poor Euwe! In the midst of all his deep delving, he has overlooked that if 7 . . . P×Kt; 8 B—Q5 leaves White the exchange ahead. Alekhine's gamble has succeeded!

| 7 . . . | B—R3 |
| 8 Q—Kt3! | Q—K2 |

If 8 . . . B×Kt; 9 B×Pch, K—Q2; 10 Kt×P! (not 10 B×Kt, R×B!; 11 Q×R??, B—Kt5ch winning the Queen) and Black's position is shattered.

| 9 O—O | B×Kt |

If 9 . . . P×Kt; 10 B—Q5, B—Kt2; 11 Q×Pch etc.

| 10 B×B | Kt—B3 |

Or 10 . . . P×B; 11 Q—Q5 and wins.

11 B—QB4	QKt—Q2
12 Kt×P	QR—Kt1
13 Q—B2	Q—B4
14 Kt—B5	

Avoiding the tempting 14 Kt×P? (if 14 . . . Q×Kt??; 15 B×Pch wins the Queen) which is answered by 14 . . . R—B1 winning a piece.

| 14 . . . | Kt—K4 |

A sly move, for if 15 Kt×Pch?, K—Q1! (if 15 . . . B×Kt??; 16 B×Pch wins the Queen) White loses a piece!

| 15 B—B4! | Kt—R4 |
| 16 B×Pch! | |

It is this clever continuation which validates his previous move. Alekhine now concludes the game in simple but vigorous fashion.

16 . . .	K×B
17 Q×Q	B×Q
18 B×Kt	R—Kt4
19 B—Q6!	

Threatening 20 P—QR4, R—R4; 21 P—QKt4 and wins.

| 19 . . . | B—Kt3 |

Or 19 . . . B×B; 20 Kt×Bch winning the exchange.

| 20 P—QKt4! | |

Threatening to win the exchange with 21 P—QR4.

| 20 . . . | R—Q1 |

So that if 21 P—QR4, R×Kt; 22 P×R, R×B.

21 QR—Q1	P—B4

What else?

22 P×P	B×P
23 R—Q5!	Resigns

Two pieces are attacked: he must lose at least the exchange (23 . . . B×B etc.). Or 23 . . . R—QB1; 24 B×B followed by the fatal 25 Kt—Q6ch!

Euwe was so crushed by this defeat that it virtually decided the fate of the World Championship!

Few experiences in a chess master's life are more disagreeable than running into an unexpected opening sacrifice in a vitally important game. As in the Alekhine—Euwe encounter, Denker's sacrifice virtually decided the result of the tournament. It is no exaggeration to say that Denker owed his title to this sensational game!

NIMZOINDIAN DEFENSE
United States Championship, 1944

WHITE	BLACK
Denker	*Fine*
1 P—Q4	Kt—KB3
2 P—QB4	P—K3
3 Kt—QB3	B—Kt5
4 P—K3	P—QKt3
5 B—Q3	B—Kt2
6 Kt—B3	Kt—K5
7 O—O!!	

A stunning surprise, the usual line being 7 Q—B2, P—KB4 with a satisfactory game for Black. The sacrifice is a speculative one: White will get a fine development, good attacking chances and the pleasant feeling that no matter what Black plays, his decision will appear faulty.

7 . . .	Kt×Kt
8 P×Kt	B×P
9 R—Kt1	B—R4

The Bishop is useless throughout the game; hence he might well have played 9 . . . O—O returning the Pawn (10 B×Pch, K×B; 11 Q—B2ch etc.).

10 B—R3!	P—Q3
11 P—B5!	O—O
12 P×QP	P×P
13 P—K4	R—K1
14 P—K5	P×P
15 Kt×P	

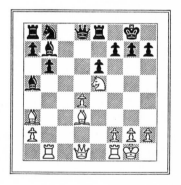

Denker has quickly built up a tremendous attacking position against Black's denuded King-side. Thus if 15 . . . Kt—B3; 16 B×Pch!, K×B; 17 Q—R5ch, K—Kt1; 18 Q×Pch, K—R1; 19 R—Kt3! wins. Or 15 . . . P—KR3; 16 Q—R5, Q—B3; 17 Kt×P!, Q×Kt; 18 B—Kt6 wins brutally.

15 . . .	Q—Kt4
16 P—Kt3	P—Kt3

On 16 . . . Kt—B3; 17 Kt×P!, K×Kt; 18 R—Kt5!! wins, for example 18 . . . P—K4; 19 Q—Kt3ch or 18 . . . Q—B3; 19 Q—R5ch etc.

17 Q—R4!   Q—Q1

17 . . . Kt—R3 is refuted by 18 Q—Q7! 17 . . . R—Q1; 18 KR—B1 virtually leaves Black without moves.

The demoralization caused by White's seventh move has taken its toll: at this late stage Black has made no progress to speak of in getting his pieces out.

18 KR—B1   P—QKt4

Sheer desperation. Against 18 . . . Kt—R3 Denker intended 19 Q×B!, P×Q; 20 R×B, Q×P; 21 B—Kt2, Q—Q4; 22 B×Kt with a winning game.

19 B×QKtP   Q—Q4
20 P—B3   B—Kt3
21 R—B5!!

Keeping up the pressure by crushing Black's counterplay.

21 . . .   B×R
22 B×B   R—KB1
23 B—B4!   B—B3

Else the Bishop is lost.

24 B×Q   B×Q
25 B×QR   Resigns

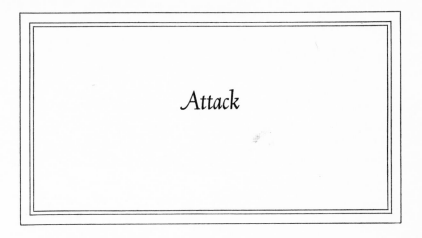

Attack

♛ Attack, to paraphrase the great Philidor's maxim, is the soul of chess. There are many ways to win a game, but attack is the most attractive of them all. Attacking chess is the kind of chess that makes our pulses beat faster—the kind of chess that gives us the greatest pleasure and the most thrills.

Not the least charm of attack is its endless variety. The King's Bishop file has often been the highway to victory, and Tartakover's utilization of the open file (p. 307) against Broadbent bears this out in a fascinating way (two sacrifices of the exchange!).

Equally deadly is the effect of two powerful Bishops trained menacingly on the hostile King. The games between Capablanca and Jaffe (p. 304), Landau and Feigin (p. 310) and between Reinfeld and Smirka (p. 306) are convincing testimony to the attacking value of the combined Bishops.

Games in which the players castle on different wings are almost invariably lively. In most of our examples, it is the player who castles Queen-side who succumbs to a withering offensive. Anderssen unleashes a pleasing series of threats against Dufresne (p. 308) which soon demolish Black's position; Noteboom, in his game with Thompson (p. 305), gives us a convincing example of the attack on the open Queen's Bishop file, supported by a murderous fianchettoed Bishop; Rossetto calmly offers his Queen a number of times to Aguilar (p. 311), serenely prepared to checkmate with the less important pieces.

To attack after the Queens have been exchanged is perhaps the rarest, certainly the most elegant, form of attack. Chalupetzky does this to perfection against Kallos (p. 312), winding up in beautiful style with an exquisite mate engineered only by minor pieces.

It would be hard to match these eight games for variety and interest. The play of the victors is, as it must be, aggressive, imaginative and inventive—"never a dull moment!" And what more can we ask of chess?

WITH his Bishops pointing balefully at Black's King, Capablanca builds up a devastating attack. Note how Capablanca provokes weaknesses in the hostile King's position and how he takes advantage of them.

QUEEN'S GAMBIT DECLINED
New York State Championship, 1910

WHITE	BLACK
Capablanca	Jaffe
1 P—Q4	P—Q4
2 Kt—KB3	Kt—KB3
3 P—K3	P—B3
4 P—B4	P—K3

4 . . . B—B4 is more promising.

5 Kt—B3	QKt—Q2
6 B—Q3	B—Q3
7 O—O	O—O
8 P—K4	P×KP
9 Kt×P	Kt×Kt
10 B×Kt	Kt—B3
11 B—B2!	P—KR3

Weakening; but White was threatening B—Kt5 in conjunction with Q—Q3.

12 P—QKt3	P—QKt3
13 B—Kt2	B—Kt2
14 Q—Q3!	P—Kt3

Another weakness; but he fears P—Q5! followed by B×Kt. If, for example, 14 . . . Q—B2; 15 P—B5!, B—K2; 16 P—Q5! (threatens 17 B×Kt, B×B; 18 Q—R7 mate), KR—Q1; 17 P—Q6 and wins.

15 QR—K1

Already threatening 16 R×P!

15 . . .	Kt—R4
16 B—B1!	

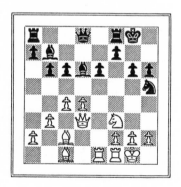

16 . . .	K—Kt2

Black is helpless: if 16 . . . B—B5; 17 R×P!, B×B; 18 R×Pch!, P×R (if 18 . . . K—R1; 19 R—Kt8ch! or 18 . . . Kt—Kt2; 19 R—Q6!); 19 Q×Pch, Kt—Kt2; 20 Kt—K5 and wins.

Or *16* . . . Kt—B5; *17* B×Kt, B×B; *18* R×P! and wins.

| *17* R×P! | Kt—B3 |
| *18* Kt—K5! | P—B4 |

If *18* . . . P×R; *19* Q×Pch, K—R1; *20* Q×Pch, K—Kt1; *21* Q—Kt6ch, K—R1; *22* R—K1, Q—K1; *23* Q—R6ch, K—Kt1; *24* R—K3 wins.

| *19* B×Pch! | K×B |
| *20* Kt×Pch! | Resigns |

Black has paid dearly for his Kingside weaknesses.

THE chess world lost a future grandmaster when Daniel Noteboom died before his twenty-second birthday.

SICILIAN DEFENSE
Ramsgate, 1929

WHITE	BLACK
Thompson	*Noteboom*
1 P—K4	P—QB4
2 Kt—KB3	Kt—QB3
3 P—Q4	P×P
4 Kt×P	Kt—B3
5 Kt—QB3	P—Q3
6 B—K3	P—KKt3
7 B—Q3?	

The Bishop has no future here: *7* B—K2 was indicated.

7 . . .	B—Kt2
8 P—KR3	O—O
9 Q—Q2	B—Q2
10 P—B4	P—QR3
11 Kt—B3?	

Another weak move: *11* P—QR4 would have restrained Black's expansion on the Queen-side.

11 . . .	P—QKt4
12 P—KKt4	R—B1
13 P—R3	K—R1
14 O—O—O?	

A notable case of "castling into it." Black's two strategical trumps (the long diagonal and the open Queen's Bishop file) are now transformed into possibilities for brilliant attack.

| *14* . . . | P—Kt5! |
| *15* P×P | Kt×QKtP |

With a strong threat of . . . Q—R4.

16 Q—K2

To make room for the King.

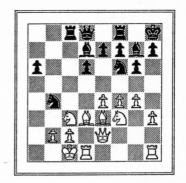

16 . . .	R×Kt!
17 P×R	Kt—R7ch
18 K—Q2	

If *18* K—Kt2, Kt×KP! is quite conclusive.

18 . . .   Kt×Pch!

Imaginative play: if *19* B×Kt, B×Pch; *20* K—Q3, B—Kt4 mate!

19 K—K1	Kt(7)×P
20 Q—Kt2	Kt×R
21 K×Kt	B—QB3!

So that if 22 K—K2, Q—R1 and the Queen's Rook Pawn can go on to queen!

22 B×P	Q—R4!
23 B—Q3	Q—R8ch
24 K—K2	Q×R!

Obvious but elegant.

25 Q×Q	Kt—Kt6ch
26 K—B2	Kt×Qch
27 K—Kt2	R—B1!
Resigns	

For if 28 B—K2, B—K5; 29 K×Kt, R×P; 30 B—Q1, R—B6 and wins. A dashing game.

In the good old days, games were generally lost as the result of large-scale mistakes. In modern chess, a trifling mistake in the opening may lead almost by force to a catastrophe.

QUEEN'S GAMBIT DECLINED
(in effect)
Marshall Chess Club Championship, 1937

WHITE	BLACK
Reinfeld	*Smirka*
1 P—QB4	Kt—KB3
2 Kt—KB3	P—B3
3 P—Q4	P—Q4
4 P—K3	P—K3
5 B—Q3	QKt—Q2
6 QKt—Q2	B—Q3

Both players are angling for the advance of their respective King's Pawns.

7 O—O	O—O
8 P—K4	P×KP
9 Kt×P	Kt×Kt

10 B×Kt	P—KR3

Avoiding the well-known trap 10 . . . P—K4?; 11 P×P, Kt×P; 12 Kt×Kt, B×Kt; 13 B×Pch! and White wins a Pawn.

11 B—B2	Kt—B3?

Correct was 11 . . . P—K4 with equal chances.

12 B—Q2	Q—K2
13 R—K1	R—Q1
14 P—QR3	P—B4
15 P—Q5!	Q—B2
16 B—B3!	

As a result of his opponent's lapse, White has all the play and his Bishops press very strongly against Black's King-side.

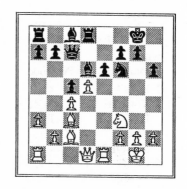

16 . . .	B—K2

Black's lagging development tells against him whenever he goes in for complications. Thus if 16 . . . P×P; 17 P×P, Kt×P; 18 Q×Kt!, B×Pch; 19 Kt×B, R×Q; 20 R—K8 mate. Or 17 . . . B—K2; 18 Q—Q3, R×P; 19 R×B!, Q×R; 20 B×Kt! with a winning game.

17 Q—Q3!	

Very painful for Black, as . . .
P×P? can always be answered decisively with B×Kt!

17 . . .   P—QKt4!

A bold bid for freedom, which fails
because of the general inferiority of
Black's game.

If 17 . . . P—KKt3 (in order to
neutralize the White Queen's mating
threat on the diagonal); 18 Kt—K5!
with the crushing threat of 19 Kt×BP
or 19 Kt×KtP.

| 18 P—QKt3 | Q—Kt3 |
| 19 QR—Q1 | B—R3 |

Threatening 20 . . . KtP×P; 21
KtP×P, R×P. But meanwhile White
has prepared for the final assault.

20 B×Kt!	B×B
21 Q—R7ch	K—B1
22 P—Q6!	

An example of what Nimzovich
called the passed Pawn's "lust to ex-
pand." The threat is 23 Q—R8 mate.
Black cannot play 22 . . . R×P because of the ensuing loss of a Rook.

| 22 . . . | P—Kt3 |
| 23 Kt—K5! | |

23 Q×RPch, B—Kt2 is too slow for
White's taste.

| 23 . . . | B—KKt2 |

On 23 . . . B×Kt; 24 R×B wins
easily, while if 23 . . . Q—Kt2; 24
P—Q7, B×Kt; 25 R×B with quick
collapse indicated for Black's position.

24 Kt×P!	K×Kt
25 Q×Pch	K—B1
26 R—K3	

Threatens 27 R—B3ch. Other ways
to win are 27 R×P followed by 28
R—K7; and 27 R—K4, P—K4; 28
R—Q3 etc.

26 . . .	B—Kt2
27 R×P	Q—B3
28 R—Q5	Resigns

If 28 . . . R—K1; 29 R—B6ch
forces mate. Or 28 . . . R—Q2; 29
R—B5ch, K—Kt1; 30 R—K8ch, R×
R; 31 Q×Rch, K—R2; 32 R—Q5
mate!

TARTAKOVER's games, like those of
Bird, are always off the beaten
track; one invariably finds in
them a touch of "something different."

SICILIAN DEFENSE
London, 1946

WHITE	BLACK
Tartakover	Broadbent
1 P—K4	P—QB4
2 Kt—K2	P—Q3
3 P—KKt3	Kt—QB3
4 B—Kt2	P—KKt3
5 P—QB3!	B—Kt2
6 O—O	Q—Kt3
7 Kt—R3!	Kt—B3
8 P—R3	O—O
9 P—Q4	

As so often happens in his games,
Tartakover has obtained a promising
position with the aid of several unconventional moves. It is already clear
that White will have all the play, but
Tartakover continues to strengthen his
position methodically.

9 . . .	P×P
10 P×P	B—Q2
11 P—Kt3!	KR—Q1
12 B—Kt2	Q—R3
13 Q—Q2!	Kt—K1

A more efficient defensive forma-

tion would result from . . . B—K1
followed by . . . Kt—Q2—B1.

14	P—B4	QR—B1
15	Kt—B4	P—QKt4
16	Kt—K3	Kt—B2
17	P—B5!	

Now that the "bizarrely" developed
Knight has been brought to the King-
side, Tartakover begins the decisive
assault.

17	. . .	Q—Kt3
18	K—R2	B—K1
19	P—B6!!	B×P

19 . . . B—R3 was the only move
that deserved consideration; but who
can blame Black for failing to see
through Tartakover's magnificent
plan?

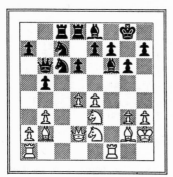

| 20 | R×B!! | P×R |
| 21 | Kt—Kt4 | P—Q4 |

The only way to give the menaced
King-side some support.

| 22 | Q—R6 | Kt—K2 |
| 23 | R—KB1 | R—Q3 |

Broadbent defends as best he can
in the absence of his precious fianchettoed King's Bishop. If 23 . . . P—
B4; 24 P×P, Kt×P; 25 R×Kt!, P×R;
26 Kt—B6ch etc.

| 24 | P—K5 | Kt—B4 |

If the attacked Rook moves, 25
P×P is fatal.

25	R×Kt!!	P×R
26	Kt×Pch	R×Kt
27	P×R	Kt—K3
28	Kt—B4	Q—Kt2

So that if 29 Kt×Kt, P×Kt guards
the mate on Black's KKt2. Or 29
B×P, R—B7ch; 30 K—Kt1 (if 30
K—R1, B—B3!), Q—B2! But . . .

29 B—R3!!

Threatens 30 Kt×Kt, P×Kt; 31
Q—B8 mate.

29 . . .   B—B3

If 29 . . . P—Kt5; 30 B×KtP!,
Q×B; 31 Kt×Kt forcing mate!

30 B—K7!!   Resigns

There is no way to guard against
the coming 31 Kt×Kt. One of the
finest combinations ever made!

THIS *is not the famous Anderssen—*
Dufresne game; yet it has very at-
tractive qualities and deserves to
be better known.

DUTCH DEFENSE
Berlin, 1852

WHITE	BLACK
Anderssen	Dufresne
1 P—Q4	P—KB4
2 P—K4	P×P
3 Kt—QB3	Kt—KB3
4 B—KKt5	P—Q4?

Instead of retaining the gambit
Pawn, this greedy move actually loses
two Pawns!

5 B×Kt	KP×B
6 Q—R5ch	P—Kt3
7 Q×QP	B—R3

If 7 . . . Q×Q; 8 Kt×Q attacking two Pawns; and if 7 . . . P—KB4??; 8 Q—K5ch winning a Rook.

8 Kt×P!	Q—K2

Of course if 8 . . . Q×Q; 9 Kt× Pch and 10 Kt×Q.

9 B—K2	Kt—Q2

If 9 . . . P—B3; 10 Kt—Q6ch, K—Q1; 11 Kt×Bch wins easily.

10 Kt—QB3	P—KB4
11 Kt—B3	P—B3
12 Q—Kt3	Kt—Kt3
13 O—O	B—K3

Both players have striven for rapid development, but it would appear that Dufresne has the better of the argument, as White's Queen is about to be forced to an awkward square.

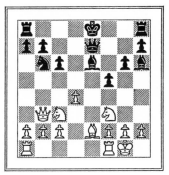

14 P—Q5!

Nicely played: he returns the extra Pawn to open up new attacking lines. Thus if 14 . . . P×P; 15 B—Kt5ch, K—B2; 16 Kt—Q4 or 15 . . . K—B1; 16 KR—K1 etc.

14 . . .	Kt×P

15 B—B4	O—O—O
16 KR—K1	Q—B3

To get out of the pin.

17 QR—Q1	K—Kt1
18 Kt—Q4	B—B2

Anderssen now makes effective use of the beautiful attacking position he has built up.

19 B×Kt!	P×B

If 19 . . . B×B; 20 Kt×B, P×Kt (if 20 . . . R×Kt; 21 Kt×Pch! wins the exchange); 21 R—K6, Q—B1; 22 R—K7! with a winning attack.

20 R—K7!	P—Kt3

20 . . . Q×R loses the Queen.

21 Q—R4!	P—R4

Forced; . . . Q×R still loses the Queen!

22 Kt—B6ch	K—B1

If 22 . . . K—R1; 23 R—R7 mate.

23 Kt—Kt5	R—Q2

The only reply to the venomous double threat of 24 R—B7 mate or 24 Kt(5)—R7 mate!

24 Kt(5)—R7ch	K—B2
25 R×Rch	K×R

Now comes a very fine move, adding force to the inevitable and deadly discovered check:

26 R—K1!	Resigns

For if 26 . . . K—Q3; 27 Q—R3ch, K—B2; 28 R—K7ch wins; or 26 . . . R—K1; 27 Kt—K5ch, K—K2; 28 Kt—Kt4ch! (not 28 Kt—Q7ch, K—Q1!), K—B1 (or 28 . . . K—Q1); 29 Q×Rch etc.

The lively succession of threats gives

us a good idea of Anderssen's genius for attack.

LANDAU received the Brilliancy Prize at Kemeri—but not for this game, beautiful as it is!

QUEEN'S GAMBIT DECLINED
Kemeri, 1937

WHITE	BLACK
Landau	Feigin
1 P—Q4	P—Q4
2 P—QB4	P—QB3
3 Kt—KB3	Kt—B3
4 P—K3	P—K3
5 Kt—B3	QKt—Q2
6 B—Q3	B—K2
7 O—O	O—O
8 P—QKt3	P—QKt3
9 B—Kt2	B—Kt2

Despite the almost symmetrical aspect of the position, it is anything but drawish: White's King's Bishop is trained on the enemy King-side.

10 Q—K2	R—B1
11 QR—Q1	Q—B2
12 Kt—K5!	Kt×Kt
13 P×Kt	Kt—Q2

If *13 . . . Q×P??; 14 Kt×P!* and Black is lost.

14 P—B4	KR—Q1
15 R—B3!	Kt—B1
16 R—R3	P—KB4

White was threatening *17 B×Pch!, Kt×B; 18 Q—R5* etc.

17 P×P e.p.

Keeping the attacking lines open.

17 . . .	B×P
18 P×P!	KP×P

On *18 . . . BP×P; 19 Kt—Kt5* is too strong.

19 Q—QB2!	P—KR3

Very debilitating, but he has no choice: *19 . . . P—Kt3; 20 Kt×P!*

20 B—B5!	R—R1

If *20 . . . Kt—Q2; 21 B—K6ch, K—B1; 22 Q—Kt6, K—K2; 23 Q—B7ch, K—Q3; 24 Kt—K4 mate;* or *21 . . . K—R1; 22 Q—Kt6, Kt—B4 (else 23 R×Pch!); 23 Kt—Kt5!* forcing loss of the Queen or mate.

21 Kt×P!!	R×Kt
22 B×B!	R×Rch
23 Q×R	Q—B2

If *23 . . . P×B; 24 R—Kt3ch, K—R1; 25 Q—R5, Q—K2 (if 25 . . . Kt—R2; 26 Q×P, R—KKt1; 27 R—R3, R—Kt2; 28 Q×P and wins); 26 Q×Pch, Kt—R2; 27 B×Kt* etc.

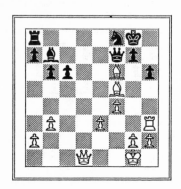

24 R×P!!

This had to be foreseen at move *21.* If now *24 . . . P×B; 25 Q—Kt4ch, Q—Kt2; 26 B—K6ch!, Kt×B; 27 Q×Ktch, Q—B2; 28 R—R8ch!* Or *24 . . . P×R; 25 Q—Kt4ch, Kt—Kt3; 26 B—K6* again winning the Queen.

24 . . .	B—B1
25 B×B	P×R

If *25 . . . R×B; 26 Q—Kt4, R—K1; 27 B—K5* wins easily.

26 Q—Kt4ch	K—R2

If *26 . . . Q—Kt3; 27 B—K6ch!* wins the Queen nicely.

27 B—Q4	Q—Kt1
28 B—B5ch	Kt—Kt3
29 P—KR4	P—B4
30 B—K5	Resigns

The pinned Knight is lost!

THE *keynote of this game is:* Tactics *before strategy! A hypermodern opening leads to a Morphy combination.*

ALEKHINE'S DEFENSE
Argentine Championship, 1945

WHITE	BLACK
Rossetto	Aguilar
1 P—K4	Kt—KB3
2 P—K5	Kt—Q4
3 P—QB4	Kt—Kt3
4 P—Q4	P—Q3
5 P—B4	

White makes no bones about his intentions: he means to play aggressive chess.

5 . . .	P×P
6 BP×P	Kt—B3
7 B—K3	B—B4
8 Kt—QB3	P—K3
9 B—K2	Q—Q2
10 Kt—B3	O—O—O
11 O—O	B—KKt5

Black's last three moves indicate that he intends to exert pressure on White's Queen's Pawn. White's counterplay?—a Pawn storming attack against the King!

12 Kt—Q2!	

The plausible *12 Kt—KKt5* is answered by *12 . . . Kt×BP!; 13 R×P, Q—K1* with a good game.

12 . . .	B—KB4

If *12 . . . B×B; 13 Kt×B* and White is ready to advance on the Queen-side.

13 Kt—Kt3	P—B3
14 P×P	P×P
15 P—QR4!	R—Kt1

Black tries counterattack, for if *15 . . . P—QR4?; 16 P—Q5!, Kt—K4 (16 . . . P×P?; 17 R×B!, Q×R; 18 B—Kt4); 17 Kt×P* etc.

16 P—R5	Q—Kt2
17 R—B2	Kt—Q2
18 B—B3	Kt(2)—K4
19 P—R6!	

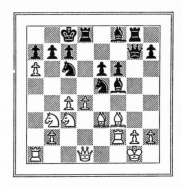

If now *19 . . . Kt×Bch; 20 Q×Kt, Q—Kt5; 21 P×Pch, K×P; 22 Kt—R5ch* wins.

Another disastrous possibility is *19 . . . Kt—KKt5; 20 P×Pch, K—Kt1; 21 B×Kt(6), Kt×B; 22 R×P!!,*

K×R; 23 Q—R1ch, K—Kt3; 24 Q—R5ch, K×B; 25 Q—Kt5ch, K—Q3; 26 Q—B5 mate!

19 . . .	B—KKt5
20 P×Pch	K—Kt1
21 B×Kt!!	Kt×B

If 21 . . . B×Q; 22 P×Kt followed by B×P mate!

| 22 P—Q5!! | P×P |

On 22 . . . B×Q; 23 P×Kt will force mate.

Or if 22 . . . Kt—K4; 23 B×Pch, K×P; 24 Kt—R5ch!, K×B (24 . . . K—B1; 25 Q—R4 with a winning attack); 25 Kt—B6ch, K—Kt2; 26 R—R7ch, K—B1; 27 R—R8ch, K—Kt2; 28 Q—Kt3ch!, K×R; 29 Q—R4ch, K—Kt2; 30 Q—R7ch, K—B1; 31 Q—R8ch, K—Q2; 32 Q×R mate.

| 23 P×P!! | Q—K2 |
| 24 P×Kt!! | |

White will not be cheated of his Queen sacrifice!

| 24 . . . | R×Qch |
| 25 Kt×R | Q×B |

The deadly Bishop must be removed.

| 26 Kt×Q | Resigns |

Black has staved off the mate, but finds himself hopelessly behind in material.

WHITE's handling of the attack is flawless throughout, but the most brilliant move of all is his exchange of Queens!

CARO-KANN DEFENSE
Gyor, 1932

| WHITE | BLACK |
Chalupetzky	Kallos
1 P—K4	P—QB3
2 P—QB4	P—Q4
3 KP×P	P×P
4 P×P	Q×P
5 Kt—QB3	Q—Q1
6 B—B4	Kt—KB3
7 P—Q4	P—KKt3?

Black's development has been rather slow, but this makes matters worse, as White's next three moves indicate. 7 . . . P—K3 was much safer.

8 Q—Kt3!	P—K3
9 B—Kt5!	B—Kt2
10 P—Q5!	P×P
11 O—O—O!	O—O
12 Kt×P	QKt—Q2
13 Kt—KB3	Q—R4

The pin is very troublesome. 13 . . . P—KR3? is answered by 14 Kt×Ktch, B×Kt; 15 B×P etc.

| 14 B—Q2 | Q—Q1 |
| 15 B—Kt4! | R—K1 |

If now 16 Kt×Ktch, Q×Kt guarding his Bishop's Pawn. Hence White strengthens the pressure with:

16 KR—K1!

Now 17 Kt×Ktch threatens to crush Black.

| 16 . . . | R×R |
| 17 R×R | Kt×Kt |

18 B×Kt	Q—B2ch
19 Q—B4!!	Q×Qch
20 B×Q	

It will soon become apparent that White's game is stronger than ever. Black's development is still in an incomplete state, and if 20 . . . Kt—B3; 21 R—K7 wins material.

20 . . .	Kt—B1
21 R—K8!	B—R3ch
22 K—Q1	P—R3
23 K—K1	P—R4
24 B—Q6	P—Kt3
25 Kt—K5!	

Imaginative play: he can win the exchange by 25 B—Q5, B—QKt2; 26 R×R etc. but he is after the Black King.

25 . . .	B—QKt2
26 B×Pch	K—R1

If 26 . . . K—Kt2; 27 B×Ktch wins at once.

27 R—K7!	B×P
28 B—B4!	B—KKt2

The threat was 29 Kt—B7ch, K—Kt2; 30 B—K5ch, K—Kt1; 31 Kt×B mate!

29 Kt—B7ch	K—Kt1
30 Kt—Q8ch	K—R1

31 R×B!!

Now White has the brilliant finish he has been angling for: the acceptance of the Rook leads to one of the most remarkable conclusions ever achieved in over-the-board play.

31 . . .	K×R
32 B—K5ch	K—R3
33 Kt—B7ch	K—R4
34 B—K2ch	K—R5
35 B—Kt3ch	K—R6
36 Kt—Kt5 mate!	

The harmonious co-operation of White's minor pieces creates a very pleasing effect which as a rule can only be obtained in compositions.

The Two-Rook Sacrifice

👑 IN THE good old days, when the two-Rook sacrifice was played instinctively, this type of combination was startling, exciting, sensational. It still is—despite the fact that the principle underlying the sacrifices is quite simple and fairly well known. In order to capture the two Rooks, the prospective victim must remove his Queen from the scene of action in a position where his King is exposed and he has little development.

Craddock—Mieses (p. 315) is an effective example. White is allowed to pick up both Rooks, his Queen is out of the game at KR8 and Black's Queen begins the final attack with 12 . . . Q—B6!

In Nield—Edwards (p. 316) the play is more complicated, as the winner has to play some very fine moves after the sacrifice of his Rooks. Nevertheless the issue is hardly in doubt, as Black's King hasn't a friend in the world.

In his celebrated game with Levenfish (p. 317), Alekhine introduces us to a very similar situation. This game, by the way, is a most impressive example of the value of superior development.

At first sight, Reti's task against Euwe (p. 318) seems simple enough, in view of Black's material advantage. But as we come to the subtle and enjoyable finish, we realize that only an artist like Reti could have wound up the game in such elegant style.

What makes the Enevoldsen—Paulsen game enchanting (p. 318) is that even after declining the second tainted Rook and taking refuge in a series of checks, Paulsen finds himself trapped after all. This example is more difficult than the rest, for Enevoldsen must *defend* as well as attack.

"That's all there is" to the two-Rook sacrifice. Looks easy, doesn't it? Try it in your own games!

WHEN a master has a reputation for brilliancy, his opponents play against him with extra caution and thus reduce his opportunities for combinative fireworks. But despite his reputation as a "Peck's bad boy," Mieses was still able to produce such light-hearted classics as this one:

ENGLISH OPENING
London, 1939

WHITE	BLACK
Craddock	Mieses
1 P—QB4	P—K4
2 Kt—QB3	Kt—QB3
3 P—KKt3	Kt—B3
4 B—Kt2	B—Kt5
5 P—K3	P—Q3
6 KKt—K2	B—Kt5
7 Q—Kt3	

Getting out of the pin and threatening to win a piece by 8 B×Ktch, P×B; 9 Q×B.

| 7 . . . | QR—Kt1 |

If now 8 B×Ktch, P×B, protecting his King's Bishop.

| 8 Kt—Q5 | B—QB4 |
| 9 Kt×Ktch | Q×Kt!! |

9 . . . P×Kt was safe enough, but the text sets a trap which White can-

not fathom: apparently 10 B×Ktch will be crushing.

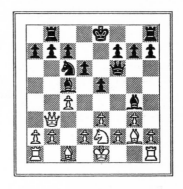

10 B×Ktch?	P×B
11 Q×Rch	K—Q2
12 Q×R	Q—B6!

Now everything becomes clear—very late in the day. Black threatens 13 . . . Q×Kt mate or 13 . . . Q×Rch; 14 Kt—Kt1, Q×Kt mate!

If 13 O—O, B—KR6 and mate follows. Or 13 K—B1, Q×Ktch with mate in the offing.

13 K—Q1	Q×Ktch
14 K—B2	Q×BPch
15 K—Kt1	Q—Q6 mate

Beautiful! Mieses was 74 when this game was played.

EVEN when you know thousands of pretty games, there is an unforgettable thrill in unearthing such a lovely game as this one.

QUEEN'S KNIGHT'S OPENING

Correspondence, 1940

WHITE	BLACK
Nield	*Edwards*
1 Kt—QB3	P—QB4
2 P—Q4?	P×P
3 Q×P	Kt—QB3
4 Q—QR4	P—Q4
5 B—B4	P—B3?

The right way to exploit White's premature Queen development was 5 . . . B—Q2! involving the crafty trap 6 Kt×P?, P—K4!; 7 B—Kt3, Kt —Q5!; 8 Q—B4, R—B1 and wins!

6 O—O—O!   P—K3

6 . . . P—Q5 will not do because of 7 P—K3, P—K4; 8 P×P!, P×B; 9 P—Q5 recovering the piece with a winning attack.

7 P—K4!	P—Q5
8 Kt—B3	B—B4

On 8 . . . P—K4; 9 Kt×QP!, P× Kt; 10 Kt—Kt5 is too strong.

9 P—QKt4!!

Beginning a deep combination which will lead to the sacrifice of both Rooks! Black cannot dodge the complications, for if 9 . . . B—Kt3; 10 P—Kt5 wins.

9 . . .	B×P
10 Kt×P!	B×Kt

If 10 . . . Q—R4; 11 Kt×Kt, Q×Q; 12 R—Q8ch, K—B2; 13 Kt×Q, P×Kt; 14 B—QR6 and wins (14 . . . B—Kt2; 15 R—Q7ch).

11 Kt×Kt   B—Kt7ch

After 11 . . . B—Q2; 12 R×B!, Q×R; 13 B—QKt5, P—QR3; 14 Kt —Q4!, P×B; 15 Q×Rch, K—B2; 16 Kt—K2 Black's game is quite shattered.

12 K×B   Q×R

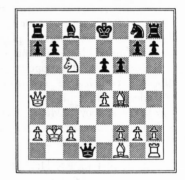

13 B—QKt5!!   Q×R

Black does not have a single square to which to retreat along the Queen's file!

14 Kt—K5ch   K—B1

14 . . . K—Q1 permits an exquisite mate: 15 Kt—B7ch!, K—K2; 16 B—Q6ch!, K×Kt; 17 B—K8 mate.

15 Q—Q4!!   B—Q2

A sorry move, but if 15 . . . P×Kt; 16 Q—Q8ch, K—B2; 17 B—K8ch, K—B1; 18 B—Kt6 mate.

16 Q×B   Resigns

The finish might have been: 16 . . . P×Kt; 17 B×P, Kt—K2; 18 B—Q6, K—B2; 19 Q×Ktch, K—Kt3; 20 Q×KPch, K—Kt4; 21 B—K7ch, K—R4; (or 21 . . . K—B5; 22 Q— B5 mate); 22 B—K2 or P—Kt4 mate. This masterpiece is a good example of the brand of chess played in Australia.

THE finest effects are achieved in chess with moves that are surprising when you first see them and logical when you come to understand them.

BENONI COUNTER GAMBIT
St. Petersburg, 1912

WHITE	BLACK
Alekhine	Levenfish
1 P—Q4	P—QB4
2 P—Q5	Kt—KB3
3 Kt—QB3	P—Q3
4 P—K4	P—KKt3
5 P—B4	QKt—Q2

Black has a constricted game, and the coming P—K5 will sadly hamper his development.

6 Kt—B3	P—QR3

The normal move 6 . . . B—Kt2 would not do because of 7 P—K5, P×P; 8 P×P, Kt—Kt5; 9 P—K6!, QKt—K4; 10 B—Kt5ch and wins.

7 P—K5	P×P
8 P×P	Kt—Kt5
9 P—K6!	QKt—K4
10 B—KB4	Kt×Ktch
11 P×Kt!	

Stronger than 11 Q×Kt, P×P!; 12 Q×Kt, P—K4 with chances for Black. White's energetic play steadily gains time either by development or by threats.

11 . . .	Kt—B3
12 B—B4	P×P
13 P×P	Q—Kt3

13 . . . Q×Qch; 14 R×Q, B—Kt2; 15 B—B7, O—O; 16 B—Kt6 holds out no hope whatever for Black. 13 . . . P—QKt4; 14 Q×Qch, K×

Q; 15 R—Q1ch, K—K1; 16 Kt×P! is equally dreary. There remains only the text, which looks quite promising with its simultaneous attack on two Pawns.

14 Q—K2!	Q×KtP

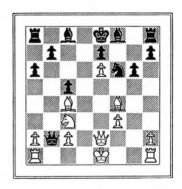

15 Kt—Kt5!!	Q×Rch

If 15 . . . Q—Kt5ch; 16 P—B3 is decisive; and if 15 . . . P×Kt; 16 B×Pch, K—Q1; 17 R—Q1ch is deadly.

16 K—B2	Q×R

Now comes White's turn!

17 Kt—B7ch	K—Q1
18 Q—Q2ch	B—Q2
19 P×B!	Resigns!

The threat is 20 Kt—K6 mate. If Black tries 19 . . . P—K4 (or 19 . . . Kt×P; 20 B—K6) there follows 20 Kt—K6ch, K—K2; 21 P—Q8(Q)ch, R×Q; 22 Q×Rch, K—B2; 23 Kt×Bch, K—Kt2; 24 Q—K7 mate.
This game unrolls like a Greek tragedy: one has an uncanny feeling that the capture of the Rooks was preordained from the first move!

This smartly played game has become one of the classics of modern chess.

TWO KNIGHTS' DEFENSE

Match, 1920

WHITE	BLACK
Euwe	*Reti*
1 P—K4	P—K4
2 Kt—KB3	Kt—QB3
3 B—B4	Kt—B3
4 P—Q4	P×P
5 O—O	Kt×P
6 R—K1	P—Q4
7 B×P	Q×B
8 Kt—B3	Q—QR4

A familiar variation, in which the routine continuation is 9 Kt×Kt, B—K3; 10 Kt(4)—Kt5, O—O—O with about even chances. But Euwe, in search of novelty, blunders:

9 Kt×P?	Kt×Kt
10 Q×Kt	P—KB4!

Retaining his booty, for if 11 P—B3??, B—B4 wins the Queen!

11 B—Kt5	Q—B4!
12 Q—Q8ch	K—B2
13 Kt×Kt	P×Kt
14 QR—Q1	

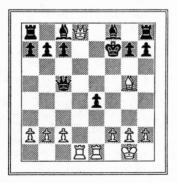

14 . . .	B—Q3!!
15 Q×R	Q×B

Threatening to win at once with 16 . . . B—KR6.

16 P—KB4

An amusing variation is 16 Q×P, B—KB4; 17 P—KR4, Q—Kt5 and White's Queen is lost.

16 . . .	Q—R5!
17 R×P	

Or 17 P—KKt3, B—B4ch; 18 K—R1, B—KKt5!; 19 R—KB1, Q—R4 and wins!

17 . . .	B—KR6!!
18 Q×R	B—B4ch
19 K—R1	

If 19 R(4)—Q4, B×Rch; 20 R×B, Q—K8 mate.

19 . . .	B×Pch!!
20 K×B	Q—Kt5ch
21 K—B1	Q—B6ch
22 K—K1	Q—B7 mate

After White's initial mistake, most players would have been content to win by mere material advantage. But not Reti!

In this game we have a cut-rate double Rook sacrifice: two Rooks are offered, but only one is accepted.

QUEEN'S PAWN OPENING

Copenhagen, 1936

WHITE	BLACK
Enevoldsen	*Paulsen*
1 P—Q4	Kt—KB3
2 P—QB4	P—K3
3 Kt—KB3	B—Kt5ch
4 QKt—Q2	P—B4

5 P—QR3	Q—R4?

The early development of the Queen will lead to trouble.

6 QR—Kt1!	B×Ktch
7 B×B	Q—B2
8 P×P!	Q×BP
9 P—K3	Kt—B3

Not 9 . . . O—O; 10 B—Kt4 winning the exchange.

10 P—QKt4	Q—B4
11 P—Kt5	Kt—K4
12 B—Kt4!	P—Q4

As a result of Black's loss of time with the Queen, he has a very bad game.

13 B—K2	P×P
14 Kt×Kt	Q×Kt
15 B×P	Kt—Q4

Getting rid of one of the Bishops.

16 B×Kt	Q×B
17 Q—Kt4!	Q—KB4

This seems to be the only chance.

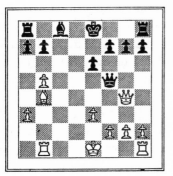

18 Q×P!!	Q×Rch
19 K—Q2!	Q—R7ch

If 19 . . . Q×R; 20 Q—B6! forces mate.

20 K—B1	Q—B5ch
21 K—Kt2	Q—K7ch
22 K—R1	P—QR4

Now Black is desperate: he has no more checks.

23 Q×Rch	K—Q2
24 Q—Q4ch	K—K1

If 24 . . . K—B2; 25 Q—Q6 mate.

25 B—Q6

Threatening 26 Q—B6 etc. There is no good way of warding off this menace, for if 25 . . . Q×BP; 26 Q—Kt7, K—Q2; 27 R—Q1 and wins; or 25 . . . Q×KtP; 26 Q—B6, K—Q2; 27 Q—K7ch, K—B3; 28 Q—B7ch, K—Q4; 29 R—Q1ch, K—K5; 30 Q—B2ch and mate next move!

25 . . .	P—K4?!

A last try: if 26 Q×Pch?, B—K3 threatening mate!

26 Q—KR4!	Resigns

Mate is forced after all!

The Two-Bishop Sacrifice

♛ EMANUEL LASKER made a great contribution to the happiness of all chess players when he discovered the pattern, back in 1889, for an explosive two-Bishop attack against a castled King. The word "explosive" is used advisedly, for the demolition of the King-side by the Bishop sacrifices gives us all the fun that youngsters get out of firecrackers.

In addition to Lasker's masterpiece, we have four later examples of this attractive theme. What makes these games particularly delightful is the crafty way in which the winner conceals his sacrificial intentions until the last possible move.

Enjoyable as these games are, they can also be useful. The pattern for the sacrifices is so clear to those "in the know" and so obscure to the uninitiated, that you have a good chance to bring off these electrifying combinations in one of your own games!

THIS was the first of the great two-Bishop-sacrifice games; and in the opinion of many critics, it is still the finest game of the genre.

BIRD'S OPENING
Amsterdam, 1889

WHITE	BLACK
Em. Lasker	Bauer
1 P—KB4	P—Q4
2 P—K3	Kt—KB3
3 P—QKt3	P—K3
4 B—Kt2	B—K2
5 B—Q3	P—QKt3
6 Kt—QB3	B—Kt2
7 Kt—B3	QKt—Q2
8 O—O	O—O
9 Kt—K2	P—B4

A modern player would find White's Bishops sufficiently threatening to play 9 . . . Kt—B4, removing most of the danger to Black's Kingside.

10 Kt—Kt3	Q—B2
11 Kt—K5	Kt×Kt
12 B×Kt	Q—B3
13 Q—K2	P—QR3?

13 . . . Kt—Q2 or . . . Kt—K5 was necessary. But Bauer is oblivious of danger!

14 Kt—R5!   Kt×Kt

Missing White's next move (and who wouldn't?). But the position was beyond salvation, for example 14 . . . Kt—K1; 15 B×KtP!, Kt×B; 16 Q—Kt4.

15 B×Pch!!

The point of this sacrifice will become clear on his 22nd move!

15 . . .	K×B
16 Q×Ktch	K—Kt1
17 B×P!!	

Only the second Bishop sacrifice can prove the soundness of the first.

17 . . .   K×B

If 17 . . . P—B3; 18 R—B3 and wins, for if 18 . . . R—B2; 19 Q—R8 mate.

18 Q—Kt4ch!   K—R2

If 18 . . . K—B3; 19 Q—Kt5 mate!

19 R—B3	P—K4
20 R—R3ch	Q—R3
21 R×Qch	K×R
22 Q—Q7!	

Winning one of the Bishops, and still retaining the attack!

22 . . .	B—KB3
23 Q×B	K—Kt2
24 R—KB1	QR—Kt1
25 Q—Q7!	KR—Q1

Making room for his King; White was threatening mate by 26 Q—Kt4ch followed by 27 R—B3.

26 Q—Kt4ch	K—B1
27 P×P	B—Kt2

Or 27 . . . B×P; 28 Q—K6! winning the Bishop. But the following Pawn advance is decisive.

28 P—K6!	R—Kt2
29 Q—Kt6	P—B3
30 R×Pch	B×R
31 Q×Bch	K—K1
32 Q—R8ch	K—K2
33 Q—Kt7ch	Resigns

Although this game is famous for the two-Bishop sacrifice, it is also a fine example of forceful Queen play. A leading critic said: "From his conduct of this game one sees something of the extraordinary talent of the rising generation of chess players."

TARRASCH and Nimzovich thoroughly despised each other and each other's theories; hence each game between them was a duel to the death. The following encounter is the most memorable of their fascinating games.

QUEEN'S GAMBIT DECLINED
St. Petersburg, 1914
(Second Brilliancy Prize)

WHITE	BLACK
Nimzovich	Tarrasch
1 P—Q4	P—Q4
2 Kt—KB3	P—QB4
3 P—B4	P—K3
4 P—K3	Kt—KB3
5 B—Q3	Kt—B3
6 O—O	B—Q3
7 P—QKt3	O—O
8 B—Kt2	P—QKt3
9 QKt—Q2	B—Kt2
10 R—B1	Q—K2

As a result of White's tame fourth

move, we have a position which is quite level. In the following phase Nimzovich makes the mistake of thinking exclusively along *positional* lines, forgetting all about the *tactical* possibilities he is creating for his hated rival.

11 BP×P?	KP×P
12 Kt—R4?	P—Kt3
13 KKt—B3	QR—Q1!
14 P×P?	P×P

Nimzovich has played to give Black the famous "hanging Pawns" in the center; but Black has a fine, free game with formidable attacking prospects.

15 B—Kt5?	Kt—K5!
16 B×Kt?	B×B
17 Q—B2	Kt×Kt!
18 Kt×Kt	

Or 18 Q×Kt, P—Q5!; 19 P×P, B×Kt; 20 P×B, Q—R5 with a winning attack.

18 . . .	P—Q5!
19 P×P?	

Pardonably oblivious of Black's brilliant plan. It is true that 19 P—K4, Q—R5; 20 P—Kt3, Q—R6 leaves Black with excellent attacking chances.

19 . . .	B×Pch!!

"Among my souvenirs": Tarrasch recalls the Lasker—Bauer setup.

20 K×B	Q—R5ch
21 K—Kt1	B×P!!

Amazingly enough, this Bishop will be miraculously preserved to give checkmate eleven moves later!

22 P—B3

If 22 K×B, Q—Kt5ch; 23 K—R1, R—Q4; 24 Q×P, R—R4ch!; 25 Q×R, Q×Qch; 26 K any, Q—Kt4ch and White's Knight is lost!

22 . . .   KR—K1!

Menacing . . . R—K7. If now 23 Q—Q3, Q—Kt6; 24 Kt—K4, R×Kt! Or 23 KR—K1, R×Rch; 24 R×R, Q×Rch; 25 K×B, Q—K7ch; 26 K any, R—Q4 etc.

23 Kt—K4	Q—R8ch
24 K—B2	B×R

An embarrassing situation for White: he cannot even play 25 R×B, for then 25 . . . Q—R7ch wins the Queen!

25 P—Q5	P—B4!
26 Q—B3	

Giving himself the pleasure of threatening mate.

26 . . .	Q—Kt7ch
27 K—K3	R×Ktch!
28 P×R	P—B5ch?!

In the heat of the battle he misses 28 . . . Q—Kt6ch!; 29 K—Q2, Q—B7ch; 30 K—Q1, Q—K7 mate.

29 K×P	R—B1ch
30 K—K5	Q—R7ch
31 K—K6	R—K1ch
32 K—Q7	B—Kt4 mate!

Because of the derivative nature of

his beautiful combination (who does not know the Lasker—Bauer game?) Tarrasch lost his chance for the First Brilliancy Prize!

THE *almost absent-minded way in which the two-Bishop sacrifice turns up here as an afterthought lends an amusing touch to this game.*

ORANGOUTANG OPENING
Portsmouth, 1923

WHITE	BLACK
Alekhine	Drewitt
1 Kt—KB3	P—Q4
2 P—QKt4	P—K3
3 B—Kt2	Kt—KB3
4 P—QR3	P—B4
5 P×P	B×P
6 P—K3	O—O
7 P—B4	Kt—B3
8 P—Q4	B—Kt3?

An anti-positional idea: the Bishop, which should have retreated along his original diagonal, is quite useless here.

9 QKt—Q2	Q—K2
10 B—Q3	R—Q1
11 O—O	B—Q2
12 Kt—K5	B—K1
13 P—B4!	QR—B1
14 R—B1	Kt—Q2

This permits White to secure a definite advantage; however, one sympathizes with Black's desire to do something before he is overwhelmed by the standard attack R—KB3—R3 etc.

15 Kt×QKt!   R×Kt

15 . . . P×Kt is equally hopeless in a positional sense, for after 16 P—

B5, B—B2; 17 Q—R4 Black's Queen-side is obviously vulnerable.

16 P—B5	Kt×P

Desperation; after 16 . . . B—B2; 17 B—Kt5 traps the Rook!

17 P×Kt	B×P

Black is happy for the first time in this game: he has two Pawns, and is about to gain a third, for the lost piece. Perhaps the reader notices what Black has overlooked: *the diagonal of White's Queen's Bishop has been opened.*

18 R—KB3

Defending the King's Pawn . . .

18 . . .	B×P
19 R×R	B×R

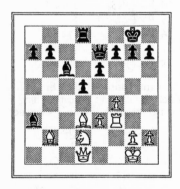

20 B×Pch!!	K×B

Or 20 . . . K—B1; 21 B×Pch!, K×B; 22 R—Kt3ch (his 18th move was more than defensive!), K—B3; 23 Q—Kt4, P—K4; 24 Q—B5 mate.

21 R—R3ch	K—Kt1
22 B×P!!	Resigns

Against 22 . . . P—B3 Alekhine intended 23 B—R6!, Q—R2; 24 Q—

R5, B—B1; 25 Q—Kt4ch, B—Kt2; 26 Q×Pch, K—B1; 27 Q×Pch and wins. Of course, if 22 . . . K×B; 23 Q—Kt4ch leads to mate.

This is a game where Drewitt didn't!

Playing over this game is like read-ing a detective story whose solu-tion we know. Such a story may still grip our attention as we won-der how all the puzzling compli-cations will be ironed out. In the following game, we know that the two Bishops will triumph; yet we marvel that a purely positional game can conclude in this fash-ion.

COLLE SYSTEM

Belgian Championship, 1936
(First Brilliancy Prize)

WHITE	BLACK
Koltanowski	Defosse
1 P—Q4	Kt—KB3
2 Kt—KB3	P—Q4
3 P—K3	P—K3
4 B—Q3	P—B4
5 P—B3	Kt—B3
6 QKt—Q2	B—Q3
7 O—O	O—O

Koltanowski has played some nota-ble games with this opening. After a slow start, White develops his pieces aggressively and Black must play with great care.

8 P×P	B×P
9 P—K4	Q—B2
10 Q—K2	B—Q3
11 R—K1	Kt—KKt5
12 P—KR3	KKt—K4
13 Kt×Kt	Kt×Kt

14 P×P!	P×P
15 Kt—B3!	Kt×Ktch

Black has brought out his pieces quickly enough, but the isolated Pawn is a headache. Thus if 15 . . . Kt×B; 16 Q×Kt and neither 16 . . . B—K3 (17 Kt—Kt5!) nor 16 . . . R—Q1 (17 Q×P!, B—R7ch; 18 Kt×B, R×Q; 19 R—K8 mate!) will do.

16 Q×Kt	B—K3
17 B—K3	QR—Q1
18 B—B2	P—QKt4
19 B—Q4!	B—QB4

The threat was 20 Q—R5, P—Kt3; 21 Q—R6 and wins; or 20 . . . P—KR3; 21 R×B!, P×R; 22 Q—Kt6 with a winning attack.

20 QR—Q1	P—Kt5
21 B—K5!	B—Q3

Or 21 . . . Q—Kt3; 22 Q—Kt3!, P—B3; 23 B—B7 and wins.

22 B×Pch!	K×B
23 Q—R5ch	K—Kt1
24 B×P!!	K×B

On 24 . . . P—B3 Koltanowski gives 25 Q—R8ch, K—B2; 26 B×R, B×B (or 26 . . . R×B; 27 Q—R7ch); 27 Q—R5ch, K—K2; 28 Q—R7ch, K—Q3; 29 R×Bch winning the Queen.

Or 24 . . . P—B4; 25 R×B, K×B; 26 Q—R6ch, K—Kt1; 27 R—Kt6ch, K—B2; 28 R—Kt7ch, K—K1; 29 R×Q, B×R; 30 Q—K6 mate!

25 Q—Kt5ch	K—R2
26 R—Q4	

Now we see the point of White's 21st move! Black's Bishop was deflected from attack on the Rook, which now threatens mate on KR4.

26 . . .	B—R7ch
27 K—R1	Q—KB5
28 R×Q	B×R
29 Q×B	KR—Kt1
30 R—K5	Resigns

White threatens mate in two; if Black tries to escape by 30 . . . K—Kt2, White polishes him off with 31 Q—Kt5ch, K—R2 (31 . . . K—R1; 32 Q—R6 mate, or 31 . . . K—B1; 32 Q×QRch); 32 Q—B6 (keeping the King fixed) and the Rook's next check at R5 will be fatal.

BEGINNING *with an almost symmetrical position which seems to offer no chance of complications, Schlechter works up a crushing attack with the simplest means conceivable. No wonder that even the great master of defense is taken in!*

QUEEN'S GAMBIT DECLINED
Vienna, 1907
(Second Brilliancy Prize)

WHITE	BLACK
Schlechter	*Maroczy*
1 P—Q4	P—Q4
2 Kt—KB3	P—QB4

3 P—K3	P—K3
4 P—B4	Kt—KB3
5 P—QR3	Kt—B3
6 Kt—B3	QP×P
7 B×P	P—QR3
8 O—O	P—QKt4
9 B—Q3	B—Kt2
10 P×P	B×P

An utterly peaceful scene.

11 P—QKt4	B—Q3
12 B—Kt2	Kt—K4
13 Kt×Kt	B×Kt
14 P—B4	B—B2
15 Q—K2	O—O
16 QR—Q1	Q—K2
17 P—K4	P—K4
18 Kt—Q5!	Kt×Kt
19 P×Kt	KR—K1?

Maroczy does not attach enough importance to the opening up of attacking lines which has resulted from the exchange of Knights. 19 . . . QR—K1 was far safer.

20 P×P	B×KP

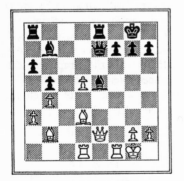

21 B×Pch!	K×B
22 Q—R5ch	K—Kt1
23 B×B	P—B3

There is no good defense. If 23 . . . Q×B; 24 Q×Pch, (this explains why Black's 19th move was faulty), K—R1; 25 R—B5! (25 Q×B is also good) and White wins quickly.

24 B×P!	P×B
25 R—Q3	Q—R2

White was threatening 26 R—Kt3ch, K—B1; 27 Q—R8ch and mate next move.

26 R—Kt3ch	K—R1
27 Q—B3	

Having calculated his combination beforehand, Schlechter does not even notice 27 Q×Qch!, K×Q; 28 R—B4! and mate follows.

27 . . .	Q—KB2

White was threatening mate in two by 28 Q×Pch etc.; he was also threatening 28 R—R3.

28 Q—Kt4!	Resigns

Black's Queen is lost, leaving his game in a state of collapse.

Slugging Matches

♛ THE popular notion of chess hardly leaves room for such a term as "slugging." But what other word could we use for such a game as Winz—Czerniak (p. 331), in which attack and defense change hands, and in which ingenious sacrifices are countered by even more elegant combinations?

Lasker's famous game with Napier (p. 328) is, if anything, even more exciting. Just as admirable as Napier's skill in keeping the attack going (and with the Queens off the board!) is Lasker's uncanny defensive technique under cruel time pressure. Study the diagram after Black's 24th move, where White is a Rook ahead, but has four pieces menaced by Black's forces!

Alekhine's victory over Nimzovich (p. 334) is not without a touch of sly humor which is likely to escape anyone playing over the game without notes. First Nimzovich offers a Pawn which, if taken, allows Nimzovich to force mate by means of an imaginative Queen sacrifice. A few moves later, Alekhine repays the compliment by making a similar offer!

Rubinstein's reputation for thorough mastery of positional chess was somewhat deceptive. That reputation was thoroughly deserved, but we must remember that he was also a past master of sacrificial play. One of his most notable games was the gem against Spielmann (p. 330), in which a double sacrifice of the exchange rates higher than Spielmann's intended Queen sacrifice!

Spielmann, great attacking player that he was, never shunned accepting a dare. It is therefore fascinating to see what happened after he accepted Stoltz's Queen sacrifice (p. 333) for only two pieces!

What makes all these slugging matches so interesting to play over is that they give us a delightful idea of the endless resources which are available to the fertile mind of a great chess master.

EVEN *after the passage of thirty years Napier was thrilled by the recollection of this incredibly wild game. The fact that he lost it did not prevent him from commenting: "This is, I think, my best game and very certainly the one I most enjoyed playing."*

SICILIAN DEFENSE
Cambridge Springs, 1904

WHITE	BLACK
Em. Lasker	Napier
1 P—K4	P—QB4
2 Kt—QB3	Kt—QB3
3 Kt—B3	P—KKt3
4 P—Q4	P×P
5 Kt×P	B—Kt2
6 B—K3	P—Q3
7 P—KR3	Kt—B3
8 P—KKt4!?	

He intends to attack, and he doesn't care who knows it!

8 . . .   O—O!?

Go right ahead, says Napier!

9 P—Kt5	Kt—K1
10 P—KR4	Kt—B2
11 P—B4	P—K4!
12 KKt—K2	P—Q4?!

This leads to glorious combinations, but the simple move *12 . . . B—*

Kt5! would have given him an excellent game.

13 KP×P

If 13 Kt×P, Black recovers the Pawn with 13 . . . P×P; 14 Kt×Kt, Q×Kt; 15 B×BP, Q—K2; 16 B—Kt2, Q—Kt5ch etc.

13 . . .   Kt—Q5
14 Kt×Kt!

Not 14 B×Kt, P×B; 15 Kt×P, Kt×P and again Black recovers his Pawn with a good game.

14 . . .   Kt×P!

Expecting 15 Kt×Kt, P×Kt; 16 B×P, Q×Kt; 17 B×B, Q×R; 18 B×R, Q×Pch and wins. But his crafty opponent has a stunning reply:

15 Kt—B5!!

Doesn't this win a piece?

15 . . .   Kt×Kt!!

Saves the piece!

16 Q×Q   R×Q
17 Kt—K7ch!

If 17 Kt×B, P×P! or 17 P×Kt, B×Kt! and in either case Black has the better of it!

17 . . .   K—R1!

But not 17 . . . K—B1?; 18 Kt×

B, Kt—Q4; 19 B—B5ch winning a piece.

18 P—R5!!

He nonchalantly continues the attack, realizing that 18 Kt×B, Kt—Q4! or 18 P×Kt, P×P!; 19 B—Q4, B×B; 20 P×B, R—K1! leaves Black with the advantage.

| 18 . . . | R—K1 |
| 19 B—B5! | KtP×P! |

If 19 . . . KP×P; 20 P×P!, P×P; 21 B—B4!! with the decisive threat of 22 B—B7!

20 B—B4!!

Stronger than 20 P×Kt, B—B1; 21 B—Kt5, R×Kt; 22 B×R, B×B and White can hardly hope to win, as his Pawns are too ragged and Black's Bishops are too powerful.

| 20 . . . | P×P!! |

What a position! And Lasker must make his next ten moves in three minutes!

21 B×BP!	Kt—K5!!
22 B×R	B×P
23 QR—Kt1	B—B6ch
24 K—B1	B—KKt5!

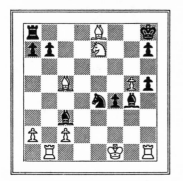

Black is a Rook down, but look at

his threats: . . . Kt×B or . . . R×B or . . . Kt—Kt6ch or . . . Kt—Q7ch. How can White defend himself?

25 B×KRP!!

Very simple, says Lasker! And it is simple.

| 25 . . . | B×B |

If 25 . . . Kt—Kt6ch; 26 K—B2, B×B (not 26 . . . Kt×B?; 27 R—R4!); 27 R×B! transposing into the text line.

26 R×B!	Kt—Kt6ch
27 K—Kt2	Kt×R
28 R×P	P—R4
29 R—Kt3!	B—Kt2
30 R—KR3!	Kt—Kt6
31 K—B3!	

At last Lasker is out of his grisly time pressure, and his King can advance decisively.

| 31 . . . | R—R3 |

If 31 . . . B—K4; 32 Kt—Kt6ch wins the Bishop.

32 K×P	Kt—K7ch
33 K—B5	Kt—B6
34 P—R3	Kt—R5
35 B—K3	Resigns

Black's game is hopeless, a likely possibility being 35 . . . R—Q3; 36 P—Kt6, R—B3ch; 37 K—Kt4, P—R3; 38 B—Q4, R—K3; 39 R×P mate.

"Dr. Lasker proposed to enter it for a brilliancy prize jointly, saying, 'It is your brilliancy, and I won it!'; which was generous" (Napier).

"One of the most beautiful, most profound, most exciting and most difficult games in the whole literature of chess!" (*Lasker's Chess Career*).

SPIELMANN and Rubinstein enriched chess literature with the memorable games they contested over a period of some twenty years. The following encounter is perhaps the liveliest of the lot.

FOUR KNIGHTS' GAME
Baden-Baden, 1925

WHITE	BLACK
Spielmann	Rubinstein
1 P—K4	P—K4
2 Kt—KB3	Kt—QB3
3 Kt—B3	Kt—B3
4 B—Kt5	Kt—Q5

The Rubinstein Defense, which can lead to a dull game or an exciting one. Is there any doubt as to Spielmann's preference?

5 Kt×P	Q—K2
6 P—B4?!	Kt×B
7 Kt×Kt	P—Q3
8 Kt—KB3	Q×Pch
9 K—B2	Kt—Kt5ch
10 K—Kt3	Q—Kt3!
11 Q—K2ch	

A curious line is *11 Kt—R4, Q—R4; 12 P—KR3, Kt—B3; 13 Kt×Pch, K—Q1; 14 Kt×R, Q×Ktch!!; 15 K×Q, Kt—K5!! and wins!*

11 . . .	K—Q1
12 R—K1	B—Q2
13 QKt—Q4	Kt—K6ch
14 K—B2	Kt×BP!

For 15 P—B5 can be answered by 15 . . . Kt×Kt! Note in the following play how Rubinstein, satisfied with his booty, does not go after more Pawns; instead he seeks to solve the problems of development, defense and counterattack.

15 Kt×Kt	Q×Kt

16 P—QKt4	P—QR4!
17 B—R3	P×P
18 B×P	Q—KB4!
19 Q—K3	P—R3
20 QR—B1	KR—Kt1!
21 K—Kt1	P—KKt4!
22 Q—B3	R—B1!
23 P×P	P×P
24 K—R1	P—Kt5
25 Kt—Q4	Q—Q4!
26 Q—K3	P—Kt6!
27 B—B3!	

Threatening a forced draw with *28 Kt—B6ch!, B×Kt; 29 B—B6ch, K—Q2; 30 Q—K7ch!, B×Q; 31 R×Bch* etc.

27 . . .	QR—R1
28 Kt—B3	P×P
29 B—B6ch	K—B1
30 Q—B3	Q—QB4!
31 Q—Q3	Q—KR4!
32 Kt—K5?!	

If now 32 . . . P×Kt?; 33 R×P winning the Queen because of the threat 34 R—K8ch! etc.

32 . . .	R×KtP!!

Bold! If now 33 Kt×B, R—Kt8ch; 34 R×R, P×R(Q)ch; 35 K×Q, Q—Kt5ch with two Pawns ahead.

33 K×R	P×Kt
34 R×P	Q—Kt5ch
35 Q—Kt3	

Leads into a lost ending, but if 35 K×P (or 35 K—R1, B—B3ch), Q—B5ch; 36 Q—Kt3, Q×Pch! wins.

35 . . .	Q×Qch
36 K×Q	B—Q3
37 K×P	R×P
38 K—Kt1	R×P!

He'd rather have the two Bishops than regain the exchange!

39 R—KR5	P—Kt3
40 B—K5	B—B4ch
41 K—B1	K—Kt2
42 B—Kt3	B—Kt4ch
43 K—K1	R—K7ch
44 K—Q1	R—KKt7
45 R—B3	

If instead 45 R—R3, B—Q2; or 45 R—Kt5, R—Kt8ch; 46 K—Q2, R×R; 47 K×R, B—K6ch.

45 . . .	B—K7ch
Resigns	

IN ANY poll of exceptionally interesting struggles, this game would be sure to take high rank.

KING'S INDIAN DEFENSE
Palestine Championship, 1939

WHITE	BLACK
Winz	Czerniak
1 P—Q4	Kt—KB3
2 P—QB4	P—KKt3
3 P—B3	P—Q4
4 P×P	Kt×P
5 P—K4	Kt—Kt3
6 Kt—B3	B—Kt2

7 B—K3	O—O
8 P—B4	

If Black is not to be bowled over by White's powerful center Pawns, he must play enterprisingly.

8 . . .	Kt—B3
9 P—Q5	Kt—Kt1
10 P—QR4	P—K4

The safe line is 10 . . . P—QB3; 11 P—R5, Kt(3)—Q2; but Czerniak does not want safety!

11 P—R5	P×P!
12 P×Kt	P×B
13 R×P	

"And wins," most of us are tempted to add. If 13 . . . R×R??; 14 P×R and the Pawn queens! Black's menaced Rook can neither flee nor secure protection. What to do?

13 . . .	Q—R5ch!!

He chuckles over the possibility 14 K—K2?, Q—B7ch; 15 K—Q3, Kt—Q2; 16 R×R, Kt—K4ch; 17 K—Q4, P—K7 mate!

14 P—Kt3	B×Ktch!
15 P×B	Q×KP!

Very baffling! If 16 R×R, Q×R;

17 R×Kt, Q×Kt; 18 Q—K2, B—Kt5; 19 R×Rch, K×R; 20 P×P!, B×Q; 21 P—B8(Q)ch, K—Kt2; 22 K×B, Q—B7ch with a draw by perpetual check.

Or 16 Q—B3, Q—B7!; 17 Q×KP, Q—Kt8ch; 18 K—B2, R×R; 19 P×R, Q—R7ch and Black stands well: the terrible Pawn will soon go lost.

16 Kt—B3!	B—Kt5!
17 R×R!	B×Kt
18 Q—Q3!	

The ingenious variation 18 R—R4!?, B×Q; 19 R×Q, B—B6; 20 R—K7!, B×R; 21 P×P is answered by 21 . . . B×P!

| 18 . . . | Q—K4 |
| 19 P×P! | Q×BP! |

Not 19 . . . B×R because of 20 P—Q6! winning.

| 20 R—Kt1 | Q—Kt3 |
| 21 P—Kt4? | |

Apparently missing the point of the following involved and masterly combination. Best was 21 B—K2 (. . . P—K7 was threatened), Q—Kt7; 22 Q×P, B×B; 23 Q×B, Q×Pch; 24 K—B2 and Black still has to work for the draw.

| 21 . . . | R—Q1! |

21 . . . P—K7; 22 Q×B, Q×R; 23 Q×P is too simple for his taste.

22 R—Kt3

If 22 P—B4??, Q—Kt5ch leads to mate. If 22 Q—Kt5?, R×P!! is decisive.

22 . . .	R×P!
23 R×Ktch	K—Kt2
24 R×B	R×Q
25 B×R	Q—B2!
26 R—K8	Q×Pch

27 K—B1	Q×Bch
28 K—Kt2	Q—Q7ch
29 K—Kt3	

Or 29 K—R3, P—R4! with a quick win.

29 . . .	P—K7
30 R(3)—K3	Q—K8ch
31 K—R3	Q—B8ch
32 K—Kt3	Q—Kt8ch
33 K—R3	Q—B7!!

If now 34 R×P, Q—B6ch; 35 K—R4, P—R3; 36 R(8)—K3 (if 36 P—Kt5, P×Pch; 37 K×P, P—B3ch; 38 K—R4, P—Kt4 mate), P—Kt4ch; 37 K—R5, Q—KB3 and mate follows.

34 R(8)—K5	P—QKt4!
35 P—Kt5	P—R4
36 R(5)—K4	

He sees that 36 P×P e.p.ch, K×P; 37 R(5)—K4, P—B4 is hopeless for him.

| 36 . . . | P—Kt5! |
| 37 R×KP | |

Otherwise the other Pawn marches down.

37 . . .	Q—B6ch
38 K—R4	P—Kt6
39 R(2)—K3	Q—B7ch
40 K—R3	P—Kt7
41 R—K8	

A parting joke: if 41 . . . P—Kt8(Q)??; 42 R—Kt8ch!!, K×R; 43 R—K8ch, K—Kt2; 44 R—Kt8ch and White will draw by stalemate with two Queens down!

| 41 . . . | Q×Rch! |
| Resigns | |

One of the most entertaining games ever played!

STOLTZ's startling surrender of the Queen reminds us of The Lady or the Tiger? No one will ever know whether Stoltz sacrificed his Queen, or merely lost it!

FRENCH DEFENSE
Match, 1930

WHITE	BLACK
Spielmann	Stoltz
1 P—K4	P—K3
2 P—Q4	P—Q4
3 Kt—Q2	Kt—KB3

This permits White to obtain a tremendous attacking formation. 3 . . . P—QB4 is safer.

4 P—K5	KKt—Q2
5 B—Q3	P—QB4
6 P—QB3	Kt—QB3
7 Kt—K2	Q—Kt3
8 Kt—B3	P×P
9 P×P	B—Kt5ch
10 K—B1!	P—B3!?
11 Kt—B4!	P×P
12 Kt(4)×KP!	P—K5!
13 B—KB4!!	

Threatening 14 B—B7 or 14 Kt—B7ch. Black seems lost; he *is* lost.

13 . . .	P×Kt!!?
14 B—B7	Kt—B3
15 Kt×Pch	K—B2
16 B×Q	B—Kt5

Momentarily Black has only a minor piece for the Queen, but he is bound to get more material.

17 P—KKt3?

This is bad because it shuts in White's King's Rook and allows Black to operate successfully with a spectacular deficiency of material.

Correct was 17 P×P!!, B—R6ch; 18 K—Kt1! If now 18 . . . KR—KKt1; 19 B—B7!, R×Ktch; 20 B—Kt3, P—KR4; 21 B—B1! Or 18 . . . P×B; 19 Kt—B5, KR—Kt1ch; 20 Kt—Kt3, P—KR4; 21 B—B1!, B—Q2; 22 P—KR4 etc.

17 . . .	B—R6ch
18 K—Kt1	K×Kt
19 B—B7	

Spielmann's analysis of 19 B—QB5 shows us another flaw of his 17th move: too many mating possibilities: 19 B—QB5, B×B; 20 P×B, KR—K1!; 21 Q×P, Kt—Q5; 22 Q—B4 (if 22 Q—Q1, R—K8ch!), R—K5!; 23 Q—B7ch, K—R1; 24 P—B3, Kt×Pch; 25 K—B2, Kt—Kt5ch; 26 K×Kt, R—B1ch; 27 Q—B4, R—K6 mate.

19 . . .	KR—K1
20 B—K5	Kt×B
21 P×Kt	R×P
22 Q—Kt3	B—QB4!!

He does not fear 23 Q×Pch, R—K2!; 24 Q×R, for then 24 . . . Kt—Kt5; 25 R—KB1, Kt×BP! wins. If 23 B—B1, B×Pch!; 24 K×B, Kt—Kt5ch; 25 K×P, R—B1 mate!

23 B—B5	B×B!
24 Q×Pch	K—Kt3

25 Q×R   R—K7

In answer to the text, 26 R—KB1 would be pointless because of 26 . . . B—KR6! leaving White helpless against 27 . . . B×Pch!

26 P—KR4   B×Pch
27 K—B1   B—Q6
28 P—R5ch   K—Kt4
     Resigns

He can no longer stave off mate. Morphy never played like this!

THIS *is just the kind of original and lively game that one would expect from these great tacticians. How many players would have seen the two amusing Queen sacrifices which were planned, but never happened?*

QUEEN'S PAWN OPENING
Vilna, 1912

WHITE	BLACK
Nimzovich	Alekhine
1 P—Q4	P—Q4
2 Kt—KB3	P—QB4
3 B—B4	Kt—QB3
4 P—K3	Kt—B3
5 Kt—B3	B—Kt5
6 B—QKt5	P—K3
7 P—KR3	B—R4

This allows White to take the initiative. 7 . . . B×Kt or 7 . . . BP×P gives an easier game.

8 P—KKt4	B—Kt3
9 Kt—K5	Q—Kt3
10 P—QR4	P—QR4
11 P—R4	P—R4
12 Kt×B	P×Kt

13 KtP×P   KtP×P
14 Q—K2   O—O—O
15 O—O—O!

15 . . .   B—Q3!

He sees through Nimzovich's fiendish plan: if 15 . . . P×P; 16 P×P, Kt×P?; 17 R×Kt!, Q×R; 18 Q×Pch, Kt—Q2; 19 Q—B6ch!!, P×Q; 20 B—R6 mate! Or 18 . . . R—Q2; 19 B×Rch, Kt×B; 20 Q—K8 mate!

16 B×B   R×B
17 B—Q3

This Bishop is headed for trouble. 17 B×Kt was better, but Nimzovich wants complications.

17 . . .   P—B5!
18 B—Kt6

The Bishop is in mortal danger; however, if 18 Kt—Kt5, P×B; 19 Kt×Rch, K—Q2 winning the Knight.

18 . . .   Kt—K2
19 KR—Kt1   Q—Kt5
20 K—Q2   R—Kt3!
21 P—B3!

He sees that Black threatens 21 . . . Kt×B; 22 R×Kt, Q×KtP; 23 R—QKt1?, Q×Ktch; 24 K×Q, Kt—K5 mate!

21 . . .   R—KR3!

Nimzovich has prevented the threatened Queen sacrifice, but there is little he can do for his awkwardly situated Bishop.

22 B—B7   Kt—B4
23 Q—R2   Q—K2!

If now 24 B—Kt6, Kt×RP! wins the Bishop (25 Q×Kt, Kt—K5ch). Reconciling himself to the loss of the piece, Nimzovich tries to get some attack.

24 Kt—Kt5   Q×B
25 Kt—R7ch   K—Q2
26 Q—Kt8   Kt—Q3

27 R—Kt5   Kt(B3)—K1
28 QR—KKt1   R—KB3
29 P—B4   P—Kt3
30 K—B1   Q—R2
31 P—B3   Q—B2
32 K—Kt1   Q—K2
33 K—R2   R—B1
34 Kt—Kt5   Kt×Kt
35 P×Kt   Kt—B2
36 Q—R7   Q—Q3
    Resigns

A final echo of the Queen-trapping theme: if 37 R×KtP, Kt×P; 38 R—Kt7ch, K—B3; 39 Q×P, R—R3 winning the Queen!

Exciting Drawn Games

♕THE masters and the rank-and-file players do not always see eye to eye. One perennial cause for disagreement is the prevalence of drawn games in master play. There are many reasons for these draws: the high level of playing strength, the risks involved, time pressure, fatigue and the like. Whatever the reasons, the average player has sour recollections of going over scrawny scores which offered little instruction and less enjoyment.

Yet there is a type of draw which gives pleasure to players and students alike. This is the draw in which ingenious and determined attacking moves are met by equally inspired parries, so that a draw becomes the justified and logical outcome.

Thus Znosko-Borovsky, finding himself in a desperate situation, sacrifices piece after piece against Vajda (p. 337) and finally works out a neat pattern for perpetual check. Material is hopelessly against him, so he *must* continue checking. As for Vajda, he too has no choice: perpetual check is the only alternative to checkmate!

Weenink, with the Black pieces, plays sharply for the initiative (p. 339). At length we reach a point where Mikenas seems clearly lost. Yet by leaving his Queen *en prise* for several moves in the course of a diabolical counterattack, he is able to work out a draw in an apparently lost ending.

Purdy (p. 338) is so full of fighting spirit that he starts making combinations as early as the seventh move! Only four moves later, he seems quite lost. Yet he manages to find a saving clause. Menaced with mate on the move, he barely escapes with a forced draw!

Excitement? These games feature it in generous measure. Many a game with a decisive outcome has nowhere near as many thrills as these brief battles in which a keen will to win is concentrated on a very few moves. So, don't condemn drawn games *per se!* These games surely merit a place in Caissa's Hall of Fame.

TARTAKOVER *would call this Wild-West chess!*

QUEEN'S GAMBIT DECLINED

Budapest, 1926

WHITE	BLACK
Znosko-Borovsky	Vajda

1 Kt—KB3	P—Q4
2 P—Q4	Kt—KB3
3 P—B4	P—K3
4 B—Kt5	P—B3
5 Kt—B3	

By playing the simple 5 P—K3, White could have saved himself an enormous amount of trouble!

5 . . .	P×P
6 P—K3	P—Kt4
7 P—QR4	P—QR3!

This looks nonsensical, in view of 8 P×P, BP×P; 9 Kt×P. But then comes 9 . . . Q—Kt3!; 10 Kt—B3, Q×KtP; 11 Q—B1, B—R6!

8 Kt—K5	B—Kt2
9 Q—B3	B—Kt5
10 B—K2	Q—Q4

As White cannot afford to exchange Queens because of his Pawn minus, Black is able to begin a powerful Queen maneuver.

11 Q—B4

If 11 Q—Kt3?, Kt—K5 wins at once.

11 . . .	Q—K5!
12 Q—Kt3!	Q—B7!

One almost expects White to resign!

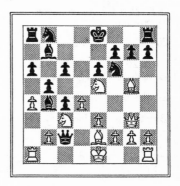

13 O—O!	B×Kt
14 B×Kt	

The counterattack; White need not fear 14 . . . Q×B; 15 Q×P, R—B1; 16 P×B nor 14 . . . B×KtP; 15 Q×P, R—B1; 16 B—R5.

14 . . .   P×B

How can White defend everything? If 15 Q—Kt7, P×Kt!; 16 Q×Rch, K—K2 etc.

15 Kt×KBP!? K×Kt

If *15* . . . R—B1; *16* Kt—Q6ch wins Black's Bishop.

16 B—R5ch K—K2

But not *16* . . . K—B1??; *17* Q—B7 and wins.

17 Q—Kt7ch K—Q3
18 Q×B!

The only chance; if *18* Q×R, Kt—Q2; *19* Q—Kt7, B×KtP with an easy win.

18 . . . B×KtP!

18 . . . Kt—Q2; *19* P×P! leaves White excellent prospects.

19 Q×R B×R
20 P×P!

Not *20* R×B, P—Kt5 with a winning position.

20 . . . BP×P

After *20* . . . RP×P White has a draw with *21* Q—R3ch etc.

21 R×B Q—Kt7?

But this is too hasty. Correct was *21* . . . R—Q1!; *22* R×Pch, K—K2!; *23* R—R1 (if *23* Q—Kt7ch?, R—Q2! or *23* R—R7ch?, Kt—Q2!), Q—Kt7! and Black's Pawns should decide the game in his favor.

22 R×Pch! Kt×R
23 Q×Ktch K—Q2
24 Q—Kt7ch Drawn!

Black cannot escape the perpetual check, as after *24* . . . K—Q3; *25* Q—Kt6ch the King must return to Q2 (*25* . . . K—Q4??; *26* B—B3 mate, or *25* . . . K—K2??; *26* Q—B7ch and mate next).

A fantastic game, rich in stratagems and spoils.

FIRST-RATE chess players are not always articulate in explaining their ideas. Similarly, first-rate chess writers are not always distinguished as players. The Australian Purdy is one of those rare people who shine in both fields. As a writer and as a player, he is profound, pungent, deeply versed in theory and keenly alive to tactical possibilities.

GRUENFELD DEFENSE
Correspondence, 1945

WHITE	BLACK
Vaughan	Purdy
1 P—Q4	Kt—KB3
2 P—QB4	P—KKt3
3 Kt—QB3	P—Q4
4 B—B4	B—Kt2
5 P—K3	P—B4!

Purdy is determined to avoid a constricted position: he intends to achieve freedom even at the cost of a Pawn or two.

6 QP×P! Q—R4!

Black's idea is to counterattack by means of combined pressure on White's Knight on QB3. This is a course which involves risk for both players.

7 P×P!

The variation which Purdy expected —a tribute to his powers of calculation—was *7* Q—R4ch, Q×Q; *8* Kt×Q, Kt—K5!; *9* P—B3, B—Q2!; *10* P×Kt, B×Kt; *11* KP×P, Kt—R3!; *12* R—Kt1, B—B7; *13* R—B1, Kt—Kt5; *14* P—QR3, B×P; *15* K—Q2, B×Rch; *16* K×B, B—Q6! and Black, with the exchange ahead, should win!

7 . . . Kt×P!

8 Q×Kt	B×Ktch
9 P×B	Q×Pch
10 K—K2	Q×R
11 B—K5!	

Now White will win a Rook, remaining a piece ahead. How can Black save the game?

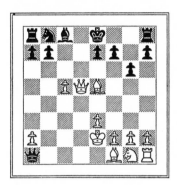

11 . . .	Q—B8!
12 B×R	B—K3!!
13 Q×P	

If 13 Q—Q1? (not 13 Q—Q2??, B—B5ch winning the Queen), B—B5ch; 14 K—K1, Q×Qch; 15 K×Q, B×B winning a Pawn.

On the other hand, after the text, 13 . . . B—B5ch? would lose: 14 K—B3 and White threatens 15 Q—B8 mate.

13 . . .	Q—B7ch!
Drawn	

For if 14 K—B3, Q—B4ch and White cannot escape from the perpetual check!

In this thrilling game both players strive with might and main for the initiative. The result of their brilliant efforts is a legitimate, hard-fought draw.

QUEEN'S GAMBIT DECLINED

Prague Team Tournament, 1931

WHITE	BLACK
Mikenas	Weenink
(Lithuania)	(Holland)
1 P—Q4	P—Q4
2 P—QB4	P—K3
3 Kt—KB3	Kt—KB3
4 P—K3	P—B3

Curious: instead of equalizing at once with . . . P—B4, he prepares for the move!

5 B—Q3	QKt—Q2
6 QKt—Q2	B—K2
7 O—O	O—O
8 P—K4	P×KP
9 Kt×P	Q—B2
10 Q—K2	P—QKt3
11 P—QKt3	B—Kt2
12 B—Kt2	KR—Q1
13 QR—Q1	P—B4!

At last! The position is about even: White has attacking chances, Black has counterplay.

14 P×P	Kt×P
15 Kt×Kt	Q×Kt
16 Kt—K5	R—Q3!
17 Kt—Kt4	Q—KKt4!
18 Kt×Ktch	B×Kt

Black does not fear 19 B×Pch, K×B; 20 R×R as he threatens . . . Q×P mate.

19 P—B4	Q—B4ch

20 K—R1   B×B
21 Q×B   QR—Q1
22 Q—K2   Q—Kt5

Somewhat premature. Before preparing to play his trump (24 . . . R—Q7) Black should have played the prudent . . . P—Kt3!

23 P—B5!   P×P
24 B×P   R—Q7

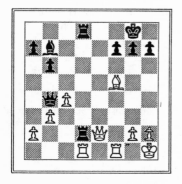

25 B×Pch!!   K—R1!

Not 25 . . . K×B?; 26 Q—R5ch, K—Kt1; 27 Q×Pch, K—R1; 28 R×R, Q×R; 29 Q×B etc.
Or 25 . . . K—B1?; 26 R×Pch!, K×R; 27 R—B1ch, B—B6; 28 R×B mate!

26 B—B2!!

If 26 Q—R5, B×Pch!; 27 K—Kt1, Q—B4ch!; 28 Q×Q, P×Q and Black has somewhat the better of it.

26 . . .   P—Kt3!

26 . . . R×Q?? allows mate in three.
Nor 26 . . . K—Kt1 (White was threatening 27 Q—R5ch); 27 R×R, Q×R; 28 R—Q1!, Q—Kt4; 29 R× Rch and White is a Pawn ahead.

27 R×P!!

So that if 27 . . . R×Q??; 28 R×Rch and mate follows!

27 . . .   B×Pch!

If now 28 K×B??, R×Q check!

28 Q×B!   R×Rch!
29 B×R   R×Bch
30 R—B1   R×Rch
31 Q×R   Q—Q7!

This assures Black the draw, despite the Pawn minus. The position of his Queen is too commanding to permit any winning possibilities by White. Thus if 32 Q—B8ch, K—R2; 33 Q—B7ch, K—R3; 34 Q×P, Q—K8ch with perpetual check.

32 P—QR4   K—Kt2
33 Q—B3   K—R3
34 K—Kt1   P—R4
35 P—R3   Q—B8ch
36 K—B2   Q—Q7ch
     Drawn

White can avoid the perpetual check only by surrendering his Knight's Pawn. A superbly contested game.

Correspondence Chess

♛ ALTHOUGH correspondence chess has been played for more than a century, it did not really begin to acquire a vogue until 1920 or so. The number of correspondence fans has risen to large proportions and still continues to increase. In this country, *Chess Review* has rendered valuable service in fostering the growth of postal chess.

In the old days, many players were prejudiced against correspondence chess because they had a mistaken notion that the games were likely to drag out interminably. The average contest of this type proceeds at the rate of about eight moves (on both sides) per month. As each player is usually conducting from ten to thirty other games at the same time, there is no danger of losing interest in the games. New, varied problems arise constantly; the games are played in leisurely fashion in the comfort of one's own home; new contacts are made and friendships are formed.

Not only has correspondence chess become popular; it has produced many beautiful games. Of the group presented here, Gonzalez—Perrine (p. 343) is undoubtedly the finest; it is, in fact, one of the best games ever played. Black's play is flawless, logical, forceful and brilliant. To make such a game known to a wider audience is one of the pleasures of chess authorship.

The best proof that postal play is not stodgy may be found in the fact that it has produced many outstanding examples of superb attacking play. Young's masterpiece against Daly (p. 344) is a case in point. From the tenth to the 23rd move, we see a thrilling contest which reminds us of a struggle between two first-rate fencers; 23 . . . P—QB4!! is a stroke of genius which decides the game in Black's favor.

Many masters, including Alekhine and Keres, started their careers as correspondence players. Maroczy was another master who produced some great games in this field. In his famous encounter with Zambelly (p. 346), he sacrificed so much and so often that he had to mate with Queen and a handful of Pawns—all the material he had left!

One of the most useful features of corespondence chess is that it offers excellent opportunities for the study of theoretical innovations in the openings. Thus Davis adopts a move recommended by Alekhine (p. 349) and carries out the ensuing attack brilliantly in the face of a clever but ultimately inadequate counterattack. Alekhine himself could not have managed the attack more impressively.

Demuth's win against Mermagen (p. 347) is a classic which emphasizes the vital importance of tactical play. For 19 moves Black holds his own in a difficult variation. One slight slip and he finds himself exposed to attack on a grand scale! Yet Mermagen's failure is excusable: how many players could have foreseen the progress of this attack, especially the exquisite 25 R—B4!!, which reminds us of the observation in *Winning Chess* that "the modern master . . . finds it highly effective, because less hackneyed, to wind up his combination with a stinging surprise."

In Dimock's fine win against Hogenauer (p. 348) the final combination is quite pretty; yet White's treatment of the whole game is captivating in its logic and simplicity. The effective Knight maneuvering is still another indication of first-class play.

The many beautiful points of these first rate games should convince even the most skeptical that postal chess is a very rewarding pastime.

HAD *this game been won by a famous master, it would have acquired the status of an "Immortal Game." It deserves that status
in any event: Black's play is perfection itself!*

NIMZOINDIAN DEFENSE
Correspondence, 1943

WHITE	BLACK
Gonzalez	Perrine

1	P—Q4	Kt—KB3
2	P—QB4	P—K3
3	Kt—QB3	B—Kt5
4	Q—B2	Kt—B3
5	Kt—B3	P—Q3
6	B—Kt5	O—O
7	P—K4	•

This is a case where "discretion is
the better part of valor." The more
modest 7 P—K3 is stronger, for if
then 7 . . . P—K4; 8 P—Q5 and
Black's Knight cannot go to Q5.

7	. . .	P—K4
8	P—Q5	Kt—Q5!

This Knight, which cannot very
well be captured, is now a thorn in
White's center.

9	Q—Q3	P—KR3
10	B—R4?	P—KKt4!!

An unexpected thrust which puts
White's Queen's Bishop out of com-
mission for the balance of the game
and prepares for a beautifully exe-
cuted attack. We now see that White should
have tried 10 B—Q2.

11 B—Kt3

Had he foreseen what was coming,
he might have tried the inadequate
but more aggressive line 11 Kt×KtP,
P×Kt; 12 B×P etc.

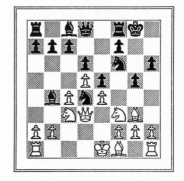

11 . . .   Kt×KP!!

A charming conception: if 12
Q×KKt?, B—KB4; 13 Q—K3, Kt—
B7ch wins the Queen!

12 Kt×Kt   P×Kt

And if now 13 Q×Kt??, R—K1
wins the Queeen.

13 Q×P   R—K1!

Practically forcing White to castle
long, for if 14 B—K2, B—KB4; 15
O—O?, Kt×B; 16 RP×Kt (not 16
BP×Kt??, B—B4 winning the unfor-
tunate Queen), B×Kt followed by
. . . R×B winning a piece.

14	O—O—O	Kt×Kt
15	P×Kt	B—R6ch

Forcing White's reply, for if 16 K—
Kt1?, B—B4ch!; 17 K—R1 (if 17 B—
Q3??, B—B4 again traps the Queen!),
B—B7 and the Rook is caught (18
R—Q2?, R—K8ch!).

16 K—B2   B—B4ch

Now White's King must venture
into the great open spaces (17 B—
Q3??, B—B4!).

17 K—Kt3   P—B4!!

Beautiful play: if 18 P×P e.p., B—
B4! attacking the Queen and threaten-

ing a quick mating attack with . . .
Q—Kt3ch etc.

| 18 | Q—Q2 | Q—R4 |
| 19 | B—Q3 | |

At last!

19 . . . P—Kt4!!

Threatens . . . Q—R5 mate.

| 20 | P×P | B×B |
| 21 | Q×B | P—B5ch!! |

The second Pawn sacrifice is the prelude to a fine finish. If now 22 K×P, Q—R5 mate.

| 22 | Q×P | QR—B1 |
| 23 | Q—Q3 | R—K5!! |

Once more threatening . . . Q—R5 mate. If 24 Q×R, R×P mate!

| 24 | K—B2 | R(5)—QB5! |
| | Resigns | |

The elegance, force and precision of Black's play remind one of Alekhine at his best!

FRANKLIN K. YOUNG *is famous as the author of several books which read as if they had been written in the Tower of Babel. This beautiful game speaks more eloquently for him than all his wordy paragraphs about "major left oblique" and similar matters.*

VIENNA GAME
Correspondence, 1911

WHITE	BLACK
Daly	Young
1 P—K4	P—K4
2 Kt—QB3	Kt—KB3

3	P—B4	P—Q4
4	BP×P	Kt×P
5	Kt—B3	Kt—QB3
6	P—Q4?	

Sadly premature. 6 Q—K2, "putting the question" to the advanced Knight, is much better.

| 6 | . . . | B—QKt5! |
| 7 | B—Q2 | B—Kt5 |

Now White has no really good way of guarding his menaced Queen's Pawn; but he does the best he can.

8	B—QKt5	B×KKt
9	Q×B	Q—R5ch
10	P—Kt3	Kt×B!!

Forcing White into the following combination, as 11 K×Kt, Q×QPch wins easily for Black.

11 Q×P Q×QP!!

Again leaving White no choice, for if 12 Q×Q, Kt—B6ch etc.

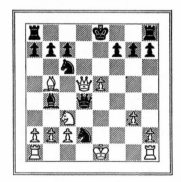

12	B×Ktch	P×B
13	Q×QBPch	K—B1!!
14	Q×Rch	K—K2
15	Q—B6	

Courteously declining the second Rook, for if 15 Q×R, B×Kt; 16 P×B,

Q—K6ch; 17 K—Q1, Kt—B5 (17 . . . Kt—K5 or 17 . . . Kt—B6 also wins) and mate cannot be stopped.

15 . . .   Q—K6ch
16 K—Q1

If 16 Kt—K2, Kt—K5ch; 17 P—B3, Q—B7ch; 18 K—Q1, R—Q1ch with a quick win.

16 . . .   R—Q1!
17 Kt—Q5ch

A little pleasanter than 17 K—B1, Kt—Kt6ch; 18 K—Kt1, Q—B8ch!!

17 . . .   R×Kt
18 Q×R   Kt—K5

Threatens 19 . . . Kt—B7 mate. If now 19 KR—B1, Kt—B7ch; 20 R×Kt, Q—K8 mate.

19 P—B3   P—QB3!!
20 Q—Q4

Forced: the Queen must be on hand to stop . . . Q—Q7 mate. White's material advantage is of no value to him.

20 . . .   Q—B6ch
21 K—B2   Q—K7ch
22 K—Kt1

If 22 K—Kt3, Kt—B4ch!; 23 K×B, Q×Pch leading to three beautiful mates depending on how White replies.

Or 22 K—B1, B×P!!; 23 P×B (if 23 Q×Pch, K—K3; 24 P×B, Q—Q7ch and mate next move), P—QB4!; 24 Q—Q1 (if 24 Q—R4, Q—Q7ch followed by mate), Q—K6ch winning the Queen and remaining with a won ending.

22 . . .   B×P!!
23 P×B

If 23 Q×Pch, K—K3; 24 Q—Kt7,

Q—Q6ch; 25 K—B1, B—Q7ch; 26 K—Q1, Kt—B7 mate.

23 . . .   P—QB4!!

A beautiful position: the Queen is lost no matter where White plays (24 Q—Kt1, Q—Q6ch and Black mates in two).

24 Q—Q6ch   Kt×Q
25 P×Ktch   K×P
26 P—QR4   K—Q4
27 R—QB1

The Rooks are as helpless as ever: if 27 R—R2, Q—K5ch wins a Rook. Black will now establish a passed Pawn, with quick victory in sight.

27 . . .   Q×P
28 P—B4ch   K—B3
29 R—R3   P—KR4!
30 R—Q3   P—R5
31 R(1)—Q1

After 31 P×P, Q×P Black would simply advance his passed Pawns.

31 . . .   P×P
32 R—Q6ch   K—Kt2
33 R—Q7ch   K—R3
34 R×P   Q—R2ch!

Much faster than 34 . . . P—Kt7; 35 R×P etc.

35 K—Kt2   P—Kt7
36 R—Q6ch   K—R4
37 R×Pch   K—Kt5
38 R—Kt7ch   K×BP
39 R—Kt3   P—Kt8(Q)
     Resigns

Some players talk a better game of chess than they play. In Young's case the reverse was true!

CIRCUMSTANCES *alter cases: Maro-czy steps out of character and un-leashes a wild attack, which ends up in a forced mate by Black when he is two Rooks and a Bishop down!*

QUEEN'S PAWN COUNTER GAMBIT

Correspondence, 1897–1898

WHITE	BLACK
Zambelly	Maroczy
1 P—K4	P—K4
2 Kt—KB3	P—Q4
3 P×P	

This gambit is one of the most in-ferior lines at Black's disposal. How-ever, White's poor handling of the position allows Black (Maroczy) to build up a crushing attack.

| 3 . . . | B—Q3 |
| 4 Kt—B3 | |

Much stronger is *4 P—Q4!, P—K5; 5 Kt—K5!* with a clear initiative for White.

4 . . .	Kt—KB3
5 B—Kt5ch	P—B3
6 B—R4?	

Another weak move which puts the Bishop out of play. Better was *6 P×P, P×P; 7 B—K2.* As played, White lets his King's Bishop wander off an im-portant diagonal.

6 . . .	P—K5
7 P×P	O—O
8 Kt—Q4	P×P
9 Kt×BP	Q—Kt3
10 Kt×Kt	R×Kt
11 B—Kt5	R—Q1!!

Black's development has made giant

strides. The text is a subtle preparation for a battering attack against White's intended castling.

| 12 O—O | B×Pch!! |

There are more sacrifices where that came from!

| 13 K×B | Kt—Kt5ch |
| 14 K—Kt3 | |

Out into the great open spaces: if *14 K—Kt1, Q—KR3; 15 R—K1, Q—R7ch; 16 K—B1, Q—R8ch; 17 K—K2, Q×P; 18 R—B1, Kt—R7* with a winning game.

14 . . .	Q—B2ch
15 P—B4	P×P e.p.ch
16 K×P	R—Q5!

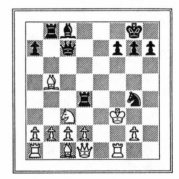

Now we see the point of Black's 11th move. The threat is *17 . . . R—B5ch; 18 K—K2, Q—K4ch* and mate next move.

| 17 P—Q3 | B—Kt2ch |
| 18 Kt—K4 | |

Or *18 K—K2, Q—K4ch* with crush-ing effect.

18 . . .	B×Ktch
19 K×Kt	Q—R7!
20 P×B	

He offers his Queen in the hope of living through the attack.

20 . . .	Q×Pch
21 K—R4	R×B!!

Spurning the Queen and playing for a quick mate.

22 Q×R	R—R4ch!!
23 K×R	Q—R6ch

Aside from his enormous material inferiority, Black is threatened with mate!

24 K—Kt5	P—R3ch
25 K—B4	P—Kt4ch
26 K—K5	Q—K3 mate!

THE classic attack against KB7 has been used so often and in so many guises that we might despair of ever seeing it in a novel form. Yet in the following game this attack is as surprising as it is rich in charming effects.

RUY LOPEZ
Correspondence, 1937

WHITE	BLACK
Demuth	*Mermagen*
1 P—K4	P—K4
2 Kt—KB3	Kt—QB3
3 B—Kt5	P—QR3
4 B—R4	Kt—B3
5 O—O	Kt×P

Tarrasch's favorite defense, which has a well-earned reputation for leading to lively play.

6 P—Q4	P—QKt4
7 B—Kt3	P—Q4
8 P×P	B—K3
9 P—B3	B—K2
10 Q—K2	O—O

11 QKt—Q2	Kt×Kt
12 B×Kt	B—KB4
13 Kt—Q4	Kt×Kt
14 P×Kt	P—B4

Getting rid of the backward Pawn on the open file.

15 P×P	B×P
16 QR—B1	Q—Kt3!?
17 B×P	QR—Q1

The surrendered Pawn must be regained: if 18 B—K4??, B×B wins a piece, or if 18 B—Kt3?, B—Q6 wins the exchange.

18 B—R5!	B×Pch
19 Q×B	Q×B
20 Q—B5!	Q—Q7?

Correct was 20 . . . B—K3!

21 QR—Q1!	Q—Kt4

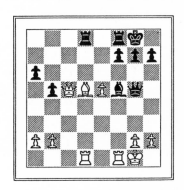

22 B×Pch!!

A stunning surprise. If now 22 . . . K—R1; 23 P—K6 wins. If 22 . . . R×B; 23 P—K6, R—Kt2 (if 23 . . . KR—B1; 24 P—K7); 24 Q×B!, Q—K2 (24 . . . Q×Q; 25 R×Rch forces mate); 25 Q—B7ch!, Q×Q; 26 R×Rch and mate next move.

22 . . .	K×B

23 P—K6ch!! K×P

If 23 . . . K—K1; 24 Q—B6ch, K—K2; 25 Q—B7ch, K—K1 (if 25 . . . K—B3; 26 R×R etc.); 26 P—K7!, Q×P; 27 R×Rch, Q×R; 28 R—K1ch and mate follows.

24 QR—K1ch! K—Q2

If 24 . . . K—B3; 25 Q—B6ch, K—B2; 26 Q—K6 mate!

25 R—B4!! Resigns

A lovely finishing touch: if 25 . . . Q×R; 26 R—K7 mate. Meanwhile Black has the insoluble problem of finding a satisfactory defense against the threat of 26 R—Q4 mate!

For all its matter-of-fact character, castling is an art. Black's failure to castle in good time leads to a sparkling finish.

SICILIAN DEFENSE
Correspondence, 1939

WHITE	BLACK
Dimock	Hogenauer
1 P—K4	P—QB4
2 Kt—KB3	Kt—QB3
3 P—Q4	P×P
4 Kt×P	Kt—B3
5 Kt—QB3	P—Q3
6 B—K2	P—KKt3
7 B—K3	B—Kt2
8 Kt—Kt3	B—K3
9 P—B4	P—Q4

He wants to break up the hostile center before White gets to play P—B5.

10 P—K5	Kt—Q2
11 O—O	

11 Kt×P is answered by 11 . . . KKt×P.

11 . . .	P—B3
12 B—Kt4!	B×B
13 Q×B	P×P?

Suicide. He should play 13 . . . P—B4; 14 Q—B3, P—K3 followed by 15 . . . O—O with a fair game.

14 Kt×P	P×P
15 Q×P	

The consequence of Black's failure to castle is that he is threatened with 16 Q—B7 mate and 16 Kt—B7ch.

15 . . .	Kt(3)—K4
16 Kt—Q4	

Threatening instant destruction with 17 Kt—K6.

| 16 . . . | Kt—B4 |

Attacks and defends.

17 Kt—Kt5!

Indirectly defending the menaced Knight and contemplating Kt—B7ch, not to mention the threat of B×Kt.
Note the astonishing line-up of all four Knights on the same rank!

| 17 . . . | Kt—K3 |

Again attacking and defending; but now White is ready for the final phase.

| 18 Q—QR4! | Kt—B3 |

The threat was 19 Kt—Q6 mate or 19 Kt(Kt5)—B7 mate!

19 QR—Q1

Getting his last piece into play. Now the threat is 20 Kt(Q5)—B7ch.

| 19 . . . | Q—B1 |

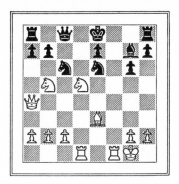

20 Kt×KP!!   Q—Kt1

If 20 . . . K×Kt; 21 Q—R3ch wins the Queen. If 20 . . . Kt×Kt White mates on the move. .

21 Kt×Kt   P×Kt
22 Kt—Q6ch   Resigns

On 22 . . . K—Q1; 23 Q×BP leaves Black completely helpless. A very enjoyable game, with instructive strategy and sharp tactical play.

HERE *is an attacking game that has everything: a farsighted combination, numerous sacrifices, sparkling finesses, able defense and masterly repulse of the counterattack!*

SCOTCH GAMBIT
Correspondence, 1939

WHITE	BLACK
Davis	*Walker*
1 P—K4	P—K4
2 P—Q4	P×P
3 P—QB3	P×P
4 Kt×P	Kt—QB3
5 B—QB4	Kt—B3

6 Kt—B3	B—Kt5
7 O—O	B×Kt
8 P×B	P—Q3
9 P—K5!	

Already a Pawn down, White gives up a second Pawn in order to open up the attacking diagonal QR3—KB8.

9 . . .	P×P
10 Q—Kt3	O—O

10 . . . Kt—QR4?? is disastrous: 11 B×Pch, K—B1; 12 B—R3ch etc.

11 Kt—Kt5!	Q—K1

Or 11 . . . Kt—QR4; 12 B×Pch, K—R1; 13 Q—Kt5, P—KR3; 14 Q×Kt, P×Kt; 15 B—Kt3 and White's attack outweighs his Pawn minus.

12 B—R3	Kt—QR4
13 Q—Kt4	P—QKt3

13 . . . Kt×B; 14 Q×Kt simply loses the exchange for Black.

14 B—Q3!

Not 14 Q×Rch?, Q×Q; 15 B×Q, Kt×B! and White's Bishop is trapped!

14 . . .   P—B4

Saves the exchange; but now White is ready for the King-side attack.

15 Q—KR4   P—Kt3

If 15 . . . P—KR3; 16 Kt—K4 with a very difficult game for Black (he cannot play 16 . . . Kt×Kt because of 17 Q×Kt winning a Rook).

16 Q—R6!!

In order to rule out the possibility of . . . P—R4 as a defense.

16 . . .	Q—R5!
17 B—K4!!	B—Kt2
18 P—KB4!!	

Leaving both Bishops *en prise*, White goes for the main chance, which is to eliminate Black's valuable defensive Knight at KB3.

| 18 . . . | B×B |
| 19 P×P! | |

The point: White is a piece down, but the attacked Knight cannot budge.

| 19 . . . | Q—B7! |

The mating threat is stronger than it looks, for if 20 R—B2?, Q×Rch!; 21 K×Q, Kt—Kt5ch and wins.

| 20 R—B3! | B×R |
| 21 P×B | KR—Q1 |

The only chance: a try for perpetual check.

22 P×Kt	R—Q8ch
23 R×R	Q×Rch
24 K—Kt2!	

He can get out of the checks, after which his mate threat decides.

| 24 . . . | Q—K7ch |
| 25 K—R3! | Resigns |

For after 25 . . . Q—B8ch; 26 K—Kt3!, Q—K8ch; 27 K—Kt4!, Q—Kt8ch; 28 K—B4! Black must surrender.

An enthralling game all the way!

Old Favorites

♛ THESE old games, and not-so-old games, wear well. Some of them are old enough to be new—games that we first saw as youngsters who were deeply impressed by the freshness of their combinative play.

Sometimes there is an element of disenchantment in these games, as for example in the famous Evans win against MacDonnell (p. 352). Viewing the game with a coldly analytical eye, we see that both players overlooked moves that are just as attractive as, but a good deal sounder than, the actual continuation!

Hoffman—Petroff (p. 353), on the other hand, could not possibly be improved upon: the striking Queen sacrifice leads to many a pretty mating tableau in which the victim's Queen is worse than useless!

Morphy performs against Marache (p. 354) just as we would expect him to. The dread Evans Gambit has no terrors for him, and the conclusion is worked out with the perfection we naturally expect in a Morphy game. The final Knight maneuvers are irresistibly droll.

That the word "dread" is used advisedly about the Evans Gambit is proved by Clemenz against Eisenschmidt (p. 355)—surely a masterly game, though not played by masters. Curiously enough, the final utilization of the Knights is, if anything, even prettier than in Morphy's game.

We come now to games of more modern vintage. The two immortal games between Lasker and Pillsbury have to be seen together to be appreciated properly. Lasker's win (p. 360) is the more profound and original of the pair; yet Pillsbury's victory (p. 361), while less flashy, has the bubbling energy which makes his games so enjoyable.

Breyer's best games, such as the one with Esser (p. 358), show that he had the stuff of genius in him. Brilliant as the numerous sacrifices are, they are less impressive than the originality of Breyer's plan of attack. Reti rightly admired Breyer's 14 K—B1!!!, which we describe as "one of the deepest moves ever made on the chessboard." Do you agree?

Capablanca's scintillating combination against Baca-Arus (p. 357) has something in common with many of the best modern games: White not only exploits a weakness, he first forces its very existence! To the connoisseur, Capablanca's provocation of . . . P—KKt3 is just as brilliant a conception as the slashing attack which follows it.

About Nimzovich's glorious win against Hakansson (p. 356) we ask, "Who but Nimzovich had the knack of getting such positions?" The answer is of course: "Nobody!" In this game we can detect that blend of sardonic humor, fiendish ingenuity and determination to wear no man's collar which are uniquely Nimzovichian. He is as indestructible as a Dickens creation!

The beauty of these games does not fade with the passage of time. From today's headlines will come tomorrow's old favorites.

It was a great day in the history of chess when Captain Evans introduced his famous gambit. Although the Captain was only a middling player while his opponent was the greatest English master of his time, MacDonnell was helpless against the gambit.

EVANS GAMBIT
London, 1838

WHITE	BLACK
Evans	*MacDonnell*
1 P—K4	P—K4
2 Kt—KB3	Kt—QB3
3 B—B4	B—B4

4 O—O	P—Q3
5 P—QKt4	B×P
6 P—B3	B—R4
7 P—Q4	B—KKt5?

MacDonnell is baffled by the new-fangled opening. 7 . . . B—Kt3! is the move.

8 Q—Kt3	Q—Q2
9 Kt—Kt5	Kt—Q1
10 P×P	P×P
11 B—R3	

The development of the Bishop on this diagonal is one of the key ideas of the opening. How is Black to castle?

| 11 . . . | Kt—R3 |

| 12 P—B3 | B—Kt3ch |
| 13 K—R1 | B—KR4 |

Or *13 . . . B—K3; 14 R—Q1,
B×B; 15 R×Q, B×Q; 16 R—K7ch*
with a winning game.

| 14 R—Q1! | Q—B1 |

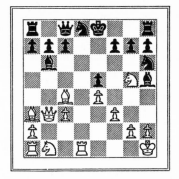

15 R×Ktch?!

There is an easy win (but without
sacrifices!) by *15 Q—Kt5ch!, Kt—B3;
16 B—Q5* and Black is helpless.

| 15 . . . | Q×R? |

After *15 . . . K×R!* White has no
good continuation of the attack!

16 Kt×BP!!

MacDonnell must have overlooked
this clever move. The point is that
after *16 . . . Kt×Kt; 17 B—Kt5ch!,
P—B3; 18 Q—K6ch*, mate follows; or
*16 . . . B×Kt; 17 B×Bch, Kt×B; 18
Q—K6ch* with the same result.

| 16 . . . | Q—R5 |
| 17 Q—Kt5ch | |

17 B—Kt5ch mates a move sooner.

17 . . .	P—B3
18 Q×KPch	K—Q2
19 Q—K6ch	K—B2

20 B—Q6 mate

History had been made; the gambit
had successfully survived its first test!

*Chess history is a procession of
names which for most of us are
no more than names. Occasionally we run across a game which
gives us a vivid notion of the personality behind the name.*

GIUOCO PIANO
Warsaw, 1844

WHITE	BLACK
Hoffman	*Petroff*
1 P—K4	P—K4
2 Kt—KB3	Kt—QB3
3 B—B4	B—B4
4 P—B3	Kt—B3
5 P—Q4	P×P
6 P—K5	Kt—K5

. . . P—Q4! is the strongest move
in such situations.

7 B—Q5	Kt×KBP!?
8 K×Kt	P×Pch
9 K—Kt3	P×P
10 B×P	Kt—K2
11 Kt—Kt5?	Kt×B
12 Kt×BP	

12 Q×Kt will not do because of *12
. . . Q×Ktch* in reply, with a winning game for Black. The text seems
very ingenious, the idea being that if
12 . . . K×Kt; 13 Q×Ktch followed
by *14 Q×B*.

| 12 . . . | O—O!! |

Foreseeing that despite the loss of
the Queen, he will have a mating attack.

13 Kt×Q

The alternative *13 Q×Kt, R×Kt* leads to some smart variations: *14 Q×B, Q—Kt4ch; 15 K—R3, P—Q3ch* winning the Queen; or *14 P—K6, B—B7ch* and *15 . . . Q—R5* mate; or *14 R—KB1, Q—Kt4ch; 15 K—R3, P—Q3ch* again winning White's Queen!

13 . . .	B—B7ch
14 K—R3	

On *14 K—Kt4, R—B5ch* there is a shorter mate: *15 K—Kt5 (if 15 K—R3, R—R5 mate; or 15 K—R5, R—R5ch; 16 K—Kt5, P—R3ch* followed by *. . . Kt—K2 mate), P—R3ch; 16 K—R5 (if 16 K—Kt6, Kt—K2ch; 17 K—R5, R—R5 mate), R—R5ch; 17 K—Kt6, Kt—K2 mate!*

| 14 . . . | P—Q3ch |

If now *15 P—Kt4, Kt—B5 mate!*

15 P—K6	Kt—B5ch
16 K—Kt4	Kt×KP!

What a situation for a waiting move! Black threatens mate beginning with *17 . . . R—B5ch.*

17 P—Kt3

White's helplessness is curious: thus if *17 K—R3, Kt—B5 mate; or 17 K—*

R5, Kt—B5ch; *18 K—Kt5, P—R3* mate; or *17 P—KR4, Kt—B4ch; 18 K—R5, P—Kt3ch* and *19 . . . B—K6 mate!*

17 . . .	Kt—Q5ch
18 Kt—K6	B×Ktch
19 K—R4	Kt—B4ch
20 K—R3	

20 K—Kt4 allows a mate beginning with *20 . . . Kt—K6ch.*
20 K—Kt5 holds out the longest, but White still succumbs.

20 . . .	Kt—K6ch
21 K—R4	

On *21 P—Kt4, P—KR4!; 22 R—Kt1, P×Pch; 23 R×P, K—B2!* leads to mate.

21 . . .	Kt—Kt7ch
22 K—R5	P—Kt3ch
23 K—Kt5	B—K6 mate

Petroff's Defense was named after the winner of this astounding game.

THINK *of Marache's effrontery in playing an Evans Gambit against the great Morphy! "It's goin' t' be fun," said Kin Hubbard, "t' watch an' see how long th' meek keep the earth after they inherit it."*

EVANS GAMBIT
New Orleans, 1857

WHITE	BLACK
Marache	Morphy
1 P—K4	P—K4
2 Kt—KB3	Kt—QB3
3 B—B4	B—B4
4 P—QKt4	B×P
5 P—B3	B—R4

6 P—Q4	P×P
7 P—K5	P—Q4!

Morphy never failed to open up lines for his pieces.

8 P×P e.p.	Q×P
9 O—O	KKt—K2

White should now play 10 B—R3, although even then his attacking prospects would not be worth a Pawn. Instead, he gets sidetracked on a puerile demonstration which Morphy thrusts back with almost insulting ease.

10 Kt—Kt5?	O—O
11 B—Q3	B—B4!

Black is not afraid to lose the exchange, as he will have three Pawns for it—not to mention a strong attack.

12 B×B	Kt×B
13 B—R3	Q—Kt3
14 B×R	Q×Kt
15 B—R3	P×P
16 B—B1	

Nobody could afford such time-wasting maneuvers against Morphy!

16 . . .	Q—Kt3
17 B—B4	R—Q1
18 Q—B2	Kt(3)—Q5

Black's Knights are poised for the kill!

19 Q—K4	Kt—KKt6!!
20 Resigns	

If 20 Q×Q, Kt(5)—K7 mate! A stunning surprise for White, but could he have done better? From the diagrammed position:

If 19 Q—Q3, Kt—KKt6!! wins the Queen for two Knights (20 Q× either Kt, Kt—K7ch) or if 20 Q×Q, Kt(5) —K7 mate.

If 19 R—Q1, Kt—K6!; 20 Q×Q, Kt—K7ch; 21 K—R1, R×R mate.

If 19 Q—R4, P—Kt4!; 20 Q×B, Kt—K7ch; 21 K—R1, Kt×B; 22 R— Kt1 (or 22 P—Kt3, Q—B3ch; 23 P— B3, Q×Pch!!), R—Q8!; 23 P—Kt3, Q—B3ch and mate next move.

Morphy's combination was as sound as it was brilliant.

THE gems which the great masters have produced with the Evans Gambit are well known. The following game, played by two amateurs, is a masterpiece which richly deserves a place of honor in any collection of fine games.

EVANS GAMBIT
Dorpat, 1862

WHITE	BLACK
Clemenz	Eisenschmidt
1 P—K4	P—K4
2 Kt—KB3	Kt—QB3
3 B—B4	B—B4
4 P—QKt4	B×P
5 P—B3	B—B4
6 P—Q4	P×P
7 P×P	B—Kt3
8 O—O	P—Q3

The famous "Normal Position" of

the Evans, from which Morphy, Anderssen, Zukertort and Tchigorin evolved some of their most beautiful games.

9 Kt—B3	B—Q2

9 . . . Kt—R4 or 9 . . . B—Kt5 gives Black better chances.

10 P—K5	P×P
11 R—K1	KKt—K2
12 Kt—KKt5	B—K3

Best under the circumstances. 12 . . . O—O would be ruinous because of 13 Q—R5!

13 B×B	P×B
14 Kt×KP	Q—Q3
15 Kt×KtPch	K—B1
16 Q—Kt4	B×P
17 Kt—K4	Q—Kt5?

Superficially tempting, as both Rooks are attacked and mate is threatened. The best defense, however, was 17 . . . Q—Kt3!

18 Kt—K6ch!

18 B—Q2 was a good enough parry, but White sees brilliant possibilities in the position.

18 . . .	K—K1
19 Kt—B6ch	K—B2

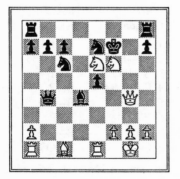

20 Kt—Kt5ch!! K—B1

If 20 . . . K×Kt; 21 Q—K6ch, K—Kt2; 22 Q—B7ch, K—R3; 23 Kt —K4ch and mate follows.

If 20 . . . K—Kt3; 21 Q—R5ch, K—B4; 22 P—Kt4ch, K×Kt; 23 Q— B7 mate.

If 20 . . . K—Kt2; 21 Kt—R5ch, K—B1; 22 Q—B3ch, K—K1; 23 Kt— B6ch, K—Q1 (if 23 . . . K—B1; 24 Kt—Q5ch wins the Queen); 24 Kt— B7ch, K—B1; 25 Q—R3 ch, K—Kt1; 26 Kt—Q7ch, K—B1; 27 Kt—Kt6ch, K—Kt1; 28 Q—B8ch!!, R×Q; 29 Kt —Q7 mate!

21 B—R3!!

Relieves the mate threat.

21 . . . Q×B

If 21 . . . Q—B5 (to prevent 22 Q—K6); 22 KR—QB1! forces Black to allow Q—K6.

22 Q—K6! Kt—Q1

If 22 . . . K—Kt2; 23 Kt—R5ch and mate next move.

23 Q—B7ch!! Kt×Q
24 Kt—K6 mate!

One of the most beautiful mating positions ever brought off in actual play!

BLACK castles with his Queen, but leaves his King in danger!

FRENCH DEFENSE
Match, 1922

WHITE	BLACK
Nimzovich	Hakansson
1 P—K4	P—K3
2 P—Q4	P—Q4
3 P—K5	P—QB4
4 Q—Kt4?!	P×P

5 Kt—KB3	Kt—QB3
6 B—Q3	P—B4?

Weak. 6 . . . Q—B2! would refute White's premature development of the Queen.

7 Q—Kt3	KKt—K2
8 O—O	Kt—Kt3
9 P—KR4!	Q—B2
10 R—K1	B—Q2
11 P—R3	O—O—O
12 P—Kt4	

In his desire to constrict Black's game, Nimzovich disdains the win of the exchange by 12 P—R5, KKt—K2; 13 Kt—Kt5, R—K1; 14 Kt—B7, R—Kt1; 15 Kt—Q6ch etc.

12 . . .	P—QR3
13 P—R5	KKt—K2
14 B—Q2	P—R3
15 P—R4	P—KKt4
16 P—Kt5	P—B5
17 Q—Kt4	Kt—QKt1

Black is in full retreat. Trust Nimzovich to do the rest!

18 P—B3!	R—K1

On 18 . . . P×P; 19 R—QB1! enables White to create havoc on the open file.

19 BP×P	K—Q1

Black's pieces are running wildly to escape the coming attack by the Rook.

20 R—QB1	Q—Kt3
21 P—R5	Q—R2
22 P—Kt6	Q—R1

Who but Nimzovich had the knack of getting such positions? As he himself said at this point, "The Queen finds herself in a position to which as a rule she would only be consigned in a problem."

23 R—B7	Kt—B4
24 Kt—B3	B—K2
25 Kt×QP!	Kt×P?

Suimate.

26 Kt×Kt	P×Kt

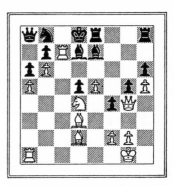

27 Q×Bch!!	Kt×Q
28 Kt—K6 mate	

An appropriate finish.

This *is a slightly flawed gem—but still a gem.*

QUEEN'S GAMBIT DECLINED
(in effect)
Havana, 1912

WHITE Capablanca	BLACK Baca-Arus
1 P—Q4	P—Q4
2 P—K3	P—K3
3 B—Q3	P—QB3
4 Kt—KB3	B—Q3
5 QKt—Q2	P—KB3

Black's Stonewall formation is not so sturdy as its name implies.

6 P—B4	Q—B3
7 P—QKt3	Kt—KR3
8 B—Kt2	O—O
9 Q—B2	Kt—Q2
10 P—KR3!!	

Threatening *11 P—KKt4!* with a tremendous attack and thereby provoking the following move, which weakens the black squares in general and the long diagonal in particular.

10 . . .	P—KKt3
11 O—O—O!	P—K4?
12 QP×P	Kt×P
13 P×P	P×P
14 Kt—B4!!	P×Kt

Declining White's extraordinarily brilliant offer (played to open the lines leading to Black's King) is also unsatisfactory: *14 . . . Kt×Bch; 15 Q×Kt, Q—K2; 16 Kt×B, Q×Kt; 17 Q—Q4!* and wins. Or *14 . . . Kt(3) —B2; 15 Kt(3)×Kt, Kt×Kt; 16 P—B4!, P×Kt; 17 B×Pch, K—R1 (. . . B—K3; 18 R×B); 18 R×B!*

15 B×Pch	Kt(3)—B2
16 R×B!!	Q×R
17 Kt×Kt	B—K3
18 R—Q1	Q—K2

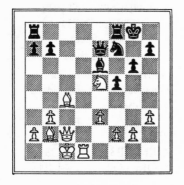

19 R—Q7!!	B×R

Again declining is futile: *19 . . . Q—K1; 20 Kt×Kt, R×Kt; 21 Q—B3!, R×R; 22 Q—R8ch, K—B2; 23 Q—Kt7 mate.*

20 Kt×B

Less accurate than *20 Kt—B6!!* (even *20 Kt×P!!* does the trick), for if then *20 . . . P×Kt; 21 Q—B3* wins at once.

20 . . .	KR—B1

White was threatening *21 Kt—B6ch, K—Kt2; 22 Kt—Kt4ch, K—Kt1; 23 Kt—R6 mate!* If *20 . . . Q×Kt; 21 Q—B3!* is decisive.

21 Q—B3!	R×B
22 P×R	Resigns

If *22 . . . Kt—Q3; 23 Q—R8ch* wins easily. Euwe: "Such an achievement in the realm of combinative chess can only be described as superb."

BREYER *was one of the leaders of the Hypermodern School, famous for their paradoxical ideas, and hatred of routine. This spectacular game, in which surprise may be said to become routine, has a grandeur which dwarfs many of the well-known "immortal games."*

QUEEN'S GAMBIT DECLINED
Budapest, 1917

WHITE	BLACK
Breyer	*Esser*
1 P—Q4	P—Q4
2 P—QB4	P—K3
3 Kt—QB3	P—QB3

4 P—K3	Kt—B3
5 B—Q3	B—Q3
6 P—B4!	O—O
7 Kt—B3	

White intends to unleash a furious attack, and his unusual sixth move has been played to keep the center securely under his control. Black could now upset this plan with 7 . . . P—B4!, giving himself enough counterplay to keep White busy in the center.

| 7 . . . | P×P |

Anticipating 8 B×P, P—QKt4 etc.

8 B—Kt1!!

The Bishop is kept on its original attacking diagonal.

| 8 . . . | P—QKt4? |

Again . . . P—B4! was the move!

| 9 P—K4! | B—K2 |
| 10 Kt—Kt5! | P—KR3 |

If 10 . . . P—Kt3; 11 P—KR4! followed by the opening of the King's Rook file.

11 P—KR4!

Threatening 12 P—K5, Kt—Q4; 13 Q—B2 (this explains why Breyer played 8 B—Kt1!! instead of the more natural 8 B—B2), P—Kt3; 14 P—R5 with a decisive attack.

| 11 . . . | P—Kt3 |

After 11 . . . P×Kt; 12 RP×P gives White a crushing attack along the King's Rook file.

| 12 P—K5! | P×Kt |
| 13 RP×P!! | |

The obvious 13 P×Kt, B×P; 14 RP×P, B×QP leaves Black with adequate defensive facilities.

| 13 . . . | Kt—Q4 |

White is a piece down. How should he continue the attack?

14 K—B1!!!

One of the deepest moves ever made on the chessboard!

14 . . .	Kt×Kt
15 P×Kt	B—Kt2
16 Q—Kt4	K—Kt2

In order to answer 17 Q—R4 with . . . R—R1.

| 17 R—R7ch!! | K×R |

Or 17 . . . K—Kt1; 18 Q—R4 winning at once.

18 Q—R5ch	K—Kt2
19 Q—R6ch	K—Kt1
20 B×P!	P×B
21 Q×Pch	K—R1
22 Q—R6ch	K—Kt1
23 P—Kt6!	

Now we see the point of 14 K—B1!!! Had this move been omitted, Black could now save himself with 23 . . . B—R5ch and 24 . . . Q—K2!

| 23 . . . | R—B2 |

The only way to stop mate.

| 24 P×Rch | K×P |
| 25 Q—R5ch | K—Kt2 |

If *25 . . .* K—B1 White's next move wins even more rapidly.

| 26 P—B5! | P×P |
| 27 B—R6ch | Resigns |

The finish might have been: *27 . . .* K—R2; *28* B—B4ch, K—Kt2; *29* Q—R6ch, K—Kt1; *30* Q—Kt6ch, K—R1; *31* K—K2, B—R5; *32* R—R1, Kt—Q2; *33* B—Kt5, Q×B; *34* Q×Q etc.

Napier sums it up in one simple sentence: "Breyer did marvelous things."

BRILLIANT *as this game is, Lasker's sacrifices acquire added luster from the fact that the loser was a very great master and not a pushover.*

QUEEN'S GAMBIT DECLINED

St. Petersburg, 1895–1896

WHITE	BLACK
Pillsbury	*Em. Lasker*
1 P—Q4	P—Q4
2 P—QB4	P—K3
3 Kt—QB3	Kt—KB3
4 Kt—B3	P—B4
5 B—Kt5	BP×P
6 Q×P	Kt—B3

6 . . . B—K2 is the more exact move; see the next game for some of the unpleasant consequences which might result from the text.

7 Q—R4

Pillsbury waited nine years after this game to play the superior *7* B×Kt! against Lasker!

| 7 . . . | B—K2 |
| 8 O—O—O | Q—R4! |

Beginning his counterattack at once against White's somewhat exposed King.

| 9 P—K3 | B—Q2 |
| 10 K—Kt1 | P—KR3! |

Sooner or later White will have to make up his mind about the disposition of his Queen's Bishop.

11 P×P	P×P
12 Kt—Q4	O—O
13 B×Kt	B×B

With the possession of the Bishop-pair, Black will soon be ready for sacrificial attack. The most prudent reply is *14* Q—Kt3, supporting his somewhat endangered King in the event of the following exchange.

14 Q—R5	Kt×Kt
15 P×Kt	B—K3
16 P—B4	QR—B1!
17 P—B5	

Unaware of the impending combination.

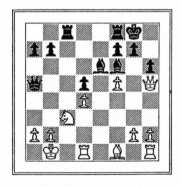

| 17 . . . | R×Kt!! |
| 18 P×B | |

The attempt to win a Rook by *18 P×R, Q×P; 19 P×B?* would be disastrous because of *19 . . . Q—Kt5ch; 20 K—B2* (if *20 K—R1, R—B1!* winning because of the threats of *21 . . . R—B8ch!!* or *21 . . . B×Pch!* or *21 . . . R—B7!*), *R—B1ch* winning easily.

It is true that *18 P×R, Q×P; 19 Q—B3, Q—Kt5ch; 20 Q—Kt3* offers a fair defense, but *20 . . . B×Pch* leaves Black with a strong game as well as two Pawns for the exchange.

18 . . .   R—QR6!!

One of the most inspired moves ever made on the chessboard! If now *19 P×R, Q—Kt3ch; 20 K—R1, B× Pch; 21 R×B, Q×Rch* with a winning attack.

Even more interesting is the postmortem analysis of these two great players: *19 P—K7, R—K1; 20 P×R, Q—Kt3ch; 21 K—B2, R—B1ch; 22 K—Q2, B×P; 23 P—K8(Q)ch, R×Q; 24 B—Q3, Q—R4ch; 25 K— B1* and now *25 . . . Q×Pch* (overlooked by both Lasker and Pillsbury!) forces mate next move!

19 P×Pch   R×P
20 P×R   Q—Kt3ch

If now *21 K—R1, B×Pch* wins easily; likewise if *21 K—B2, R—B2ch* etc.

21 B—Kt5   Q×Bch
22 K—R1   R—B2

Threatening mate in three beginning with *23 . . . R—B8ch!* The remainder of the game was played in the most harrowing time pressure.

23 R—Q2   R—B5
24 KR—Q1   R—B6
25 Q—B5

If *25 Q—K2, R—B8ch!; 26 R×R, B×Pch; 27 R×B, Q×Q* and Black should win.

25 . . .   Q—B5

Threatens *26 . . . R—B8ch; 27 R×R, Q×Rch; 28 Q—Kt1, Q×R.*

26 K—Kt2

Relatively better was *26 K—Kt1, R×P; 27 Q—QB2, R—B6; 28 Q— Kt2, P—QKt4* and White will eventually succumb to the pressure.

26 . . .   R×P!!
27 Q—K6ch   K—R2
28 K×R

Or *28 K—Kt1, B×P!* and Black wins rapidly.

28 . . .   Q—B6ch

Black mates in four: *29 K—R4, P—Kt4ch!; 30 K×P, Q—B5ch; 31 K—R5, B—Q1ch* and mate next move. One of the finest games ever played between great masters.

Lasker himself considered this the best game he had ever played.

HERE *we see how Pillsbury gained his revenge by finally adopting the move which he had saved for nine years! Note the practiced skill with which Pillsbury handles the Queen's Knight: it goes to QB3—K4—Q6—B4—K5—Kt4— K5. In fact, it is on these clever moves that his victory depends.*

QUEEN'S GAMBIT DECLINED

Cambridge Springs, 1904

WHITE	BLACK
Pillsbury	*Em. Lasker*
1 P—Q4	P—Q4
2 P—QB4	P—K3
3 Kt—QB3	Kt—KB3
4 Kt—B3	P—B4

5 B—Kt5	BP×P
6 Q×P	Kt—B3

As previously pointed out, 6 . . . B—K2 is the right move to avoid the ensuing difficulties.

7 B×Kt!

This is the baleful move saved up by Pillsbury.

7 . . .   P×B

7 . . . Q×B loses a Pawn. 7 . . . Kt×Q; 8 B×Q, Kt—B7ch looks attractive, but after 9 K—Q2, Kt×R; 10 B—R4 Black will lose his venturesome Knight, leaving him with the material disadvantage of a Rook for two pieces.

8 Q—R4	P×P
9 R—Q1	B—Q2
10 P—K3	Kt—K4
11 Kt×Kt	P×Kt
12 Q×BP	Q—Kt3
13 B—K2!?	Q×KtP

Courageously accepting the proffered Pawn, although he realizes the dangers involved in the capture.

14 O—O!	R—B1
15 Q—Q3	

Threatening mate and thus saving his Knight.

15 . . .   R—B2?

A serious error of judgment. 15 . . . B—B3 was the best chance.

16 Kt—K4!	B—K2
17 Kt—Q6ch	K—B1

Or 17 . . . B×Kt; 18 Q×B, Q—B6 (if 18 . . . Q—Kt3; 19 Q×P with a powerful attack); 19 B—Kt5! and wins.

18 Kt—B4	Q—Kt4
19 P—B4!	

This is the move which Lasker must have missed. It opens up powerful attacking lines.

19 . . .	P×P
20 Q—Q4!	P—B3

Not 20 . . . R—Kt1?; 21 Q×BP winning a Rook because of the mate threat.

21 Q×BP	Q—QB4
22 Kt—K5	B—K1
23 Kt—Kt4	P—B4
24 Q—R6ch	

This is a real Pillsbury attack: one threat after another!

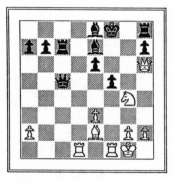

24 . . .   K—B2

On 24 . . . K—Kt1 there is a pretty win by 25 Q×KPch, B—B2; 26 Kt—R6ch, K—Kt2; 27 Q×Bch, K×Kt; 28 R×P, Q×Pch; 29 K—R1, Q×B; 30 R—Q6ch!, B×R; 31 Q—B6 mate.

25 B—B4!

Beautiful play! The Bishop, which is immune from capture (25 . . . Q×B; 26 Kt—K5ch) prepares White's next move.

25 . . .	R—B3
26 R×Pch!	Q×R

27 R—KB1	Q×Rch	Q×R mate!
28 K×Q	B—Q2	30 Kt—K5 Resigns
29 Q—R5ch!	K—Kt1	

If 29 . . . K—Kt2; 30 Q—K5ch, K—Kt1; 31 Kt—R6ch, K—B1; 32

This was Pillsbury's last great game. He died two years later at the age of thirty-four.

"*A little less quiet up there!*"

Positional Masterpieces

♛ THE tenacity of the misconceptions about positional play is really remarkable.

It is thought, for example, that tactical play is a method of winning quickly, while positional play wins slowly and laboriously. In many cases, as we shall see in these games, positional play wins neatly, convincingly and rapidly.

In any event, there are innumerable instances where tactical play is not feasible, or is not likely to be successful. What then is so attractive about tactical play which leads to quick defeat?

The great fallacy, however, is the belief that tactical play and positional play are mutually exclusive. Be it ever so positional, a *game cannot be decided without tactical means!* It would be difficult, for example, to imagine a simpler game than Domenech—Flohr (p. 366), in which the Queens are exchanged on the seventh move. Flohr's objective is quite humdrum: simplification and more simplification— yet he relies in the last analysis on a surprising tactical interlude (moves 20–22) to make the win clear. Similarly with another "simple" positional game, Nimzovich—Mieses (p. 367), which concludes with a delightful tactical flourish.

In his unobtrusively elegant game against Salve (p. 369), Suechting's masterly play on the black squares makes a very pleasing impression. But in the end the decision comes, as it must, by tactical means. A more complicated example of the same idea is seen in Alekhine—

Freymann (p. 368), in which weak Pawns are compelled to become still weaker. But once this process has been completed, Alekhine characteristically turns to devastating attacking play. Capablanca—Villegas (p. 372) is a paradoxical affair: superficially, it seems nothing more than an outstanding example of utilizing the Queen-side majority of Pawns. The real point, however, is that the advantage is established by the offer of a Queen sacrifice and is ultimately exploited by means of a second Queen sacrifice!

We also describe Spielmann—Maroczy (p. 374) as a paradoxical game, yet it again proves our thesis: the great master of attack uses tactical means to execute his brilliantly conceived positional plans. How shall we appraise Steinitz—Sellman (p. 370), which is surely the archetype of the Steinitz games famous for their massive maneuvers on a large scale? Here again we find that the game is full of crucial tactical possibilities! In Mieses—Alekhine (p. 375) we have another game which on the surface is all strategy; yet the notes to Black's 24th and 35th moves teach us otherwise. The progress of the Reinfeld—Denker game (p. 376) is again typical; once White's strategical plan has been crossed, he must resort of tactics. In this case, the switch to tactics was sudden enough to surprise a great tactician!

Mikenas—Petrov (p. 378) comes near to being the perfect game, for here tactics and strategy are inextricably mingled. Petrov uses tactics to further his positional aims; he uses positional play to drive home his attack. Who can doubt, after playing over these absorbing games, that positional play and tactical play go hand in hand?

How simple is simple? It takes a great technician like Flohr to show us the hidden beauty of economical end-game play.

SICILIAN DEFENSE
Rosas, 1935

WHITE	BLACK
Domenech	Flohr
1 P—K4	P—QB4
2 Kt—KB3	P—K3
3 P—B4	Kt—QB3
4 P—Q4	P×P
5 Kt×P	Kt—B3
6 Kt×Kt	QP×Kt
7 Q×Qch	K×Q
8 P—B3	

Securely guarding the King's Pawn, but at the cost of limiting his King Bishop's scope.

8 ...	P—K4!
9 B—K3	K—B2
10 P—QR3?	Kt—Q2!
11 Kt—Q2	P—QR4!
12 B—K2	P—R5!
13 K—B2	B—QB4!

By advancing his Rook's Pawn, Flohr has ensured permanent occupation of his QB4. With the text he forces the removal of White's "good" Bishop, leaving him with a white-squared Bishop which is starved for moves.

14 B×B	Kt×B
15 QR—QB1	B—K3

This Bishop is aggressive, White's Bishop is passive.

16 KR—Q1	KR—Q1

Intending to double Rooks on the open file. If White attempts to dispute the file by 17 Kt—B1 then . . . Kt—

Kt6 followed by . . . Kt—Q5 gives Black a strong pull. It is now clear that White's troubles began, instead of ending, with the exchange of Queens!

17 K—K3	R—Q2
18 P—KKt3	

This and his next move are part of a perfectly natural attempt to get some more room for his pieces. But Flohr has something to say about that!

18 ...	QR—Q1
19 P—B4?	P×Pch
20 P×P	

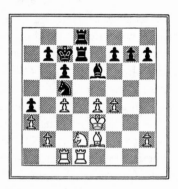

20 ...	R—Q6ch!!

Who would expect a sacrifice in this simple position?

21 B×R	R×Bch
22 K—B2	

Or K—K2, B—Kt5ch; 23 K—K1, B×R; 24 R×B, Kt×P!; 25 Kt×Kt, R—K6ch etc.

22 ...	B—Kt5

Threatening an easy win by 23 . . . B×R; 24 R×B, Kt×Pch etc. or 24 . . . R×Ktch!

23 P—K5	B×R

24 R×B   Kt—K3!

Forcing new weaknesses before exchanging all the pieces.

25 P—KB5   Kt—Q5
26 P—B6   P×P
27 P×P   Kt—Kt6
28 K—K2   R×Ktch

Now exchanges are in order.

29 R×R   Kt×R
30 K×Kt   K—Q3
     Resigns

Black picks up the King's Bishop's Pawn, with an easy win. Superior technique has triumphed!

NIMZOVICH demonstrates his opponent's errors to him with almost geometric exactitude. The game is much simpler than we expect from Nimzovich, but the finish has his characteristically sardonic touch!

DUTCH DEFENSE
Baden-Baden, 1925

WHITE	BLACK
Nimzovich	Mieses
1 P—Q4	P—KB4
2 Kt—KB3	P—K3
3 B—B4	Kt—KB3
4 P—B4	P—Q3

Mieses plays the opening in a strangely uninspired mood.

5 Kt—B3	P—B3
6 P—K3	QKt—Q2
7 B—K2	Kt—K5?
8 Kt×Kt	P×Kt
9 Kt—Q2	Kt—B3
10 O—O	B—K2

11 Q—B2   P—Q4

Now that he has forced this advance, White's game plays itself: he controls K5, he can initiate Queen-side play with P—B5 and take the offensive in the center with P—B3.

Meanwhile a serious flaw turns up in Black's development: there is no good square for his Queen's Bishop, which is hemmed in by his own Pawns.

12 P—B3   KP×P
13 Kt×P!

Next stop: K5. Occupation of this square is strategically decisive.

13 . . .   O—O
14 P—B5!   P—QKt3
15 P—QKt4   P—QR4

Despite Black's writhing, the encirclement process goes on.

16 Kt—K5   B—Kt2

At last the Bishop is "developed."

17 P—QR3   Kt—K5
18 B—Q3   B—Kt4

Giving up a Pawn in a futile effort to propitiate Nimzovich.

19 B×Kt   P×B
20 Q×P   B×B
21 P×B   RP×P
22 RP×P   P×P
23 KtP×P   Q—Q4
24 Q×Q   KP×Q

Ordinarily exchanges help the player with a constricted game—but not in this case.

25 R×R!   B×R

Or 25 . . . R×R; 26 R—Kt1, R—R2 (forced); 27 R—Kt6 and wins.

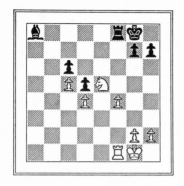

26 R—R1!   B—Kt2

Else 27 R—R7 followed by Kt—
Q7—Kt6 wins the imprisoned Bishop!

27 R—R7   B—R1

If 27 . . . R—Kt1; 28 Kt—Q7
wins.

28 Kt—Q7   Resigns

For after 28 . . . R—Q1; 29 Kt—
Kt6 still wins the Bishop. A game that
goes like clockwork!

WHILE this game lacks the driving
    nervous tension which Reti gave
    as the chief ingredient of Alek-
    hine's play, there are rewarding
    compensations: we have a model
    positional game in which a sim-
    ple idea is carried remorselessly
    to its logical conclusion.

RUY LOPEZ
Cologne, 1911

WHITE	BLACK
Alekhine	*Von Freymann*
1 P—K4	P—K4
2 Kt—KB3	Kt—QB3
3 B—Kt5	Kt—B3

4 O—O	P—Q3
5 Kt—B3	B—Q2
6 P—Q4	P×P
7 Kt×P	B—K2
8 Kt×Kt	B×Kt
9 Q—K2	

As usually happens in the Steinitz
Defense, White has come out of the
opening with the freer game.

9 . . .	O—O
10 B—Kt5	R—K1
11 KR—K1	

Black was threatening 11 . . .
Kt×P!

11 . . .	P—KR3
12 B—KB4	Kt—Q2

12 . . . Kt—R2; 13 B—B4, B—
KKt4; 14 B—KKt3, B—KR5? is not
feasible because of 15 Q—R5!; but 12
. . . B×B should have been tried.
The text leads to a Pawn weakness
which proves fatal.

13 B×B!	P×B
14 Q—B4!	B—Kt4

A clever defense, as far as it goes;
but it doesn't go far enough.

15 B—Kt3!

But not 15 B×B, Q×B; 16 Q×P?,
Kt—K4 followed by . . . Kt—B6ch.

15 . . .	P—B4
16 QR—Q1	B—B3

Else P—K5 ruins his Pawn position.

17 P—Kt3	Kt—K4
18 Q—K2	P—Kt3
19 Kt—Q5!	B—Kt2
20 Q—R6!	

Threatening to win a Pawn by 21
B×Kt and 22 Q—Kt7. The weak

Queen-side Pawn formation proves Black's undoing.

20 . . .	Q—B1
21 Q—R5!	P—QB3
22 Kt—K3	R—Q1

If 22 . . . Q—Q2; 23 B×Kt, B×B; 24 Q×BP or 23 . . . R×B; 24 Kt—B4.

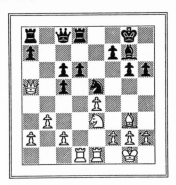

23 B—R4!	P—Kt4

This creates a King-side weakness which makes direct attack possible; but 23 . . . P—B3 is not inviting, and 23 . . . R—Q2? is refuted by 24 P—KB4!

24 B—Kt3	Q—K3
25 Kt—B5	B—B1
26 Q—B3!	P—B3
27 P—B4!	Kt—Kt3

If 27 . . . Kt—B2 White infiltrates decisively with Q—B3—R5.

28 Kt×Pch!	B×Kt
29 P—B5	Q—K2
30 P×Kt	B—B1
31 Q—B4ch	K—Kt2

If 31 . . . K—R1; 32 Q—K2 (threatening to capture the Queen's Pawn) wins easily.

32 B×P!	Resigns

32 . . . R×B; 33 R×R, Q×R; 34 Q—B7ch leads to mate. Retreating the Queen leaves Black hopelessly behind in material.

A POLISHED example of position play—nothing flashy, but impressive all the same. The fact that a minor master like Suechting could produce such a beautiful game shows the extent to which position play has been perfected.

RUY LOPEZ
Karlsbad, 1911

WHITE	BLACK
Suechting	*Salve*
1 P—K4	P—K4
2 Kt—KB3	Kt—QB3
3 B—Kt5	P—QR3
4 B—R4	Kt—B3
5 O—O	B—K2
6 R—K1	P—Q3
7 P—B3	O—O
8 P—KR3	Kt—Q2
9 P—Q4	B—B3
10 B—K3	Kt—K2
11 QKt—Q2	P—KKt3

The opening has followed a familiar form of the Lopez in which Black regroups his pieces to get more maneuvering space. Instead of his last move (which led to a weakness on the black squares), Black should have played the more solid 11 . . . Kt—Kt3.

12 B—R6!	R—K1
13 Kt—B1	P—QKt4
14 B—Kt3	Kt—B1
15 Kt—K3	B—K3
16 B×B!	P×B

This leads to a serious weakening of his Pawn structure, but if *16 . . . Kt×B; 17 Kt—Kt4!* wins a Pawn, *17 . . . Kt—B3* being impossible because of *18 P—Q5.*

17 Kt—Kt4!	Kt—B3
18 P×P!	Kt×P

He has no choice: if *18 . . . P×P; 19 Q×Q* wins a Pawn. If *18 . . . B×P?; 19 B—Kt5!* followed by *20 Kt(3)×B* and *21 Kt—B6ch* wins the exchange.

19 Kt(3)×Kt!	B×Kt
20 Kt×B	P×Kt

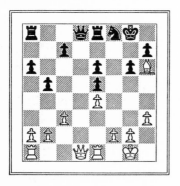

The exchanges have left White with a won game because (a) he can operate on the weak black squares; (b) he can attack the weak Pawns; (c) he will have exclusive control of the open file.

21 Q—Kt4	Q—K2
22 B—Kt5!	Q—Kt2
23 Q—R4	Kt—Q2

B—B6 was threatened.

24 QR—Q1	P—KR4

White threatened to force the Knight away by doubling Rooks on the Queen file. Black wants to protect the Knight by *. . . R—KB1—2;* but first he must prevent B—R6.

25 R—Q2	R—KB1
26 KR—Q1	R—B2
27 Q—Kt3	Kt—Kt3
28 P—Kt3!	K—R2
29 Q—K3!	Q—B1

To prevent Q—B5, which would have a paralyzing effect.

30 Q—Kt3	Q—B4

If he tries *30 . . . Q—Kt2,* White can now switch to the following idea: *31 Q—K3, Q—B1; 32 B—R4!* followed by *33 B—Kt3!* Black will either have to allow Q—B5 or give up the Pawn at K4—or more likely, he will have to give way on both points.

31 B—K3!	Q×P

Else he loses the Pawn at K4.

32 Q—Kt5!	Resigns

There is no defense to the threat of *33 Q—R6ch* followed by *34 R—Q8ch.* If *32 . . . R—Kt2; 33 R—Q8* and wins. If *32 . . . K—Kt2; 33 Q—R6ch, K—B3; 34 B—Kt5* mate.

THERE was something peculiar about the Steinitz style: he insisted on accumulating small advantages, but he played in the grand manner!

FRENCH DEFENSE
Match, 1885

WHITE	BLACK
Steinitz	*Sellman*
1 P—K4	P—K3
2 P—Q4	P—Q4
3 Kt—QB3	Kt—KB3

4 P—K5	KKt—Q2
5 P—B4	P—QB4
6 P×P	B×P

Steinitz has "given up the center" because he hopes to occupy the square Q4 later on with his pieces.

7 Kt—B3	P—QR3
8 B—Q3	Kt—QB3
9 Q—K2	Kt—Kt5
10 B—Q2	P—QKt4
11 Kt—Q1	Kt×Bch
12 P×Kt	

Black has obtained the Bishop-pair, but his Queen's Bishop has very little scope, as it is hemmed in by Black Pawns on white squares. The right move was therefore 12 . . . P—Kt5! intending . . . P—QR4 followed by . . . B—R3 when Black would have a splendid game.

12 . . .	Q—Kt3?
13 P—QKt4!!	

This fixes the Black Pawn at QKt4, and it also drives Black's "good" Bishop off its best diagonal. White will soon assert himself on the black squares.

13 . . .	B—K2

Not 13 . . . B—Q5?; 14 QR—Kt1! and Black is helpless against the threat of 15 Kt×B, Q×Kt; 16 B—K3 winning the Queen!

14 P—QR3	P—B4
15 QR—B1	B—Kt2

This Bishop is as good as dead.

16 B—K3!

Beginning the process of obtaining complete mastery of the black squares.

16 . . .	Q—Q1
17 Kt—Q4	Kt—B1

18 O—O	P—KR4

To restrain a possible attack by P—Kt4. Even at this stage Black is "cabin'd, cribb'd, confin'd."

19 Kt—QB3	K—B2
20 Kt—Kt1!	P—Kt3

Now every one of his Pawns is on a white square, which completes the smothering of his Queen's Bishop and the weakening of his black squares. He wants to play . . . Kt—Q2, but if 20 . . . Kt—Q2?; 21 Kt×BP!, P×Kt; 22 P—K6ch! regaining the piece and advantageously opening up the game (22 . . . K×P??; 23 B—Kt6ch).

21 Kt—Q2!	Kt—Q2
22 Kt(2)—Kt3!	QR—B1
23 Kt—R5!	

Still working on the black squares! The Knight will go to QB6 at the right moment.

23 . . .	B—R1
24 R×R!	Q×R
25 R—B1	Q—QKt1
26 Q—QB2!	

Naturally he monopolizes the only open file!

26 . . .	B—Q1

The removal of this Bishop will leave him disastrously weak on the black squares, but there is not much that he can do about it.

27 Kt(5)—B6!	Q—Kt2

If 27 . . . B×Kt; 28 Q×B, Kt—B1; 29 Kt×KP!, Kt×Kt; 30 Q—Q7ch, B—K2; 31 R—B6! Kt—B1; 32 R—B6ch and wins.

28 Kt×Bch	R×Kt
29 Q—B7!	Q—Kt1
30 B—B2!	

Threatening to win at least the exchange with 31 B—R4. Note the play on the black squares!

30 . . .	Q—Kt3
31 Kt—B3	Q×Q
32 R×Q	K—K1

The only way to save the Knight.

| 33 Kt—Kt5 | Kt—B1 |
| 34 B—B5! | Kt—Q2 |

He could not answer the threat of 35 R—K7 mate with 34 . . . R—Q2 for then 35 R—B8ch wins a piece. Or if 34 . . . R—Kt1; 35 R—K7ch, K—Q1; 36 Kt—B7ch, K—B1; 37 R—K8ch winning a piece.

| 35 B—Q6! | Resigns |

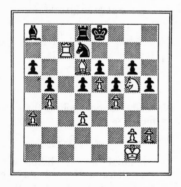

Black is crippled: he cannot move his King or Bishop, and if 35 . . . R—Kt1; 36 R×Kt! wins a piece. If 35 . . . Kt—Kt3 (or 35 . . . Kt—B1; 36 R—K7 mate!); 36 R—K7ch, K—B1; 37 Kt—R7ch, K—Kt1; 38 Kt—B6ch etc. If 35 . . . P—Q5; 36 Kt×P, R—Kt1; 37 Kt—Kt7ch, K—Q1; 38 P—K6 is decisive.

A magnificent example of constriction strategy.

IN ANDERSSEN's *time, a Queen sacrifice was played to lure the hostile King to his doom. Here, a spectacular Queen sacrifice has the humble objective of gaining a slight positional advantage!*

QUEEN'S GAMBIT DECLINED
(in effect)
Buenos Aires, 1914

WHITE	BLACK
Capablanca	Villegas
1 P—Q4	P—Q4
2 Kt—KB3	Kt—KB3
3 P—K3	P—B3
4 B—Q3	B—Kt5
5 P—B4	P—K3
6 QKt—Q2	QKt—Q2
7 O—O	

Black has a fine, free development, which he could now continue suitably with . . . B—Q3 and . . . Q—K2. Instead, he turns cautious.

7 . . .	B—K2
8 Q—B2	B—R4
9 P—QKt3	B—Kt3
10 B—Kt2	B×B
11 Q×B	O—O
12 QR—K1	Q—B2
13 P—K4	

As a result of Black's loss of time with his Queen's Bishop, Capablanca now has some initiative. The text leads to exchanges which make White's Queen's Rook a formidable attacking weapon.

13 . . .	P×KP
14 Kt×P	Kt×Kt
15 R×Kt	B—B3
16 Q—K3	P—B4

17 Kt—K5

If now 17 . . . Kt×Kt; 18 P×Kt, B—K2; 19 R—Kt4 with good attacking chances.

17 . . .   P×P

In order to simplify advantageously: 18 B×P, Kt×Kt; 19 B×Kt, B×B; 20 R×B, KR—Q1! when White cannot hope to dispute Black's control of the only open file.

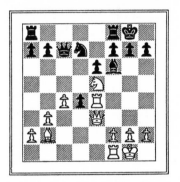

18 Kt×Kt!!

What a shock for Black! If 18 . . . P×Q; 19 Kt×Bch, K—R1 (not 19 . . . P×Kt??; 20 R—Kt4ch, K—R1; 21 B×P mate!); 20 R—R4!, P—KR3; 21 R×Pch!!, P×R; 22 Kt—K8ch followed by 23 Kt×Q and White has the winning advantage of two pieces for a Rook.

18 . . .   Q×Kt
19 B×P   B×B
20 R×B

Black has achieved the desired simplification, but it is White who controls the Queen file.

20 . . .   Q—B2
21 KR—Q1   KR—Q1

22 P—QKt4!

A cruel paradox: now that the game is simplified, White can proceed to turn his Queen-side majority of Pawns into a passed Pawn!

22 . . .   R×R
23 Q×R   P—QKt3
24 P—Kt3   R—QB1
25 R—QB1   R—Q1

Now he has the open file; but this is of slight consequence, as there is no useful point of invasion available to Black.

26 Q—K3   K—B1
27 P—B5   P×P
28 Q—K4!   R—Q4
29 P×P   P—Kt3

29 . . . R×P?? loses a Rook after 30 Q—QKt4!

30 P—B6   K—Kt2
31 P—QR4!

In order to play Q—QKt4—Kt7. Then, after Black plays . . . Q×Q and White replies P×Q, Black must play . . . R—Q1 (. . . R—QKt4 is impossible!), whereupon R—B8 wins. Note the enormous power of White's passed Pawn!

31 . . .   R—Q3?

This loses at once; but if 31 . . . P—QR4 (to prevent 32 Q—QKt4), White wins by Q—QB4—R6—Kt7 etc.

32 Q—K5ch!   Resigns

For any move of Black is answered by 33 Q×R!, Q×Q; 34 P—B7 and the passed Pawn must queen!

A PARADOX, a paradox: Spielmann, the great master of attack, meets Maroczy, the great master of strategy, and bests the latter with his own weapons!

FRENCH DEFENSE
San Sebastian, 1911

WHITE	BLACK
Spielmann	*Maroczy*
1 P—K4	P—K3
2 P—Q4	P—Q4
3 Kt—QB3	Kt—KB3
4 B—Kt5	B—Kt5
5 P—K5	P—KR3
6 P×Kt	P×B
7 P×P	R—Kt1
8 P—KR4	P×P
9 Q—R5	

The variation is one which Black need not fear if he plays accurately.

9 . . .	Q—B3
10 Kt—B3	Kt—Q2

This impedes the development of his Queen's Bishop with a consequent delay in castling. 10 . . . Kt—B3 is correct.

11 O—O—O	Q×KtP
12 Q×RP	P—R3

Black is afraid of Kt—Kt5 followed by Q—B4.

13 B—Q3!	Kt—B3

White was threatening 14 Kt×P!

14 QR—K1	B—Q2
15 P—Kt4!	

This advance is difficult to meet. If, for example, 15 . . . Kt×P; 16 Kt×P!, B—Q3 (not 16 . . . B×R??; 17 Q—K7 mate); 17 B—R7! and wins

(17 . . . R—R1; 18 Q×Kt!, R×B; 19 R×R!).

15 . . .	B×Kt
16 P×B	O—O—O

16 . . . Kt×P? is refuted by 17 KR—Kt1.

17 P—Kt5	Kt—K5
18 B×Kt	P×B

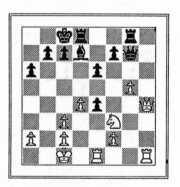

19 Kt—K5!

Black was hoping for 19 Q×P (if 19 R×P??, R—R1 wins), B—B3 followed by . . . B×Kt and . . . Q×Pch with an ultra-safe position.

19 . . .   B—K1

And not 19 . . . Q×Pch?; 20 Q×Q, R×Q; 21 Kt×P winning the exchange. Spielmann has an active Knight against a "bad" Bishop, and a stranglehold on the black squares.

20 QR—Kt1	Q—B1
21 Q×P!	Q—R6ch
22 K—Q2!	Q×P
23 R—R1!	Q—Q4
24 Q×Q	P×Q

Spielmann has forced a won **end** game.

25 P—KB4	R—Q3

Hoping for . . . P—KB3.

26 Kt—Kt4!	B—Q2
27 Kt—B6	R—B1
28 QR—K1	P—B3
29 R—K5!	

All very simple, and all very forcing.

29 . . .	R—K3
30 Kt×B!	K×Kt
31 P—B5	

Spielmann has exchanged his Knight because he now has a Pawn mass which is bound to yield a winning passed Pawn, for example 31 . . . R×R; 32 P×R, R—KKt1; 33 P—Kt6!, P×P; 34 R—R7ch followed by 35 P—B6!

31 . . .	R—K2
32 R—R7!	K—Q1

Or 32 . . . R(1)—K1; 33 P—Kt6!, P×P; 34 R(5)×Rch, R×R; 35 P×P, K—K3; 36 P—Kt7, K—B2; 37 P—Kt8(Q)ch!

33 P—Kt6!	R×R
34 P×R	P×P
35 P—B6!	K—B1

An attractive possibility is 35 . . . R—K1; 36 R×P (the seventh rank absolute works wonders!), R×P; 37 R—Kt8ch, K—B2; 38 P—B7! and wins!

36 R—K7	Resigns

If 36 . . . P—KKt4; 37 P—B7, K—Q1; 38 R×P, P—Kt5; 39 P—K6 wins. A really enchanting game!

A DEEPLY satisfying game: far-sighted positional plans are brought to fruition by means of sparkling tactical finesses. To outplay a great master of combination in this style is no small feat!

GIUOCO PIANO
Mannheim, 1914

WHITE	BLACK
Mieses	*Alekhine*
1 P—K4	P—K4
2 Kt—KB3	Kt—QB3
3 B—B4	B—B4
4 Kt—B3	P—Q3
5 P—Q3	B—K3
6 Kt—Q5	Kt—R4!
7 B—K3	Kt×B
8 P×Kt	

8 B×B is answered by 8 . . . Kt×P!

8 . . .	B×B
9 Kt×B	Kt—B3
10 Q—Q3	Kt—Q2!

Black has outplayed his opponent by creating a weakness on the Queen-side (doubled Queen's Bishop Pawn). Now Alekhine threatens to win a Pawn by . . . Kt—B4 and thus provokes a new weakness on the Queen-side.

11 P—QKt4	P—QR4!
12 P—B3	O—O
13 O—O	P—KKt3!
14 Kt—Q2	P—KB4
15 P—B3	

After 15 KP×P, KtP×P Black has a powerfully compact Pawn mass in the center and attacking chances on the King's Knight file.

15 . . .	P—B5!

Severely restricting the mobility of White's Knights (if 16 Kt—Q5?, P—B3!).

16 Kt—Q1	P—KKt4
17 Kt—B2	P—R4
18 P—R3	Kt—B3
19 KR—Q1	Q—K2
20 P—B5	

Mieses decides to divert his opponent from the contemplated doubling of his Rooks on the King's Knight file —else the eventual . . . P—Kt5 will shatter White's King-side.

20 . . .	RP×P
21 P×QP	Q×P!
22 P×P	R×P!
23 R×R	Q×Q!
24 Kt×Q	B×R

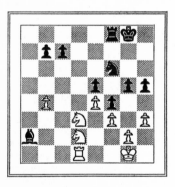

Apparently Mieses has done an excellent simplifying job, and can now regain the lost Pawn with 25 Kt×KP. But on closer examination we see that this move will not do: 25 Kt×KP?, R—Q1! and White is lost because of the coming . . . B—Kt6!

25 R—R1	R—Q1!
26 R×B	R×Kt
27 Kt—B4	R—Q5!
28 R—QB2!	

Expecting the obvious 28 . . . Kt —Q2; 29 Kt—R5, P—Kt3; 30 Kt— B6 when the win presents inordinate technical difficulties.

28 . . .	Kt—K1!
29 P—Kt5!	P—Kt3!
30 Kt×KP	R—Kt5
31 R—B6	R×KtP
32 R—Kt6ch	Kt—Kt2
33 R×KKtP	P—R5!

Now we see the point of Alekhine's ingenious maneuvers. Both of White's pieces are amusingly prevented from moving (if 34 Kt—B7, R—Kt8ch!).

| 34 K—B2 | R—B4! |
| 35 K—K2 | |

Hoping for 35 . . . P—Kt4? (he must keep his Rook protected!); 36 Kt—B7!, R—B7ch; 37 K—Q3 and White is safe.

| 35 . . . | K—R2!! |
| Resigns | |

A delightful Zugzwang situation: White's King cannot cross to the Queen-side, his Knight is pinned, his Rook must stay put. Black's threat is simply to advance his Knight's Pawn and queen it! If 36 Kt—B7, R×R; 37 Kt×Rch, K—Kt3 and the Knight is lost!

WHAT *gives this game its fascination is the way in which the positional struggle is decided by tactical means.*

DUTCH DEFENSE
Syracuse, 1934

WHITE	BLACK
Reinfeld	*Denker*
1 Kt—KB3	P—KB4
2 P—KKt3	P—QKt3

3 B—Kt2	B—Kt2
4 P—Q4	Kt—KB3
5 P—B4	P—K3

Black's combination of . . . P—KB4 with the Queen fianchetto is bad; for another proof of this point, see the game Denker—Feit, p. 257.

6 O—O	P—Kt3
7 Kt—B3	B—Kt2
8 P—Q5!	P×P
9 P×P	O—O
10 Kt—Q4	Kt—R3
11 B—K3	Kt—B4
12 Kt—Kt3!	

In order to exchange Black's Queen's Knight, which is too well posted now. In addition, White's Queen will come to QKt3, creating new difficulties for Black.

12 . . .	Kt×Kt
13 Q×Kt	

Threatening to win a piece with 14 P—Q6ch. If 13 . . . K—R1; 14 QR—B1 leaves White with a considerable positional advantage.

13 . . .	P—Q3

Black has parried all threats on the diagonal, but now his K3 is a hole. If White can occupy this square with his Knight, he will have a winning game.

14 Kt—Kt5	Kt—Q2
15 B—Q4	Kt—B4
16 Q—B2	P—QR4

Preventing White from driving the Knight away with P—QKt4.

17 B×B	K×B
18 P—Kt3	

Intending to drive away the Knight with 19 P—QR3 and 20 P—QKt4.

18 . . .	B—R3
19 Kt—Q4	Q—B3
20 KR—Q1	P—QKt4
21 P—QR3	P—Kt5

Preventing White's P—QKt4 and in this way keeping his Knight on QB4 and thus protecting his weak square K3.

22 P×P	P×P

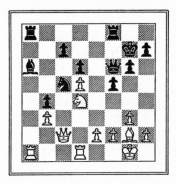

23 Kt—K6ch!!

Completely refuting Black's plan.

23 . . .	Kt×Kt

Else he loses the exchange.

24 P×Kt	R—R2

After this the pin on the Rook file decides: but if 24 . . . B—Kt2; 25 Q×Pch, K—R3; 26 Q—B1ch followed by 27 B×B and Black can resign.

25 R—R4	Q×P
26 KR—R1	P—Q4
27 Q—B5	R(1)—QR1
28 B×P	Q—K4
29 P—B4	Q×KP

Disastrous loss of material was un-avoidable.

30	B×R	R×B
31	Q—K5ch!	Q×Q
32	P×Q and wins	

Black must lose the Bishop as well, leaving him a Rook down.

TARRASCH *was delighted with this game because it put his beloved defense in a very favorable light!*

QUEEN'S GAMBIT DECLINED
Team Match, 1933

WHITE	BLACK
Mikenas	*Petrov*
(Lithuania)	*(Latvia)*
1 P—Q4	P—Q4
2 P—QB4	P—K3
3 Kt—KB3	P—QB4
4 BP×P	KP×P
5 Kt—B3	Kt—QB3
6 P—KKt3	Kt—B3
7 B—Kt2	B—K2
8 O—O	O—O

A much-mooted position, in which the usual continuation is 9 P×P in order to concentrate on Black's iso-lated Pawn. Advocates of the defense consider that Black has sufficient com-pensation in the free development of his forces.

9 P—KR3	B—K3
10 B—K3	P—QKt3!
11 Kt—K5	Kt×Kt!
12 P×Kt	P—Q5!

Black's positional sacrifice of the ex-change, which he has had in mind for several moves, testifies to masterly po-sitional insight. He relies primarily on

the strength of his Bishops—a well-founded speculation.

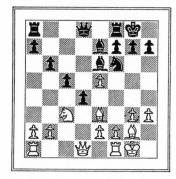

13 P×Kt	B×BP
14 B×R	

If instead 14 Kt—K4, P×B; 15 Kt×Bch, Q×Kt; 16 B×R, R×B; 17 P×P, Q×P leaving Black with a Queen-side majority of three Pawns to one and a strong attack on the other wing—adequate compensation for the exchange.

14 . . .	Q×B

The Queen commands the diagonal leading to White's King. The threat is 16 . . . B×KRP.

15 K—R2	P×B
16 P×P	B—K4!

Preventing White from returning the exchange with R×B, and also threatening . . . P—KR4—5. Black's Bishops are formidable!

17 Q—K1	P—KR4!
18 P—KR4	P—QKt4!

So that if 19 Kt×P, Q—Kt1; 20 Kt—B3, Q×P; 21 R—B1, R—Q1 with a strong game. Meanwhile Black prepares for . . . Q—K5.

19 P—R3	P—Kt5
20 P×P	P×P
21 Kt—Q1	Q—K5!

Powerful centralization! If now 22 K—Kt1 (Black threatens 22 . . . Q×Pch), B—Q4; 23 R—B3, Q—Kt3; 24 K—R2, B×R; 25 P×B, R—B1 with a winning position.

22 R—B4	B×R
23 KP×B	B—Q4!
24 Q—B1	R—K1!

Every move tells.

25 P—K3   R—QB1!

Now that the King's Pawn has been forced to move, the Rook comes in decisively on the seventh rank.

26 Kt—B2   R—B7!
   Resigns

There is no defense to . . . Q—B6. A beautiful game, artistically of the highest order.

"Quick! Take down the position Bert, 'ere comes the foreman!"

From *Chess Magazine,* by courtesy of the publisher, B. H. Wood, Sutton Coldfield, England.

The Perfect Game

♛ To DEFINE perfection on the chessboard is more difficult than to explain what perfection is *not*. A game in which neither side has made a mistake does not add up to perfection; in such games we find only a sterile dullness which lacks every memorable feature.

Thus we have a paradox: chess perfection is made possible only by the mistakes of one's opponent. How skillfully are these mistakes exploited? How deep are the plans for taking advantage of the mistakes? How flawless is the execution of these plans? When we have the answers to these questions, we know whether or not a game is perfect.

In some games we get an intimation of perfection from the iron consistency of the winner's play. In such games as Capablanca—Mieses (p. 381), Bogolyubov—Reti (p. 382), and Reshevsky—Treystman (p. 384), one gets the feeling, as unreal as it is irresistible, that the loser has not made a mistake, that he simply *had* to lose no matter what moves he might have made. In these encounters, the winner's play is so powerful that seeking the conclusive mistake is like trying to discover the first cause uncaused.

Another type of game is easier to understand: the kind of game in which a tangible positional weakness, created in the opening, is kept under withering fire. Tarrasch—Scheve (p. 387), Alekhine—Yates (p. 385), and Chernev—Gustafson (p. 389) all belong in this category.

Similarly, perfect attacking technique against a clearly indicated target also makes for fascinating play. There are absorbing examples in

Saemisch—Johner (p. 390), Mannheimer—Kashdan (p. 388), Rellstab—Petrov (p. 391) and Parr—Wheatcroft (p. 392). In the opinion of the writers, Parr's masterpiece has well-founded claims to being considered the finest attacking game of all time.

Alekhine—Yates (p. 393) and Keres—Mikenas (p. 395) are games which evade easy classification. In the former we see an enterprising opening, an adventurous middle game, and a neatly pointed ending which can be won only by guile—and Alekhine had plenty of that! In the other game, Keres starts off on the defensive, wards off the hostile pressure, and conjures up a series of smashing threats from components of almost gossamer delicacy. An astonishing variety of tactical motifs appears in this "simple" end game.

These, then, are the perfect dozen. Above all, we pride ourselves on the unhackneyed character of the selections.

THE standard comment on a typical Capablanca game is: "Quite simple." Then: "Very obvious." And finally: "But how does he do it?"

BENONI COUNTER GAMBIT

Berlin, 1913

WHITE	BLACK
Capablanca	Mieses
1 P—Q4	Kt—KB3
2 Kt—KB3	P—B4
3 P—Q5	P—Q3
4 P—B4	P—KKt3
5 Kt—B3	B—Kt2
6 P—K4	O—O

One of the great drawbacks of the defense chosen by Black is that it is difficult for him to develop the Queen-side in normal fashion.

7 B—K2	P—K3
8 O—O	P×P
9 KP×P	Kt—K1
10 R—K1!	B—Kt5

11 Kt—KKt5!

Capablanca is not worried about the possible weakening of his Pawn position by . . . B×Kt. He is more interested in getting control of the open King file.

11 . . .	B×Kt?
12 P×B	B×B
13 Q×B	Kt—Kt2

Now we realize that in parting with the valuable Bishop which was posted at KKt2, Mieses has left his black squares vulnerable to attack and occupation. Capablanca now proceeds to exploit this weakness, at the same time making good use of the superior mobility of his Rooks. The fact that his doubled Pawns are theoretically weak is of no importance.

14 Kt—K4!

This concentration on the Queen's Pawn makes the normal development . . . Kt—Q2 impossible.

| 14 . . . | P—B3 |

Not *14 . . . R—K1?*; *15 B—Kt5!* and White wins the exchange!

| 15 B—B4! | Kt—K1 |
| 16 B—R6 | Kt—Kt2 |

The clever Bishop moves have gained a whole tempo for White.

| 17 QR—Q1! | Kt—R3 |
| 18 R—Q3 | |

The Rook has three possibly useful squares on this rank: K3, KB3 or R3.

| 18 . . . | P—B4 |
| 19 Kt—Kt5 | |

Threatening to win at least the exchange by 20 B×Kt etc.

| 19 . . . | Kt—B2 |

20 Q—K7!

Forcing the following exchange because of the mate threat.

20 . . .	Q×Q
21 R×Q	Kt(B2)—K1
22 R—R3!	P—B5

Despite the absence of the Queens, White has a killing attack.

| 23 B×Kt | Kt×B |
| 24 R×RP | Kt—B4 |

| 25 R—K6 | KR—K1 |
| 26 R×Pch | Resigns |

If *26 . . . K—B1*; *27 R—B7 mate*. If *26 . . . Kt—Kt2*; *27 R(7)×Ktch* and mate next move.

RETI's play is versatile: *he performs many tasks here, and performs them well. He thrusts back a premature attack, he demonstrates the power of a compact center, he steadily cuts down his opponent's mobility, he maneuvers his Knight with exquisite skill, he obtains and exploits a passed Pawn according to plan.*

FRENCH DEFENSE
Mährisch-Ostrau, 1923

WHITE	BLACK
Bogolyubov	*Reti*
1 P—K4	P—K3
2 P—Q4	P—Q4
3 Kt—QB3	Kt—KB3
4 P—K5	KKt—Q2
5 Q—Kt4	

The Gledhill Attack, which is premature because it neglects the center.

5 . . .	P—QB4!
6 Kt—Kt5	P×P!
7 Kt—KB3	Kt—QB3
8 Kt—Q6ch	B×Kt
9 Q×KtP	B×P!
10 Kt×B	Q—B3!

Forcing White to exchange, which leaves him with a very poor game.

11 Q×Q	Kt×Q
12 B—QKt5	B—Q2
13 Kt—B3	Kt—K5!

14 O—O	P—B3!

Threatens . . . P—K4.

15 B×Kt	P×B
16 Kt×P	P—QB4

Black has a compact Pawn mass in the center which must eventually result in a passed Pawn, and which also has the virtue of cutting off White's Knight from useful squares.

17 Kt—K2	K—B2
18 P—KB3	Kt—Q3
19 P—QKt3	P—K4
20 B—R3	QR—QB1
21 QR—Q1	P—Q5
22 Kt—B1	Kt—B4!

Watch this Knight!

23 R—B2	Kt—K6
24 R—K1	

24 . . .	P—B5!

Very powerful. White cannot very well capture, for if 25 P×P, R×P; 26 R(1)—K2, KR—QB1 winning the weak Pawn.

25 P—QKt4	B—R5!
26 R(1)—K2	

If 26 P—B3?, Kt—B7 wins.

26 . . .	Kt—Q8
27 R—B1	Kt—B6
28 R(2)—B2	Kt—Kt8!

The antics of this Knight are very amusing.

29 B—Kt2	P—B6

Forcing White's reply, for if 30 B—R1, Kt—Q7; 31 R—K1, B×P with an easy win.

30 Kt—Kt3	B×Kt
31 RP×B	

Again there is little choice, for if 31 BP×B, P—B7 followed by . . . P—Q6; or 31 R×Kt, B×RP; 32 R—R1, P×B etc.

31 . . .	Kt—Q7
32 R—K1	KR—Q1
33 B—B1	P—Q6!

Now he gets his passed Pawn: if 34 B×Kt, P×B; 35 R×KP, P×P; 36 R×R, R×R and Black gets a Queen.

34 P×P	R×P
35 B×Kt	R×B!
36 R—R1	

36 R×R loses at once.

36 . . .	K—K3!
37 K—B1	R×Rch!
38 K×R	P—B7
39 R—QB1	K—Q4
40 K—K3	R—B6ch!
41 K—Q2	K—Q5!

So that if 42 R×P, R×Rch; 43 K×R, K—K6; 44 K—B3, K—B7 with an easy win.

42 P—R4	R—Q6ch!
Resigns	

If 43 K×P, R—B6ch; 44 K—Q2, R×R; 45 K×R, K—B6 wins; or 43

K—K2, K—B6 with *44* . . . R—Q1 and *45* . . . K—Kt7 to follow. Slick technique!

ALTHOUGH Reshevsky's games often contain many dreary stretches, he shows here how artistry can be applied to the routine task of scoring a valuable point in an important tournament.

CATALAN SYSTEM
United States Championship, 1938

WHITE	BLACK
Reshevsky	Treystman
1 P—Q4	Kt—KB3
2 P—QB4	P—K3
3 P—KKt3	

With this move, which gives the opening its name, White prepares to give his King's Bishop an influential position on the long diagonal.

3 . . .	B—Kt5ch
4 B—Q2	Q—K2
5 B—Kt2	O—O
6 Kt—KB3	P—Q4
7 Q—B2	Kt—K5
8 O—O	Kt×B
9 QKt×Kt	P—QB3
10 P—K4!	B×Kt
11 Kt×B	P×KP
12 Kt×P	Kt—Q2
13 P—B5!	P—K4
14 P×P	Kt×KP
15 KR—K1!	

White's opening strategy has been vindicated. He is ahead in development (watch that Bishop!); his Rook has seized the open King file; he has a magnificent post at Q6 for his Knight.

15 . . .	Kt—Kt3
16 Kt—Q6	Q—B2
17 P—B4!	B—Q2

Or *17* . . . Kt—K2; *18* P—B5 and Black is badly tied up.

18 P—B5!	Kt—R1

The Knight never makes another move for the remainder of the game!

19 R—K7!	P—QKt3

A desperate attempt at freedom; Black is panic-stricken because he cannot dislodge the powerfully posted Rook from the seventh rank.

20 P—QKt4!	P×P
21 Q×P!	QR—Q1
22 P—Kt5	Q—Kt1

So that if *23* P×P, B×QBP!; ingenious but unavailing.

23 P—QR4!	P×P
24 P×P	B—B1
25 R—B7!	Q—Kt3

He struggles like a fish on a hook. The text is the only way to stave off the loss of a Pawn . . . for a while.

26 Q×Q	P×Q
27 R—B6	P—Kt3
28 P—Kt4!	

Reshevsky does not mean to win the Pawn at the cost of allowing Black to free himself on the other wing.

28 . . .	P—R4
29 P—R3!	RP×P
30 RP×P	K—Kt2

Amusing (but not for Black) is *30* . . . P×P; *31* P×P, B—Q2; *32* R×P, R—Kt1; *33* R×R, R×R; *34* R—R8!, R×R; *35* B×R and Black must give up a piece if the passed Pawn is to be prevented from queening.

31 K—B2!	B—Q2
32 R×P	R—QKt1
33 P—B6ch!	K—R3

Or 33 . . . K×P; 34 Kt—K8ch! winning the exchange.

34 K—Kt3!

He can leave the Rook *en prise* with a clear conscience: if 34 . . . R×R; 35 R—R1ch, K—Kt4; 36 Kt—K4 mate!

34 . . .	K—R2

Not 34 . . . P—Kt4; 35 B—K4, Kt—Kt3; 36 R×R, R×R; 37 R—R1ch, Kt—R5; 38 Kt×P mate!

35 R×R	R×R
36 P—Kt5!	

Now the Knight and the King are out of play—a fearful handicap for Black.

36 . . .	R—Kt3

If 36 . . . B×P?; 37 R—QKt1 wins a piece.

37 R—R6	R—Kt1
38 B—B6!	

At last the Bishop plays an active role, after having strongly influenced

the proceedings by merely staying at Kt2.

38 . . .	B—B4
39 R—R8!	R×R
40 B×R	B—Q6
41 P—Kt6	B—R3
42 B—Kt7!	Resigns

For if 42 . . . B—Q6 or 42 . . . B—K7; 43 B—B8! and the Pawn queens while Black's forces look on impotently. A triumph of merciless logic!

This superb game has a double personality. Its basic ideas are subtle and yet transparent; its technical finish is perfection itself, yet it makes us feel that great chess is a very simple matter.

QUEEN'S GAMBIT DECLINED
London, 1922

WHITE	BLACK
Alekhine	Yates
1 P—Q4	Kt—KB3
2 P—QB4	P—K3
3 Kt—KB3	P—Q4
4 Kt—B3	B—K2
5 B—Kt5	O—O
6 P—K3	QKt—Q2
7 R—B1	P—B3
8 Q—B2	R—K1
9 B—Q3	P×P
10 B×P	Kt—Q4
11 Kt—K4	P—KB4?

He removes the tension, but only at the cost of seriously weakening his black squares.

12 B×B	Q×B

13 QKt—Q2   P—QKt4?

This completes the ruination of his black squares.

14 B×Kt!	BP×B
15 O—O	P—QR4
16 Kt—Kt3!	P—R5
17 Kt—B5	Kt×Kt
18 Q×Kt!	Q×Q
19 R×Q	

The exchanges have left White with just the position he wanted: he has control of the open Queen's Bishop file, and will eventually play to the seventh rank and double his Rooks on it; he dominates the black squares, and will post his Knight unassailably on K5; he has easy play against Black's weak Pawn position; finally, Black has the "bad" Bishop, which is limited to purely defensive functions.

19 . . .	P—Kt5
20 KR—B1	B—R3
21 Kt—K5!	KR—Kt1

To oppose Rooks would be suicidal: 21 . . . KR—QB1; 22 R×Rch, R×R; 23 R×Rch, B×R; 24 Kt—B6 winning the Knight's Pawn because of the threatened Kt—K7ch.

22 P—B3!

A new advantage: he can bring his King into aggressive play, while Black's King must stay put.

22 . . .	P—Kt6
23 P—QR3!	P—R3
24 K—B2!	K—R2
25 P—R4!	R—KB1
26 K—Kt3	KR—QKt1
27 R—B7	B—Kt4
28 R(1)—B5	B—R3
29 R(5)—B6	R—K1

Not 29 . . . R—QB1?; 30 R×B!

winning a piece. Black is now severely constricted, and the doubling of White's Rooks on the seventh rank will soon be an accomplished fact.

30 K—B4!	K—Kt1
31 P—R5!	

As will be seen, these moves are essential factors in White's plan.

31 . . .	B—B8
32 P—Kt3	B—R3
33 R—B7!	K—R2
34 R(6)—B7	R—KKt1
35 Kt—Q7!	K—R1

Else 36 Kt—B6ch wins the exchange.

36 Kt—B6!   KR—KB1

Apparently forcing the exchange of a pair of Rooks (not 36 . . . P×Kt?; 37 R—R7 mate). But Alekhine has other ideas!

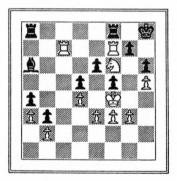

37 R×P!!	R×Kt
38 K—K5!!	Resigns

Black can play neither 38 . . . R(3)—B1 nor 38 . . . R(1)—KB1 because of 39 R—R7ch, K—Kt1; 40 R(B7)—Kt7 mate. He must therefore permit his Rook to be captured, after which he will still succumb to mate. A much-admired finish.

TARRASCH was the great master of method: methodical planning, methodical execution. Even the loser of this game must have been charmed by Tarrasch's relentless logic!

QUEEN'S GAMBIT DECLINED

Leipzig, 1894

WHITE	BLACK
Tarrasch	Von Scheve
1 P—Q4	P—Q4
2 P—QB4	P—K3
3 Kt—QB3	Kt—KB3
4 Kt—B3	B—K2
5 B—B4	P—B3
6 P—K3	QKt—Q2
7 P—KR3	Kt—K5?

This move, says Tarrasch, loses the game! It sounds incredible, but he proves his point.

8 Kt×Kt	P×Kt
9 Kt—Q2	B—Kt5
10 P—R3	B×Ktch
11 Q×B	O—O
12 Q—B2!	P—KB4
13 B—Q6	R—K1

Tarrasch's plan is as convincing as it is simple: he will play P—B3, forcing . . . P×P. Once the King's Knight file is opened, he will double Rooks on it, securing a winning attack because of his greater mobility.

14 O—O—O	Kt—B3
15 B—K5	B—Q2
16 P—B3!	P×P
17 P×P	

The file is open. Part two follows immediately.

| 17 . . . | P—QKt4 |

18 R—Kt1!	R—KB1
19 R—Q2!	R—B2
20 QR—Kt2	

The Rooks are doubled. The next step is to strengthen the pressure.

20 . . .	P—QR4
21 Q—B2!	Kt—K1
22 R—Kt5!	Q—K2

The participation of the White Queen in the attack means that the final smash is approaching. Thus if 22 . . . P—R3; 23 R—Kt6, K—R2; 24 Q—Kt3, Q—K2; 25 R×RPch! and wins.

| 23 Q—R4 | Kt—B3 |
| 24 Q—R6 | R—R2 |

There is no good move. If 24 . . . B—K1; 25 B×Kt, Q×B; 26 Q×Q, R×Q; 27 R×Pch wins.
Or 24 . . . P—Kt3; 25 R×Pch!, P×R; 26 R×Pch, R—Kt2; 27 B×Kt with crushing effect.

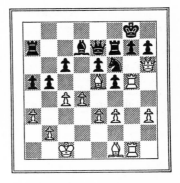

| 25 B—Q6!! | Q×B |
| 26 R×Pch | K—B1 |

If 26 . . . K—R1; 27 Q×Pch!!, Kt×Q; 28 R—Kt8 mate!

| 27 R×Pch! | K—K2 |
| 28 R×Rch | K×R |

29 R—Kt7ch K—K1
30 Q×Kt   Resigns

For if 30 . . . Q—B1; 31 Q—
Kt6ch wins the Queen. One of Tarrasch's many perfect games!

A GAME *without sacrifices—but Black's relentless threats keep White's position in a state of constant turmoil.*

QUEEN'S GAMBIT DECLINED
Frankfort, 1930

WHITE	BLACK
Mannheimer	*Kashdan*
1 P—Q4	P—Q4
2 P—QB4	P—K3
3 Kt—KB3	Kt—KB3
4 B—B4	P×P
5 P—K3	

5 Q—R4ch gives an easier game.

5 . . .   B—Kt5ch

For now Black can defend the gambit Pawn. White will eventually regain it, but only after a serious loss of time, allowing Black to prepare threats which are numerous and formidable.

6 KKt—Q2	P—QKt4
7 P—QR4	P—B3
8 P×P	P×P
9 B×Kt	R×B
10 R×P	B—R4!

Threatens 11 . . . Q—Kt3, winning the exchange. Black has a considerable lead in development, and what is even more heartening for Kashdan, he has his favorite Bishop-pair.

11 Q—B3	Q—Kt3
12 R—R8	R×R
13 Q×R	O—O!

Threatening to win the Queen by 14 . . . B—Kt2.

14 Q—B3	B—Kt2
15 Q—B4	Kt—K5

Threatening 16 . . . B×Ktch; 17 Kt×B, Q—R4 and wins.

16 P—B3	Kt×Kt
17 Kt×Kt	R—K1!

A new threat: 18 . . . P—K4; 19 P×P, R—Q1! and wins.

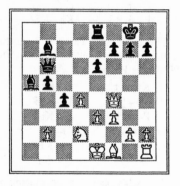

18 Q—R4	P—K4
19 Q—B2	P×P
20 P—K4	P—B4!
21 K—Q1	B×Kt
22 K×B	P×P
23 P×P	Q—R4ch
Resigns	

Wherever the King moves, he runs into a deadly check. Black's masterly simplicity has led to an impressive finish.

It is a truism that when bad moves are not refuted, they often yield their perpetrator a good game. It is therefore interesting to see how Black's bad moves are refuted here. Particularly useful are the zigzag moves of White's King's Knight, which executes the following tour: KB3—R4—B5—R6 —B7—Q6, involving three sacrifices!

QUEEN'S GAMBIT DECLINED
New York, 1937

WHITE	BLACK
Chernev	Gustafson
1 P—Q4	P—Q4
2 Kt—KB3	Kt—KB3
3 P—B4	P—K3
4 Kt—B3	B—Q2?
5 B—Kt5	B—Kt5
6 P—K3	P—KR3
7 B×Kt	P×B?
8 P×P!	P×P

White's last move is the key to all the remaining play. Black's King-side Pawns are permanently weak; Black's KB4, being unguarded by Pawns, is vulnerable to invasion; finally, if and when Black castles on the King-side, his King will immediately be exposed to attack.

| 9 Q—Kt3! | B×Ktch |
| 10 P×B | B—B3 |

Leaving his KB4 completely open to occupation and attack; but 10 . . . B—B1 is not inviting.

11 P—Kt3!	Q—Q2
12 B—Kt2	P—Kt3
13 O—O	B—Kt4
14 KR—K1	O—O

| 15 Kt—R4! | B—B5 |
| 16 Q—Q1 | |

Threatening 17 Q—R5, K—Kt2; 18 Kt—B5ch with a winning game.

16 . . .	K—Kt2
17 Q—R5	R—R1
18 B—R3!	Q—B3

And not 18 . . . Q×B??; 19 Kt—B5ch winning the Queen.

19 Kt—B5ch	K—B1
20 Kt×P	R—R2
21 B—B5	R—Kt2
22 P—K4!	Kt—Q2
23 Kt×P!	R—K1

If 23 . . . R×Kt; 24 P×P wins the Queen! (chief threat: 25 Q—R8 mate!).

| 24 P×P | R×Rch |

In the event that Black captures the Queen's Pawn, there follows 25 Q—R8ch, R—Kt1; 26 R×Rch, K×R; 27 Q×Rch followed by 28 R—K1ch and wins.

| 25 R×R | Q×P |

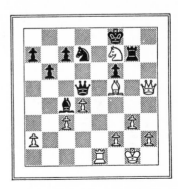

A final zigzag move ends it all:

| 26 Kt—Q6!! | Resigns |

If the Knight is captured, then 27
Q or R—K8 mate. If 26 . . . R—
K2; 27 Q—R6ch, K—Kt1; 28 R×R
forces mate.

Every chess player worships perfection, but how often does he achieve it?

QUEEN'S GAMBIT DECLINED
Teplitz-Schönau, 1922

WHITE	BLACK
Saemisch	Johner
1 P—Q4	P—Q4
2 P—QB4	P—K3
3 Kt—QB3	Kt—KB3
4 B—Kt5	B—K2
5 P—K3	QKt—Q2
6 Kt—B3	O—O
7 R—B1	P—B3
8 Q—B2	P—QR3
9 P—QR3	P×P
10 B×P	P—Kt4
11 B—Q3	P—B4?

The thematic move with which
Black frees himself in the Orthodox
Defense. But here the advance is sadly
premature.

12 B×Kt!	Kt×B
13 P×P	B×P
14 Kt—K4!	

If now 14 . . . Kt×Kt?; 15 B×Kt
simultaneously attacking Black's King
Bishop and Queen Rook. If 14 . . .
B—K2; 15 Kt×Ktch, B×Kt; 16 B×
Pch etc.

14 . . .	B—Q3?

Allows White to unleash a veritable
avalanche of tactical motifs.

15 Q—B6!	B—K2

Amusing would be 15 . . . Kt×Kt;
16 Q×Kt! winning the Rook after all
because of the mating threat.

16 Kt×Ktch	P×Kt

16 . . . B×Kt leads to a pretty
finish: 17 Q×R, Q×B; 18 R×B, Q—
Kt8ch; 19 K—K2 and Black loses because of the mating threat.

17 B×Pch	K×B
18 Q×R	Q—Q6

After 18 . . . Q—R4ch; 19 K—
K2, B—Q2 White wins a piece neatly:
20 Q—Kt7, R—Q1; 21 KR—Q1 etc.

19 R×B!	

Beginning a series of exchanges
which will leave him a clear piece
ahead.

19 . . .	R×R
20 Q×R	Q—Kt8ch
21 K—K2	Q×R
22 Q—K8	Resigns

For if 22 . . . B—B4; 23 P—
QKt4 wins the Bishop or leads to
mate: 23 . . . B—Kt3 (23 . . . B—
Q3 loses the same way); 24 Q×Pch,
K—R1 (or 24 . . . K—R3; 25 Q×
Pch, K—R2; 26 Kt—Kt5ch and mate

follows); 25 Q×Pch, K—Kt1; 26 Kt
—Kt5 forcing mate.

Saemisch has blended accuracy and
verve in just the right proportions.

HERE *is one of those rare games in
which every move meshes inexo-
rably with the previous one.*

QUEEN'S PAWN OPENING
Kemeri, 1937
(Special Prize)

WHITE	BLACK
Rellstab	*Petrov*

1	P—Q4	P—Q4
2	Kt—KB3	P—QB4
3	P—K3	Kt—KB3
4	B—Q3	P—KKt3!
5	QKt—Q2	QKt—Q2
6	P—QKt3	B—Kt2
7	B—Kt2	O—O
8	P—KR3?	P×P!
9	P×P	Kt—R4!

Black has already secured the initiative: . . . Kt—B5 is a troublesome
threat.

| 10 | P—Kt3 | Q—B2! |

So that if 11 O—O, Kt×P! with a
lasting attack.

11	Q—K2	Kt—B4!
12	Kt—K5	Kt×Bch
13	Kt×Kt	B—B4!

Threatening to win with 14 . . .
Q×BP etc. Note that if 13 . . .
Q×BP??; 14 QR—B1 wins the
Queen.

| 14 | QR—B1 | |

If 14 P—KKt4, B×Kt followed by
. . . Kt—B5 with a winning game.

| 14 . . . | QR—B1! |

So that if 15 P—KKt4, B×Kt; 16
Q×B (if 16 P×B?, Q×Rch!), Kt—
B5; 17 Q—KB3, P—K4! with a win-
ning position.

| 15 | Q—K3 | Q—Q3! |

Again providing for 16 P—KKt4,
which would be answered by 16 . . .
B×Kt; 17 P×B (Black's Queen is not
attacked!), R×Rch; 18 B×R, Kt—B5
and White is in serious difficulties (19
O—O, B×P!).

| 16 | P—QB3 | KR—K1! |

A new idea: if 17 P—KKt4, P—
K4! and wins.

| 17 | P—KB4 | P—KKt4! |
| 18 | O—O | |

He is desperate.

| 18 . . . | P×P! |

Stronger than the obvious 18 . . .
B×RP etc.

| 19 | Kt×P | |

On 19 P×P?, Q—Kt3ch wins a
piece.

19 . . .	B—R3!
20	Q—B3	Kt×Kt
21	P×Kt	K—R1!
22	R—KB2	R—Kt1ch
23	K—R2	

Now there will be threats on the
diagonal; 23 K—R1 was a little better.

| 23 . . . | R—Kt3 |
| 24 | P—B4 | |

If 24 R—KKt1, QR—KKt1; 25
R×R, Q×R; 26 R—Kt2, B×Pch!
wins a piece.

| 24 . . . | QR—KKt1 |
| 25 | P×P | |

Had he seen through the superb final combination, he could have prolonged his resistance with *25 P—B5.*

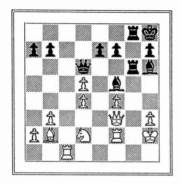

25 . . .   B×Pch!!

If now *26 K—R1, R—Kt6!; 27 Q—R5* (if *27 Q×B, Q×Q; 28 R×Q, R×P* mate!), *Q×Pch; 28 Kt—B3, B—K5!* and White can resign.

26 Q×B   R—Kt6!!
Resigns

For if *27 Q×B, R—Kt7ch* or *27 . . . R×RPch!* and mate next move. Surely one of the most elegant games ever played!

THIS *game is cut very sharply in two contrasting halves: the first, purely strategical, the second, purely tactical.*

KING'S INDIAN DEFENSE
City of London Chess Club Championship, 1938

WHITE	BLACK
Parr	Wheatcroft
1 P—Q4	Kt—KB3
2 P—QB4	P—KKt3

3 P—KKt3	B—Kt2
4 B—Kt2	P—Q4
5 P×P	Kt×P
6 Kt—QB3	Kt×Kt
7 P×Kt	P—QB4

At first sight, Black seems to have a fine game, with his thematic pressure on the long diagonal. But the target of this pressure, White's Queen Pawn, can be solidly protected. What really matters is that White's development will be quicker and more harmonious.

8 P—K3	O—O
9 Kt—K2	Kt—B3
10 O—O	P×P
11 BP×P	P—K4?
12 P—Q5!	Kt—K2
13 B—QR3	R—K1
14 Kt—B3	Q—R4
15 Q—Kt3	P—K5?!

Black is troubled by his opponent's powerful concentration of force converging on the center. He decides to embark on tactical play, but finds that White is well prepared for the coming complications.

16 Kt×P!   Kt×P

If *16 . . . B×R; 17 R×B, Kt×P; 18 R—Q1!* and White has too many threats.

17 QR—B1	B—K3
18 R—B5	Q—Kt3

White's success will be due to his superior development; thus if *18 . . . Q—Q1; 19 R—Q1* wins.

19 R—Kt5!	Q—R3
20 Kt—B5!	

If now *20 . . . Q—B3* (or *20 . . . . . . Q—Q3; 21 Kt×B*); *21 Kt×B, P×Kt; 22 R×Kt!* wins.

20 . . .   Kt×P?!

Counterattack: if 21 Kt×Q, B×Q; 22 P×Kt, B—B5; 23 Kt—B7, B×QR; 24 Kt×B, R×P etc.

21 Kt×B!	Kt×R

Still fighting: if 22 Kt—B7, Kt—Q7!

22 Kt—Kt5!!	Kt—Q7
23 Q×Pch	K—R1

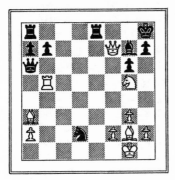

White is not worried about his material minus: he heads for Black's King:

24 B—Q5!!	P—R3

Guarding against the venomous threat 25 Q—Kt8ch!!, R×Q; 26 Kt—B7 mate!

25 B—QKt2!	R—KKt1
26 Q—Q7!!	Q—R5

If 26 . . . P×Kt; 27 Q—R3 mate! If 26 . . . Q×R; 27 Kt—B7ch! followed by 28 Q×Q.

27 B—Kt3!

Black was threatening mate in two!

27 . . .   Kt×B

27 . . . Q—R3 allows this pretty finish: 28 Q—R3!, P—R4; 29 Q×Pch!!, P×Q; 30 Kt—B7ch, K—R2;

31 B—B2ch, Q—Kt3; 32 R×Pch, B—R3; 33 R×B (or Kt—Kt5) mate.

28 Kt—B7ch	K—R2
29 R—KR5!!	Q—R4

If 29 . . . P×R; 30 Q—B5 mate. If 29 . . . Q×Q; 30 Kt—Kt5ch, K—R1; 31 R×P mate. If 29 . . . B×B; 30 Kt—Kt5ch and mate next move.

30 R×Pch!	Resigns

If 30 . . . B×R; 31 Kt—Kt5 mate. One of the greatest combinative games on record!

ALTHOUGH this game was played in Alekhine's first international master tournament, it is astonishingly mature, with many interesting features.

QUEEN'S GAMBIT DECLINED
Hamburg, 1910

WHITE	BLACK
Alekhine	Yates
1 P—Q4	P—Q4
2 P—QB4	P—K3
3 Kt—QB3	Kt—KB3
4 B—Kt5	B—K2
5 Kt—B3	QKt—Q2
6 P—K3	O—O
7 Q—B2	P—QKt3

Too slow: 7 . . . P—B4! is the move to discourage White from castling Queen-side.

8 P×P	P×P
9 B—Q3	B—Kt2
10 P—KR4!	

It is always useful in this variation to protect the Bishop at Kt5.

10 . . .	P—B4
11 O—O—O	P×P
12 KKt×P	R—K1
13 K—Kt1	P—QR3
14 P—KKt4	P—Kt4

Black is very uncomfortable because he must reconcile himself to defending an attack in the center and on the King-side as well. He calculates the following play five moves deep—but Alekhine calculates it *six* moves deep!

15 B×Kt	Kt×B
16 P—Kt5	Kt—K5
17 Kt×Kt	P×Kt
18 B×KP	B×B
19 Q×B	B×P

Yates has played all this with his usual tactical skill—but the next move is what counts.

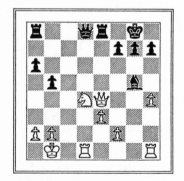

20 Kt—K6!!	Q—K2

The Knight could not be captured.

21 P×B	P—R3

But not 21 . . . P—Kt3; 22 R×P!!, Q×Kt (if 22 . . . K×R; 23 Q—R4ch, K—Kt1; 24 R—R1 forcing mate); 23 Q—KR4, Q—K5ch; 24 Q×Q, R×Q; 25 QR—R1 and now the mating threat wins a Rook for White!

22 P×P	Q×Kt
23 Q—Q4	Q—K5ch
24 Q×Q	R×Q
25 P×P	K×P

Alekhine's excellent handling of the middle game has left him an ending in which he is a Pawn ahead and has the initiative.

26 QR—Kt1ch	K—B3
27 R—R6ch	K—K2
28 R—QB1	R—R2
29 R(1)—B6!	P—R4

29 . . . R—K3? loses a Rook!

30 R—R6	R×R
31 R×R	P—R5
32 R—QKt6	R—K4
33 K—B2	R—B4ch
34 K—Q3	K—Q2
35 P—R3	R—B4
36 P—B4	K—B2
37 R—KR6	R—Q4ch
38 K—B3	P—B4

Else White drives the Rook off the rank with P—K4.

39 R—K6!	K—Q2
40 R—K5!	R×R
41 P×R	K—K2!

If 41 . . . K—K3; 42 K—Q4 wins easily.

42 K—Q3!

If 42 K—Q4, K—K3 regains the Pawn. 42 K—Kt4, K—K3; 43 K×P, K×P yields only a drawn ending.

42 . . .	K—Q2
43 P—K4!	P—B5
44 K—K2!	K—K3

On any other move, 45 K—B3 wins.

45 K—B2!!	Resigns

If 45 . . . K×P; 46 K—B3 winning the Bishop's Pawn. Black had hoped for 45 K—B3?, K×P and White is lost!

A brightly played ending by Alekhine.

There are times when even the most dashing player realizes, however reluctantly, that the Queens must be exchanged. Yet the absorbing play here shows how enjoyable such a game can be when it is handled by a player who has an inexhaustible richness of ideas.

FRENCH DEFENSE
Kemeri, 1937

WHITE	BLACK
Keres	*Mikenas*
1 P—K4	P—K3
2 Q—K2	

The famous move introduced by the great nineteenth-century master Tchigorin. It has the doubtful merit of creating complications which are likely to be unpleasant for White because of his premature development of the Queen.

2 . . .	P—QB4
3 P—KB4	Kt—QB3
4 Kt—KB3	KKt—K2
5 P—KKt3	P—Q4
6 P—Q3	P—QKt3
7 B—Kt2	P×P
8 P×P	Kt—Kt5
9 Kt—R3	B—R3
10 Kt—B4	Kt(K2)—B3

White's situation is a difficult one: if 11 O—O?, Kt—Q5! wins; if 11 P—B3?, Kt—Q6ch wins; if 11 B—K3, Kt—Q5; 12 B×Kt, P×B and

Black will increase the pressure on the pinned Knight with a winning game.

11 P—QR3!	Kt—Q5
12 Kt×Kt	Q×Kt
13 P×Kt	B×Kt
14 Q—K3!	P—QR3

If instead 14 . . . Q×Qch; 15 B×Q, P×P; 16 P—K5!, B—Q4; 17 B×B, P×B; 18 B×P, P—QR3; 19 R—R5 and White wins a Pawn.

15 P×P	B×P
16 Q×Q!	B×Q
17 P—B3	B—B4
18 P—QKt4!	B—K2
19 B—K3	

Starting from very modest beginnings, Keres has played his cards craftily and worked up decisive pressure against Black's Queen-side Pawns. If now 19 . . . QR—Kt1; 20 B—KB1! wins a Pawn!

19 . . .	B—Q1
20 K—B2	O—O
21 KR—Q1	B—B2

He cannot guard his second rank with 21 . . . B—QKt4 because of 22 B—KB1!

22 R—Q7	R—R2
23 B—KB1!	

The key to the ending: Black's Queen's Bishop must go.

23 . . .	B×B
24 K×B	KR—R1
25 P—B4!	

The "weak" Pawn suddenly becomes a strong Pawn! The rapidity with which Keres now forces the game is astonishing.

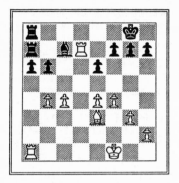

25 . . .   R—QB1

There is no time to bring his King to the defense: if 25 . . . K—B1; 26 P—QB5!, K—K1 (if 26 . . . P—QKt4?; 27 P—B6! wins quickly); 27 P×P!, K×R (or 27 . . . B×KtP; 28 R×R, B×R; 29 R×P wins); 28 P×R, B—Q3; 29 R×P, B×KtP; 30 R—Kt6, B—Q3; 31 R—Kt7ch and wins.

26 P—Kt5!   P—QR4

If 26 . . . KR—R1; 27 R×RP leaves Black without a good move.

27 P—QB5!   P×P
28 B×P   R—Kt2

Or 28 . . . R(2)—R1; 29 P—Kt6 attacking the Bishop and threatening P—Kt7 as well.

29 P—Kt6   B×KtP

Amusing would be 29 . . . R×P; 30 R×B!

30 R×R   B×B
31 R—QB1   Resigns

The pin is decisive: if 31 . . . P—R3 (32 R×B was threatened); 32 R—Kt5 wins the Bishop.

To win this game only 15 moves after the exchange of Queens shows the touch of a master!

"Now watch out for the fireworks!"

Cartoon by Whitney Darrow, by permission of the artist. Copyright 1948
The New Yorker Magazine, Inc.

1. Black charmingly illustrates the power of the Queen by playing 1 . . . Q—R1 mate!

2. 1 P—B8(Q) would win, but would not meet the condition of mating in one move. The right way is 1 P—B8(Kt) mate!

3. Black's well-meaning Rooks crowd his King too closely for comfort: 1 Q—B6 mate!

4. Unless you have your eye on Black's self-effacing Bishop at QR2, you are apt to miss this one: 1 . . . Kt—Kt6 mate!

5. White begins with the remarkable move 1 Kt—Q6ch!! If 1 . . . Q×Kt; 2 Q—Kt7 mate.

   If 1 . . . Kt (either one!) ×Kt; 2 Q×Q mate.

6. This happened in actual play, although it looks like the conclusion of an end-game composition: 1 Kt—B4ch, K—R3; 2 P—Kt5 mate.

   Or 1 . . . K—B3; 2 B—K4 mate.

7. Black can mate in three ways: 1 . . . B×Ktch; 2 R×B, R—Kt6 mate. Or 1 . . . R—Kt6ch; 2 Kt×R, R—B7 mate. Or 1 . . . R×Kt; 2 R×R, R—Kt6 mate.

8. Black's pieces are poorly placed for defensive purposes: 1 Q×Pch!, K×Q; 2 R—R3 mate.

9. White's neglected development results in disaster. The power of Black's Bishops is the key to the situation: 1 . . . Q×Bch!; 2 R×Q, B—B6 mate.

10. Black is so boxed in that White can mate in two ways, 1 R×Ktch, R×R; 2 Kt—R7 mate.

    Or 1 Kt—R7ch, R×Kt; 2 R×Kt mate.

11. White has sacrificed a Rook to get this finish: 1 P—B5ch!!, B×P (forced, but he blocks the King's escape); 2 Q—R5 mate.

12. White has set up a very elaborate defensive formation which is nevertheless inadequate: 1 . . . Q×Pch!; 2 K×Q, R—R3 mate.

13. The White Queen's lack of mobility leads us infallibly to 1 . . . B—K2! after which the Queen is trapped!

14. As Black's Queen must guard the Rook at KKt2, 1 R—KR3! wins the unfortunate Queen.

15. With Black's King and Queen on the same diagonal, try 1 B—B4!
16. Black has gone after an enticing Pawn at KKt7. Now comes 1 Kt—B4! and despite all the moves available to Black's Queen, there is no escape!

ABOUT THE AUTHORS

IRVING CHERNEV has written many successful chess books, including the best-selling chess primer Invitation to Chess, which he co-authored with Kenneth Harkness. Chernev is a deep student of the game, but he writes about it in a witty and entertaining manner; his scholarly approach is combined with a light touch.

FRED REINFELD is credited with being the world's most prolific chess writer. He has also defeated many of America's leading masters in tournament competition. After annexing the Intercollegiate Championship in his undergraduate days, he won the New York State Championship twice and subsequently became the titleholder of both the Manhattan and Marshall Chess Clubs.

BOTH Chernev and Reinfeld have a phenomenal knowledge of chess literature. They can (and do!) spend hours discussing the details of hundreds of master games without bothering to consult any texts or sources. Their love for the game is enormous and, they hope, contagious.